THE WINDOW OF MEMORY

THE
WINDOW OF
MEMORY

The Literary Career of Thomas Wolfe

by

RICHARD S. KENNEDY

"You want to make a perfect thing, but I want
to get the whole wilderness of the American
continent into my work."

—Thomas Wolfe to John Hall
Wheelock in conversation.

CHAPEL HILL
THE UNIVERSITY OF NORTH CAROLINA PRESS

for ELLA

PREFACE

THIS BOOK IS THE RESULT OF A NUMBER OF YEARS OF STUDY
and research, including a thorough examination of the voluminous
materials at the Harvard Library and extensive travel to interview
people who had been associated with Wolfe in his career. Some years
ago I had planned a comprehensive two-volume work. The first
volume, entitled "The Long Apprenticeship" (parts of which are
included in the present work), was ready in 1953. Circumstances
beyond my control altered those plans, forced some changes
in the nature of the work, and held up the publication of the final
product for more years than one would wish. Although this delay in
publication has not improved my disposition, it has perhaps improved the manuscript, which has undergone overhaul several times.
Also, readers who differ in taste from George Webber (he "liked big
books") will be happy that this work is considerably shorter than had
been originally intended.

During these years I received help from many people and I welcome the opportunity to express my gratitude. My study was made
possible by the generosity of William B. Wisdom of New Orleans,
who made his magnificent Thomas Wolfe Collection available for
research. In 1947, when he placed the papers in the Harvard Library,
where gifts from Mrs. Aline Bernstein, Gabriel Wells, and James B.
Munn already formed a large block of Thomas Wolfe material, he
made Harvard the center for all research on Thomas Wolfe. Further
material has been added each year. I am grateful to Paul Gitlin,
the Administrator of the Estate of Thomas Wolfe, and to William
Jackson of the Harvard Library for allowing me to quote from this
treasure of unpublished writings. The staff of the Houghton Library
at Harvard, particularly William Bond and Carolyn Jakeman, have
been efficient and helpful at all times.

I owe thanks to Jerrold Orne of the University of North Carolina
Library and again to Mr. Gitlin for permission to quote from letters

of Thomas Wolfe and of Maxwell Perkins in their possession. I am deeply indebted to Myra Champion of the Pack Memorial Public Library, Asheville, for making available to me her splendid collection of material about Thomas Wolfe and for answering countless questions.

To Charles Scribner's Sons, and particularly to John Hall Wheelock, I owe thanks for permission to study the unpublished letters of Thomas Wolfe to Maxwell Perkins and John Hall Wheelock which are in their files.

But Thomas Wolfe's manuscripts and published work alone could not have provided all the authority for facts and interpretations. I owe a debt of gratitude to a host of Wolfe's friends and acquaintances for information about his career or his writings: Edward C. Aswell, Mrs. Charles Bolster, Mrs. Madeleine Boyd, Mrs. Roscoe Brink, Rose and Sanford Brown, John Warner Brown, Mrs. George P. Baker, Philip Barber, Melville Cane, Henry F. Carlton, Mrs. D. J. Casey, Edmund Casey, Francis Casey, Mrs. Virginia Hulme Chapman, Grant Code, Malcolm Cowley, Mrs. Mina Curtiss, Mrs. Edla Cusick, Rev. Calvin Davis, Elmer Davis, Mrs. Monroe Day, Frederick L. Day, Robert Bruce Dow, Wilbur Dunkel, Edward P. Goodnow, Elizabeth and Douglas Gorsline, Mrs. Elaine Westall Gould, Doris Halman, Henry Harris, William E. Harris, Mr. and Mrs. Hubert Hays, Laura M. Hearne, James Howell, Max Israel, Parnell Kennedy, Rev. Arthur Ketchum, Donald Keyes, Stanley McCandless, Mr. and Mrs. George McCoy, Mrs. Edward McDowell, James Leon Mandel, Mrs. Thora Meredith, Mrs. Osmer Meunch, Wallace Meyer, W. Northrup Morse, Ernest Mosley, James B. Munn, Mrs. Martha Wrenshall Osbourne, Frederick C. Packard, Mrs. Hortense Pattison, Kate Pearson, Norman Holmes Pearson, Mrs. Albert Rivers, Edward C. Ruge, Dorothy Sands, William Sloane, James Stokely, John Terry, William Tindall, John Varney, Henry Volkening, Mary V. Walker, Mrs. Eda Lou Walton, Dixon Wecter, Charles Westall, Sophus K. Winther, Francis Wolle.

Members of the Wolfe family have been extraordinarily kind and helpful on the occasions of my visits to Asheville: Mrs. Julia Wolfe in 1943; Mabel and Ralph Wheaton and Frank Wolfe in 1954. A scholar is particularly fortunate when members of a family take an objective attitude toward his writing about them. In a letter dated October 12, 1954, Mabel Wheaton said to me, "There is only truth in your past writings of Tom. Don't 'whitewash' him or any of us—just be honest and truthful and it won't hurt."

Mrs. Aline Bernstein has been helpful and gracious to me. She not only told me about Thomas Wolfe in his early days in New York, but she kindly permitted me to see excerpts from Thomas Wolfe's letters to her.

Without the help of Mrs. Elizabeth Nowell Perkins, my task in its early stages would have been beset with twice as many difficulties and uncertainties. She generously opened to me the files of her collection of Thomas Wolfe's letters while she was gathering it, and she continually provided information and advice. She read through my early manuscript and filled my margins with pungent comments and suggestions for its improvement.

Howard Mumford Jones was the first to encourage and guide me in this project. For this and for enlightening criticism of the manuscript in its earliest form, I am deeply grateful.

To Dean Lewis Beck and the Committee on Grants-in-Aid at the University of Rochester, I owe my thanks for a summer travel grant in 1954 and for summer fellowships in 1955 and 1956. To Dean Margaret Habein and the University of Wichita, I owe thanks for financial help in preparing the final typescript.

My friends and colleagues have provided an agreeable climate of criticism and advice in which to work. For help and encouragement of various sorts I am aware of the thanks I owe to Katherine Koller, Bernard Schilling, Hyam Plutzik, Robert Hinman, and Walter Merrill. The careful scrutiny of Lucian Cohen and James Ruoff, who read portions of the manuscript, saved me from many errors.

One could not find better editorial associations than those with the University of North Carolina Press. To members of the staff of the Press I am deeply indebted for aid and concern that went far beyond the province of mere editorial assistance.

My wife, Ella D. Kennedy, deserves the most thanks and recognition for her constant help during the years these pages were in the making. The best of "chimney critics," she brought me to earth innumerable times with her penetrating, common-sensical queries. Her ideas and suggestions are scattered in more places in this book than I can acknowledge. For her unshakable serenity during this period I have no words to express my tribute.

Wichita, Kansas   RICHARD S. KENNEDY

CONTENTS

ABBREVIATIONS

The following abbreviations are used in the notes:

AO — Autobiographical Outline, HCL*46AM-7(25), set down by Wolfe to use as a guide for writing *Look Homeward, Angel.*

CSS — Charles Scribner's Sons.

FDTM — *From Death to Morning* (New York, 1935).

HB — *The Hills Beyond* (New York, 1941).

HCL — Harvard College Library. The accession number for unpublished materials and Wolfeana in the William B. Wisdom Collection is placed after the abbreviation.

Letters — *The Letters of Thomas Wolfe,* ed. Elizabeth Nowell (New York, 1956). Wolfe's punctuation and spelling have been followed, however, for all letters in the Harvard Library.

LHA — *Look Homeward, Angel* (New York, 1929).

LTM — *Thomas Wolfe's Letters to His Mother,* ed. John Terry (New York, 1943).

Nowell — Elizabeth Nowell, *Thomas Wolfe: A Biography* (New York, 1960).

OT&R — *Of Time and the River* (New York, 1935).

PN — Pocket Notebook. There are thirty-three pocket notebooks, HCL*46AM-7(69), in the Wisdom Collection at Harvard. When cited in the notes, the number and date of the pocket notebook are given.

SN	*The Story of a Novel,* reprinted in *The Viking Portable Thomas Wolfe,* ed. Maxwell Geismar (New York, 1947).
Short Novels	*The Short Novels of Thomas Wolfe,* ed. C. Hugh Holman (New York, 1961).
UNCL	University of North Carolina Library.
W&R	*The Web and the Rock* (New York, 1939).
Walser	*The Enigma of Thomas Wolfe,* ed. Richard Walser (Cambridge, Mass., 1953).
Wheaton	Mabel Wolfe Wheaton and Legette Blythe, *Thomas Wolfe and His Family* (New York, 1961).
YCGHA	*You Can't Go Home Again* (New York, 1940).

THE WINDOW OF MEMORY

INTRODUCTION: AN AMERICAN BARD

IN JULY, 1928, THOMAS WOLFE JOTTED THE FOLLOWING ENTRY in his pocket notebook: "Some Conclusions about the good life: the only happiness comes in finding the work you want to do, and to do it without obstruction—." [1] At this point of his life, when he was twenty-seven, Wolfe had written three full-length plays, a complete novel, a semi-fictional travel journal, and numerous stories and sketches—well over half a million words. But aside from student work, he had not published a line. Yet, with a propensity for self-expression and with the soundest artistic impulse, a passion to re-create life, he continued to write, to tell his story, and to surround it with an imaginative rendering of the life of his time: already he had begun a second novel. Wolfe had found his work while he was a student at Harvard, and with a fervor of purpose he had written his mother: "...I think of the devotion of a woman of frail physique to a father, I think of the daisy meadows on the way to Craggy Mountain, of the birch forests of New Hampshire, of the Mississippi River at Memphis—of all of which I have been a part—and I know there is nothing so commonplace, so dull, that is not touched with nobility and dignity. And I intend to wreak out my soul on paper and express it all." [2] At length he found success and fame, too, but even if he had not, he would have followed his chosen course until death overtook him at the age of thirty-seven.

This study of the mind and art of Thomas Wolfe will present the story of those years. Though it employs the narrative form, it is not a biography. Readers interested in the story of Wolfe's life will find a fully detailed treatment in the official biography, Elizabeth Nowell's *Thomas Wolfe, A Biography*. But since Wolfe's life and work were intimately bound together, enough biographical detail has

1

been included in the present study to flesh out the figure of the man.[3]
We can best understand Wolfe's work if we see the author not as
a writing machine but as a human being.

The early portion of the work, accordingly, attempts to trace the
literary development of Thomas Wolfe and the intellectual growth
and change that provided impetus and direction. This study fills in
the context within which Wolfe's talents were formed, necessarily
inquiring into his parentage, his surroundings, his reading, his
studies, his travels, and the friendships that influenced him as a
writer. The remainder and the bulk of the study is concerned with
what those talents produced. Above all, this whole critical effort attempts to answer the question of why Wolfe wrote the kind of books
that he did. Following Wolfe's literary output chronologically, this
study offers not only critical analysis of each work but also gives,
where possible, the facts in the shaping of each work. Since Wolfe
profited less than most writers do from the instruction and criticism
he received and since he learned always the most difficult way, by
his own mistakes, we shall see him through a period of great flounder-
ing. We shall follow his course through his failures and successes,
through new problems arising from the greater breadth of his intentions and from changing responses to his world, up to the point
at which his life was cut short before he could complete his huge
final manuscript.

II

Wolfe was not a careful artist, a skillful craftsman who took pains
with every detail of his work. He was an instinctive writer, a natural
genius, a bard somehow left over from the days of spoken literature.
One characteristic provides the key to all his virtues and his faults—
his approach to his work was oral and not literary. He was a storyteller, like the scop or the minstrel, except that he sang not of traditional heroes but of his own life.[4] Wolfe was always loath to revise
his work carefully, preferring to rewrite an episode in its entirety;
in other words, he would tell the story again and improve it. Like
most oral literature, Wolfe's work is imperfect. It is in style lacking
in precision of word and compactness of statement, in pace digressive, in organization often crude and unwieldy. Yet the virtues of
primitive poets and storytellers are there, too. His work, vigorous,
robust, rhythmic, capable of great emotional intensity and evocative

detail, lightened by broad humor and dignified by a concern with the general experience of men, is a mixture of ecstatic frenzy and common sense.

Wolfe is compared most often to another American primitive, Walt Whitman. Both composed spontaneously. Both produced uneven writing. Both were uncritical: they had difficulty distinguishing their good work from their bad. They are alike in their white-heat intensity of tone; and in their emotional outbursts, they both have a naive sincerity. In technique both made use of parallelism, cataloguing, and simple repetition; for both, having the poet's sensibility but finding the discipline of verse too rigorous, had returned to these simple rhythmic devices.

In order to re-emphasize this description of Wolfe as the storyteller, the improviser, the bard, I remind the reader that the adjective "Homeric" is applied to Wolfe's work. In addition to his epic intentions, Wolfe has stylistic characteristics which make the application just. He was brash enough to attempt an elevated style, and as a result in many passages his rhythm, his imagery, and his conscious poetic diction combine to give him the epic manner. More than this, he includes a number of long declamations, both by character and by narrator, that are uncommon in modern literature. Nor did he shun the use of variation and epithet, as did his contemporaries; the crowded city streets are trodden by the "manswarm" and the sound-filled night is "million-noted." With these devices, he adds heroic stature to his characters, as, for example, old Gant, the "Far Wanderer" with his "earth-devouring stride." Wolfe's presumptuous reach, his national consciousness, and his use of stylistic formulas, then, make him a kind of American bard.

The question immediately arises, why does Wolfe appear the natural writer when his formal education was so extensive? When we add up his preparatory school introduction to Latin and Greek and to English literature; his further training in classics at the University of North Carolina, as well as the discipline in English literature under Edwin Greenlaw, one of the most judicious scholars of the century; and his final training at Harvard, we could expect a surer sense of artistry. In a statement sympathetic to Wolfe but critical of educational advantages in general, Edward Aswell has posed the same question: "Somehow...Thomas Wolfe acquired an education without acquiring blinders." [5] To say that Wolfe remained suspicious and anti-intellectual throughout his sorties into higher learning would answer this question only in part. To say that Wolfe failed to acquire a critical sense during these years but instead absorbed the imaginative truth of the literature he read would add very little. But to say that Wolfe accepted only what critical tenets suited his instinct for self-expression (for example, his literal acceptance of Greenlaw's theory of "literature as a transcript of life" and his interest in John Livingston Lowes's probing into "the deep well" of the unconscious) would supply a large part of the explanation.

Nor can we lose sight of Wolfe's native background. Born and brought up in the Southern Appalachians, he never lost the outlook of the provincial. Here, however, is one of the sources of his strength. Looking with fresh, innocent eyes upon twentieth-century civilization, Wolfe recorded it in full scale more faithfully and more sensitively than Dos Passos, the only other American contemporary who attempted an imaginative compendium of his time. Further, as Wolfe's world widened he gradually adopted the attitude of a national spokesman because his instincts were clannish. As he expressed his aim in a letter to John Hall Wheelock about his second novel, we sense that he felt a deep tribal impulse: "I've just finished the first section of the first part. . .and it is as if I had become a voice for the experience of a race." [6]

To characterize Wolfe as an American primitive is not to say, certainly, that all of his undisciplined traits are welcome. It is a commonplace that great literature is the product of powerful feeling and a sense of form. Had Wolfe been able to channel his emotional resources with more careful planning, had he learned to govern his natural talents earlier in his life, he might have developed into the Great American Novelist. In shorter works and in parts of his novels, he did demonstrate a mastery of his powers. But whether he could have attained the same control in his longer works, whether he could have measured up to his ever more elevated intentions, no one can say. So we must take what we have and feel with Joseph Warren Beach, "There is in Wolfe a power of feeling and imagination that overrides a hundred faults." [7]

Beach's remark applies both to Wolfe himself and to his work, for his keen sensibility permeates and quickens all of his writing. Such scenes as Eugene Gant's introduction to his teacher, Mrs. Leonard, leaning on her broom, his parting from his aged mother with a pitying glance at her false teeth in the water glass, his recapture of home as he hears the bells in Dijon, were possible because Wolfe's memory allowed him to relive the past with the pulse of the present. He trusted his store of experience faithfully. Again and again he paraphrased Tennyson's Ulysses, saying, "We are a part of all that we have touched." Seeking experience, he became a wanderer, an observer, a listener. He tried to move in all the strata of life; he tried to peer into all of life's compartments. Before he could write about anything, he had to make it a part of himself. For example, after he visited Beethoven's house in Bonn and then thought to make the main character in "The River People" grow deaf, he walked around for a week with cotton in his ears to see how it felt.

With this hoard of experience, Wolfe strove to reproduce in his work the force of his own emotional responses. He never hesitated to defend passion in literature; he always argued against moderation or emotional restraint. Remembering the discussions in the 47 Workshop at Harvard, he set down these notes:

. . . the ancient lies about restraint and decorum—But nowhere is fury, madness, the vast unleashings of human passion more noticeable than with the Greeks—No one can curse like Sophocles—Madness is made more terrible because ruddered and constrained to a choral movement—What Moderation is there in *Oedipus Rex?* Compare with it even the terrible Banquet scene in the Elizabethan play—*Tis Pity She's a Whore*— this contrasted—bloodiness is tame by comparison.[8]

An overcivilized debility, he felt, endangered modern literature: "The European temper is one that has learned control—that is it has learned indifference." [9] Of course, a little more control in his own work, especially in *Of Time and the River,* would have "ruddered and constrained" his own "vast unleashings" for greater effect, for his tendency was to overuse loaded words like death, defeat, exile, despair, terror, desire, joy. Yet the over-all effect of the emotional intensity with which Wolfe communicated Eugene Gant's awareness of life prompted the historian of ideas, Crane Brinton, to point to Wolfe as the best modern example of Renaissance exuberance.[10]

Seeing this zeal for self-expression, we well might ask whether Wolfe had any aesthetic theory at all. What we find is that Wolfe was an artist in the broadest sense, a man with the natural impulse to re-create life. His idea of the beautiful was a "distillation" of life in all its complexity, with all its minute and mysterious detail. At the age of twenty-two, while he was still a student at Harvard, he declared his purpose to his mother in a long letter bursting with a frenzy of self-dedication.

It is not all bad, but it is not all good, it is not all ugly, but it is not all beautiful, it is life, life, life—the only thing that matters. It is savage, cruel, kind, noble, passionate, selfish, generous, stupid, ugly, beautiful, painful, joyous,—it is all these, and more, and it's all these I want to know, and, by God, I shall, though they crucify me for it. I will go to the ends of the earth to find it, to understand it, I will know this country when I am through as I know the palm of my hand, and I will put it on paper, and make it true and beautiful.[11]

But the hardest lesson of Wolfe's career was to learn the limits which had to be imposed on his display of life. His first important wrestle with the problem came with his Harvard play, *Welcome to Our City*, into which he tried to cram a full picture of life in a small Southern town. After three years had passed, Wolfe realized that he had to turn to prose narrative before he could present the spectacle of life he visualized. Even then, he still had the problem of distinguishing between distilling and mere recording, and he grappled with it for the rest of his career.

In spite of Wolfe's instinctive sense of what he wanted to do, he was greatly troubled by the problem of craftsmanship and particularly by his isolation from the main aesthetic current of his time. This tension often worked to his disadvantage, as in the murky, derivative play, *Mannerhouse,* and the incoherent conclusion to *Look Homeward, Angel.* He was more successful when he did not seek to be imitative or when he did not fret about form; "You want to make a perfect thing," he told John Hall Wheelock, "but I want to get the whole wilderness of the American continent into my work." [12] In this frame of mind, he went ahead to produce better work: he followed his own inclinations and learned by trial and error.

Actually, in organization his models were the vast Victorian and Edwardian chronicles of Dickens, Thackeray, Bennett, and Galsworthy. He even looked back for confidence to Fielding and Smollett, for he enjoyed their gusto and drew some encouragement from the fact that their narratives were loose and digressive. In another way, his models were those anomalous works which contain a mixture of genre and seem to burst beyond the restrictions of recognized forms —like *Moby Dick, Don Quixote, Lavengro, Tristram Shandy,* or *Sartor Resartus.* He admired departure from the norm: he saw Burton and Frazer "leaving method and with a purpose." [13] He followed no contemporaries save James Joyce, and here he was interested most of all in Joyce's expression of the inner life and in his brilliant language.

Wolfe was always concerned with language, delighting to read through pages of the dictionary or to make note of unusual usage in a book he was reading. What he appreciated in *Ulysses* was the same tumbling profusion that he relished in Burton's *Anatomy of Melancholy* and in Urquhart's translation of Rabelais. Although these writers charmed his ear, unfortunately he often substituted sound for sense when he imitated them. The question of the exact word was a touchy one with Wolfe. He looked back with scorn upon the 47 Workshop "Artist Myth," that a writer should continue to revise his work to a point of perfection, "Work on it for years if necessary—Make it perfect—Every man his own Flaubert." He disdained the opinion that Shakespeare had "the inevitable way of saying a thing," declaring, "Why, there are seven hundred inevitable ways, each of which if you could find it, would seem the only one to your reader." [14] Although Wolfe was right in his judgment that readers are timid about questioning an author's word choice, his belligerence about precise diction betrays his vulnerability. Often he seemed to forget what he had taught his students at New York University, that concrete details communicate emotion better than abstract gropings. At times he depended on vague personal associations of words. A shocking example is his statement to Alfred Dashiell, the editor of *Scribner's Magazine,* about one of his stories: "As to the title, will you consider this one tentatively—*Dark In the Forest, Strange As Time* (or *Dark In The Forest, Dark as Time* as a variant)—Don't ask me what the title means, I don't know, but think it may capture the feeling of the story which is what I want to do." [15] In spite of these lapses, Wolfe could be rigorous in his word choice. When the "inevitable" word did not fly to his pen he paced and pondered, or made a list of words for consideration, or consulted his well-worn Webster's Collegiate Dictionary. After the publication of his first novel, however, he became much more careless.

Wolfe's semi-bardic mode of expression made him unique in a period when critical opinion increasingly demanded form and precision and placed a value on compact, elliptical style in verse and simple unadorned statement in prose. That Wolfe was more at home with the literature of the past and somewhat bewildered by the literary experiments of his time further separated him from his contemporaries. He knew that his narrative method, the presentation of a fully detailed, straightforward chronicle, had become outmoded, and yet he was undaunted by his knowledge that the more crowded his canvas became, the less orderly his created world would appear to the new generation of critics. On the other hand, there is some bitterness in his remark to Henry Volkening: "I have found out that although there are millions of people who swear they are willing to live and die for what is good and beautiful, I have never known a half dozen who were willing to be out of fashion." [16] He was defensively opposed to special cults in the literary world. He vociferously denounced what he called "Van Vechtenism," [17] the pursuit of literary fads. And he was uncritically antagonistic to the writers in the little magazines—though still awed and envious, even offering, after he had first broken into print, to write something "practically unintelligible, even to the author" [18] for his agent to send to the *Dial*. But what annoyed him most was literary cocktail-party chatter reflecting attitudes of boredom, cynicism, and defeat. He summed up this atmosphere in the term "wastelanderism," for he was especially repelled by those who clutched *The Waste Land* to their bosoms and enjoyed echoing Eliot's lines about rat's feet, dead men's bones, or handfuls of dust. After a brief contact with the literary life in London and Paris in 1930, he sent Maxwell Perkins one of his outbursts (which was not entirely free from his sense of social and cultural inferiority to his enemies): "I grind my teeth when I think how we have been cheated and intimidated by these people—we have been secretly filled with horror and weariness by wastelanderism, but we have stood for it because we thought these exalted people were better and wise and had some truth and beauty to offer—well they haven't a damn thing, and they lie...." [19]

Wolfe's hostility to "wastelanderism" arose from the natural repulsion he felt for any attitude of resignation, any suggestion that man should retire without a fight to overcome his obstacles. This activism, this belief in continual striving, is an offshoot of Wolfe's biological view of life, which could be called vitalism, or the philosophy of emergent evolution or creative evolution,[20] although nowhere in his writing does he use terms of this sort. He was acutely aware that he lived in a naturalistic world of change and that human life was surrounded by powerful determinants; and he felt compelled, if he was going to present life fully, to illuminate this awesome vision. Yet, an optimism seems always to color his outlook. Even when he is trying to face up to the harshest naturalistic truths, his exuberant style reveals an enjoyment of life in all its aspects, dark or bright, bloody or peaceful.

Vitalism, emergent evolution, and creative evolution, all somewhat alike and all somewhat vague, are theories more poetic than scientific. They personify the organic principle of growth and reproduction as Nature, Life, Life Principle, Life Force, Procreant Urge, and the like; and they are all optimistic views of evolutionary "progress." "Ever since Aristotle," says Bertrand Russell, "men whose preoccupations were biological have thought they could discern Purpose in Nature." [21] In Wolfe's view the evolution of life is purposive and man participates in its forward march, although the purpose is unknown and man's specific role is unstated. But for the artist the philosophical details are less important than the question, what is the individual's lot in such a world? "[Man] is only big enough to hold a little ounce of God which burns him up at length like radium," [22] Wolfe wrote, but his emotional response to this thought was not always the same. At times he was stirred with sorrow for the "bitter briefness of our days," at times he reflected with pride that, though man's years are fleet, he leaves enduring intellectual and artistic monuments. Although Wolfe's evolutionary view becomes a unifying scheme underlying much of his work, the enormous gusto in his psalm of life reflects his own vitality as much as it does any theory of Life Principle.

This cosmic outlook was a common one in the late nineteenth and earlier twentieth centuries and was given wide circulation in the work of such figures as Butler, Shaw, and Bergson. But in addition to his probable brushes with the idea in their writings, Wolfe absorbed it fully from H. G. Wells's *The Undying Fire*, a novel whose plot he borrowed for an unfinished play at Harvard. Wolfe never gave a full, coherent exposition of his philosophic views, but they may be discerned in the symbols, metaphors, and patterns of his fiction and occasionally in the meditations and dilemmas of his central character, Eugene Gant–George Webber. Since Wolfe gives his vitalism its fullest statement in *Look Homeward, Angel*, it will more thoroughly be presented in the discussion of that book in Chapter 9.

But Wolfe's view of man required something more comprehensive than vitalist doctrine. He was aware of "the terrible fusion of brute and spirit" (as he wrote of his alter ego in "Dark in the Forest, Strange as Time").[23] Thus he attempted to link a Platonic view of man with his biological interpretation of life. In *Look Homeward, Angel*, Wolfe depicts the spirit of man come from a timeless world of reality and joined at birth to a body. During its sojourn in the world of change and imperfection, man's spirit struggles to communicate, to learn, and to adjust to the limitations of the physical self. This Platonic idealism stands opposed to the evolutionary naturalism in a conflict which surges throughout Wolfe's work. According to his mood, the tide of emphasis shifts. Sometimes the idealism of a world of spirit is held up as something to aspire toward; at other times it is seen as only a retreat into illusion, an escape from facing "the way things are." Sometimes he attempts to integrate the two views of life, but the result is by no means a perfect synthesis and leads to some confusion in his thought.

Other difficulties in his mixture of the old and the new he met with more success. For example, a vitalist like Shaw foresaw that a gradual evolution of Man would increase his intellectual capacity and shake off the disabilities of the flesh; whereas Wolfe, realizing that within recorded time man's nature has always been the same, accepted the limitations of the flesh as man's lot ("What have we but the pinion of a broken wing to soar half-heavenward?").[24] In his commentary on living, he did not speculate upon the future of the race but narrowed his view to Man the individual. "Mankind was fashioned for eternity, but Man-Alive was fashioned for a day,"[25] he had George Webber write in his credo. For "Man-Alive," then, he celebrated both the life of the mind and the life of the flesh, calling for a proper balance between the two in Man's nature.

It is fortunate that Wolfe clung to a traditional view of Man, for vitalism alone is an inadequate intellectual position. It can produce an ethic in which good is equated with health, strength, and fertility and the only evils are weakness, disease, and impotence. It is open to the same criticism that Butler leveled at Darwinism in *Erewhon*, where a slight headache is a misdemeanor and illness, a crime. And it is true that Wolfe tended toward this kind of morality. In his vocabulary, words like lively, potent, fruitful, yolky, opulent are "good" words, whereas words like sterile, barren, life-destroying, withered, shrunk suggest the utmost evil. But any novelist must hold a more human ethical standard than the mere preservation of the species. Thus Wolfe focused his attention on the individual in spite of his more inclusive assumption that Mankind participates in the evolution of life. For Wolfe, "Man-Alive" has a moral responsibility. Hence, a very real sense of evil, Wolfe's Presbyterian heritage, keeps cropping up in his writings, from the Harvard play, *Welcome to Our City*, written to oppose "a spirit of world-old evil," [26] to George Webber's credo in *You Can't Go Home Again*, where he says, "I think the enemy is old as Time, and evil as Hell, and that he has been here with us from the beginning." [27] Wolfe's repudiation of the idea that values only concern growth and reproduction is obvious not only in the statements of his characters but also in passages such as this:

Was no love living in the wilderness, and was there nothing but unceasing dying and begetting, birth, growth, pollution, and the cat's great snarl for blood and honey? Was there no love?

We shall scorn scorners, curse revilers, mock at mockers. Have they grown wise on dust and alum? Do they speak truly because their tongues are bitter? Have they seen clearly because their eyes are blind? Is there no gold because the sands are yellow? It is not true. They'll build great bridges yet and taller towers. But a vow has lasted where a wall has fallen; a word has been remembered where a city perished; and faith has lived when flesh grew rotten.[28]

This quotation leads us to an important corollary to Wolfe's world view. He had a powerful hatred of urban civilization, and he attacked it, using the city as a symbol, in his notebooks and letters as well as in his books. Since he had grown up within sight of the Great Smoky Mountains, the immensity of nature did not trouble him, but the towers of men oppressed his spirit. "Why is it that the vastness of nature never humiliates me, but the vastness of a city does?" [29] he wrote from the Alps. Although he was dazzled by metropolitan life, staring at its rush and variety through the eyes of a country boy (in the same way that he admired express trains and transatlantic liners as symbols of man's power), he felt that urbanization had dehumanized men and had enfeebled the family and community values that give nations their strength. In one of his long letters to Maxwell Perkins about his love for Aline Bernstein, he points to the city as the terrible angel of "fact" who destroys "ideal belief":

...it is true, for example, that not war, Darwin, or science has destroyed the ancient conception of God, so much as the life of the modern city: the inhuman scenery, the strong architecture, and the vast hordes of swarming maggots—crawling, pawing, cursing, cheating, pushing, betraying, dying or living, surviving or [perishing?]—the spectacle of the subway rush hour, for example, is sufficient to destroy all ideas of man's personal destiny, his personal importance and salvation. So it is with the other Ideal Beliefs—the belief in Courage, Honor, Faithfulness, and Love—in that great stain of crawling filth which is the city's life—that stain which is horrible and yet has so much beauty in it—we see the infinite repetitions of lust, cruelty, and [——?], of hatred, defeat, and dishonor, of gouging and killing—we see, moreover, the horrible chemistry of flesh, of millions of pounds and tons of flesh: we see flesh soothed, or irritated, or maddened, or appeased in a million different patterns daily, and our belief fails: how can one memory be here where a million memories pass before us in a second? How can one face be cherished and remembered out of a million faces? How can one grief, one joy, endure among ten million griefs and joys? How, finally, can love endure here—where treason can be consummated in 30 seconds? How can faith live, where a million faiths have died? [30]

Yet the fascination of the multitude of struggling men forming the huge organism of a metropolis drew him to New York City and held him there looking with revulsion, wonder, and pity upon the unceasing pageant of its streets. He never made his home elsewhere after the age of twenty-three.

III

Thomas Wolfe may seem a man who made a calculated attempt to play the role of the artist alienated from his time. But his extreme behavior was never a pose, and his good humor, natural warmth, and naiveté balanced his idiosyncrasies. He was volatile and was afflicted with an overweening egoism, but his moods shifted easily. He was now unbearably arrogant, later embarrassingly humble; he was now irrationally suspicious, again childishly innocent; he was at times quarrelsome and cruel, at other times gentle and kind; he hoped he was the greatest writer in the world, he despaired he was the worst hack that ever defaced paper. Because his personality was so full of extremes, we can call his winning a place as a writer a triumph over his own temperament. This is, of course, the secret of the artist. He is able to dominate his neuroses and use them in his work.[31] On the other hand, we cannot fail to note, as the biographies of artists reveal, that the emotional power which the artist possesses and which gives vitality to his work can make his actions irregular and at times ridiculous.

Some of Thomas Wolfe's personal characteristics are well known. He was of enormous size: he was six and a half feet tall, and although a slim, Abe-Lincoln-like figure until he was twenty-eight, he weighed over two hundred and fifty pounds in his later years. His face seemed small in proportion to his body. He had a protruding lower lip, a sharp, turned-up nose, and dark, penetrating eyes. He seldom concerned himself about his appearance. His hair was long and usually unkempt, not because he wanted to look like a Greenwich Village artist, but because he neglected to have it cut. Although his clothes looked hastily donned, or even slept in (which was often true), and although for years an old raincoat was his only article of winter gear, he was making no attempt at frugality, for Wolfe seemed to have no responsibility about money at all. Though his ordinary needs were few, his capacity for food and drink was immense. His "ravening gut," as he said, kept his pocket empty, for he liked steak for breakfast and his bills for prohibition liquor ran high. His apartments were skimpily furnished and disordered with papers and soiled clothes. Here he wrote late into the night—part of the time on his "lucky" table, massive, scarred, and column-legged, and part of the time on his icebox, which was a convenient height for writing as he paced the room—and after he had exhausted his energies, he went out to walk the streets until he had calmed his mind for sleep.

Habits like these give rise to legend. We find such apocryphal stories as this: "When hungry he reached for a can, opened it, ate the contents, and threw the can over his shoulder. When the apartment was full of cans, he moved to another." [32] Yet others just as fantastic were true. These outward details of Wolfe's life, however, are only the trivia of literary anecdote. The real man is revealed more clearly in glimpses of his behavior that show polarity of temperament and egocentricity.

His oversize body had made him so shy that among strangers he stammered when he talked. Yet among friends he was gay and convivial, pouring forth a torrent of earnest argument or humorous narrative. His sensitivity about his huge, awkward frame combined with his mountain background to make him extremely suspicious of others. His fear that they would take advantage of his naiveté or laugh at him behind his back led to such eccentricities as making people precede him downstairs. When he came upon the passage about suspicious men in his Burton's *Anatomy of Melancholy,*

If two talk together, discours, whisper, jest or tell a tale in general, he thinks presently they mean him, applies all to himself. Or if they talk with him, he is ready to misconstrue every word they speak and interpret it to the worst; he cannot endure any man to look steadily upon him, speak to him almost, laugh, jest, or be familiar, or hem, or point, cough, or spit, or make a noise sometimes, &c. He thinks they laugh or point at him...,[33]

he marked it and wrote in the margin, "Aye Aye." He was especially on his guard at literary social gatherings and after a few drinks got a chip on his shoulder. A quarrel was the inevitable result. But usually Wolfe had a right to feel irascible, for his innocence was the perfect target for the malicious jibe. When it came, he made a blunt, ineffectual retort, feeling boorish and miserable. He left many parties as he did one in England, when he recorded in his notebook: "stalked away again, feeling like a callow, over-sensitive damned fool who had acted badly."[34] He also carried this sensitivity into his work. When he saw a mildly dissenting review, he was furious; when he read a more strident attack, he girded himself for vengeance, keeping "a little list"[35] of the enemies he planned to annihilate with his satire.

Wolfe was the complete man of feeling: his anger, love, hate, sympathy, jealousy—all his emotional states—were violent. Often he entertained contradictory attitudes toward people or places, switching unexpectedly back and forth as his humor changed. Thus he loved and hated his mother, his family, Mrs. Bernstein, Maxwell Perkins, many friends, teachers, America, the South, New York, Paris, London, Germany, the Jews, the English, Bostonians, and so on. Since the greater his bond to anyone, the deeper the resentment

Wolfe could feel, his bitterness toward the living members of his family in *Look Homeward, Angel* reflects his strong attachment. Though he was most of his life frankly anti-Semitic, a Jewish woman meant more to him than any other person in his life.

When friends describe Wolfe's expansive nature, his bringing to a room a glow of life with his flood of eager talk, his exploding laughter, his mimicry, his mock-serious declamations, and his kindly inquiries about friends and families, it is hard to conceive of his quarrelsome moods, in which he turned from an amiable St. Bernard to a snapping hound. But the dark side of his nature was always there, and it came forward most frequently during, or just after, periods of intense creative activity. He even dramatized his unreasonable streaks as the madness of genius. As we read of George Webber's or Eugene Gant's insane jealousy or vertiginous wanderings in European cities, or when we read Wolfe's report to Perkins about a hallucination ("the horrible experience of seeming to disintegrate into at least six people—I was in bed and suddenly it seemed these other shapes of myself were moving *out* of me"),[36] we see that he enjoyed the idea of mental instability. He saw in himself an example of the truism that the man who exerts extraordinary powers in his daily tasks has not much control left for social situations. For he theorized in his pocket notebook: "I believe that a work that causes a tremendous expenditure of man's spiritual and mental energy may cause temporarily a profound disintegration in his nervous and physical self as well. . . .The artist in his perception may be a man of the greatest and most compassionate understanding, but the artist at work may be a kind of maniac."[37] As his letters of apology indicate, liquor combined with tension about his work caused some of his ugliest fits of temper. "I had been drinking," he wrote Henry Carlton on one occasion, "and have also been doing a big piece of work which is going very well but for several days now I have snarled at the whole world and spoken to several of my friends in a way I now bitterly regret."[38] Besides making Wolfe a great many outright enemies, these unfortunate rages strained his relations with all of his friends—with the result that only a handful stood by him to the end of his life.

Wolfe recognized his Jekyll-and-Hyde behavior,[39] for he had learned to stand off and take his own measure. From the time he conceived that a full presentation of life was his literary aim, he gradually, if sporadically, came to know himself with all his inconsistencies. "He can be cruel," Wolfe wrote of the young artist, "and yet hate cruelty with the hate of hell; he can be so unjust, and give his life to fight injustice; he can, in moments of anger, jealousy, or wounded vanity, inflict a grievous hurt on others who have never done him wrong. And the next moment, thrice wounded, run through and pinioned to the wall upon the spear of his own guilt, remorse, and scalding shame, he can endure such agonies that if there really were a later hell there would be no real damnation left in it." [40] Hence, in spite of his oddities of conduct, his moral sense cut through so that he could view himself nakedly for his autobiographical narrative. [41]

Thomas Wolfe was egoistic, over-emotional, illogical, ruthless, irascible, petty, and tedious, and yet at the same time was warm, vital, knowing, humble, gay, curious, and hard-working. His personal traits, though interesting in themselves, do not account for his literary achievement, but we need an acquaintance with Wolfe's difficult personality in order to look with proper perspective at him and his work. Fortunately, his combination of personal characteristics included an irrepressible impulse to express himself. He became a latter-day Ancient Mariner who fixed his gaze on his hearer and poured out his tale. Out of this need arose Wolfe's greatest dilemma, whether to enjoy a gregariousness or to seek solitude so that he could get his work done. He chose the loneliness of the artist, even severing his two closest ties to the world of companionship, that with his family and that with Aline Bernstein.

NOTES

1. PN 3, Fall, 1927 to September, 1928.

2. LTM, pp. 51-52.

3. The metaphor was suggested by Elizabeth Nowell when she read through an early version of some of these pages several years ago. She complained that Wolfe seemed only a skeleton and urged me to "clothe these bones with the flesh and blood of reality." Letter dated May 9, 1949.

4. Malcolm Cowley in "Thomas Wolfe," *Atlantic Monthly*, CC (November, 1957), 202-12, has also recognized the bardic quality in Wolfe's creative practice.

5. Introduction to a paperback edition, *Look Homeward, Angel: II. The Adventures of Young Gant* (New York, 1948).

6. *Letters*, p. 234.

7. *American Fiction, 1930-1940* (New York, 1948), p. 214.

8. AO.

9. PN 5, October 24 to *ca.* November 15, 1928.

10. *Ideas and Men* (New York, 1950), p. 283.

11. LTM, pp. 49-50.

12. Interview, December, 1950.

13. AO.

14. AO.

15. *Letters,* p. 400.

16. *Letters,* p. 227.

17. Wolfe later developed his term into the character, Van Vleeck, for W&R, in which he pilloried Carl Van Vechten as the author of "books about tattooed duchesses, post-impressionist moving picture actresses, and negro prize fighters who read Greek." See Chapter 30, "First Party."

18. *Letters,* p. 175.

19. Unpublished letter, January 7, 1931, in the files of CSS.

20. The term, vitalism, was first applied to Wolfe's philosophy by Bella Kussy, "The Vitalist Trend and Thomas Wolfe," *Sewanee Review,* L (July-September, 1942), 306-24.

21. "Non-Materialistic Naturalism," *Kenyon Review,* IV (Autumn, 1942), 361-65.

22. HCL*45M-156F, typescript of "O Lost" (the first version of LHA), p. 49.

23. FDTM, p. 107.

24. W&R, p. 693.

25. YCGHA, p. 737.

26. *Letters,* p. 33.

27. YCGHA, p. 742.

28. W&R, pp. 368-69. The similarity to the passage in *A Portrait of Bascom Hawke* (*Scribner's Magazine,* XCI, 256) and in "The Train and the City" (*Scribner's Magazine,* XCIII, 293) is typical of Wolfe's bardic repetition.

29. PN 14, May to August, 1930.

30. Unpublished letter in the files of CSS, January 19, 1931.

31. When Lionel Trilling's article "Art and Neurosis," in *The Liberal Imagination* (New York, 1950), established this point, a new era in psychological criticism began.

32. Ann Preston Bridgers, "Thomas Wolfe, A Legend of Man's Hunger in his Youth," *Saturday Review of Literature,* XVII (April 6, 1935), 599-600, 609.

33. HCL*46A-110, p. 265.

34. PN 26, March 21 to April 26, 1935.

35. PN 31, August 20 to *ca.* September 30, 1936. Bernard de Voto, Henry Seidel Canby, and Edwin Berry Burgum are among others on the list. Before his death, Wolfe settled his score with Canby in "Portrait of a Literary Critic" (HB, pp. 150-61) and with Burgum in the character of Chester Spurgeon (YCGHA, p. 410).

36. *Letters,* p. 438.

37. PN 24, November, 1934 to *ca.* January, 1935.

38. HCL, unpublished letter, August 25, 1933. This is one of three such notes, all unsent. Mr. Carlton reports that Wolfe, unable to reach him by written message, made his apologies by telephone.

39. *Letters,* p. 366.

40. W&R, pp. 347-48.

41. C. Hugh Holman, in his pamphlet *Thomas Wolfe* (Minneapolis, 1960), sees the contradictions in Wolfe's life and the paradoxes in Wolfe's reading of life as his outstanding characteristic.

Part I

FORMATIVE YEARS

2

THE HOME PLACE

THERE IS NOTHING EXTRAORDINARY ABOUT ASHEVILLE, NORTH Carolina, in the same way that there is nothing extraordinary about Concord, Massachusetts, or Sauk Center, Minnesota. A walk through this small city near the western border of North Carolina provides no answer to the question, what is it about this place that it should produce one of America's most gifted writers? Or, as Wolfe put the question so frequently, "Why here?" In Leanne Zugsmith's phrase, home is where you hang your childhood. And Thomas Wolfe, born October 3, 1900, spent his first sixteen years in Asheville. The stamp of this region is strong upon his life and his literary work.

We should not think of cotton and tobacco country as his background. Western North Carolina, culturally associated with Virginia's Blue Ridge Mountains and with the hills of Tennessee, feels its independence from the eastern part of the state—Wolfe described a similar rivalry between the East and the West of "Old Catawba" in *The Hills Beyond*. From Asheville it is only a short trip to Knoxville, Tennessee, whereas it is a long way to Raleigh, North Carolina's capital, and a day's journey to North Carolina's coastline. Because Asheville is on the edge of real mountain country, Wolfe had an early acquaintance with natural grandeur, in a boyhood surrounded by "the everlasting rim of hills." [1] In the western part of the state, where the Appalachians reach their highest peaks, the local ranges, the Black Mountains, the Bald Mountains, and the Great Smoky Mountains, constitute the greatest mountain mass in the eastern United States. Any stranger traveling west by train to Asheville becomes aware of a long slow climb, and he knows he is reaching heights as he peers out of the window through patches of cloud at the red clay and scrub pine.

These mountains were long the barrier to the westward migration of early settlers; hence, the old families are for the most part descended from pioneer stock. Self-sufficient farming was the mainstay of the people, for there were no large Southern plantations here, nor was slaveholding common. Since Thomas Wolfe's maternal relatives had long been established in this region, he felt proud of his mountain background (including a remote family connection with David Crockett) [2] and especially of the exploits of his forebears in the Confederate Army. But he also thought he felt a sense of restriction because of the generations of mountain isolation that lay behind him. Indeed, after leaving North Carolina, he frequently behaved as if the restriction really did exist. Although he always felt at home with Southerners and although he generally was at ease among any hearty, unpretentious people, he often seemed the proverbial mountaineer, shy, suspicious, awkward, independent. His brothers and sisters, it should be noted, never seemed to feel this regional confinement.

Still, Asheville, a city of some sixty thousand, comparable in size to such small cities as York, Pennsylvania, or Waterloo, Iowa, is not a typical mountain community. A visitor approaching the city by bus is struck not only by the sense of unending ascent but also by the odd mixture of Asheville-bound passengers. The dusty hats and blue denim shirts, the bonnets and aprons of the rural folk mingle with the business suits, the tailored jackets, the slacks and sweaters of vacationers from all over the North and South. For besides serving as county seat and commercial center for the surrounding countryside, Asheville, boasting a year-round moderate climate, is a resort city that had once hoped to attract as many summer tourists as Florida cities did in winter.

Asheville, which was reputed to be John C. Calhoun's favorite resort,[3] rose from a small mountain town of about 2600 people in 1880 to become a flourishing tourist center where seekers of pleasant summer weather and beautiful natural scenery far outnumbered the "lungers" who came to breathe the healthful mountain air. Citizens began to feel particular pride when, about 1890, George W. Vanderbilt, behaving like the typical American millionaire, bought 120,000 acres near Asheville, reconstructed a model English village which he called Biltmore, and carried out a private reforestation program that became the estate area, Biltmore Forest. As his crowning achievement, he erected Biltmore House, an architectural copy of the Château de Blois.[4]

The vision of money to be made from Asheville's climate had its culmination in a real estate boom in the early 1920's, the subject of Wolfe's best play, *Welcome to Our City*. The decline, which Wolfe pictured in *You Can't Go Home Again*, occurred in two stages, the explosion of the real estate bubble about 1926 and the economic slump of the 1930's, including a scandalous bank failure and consequent loss of city and county funds. Asheville still points with civic pride to certain landmarks of the boom days, such as The Grove Park Inn, a luxurious resort hotel built by Asheville's other millionaire, E. W. Grove (whom Wolfe in his fiction called "Dr. Doak, the quinine king")[5] and the Asheville "skyscrapers," a couple of tall office buildings. But it is only since World War II, thanks to such humble activities as the manufacture of textiles, furniture, chemicals, and paper, that Asheville has grown and prospered in the way the city fathers had hoped thirty years before.[6]

II

In the Asheville of less pretentious days, a slow-moving community of 15,000, Thomas Wolfe was born in the Wolfe family house at 92 Woodfin Street. He was the youngest of eight children, one of whom died in infancy. The boy's father, William Oliver Wolfe (whom his son built into the towering figure, W. O. Gant, in his novels), was a mason and stonecutter, a vigorous, masculine craftsman from Adams County, Pennsylvania, who wandered into the South in the 1870's, adding the final "e" to his name during his travels. Pictures show the well-built frame which supported his six feet four inches, and close-ups reveal a strong face made somewhat mournful by a drooping mustache.[7] Readers familiar with the W. O. Gant of the novels need not be told that Thomas Wolfe's father led a strenuous life. He was a hard worker, a traveler, a great eater, a heavy drinker (a "spree drinker" in Mrs. Wolfe's words, "he would go through a brick wall to get it when one of those spells came on"),[8] and a man who prided himself on his openhandedness and on his being a "good provider."[9] After he opened his tombstone shop in Asheville, his life and his livelihood were in constant association with death, and that may account for the periodic spells of melancholy during which he took to whisky.[10] As a Northerner and outspoken Republican, he was looked on as somewhat of an outsider in Asheville; and as a drinker and a person who was on speaking terms with Irene Irvine (or Ervine), the proprietress of one of the local bawdy houses, he was no doubt looked down on as vulgar, particularly by some of his wife's prosperous relatives. Nevertheless, with his friendly, hearty manner, this man whose shop displaying the sign "W. O. Wolfe, Tombstones and Monuments, Cements and Plaster" faced Pack Square, the center of Asheville's life, was well liked and made himself respected as a man who did good work. This reputation was enhanced by his genteel formality with the ladies, by his habit of removing his granite-dusty apron (made from mattress ticking) before he came to speak to any customer in the front of his shop, and by his middle-class pretensions in Sunday dress— a well-tailored coat, a wing collar, a carefully folded necktie held in place by a fancy stickpin.

Thomas Wolfe was in many ways his father's son, and he drew from him more than a zest for life. W. O. Wolfe had a natural artistic impulse; he was a competent craftsman who took pride in his marble and granite carving. His daughter Mabel reports that he could chip out the lettering and the ornamental roses on the face of a gravestone free hand. Besides being a master of his craft, Mr. Wolfe was a great talker. He relished rhetorical phrase. "Papa could floor you with words," Mabel said, and he sometimes even coined words for the occasion. Since he held a secret yearning to be a lawyer, he liked to picture himself as a prosecuting attorney; and, striding up and down the Wolfe living room, he would stun an imaginary courtroom: "Your honor and members of the jury, cast your eyes upon this defenseless woman and her little child. . . ." [11]

Along with this delight in oratorical bluster, the man had a taste for poetry of a rhythmic, declamatory sort, Hood's "I Remember, I Remember," Gray's "Elegy," Poe's "Raven," and other such works from his well-thumbed volume of Stoddard's *Golden Treasury of Poetry and Prose* or from *Songs of Spur and Saber*. He had attended the theater often in his youth in Baltimore, and now for the assembled Wolfe family he loved to recite soliloquies from *Hamlet, Macbeth, Othello,* Portia's mercy speech from *The Merchant of Venice,* or Antony's funeral oration from *Julius Caesar*.[12] "I heard it as a child," Thomas Wolfe recalled in *The Story of a Novel;* "I memorized and learned it all." [13]

Thomas Wolfe's mother, Julia Elizabeth Westall, was a mountain girl who had come to the city. The Westall family headquarters had been at Burnsville (near Mt. Mitchell, the highest peak east of the Rockies) in Yancey County, which is the mountain capital of North Carolina. Grandfather Thomas Casey Westall, for whom young Thomas had been named, had settled at Burnsville after the Civil War to raise a family of nineteen children (six by his first marriage) in Scotch Presbyterian orthodoxy. T. C. Westall was an eccentric, a sometime builder and "contractor," a religious zealot who left the church on the question of predestination and infant damnation, an editor of a temperance newspaper, and a mystic who in his final illness, so the story goes, predicted the hour of his death, as his father, William Westall, had before him.[14]

Julia Wolfe, born in Swannanoa, nine miles from Asheville, had been brought up in the hill country during Reconstruction days. Although her girlhood was spent in poverty, she enjoyed the pleasures of the Carolina mountain people: family life, church-going, quiltings, corn-shuckings, and country dances. She played the violin by ear, she became a temperance worker, she taught "readin', writin', and figgerin' " in a country school. She extended her education with a couple of years at a small college.[15] Her innumerable stories of the prodigious Westall family supplied her son, Thomas, with an abundance of material for the Pentlands and Joyners of his novels. Her Uncle William's bear-trapping was the basis for Wolfe's legends of "Bear" Joyner; her half-brother Bacchus, the saintly prophet with the odoriferous feet, played his role both as a Pentland and a Joyner; her father provided the shiftless character of "Major" Joyner in *The Web and the Rock;* his children became the populous tribe of "Bear" Joyner in *The Hills Beyond*—the list is endless. It is interesting to note in passing that Wolfe used his grandmother's maiden name, Penland, in early writing, but later altered it to Pentland in order to make use of Walter Scott's phrase from "Bonny Dundee," "There are hills beyond Pentland," for the title of a proposed book.[16]

Thomas Wolfe's mother was a diminutive, soft-spoken, strong-willed woman and a great egoist. Like Eliza Gant, she was, because of the poverty of her youth, parsimonious, even grasping; and as a housewife, a boarding house keeper, and a real estate speculator, she was a driver of hard bargains. Anecdotes stress her squeeze of the nickel and her practice (in her old age) of bringing home sugar lumps, crackers, rolls, and parts of uneaten steak whenever she went to a restaurant. But anecdotes always tend to caricature; these stories overshadow her humanity. She was a vigorous and kindly woman who exhibited the enterprise and resourcefulness that were considered virtues in the mountain country. She strove hard to improve her family's economic position, partly because she wished to keep up with her older brother, William Westall, who had made himself (according to Wolfe family talk) "the richest man in Asheville, outside of Mr. Vanderbilt"—a statement always qualified: "At least he paid more taxes than anybody except Mr. Vanderbilt."

Thomas Wolfe's heritage from his mother was a mixed blessing. For one thing he had inherited her faculty of total recall. In telling an incident from the past, she could not only give the date and the year, but the time of day and prevailing weather conditions. Yet she could not organize her thinking, and associations led her astray. Her train of thought would be interrupted by "I remember because I was just stepping out the front door to...," and the chain of references would link out endlessly. Thomas Wolfe's memory, similarly exact but powerfully emotional, was one of his greatest gifts. The remembrance of an event brought with it an entire context, not only sight, sound, and other sensory details but the emotional impact that was felt at the time, so that the past came alive with painful immediacy. Thus Wolfe's entire experience was available for him as a rich treasury of material for his writing. But as far as his personal life was concerned, past insults or misfortunes always caused present suffering if he recalled them—which may partly explain the violence of his hates and prejudices. Further, his memory was often a hindrance to his creative efforts, bearing down upon him with a crushing multiplicity of detail as he tried to restrict his autobiographical narrative.

Another characteristic that Julia Wolfe passed on to her son was her interest in the realm of the irrational—popular superstitions, prophetic senses, visions, voices from nowhere, mental telepathy, and the like. "Any visiting spiritualist," said Mabel, "somehow got around to the Wolfe home." Indeed, Thomas' middle name, Clayton, was given him in honor of Clayton Bowman, a close friend of Julia Wolfe's who was a devout believer in spiritualism. All his life, Thomas Wolfe was attracted to the fantastic and the supernatural, and he discussed reports of incredible happenings with the greatest interest. Although this tendency lent a flavor of ignorance and un-healthiness of mind to his life, it did not impair his writing. In fact, early use of the supernatural, in the juvenile play, "The Third Night," and in his first attempt at prose narrative, "Passage to England," was quite successful. And whatever is revealed of the Westall mysticism in his later writing certainly does not harm it. The family stories, such as the appearance of T. C. Westall's *Doppelgänger*, contribute to the atmosphere of eerie madness with which Wolfe wished to surround his Pentlands and Joyners. And an occasional passage of Wolfe's own direct commentary takes us out of the world of sense, as, for example, this prophetic statement at the close of *I Have a Thing to Tell You:* [17]

Something has spoken to me in the night, burning the tapers of the waning year; something has spoken in the night, and told me I shall die, I know not where. Saying:

"To lose the earth you know, for greater knowing; to lose the life you have, for greater life; to leave the friends you loved, for greater loving; to find a land more kind than home, more large than earth—

"—Whereon the pillars of this earth are founded, toward which the conscience of the world is tending—a wind is rising, and the rivers flow."

In later years, Thomas Wolfe's analysis of the opposing personali-ties of his father and mother provided one of the principal conflicts in *Look Homeward, Angel,* and their backgrounds stood as the "Two Worlds Discrete" in *The Web and the Rock.* He probably felt some of the tension of their incompatibility early in his childhood, for he recorded in his Autobiographical Outline his remembrance of W. O. Wolfe's half-comic denunciations of Julia when he returned from work in the evening; "The daily tirades did not matter [—] indeed she herself got a kind of stimulation from them: there was in her, however, a fear of the periods of drunkenness, and a stubborn and unforgiving recollection of the past—Slow to forgive." [18] Occasion-ally, he was traumatized by his father's violent outbreaks, such as the time W. O. Wolfe pursued Julia to her bedroom and tried to break down her locked door while she crept out the window onto the roof. This household situation obviously disturbed the children. Frank, the oldest, showed tendencies to juvenile delinquency. Fred and Tom stuttered. Fred, Mabel, and Tom all became compulsive talkers.

But this tension should not be isolated and stressed. On the whole, Tom's early childhood was spent happily in the midst of the demon-

strative, garrulous Wolfe family. The many-roomed house on Woodfin Street had been built by W. O. Wolfe "with his own hands," he
was proud to say.[19] In winter, a sense of warmth prevailed: it had
two fireplaces downstairs and one upstairs, a great Franklin stove in
the dining room, besides a good-sized wood stove in the kitchen.
Many of Wolfe's earliest memories are of dressing in front of the
stove or leafing through a book by the fireplace. One hearthside
recollection goes back to nursery-rhyme days: "Winter 1903 aetat
2½: the owl an' th' puthy cat went to thea in a bewteeful pea-green
boat. . .And the hot feel of the fire on the side of my face—and the
smell of the warm leather and the blistered varnish and of apples
and looking at the book all the time as I reeled it off and not knowing
one word from the other but thinking that I did." [20] In other seasons,
the well-planted lot was the pre-eminent feature of the home. The
back yard, full of fruit trees, cherry, plum, quince, and apple, with
ample space for the annual vegetable garden and with a playhouse
that W. O. Wolfe had built for the children, was a youngster's paradise. Here Tom grew up in close association with the younger Wolfe
children, Fred, Mabel, and Ben. Frank and Effie, who had left home
early in his life, he hardly knew. Grover, Ben's twin, who had died
when Tom was three years old, was only a shadowy memory. Here
the dark-faced, curly-haired boy played with his sister and brothers
and with the neighbor children, Max Israel and Charley Perkinson;
savored the orchard fruit; smelled the burning leaves in October;
stored up the memories upon which he drew for the nostalgic reminiscence of "Three O'Clock" in *The Web and the Rock.*

The Wolfe household, dominated by the powerful voice and
earthy humor of W. O. Wolfe, was full of laughter and noise. Moreover, Mr. Wolfe made the routine of ordinary living seem grand by
establishing family traditions. "My Father, before his sickness, had
the instinct for ritual," Wolfe recalled, "the order of rising, washing,
fire-making, etc.—his comings and goings." [21] It was W. O. Wolfe who
made Christmas an exciting event for the children, Mabel Wolfe has
said.[22] Remembering this atmosphere, Wolfe later jotted this question
in his notebook: "Why have I liked Christmas always as a child?
Because of the sense of ritual in it." [23]

It was family ritual that Wolfe associated with Christmas; religion
did not penetrate deeply into the family life of the Wolfes. But the
simple externals of American Protestant life were present. Julia

Wolfe had come from a Bible-reading, Bible-quoting family, and she sent Tom off to the First Presbyterian Sunday School at an early age. W. O. Wolfe said his prayers on his knees before going to bed at night. Grace was asked at the table for formal meals. In fact, one of the earliest records of Tom's writing is a prayer inscribed in a family autograph book:

> Now I lay me down to sleep
> I pray the Lord my sole to keep
> If I die before I wake
> I pray the lord my sole to take
> God bless papa and mama
> Make papa well
> don't let none of the children
> get sick   we thank you for
> our food
> for Christ sake
>   Amen
> Thomas Clayton Wolfe
> Tom Wolfe
> 8 [years] old [24]

As a young child, Tom received great attention from both his parents. To his mother he was the baby of the family, and she kept him a baby as long as she could, nursing him, as she has said, until he was three and a half years old.[25] Although we may be tempted to place this report with some of her motherly exaggerations—that Tom learned to read at the age of two and went to school at four [26]— Wolfe supports it in his story of Eugene Gant.[27] He was very closely tied to his mother and he slept with her until he was nine years old. He was also his father's favorite and the receiver, as he later recalled, of bristly, mustached kisses. He sat next to his father at the table, where W. O. Wolfe would heap his plate with food. His father liked to take him down to his shop during the day and later, when Tom could read, gave him money for dime novels. Since both his mother and father frequently took him on trips, he had traveled all over the South by the time he was twelve. Beginning at the age of three, when he went with the family to the St. Louis Fair, he traveled almost every year, going several times to Florida, once to New Orleans, and, most memorable of all, to Washington for the Wilson inauguration in 1913.

In sum, this is the cultural matrix that formed the child, Thomas Wolfe: the ordinary family life of pre-World-War America in the home of a prosperous tradesman in a small, isolated city to which travelers brought some cosmopolitan flavor. It is well known that the life of Eugene Gant in *Look Homeward, Angel* corresponds closely to Thomas Wolfe's own life; Altamont is Asheville, the Gant family is the Wolfe family, Dixieland is Julia Wolfe's boarding house, the Old Kentucky Home, and all of the characters are modeled on real persons.[28] Since this is a critical study of Thomas Wolfe as a writer and in no sense a biography, we need not retrace the details of the twenty years which Wolfe himself rendered into autobiographical fiction. But in order to follow the growth of young Wolfe's mind, we should focus on his reading and his schooling, and in order to account for a striking feature of his personality, we must note that when he was six years old the weather turned around and blew away the warmth and security he had known in his first years.

III

In August, 1906, Julia Wolfe purchased a large, rambling frame house at 48 Spruce Street, two blocks from the Wolfe home, and established the Old Kentucky Home boarding house. It was apparently ready for the vacationers by the following summer. She took six-year-old Tom there with her and left the rest of the family at home.[29] Neglected by his busy mother, Tom frequently wandered back to the Woodfin Street home to join his brothers and sisters until she tracked him down at the end of the day. Over the next years, the Wolfe home life gradually began to disintegrate. The father and mother began to live separately. Living conditions for the children became fluid; sometimes they lived in the old house, sometimes in the boarding house, depending upon the season and Julia's Wolfe's whim. W. O. Wolfe, weakened by a recurrent prostate disorder and stricken severely with arthritis in his hands, became less the dominant figure of the family. Although he finally underwent surgery in 1913, he was not freed of his prostate difficulty, which developed a few years later into cancer. "After Woodfin Street," Tom noted, "the almost total lack of ritual in our life." [30]

Since Tom was the youngest, this disruption of family life affected him more than the other children and left a permanent mark on his personality. He was especially bewildered by the treatment he received from his mother, who lost him in the disorder at the Old Kentucky Home but who was possessively determined to baby him when she had time. He had no sense of home during his boyhood; and further, the intermittent absence and the illness of his father left him without a figure of authority in his life. During these years he developed his stutter. During these years he formed the deep need for love and for order and direction that he sought constantly to fill in his adult life.

This was the price that the family paid for Julia Wolfe's ambitions to complete its transition from the working class to the middle class. The rise of W. O. Wolfe from an itinerant stonemason to a man who owned his shop and ran his own business had taken place long before young Tom was born, and the economic prosperity (especially as it was increased by the profits from Julia's boarding house) grew while Tom was a boy. Although W. O. Wolfe worked with his hands and although the family prestige was tarnished by his occasional rampages, the growth of the family possessions gradually solidified its standing in the middle class. All the way along, in fact, the family had held by the middle-class values of money-making and indi-vidualism and had reflected what has come to be called the Protes-tant Ethic. Toward the end of his life, Thomas Wolfe, readying him-self for an attack on the overemphasis of utilitarian values in American life, set down some notes on the beliefs held in "Altamont" in 1916, beliefs that were inculcated by the Wolfe parents:

> —that the richest man in town was the best
> —that it was a disgrace bordering on crime to be poor
> —that there was a personal God regulating the affairs of
> the universe and that if we saw things amiss in the life
> around us they seemed amiss because we didn't know as
> much about them as God knew
> —that it was the duty of every "real man" to get and hold
> a job and that if he didn't, it was his fault
> —that the American way of life was incomparably the
> best on earth [31]

But Julia Wolfe had waited until her youngest child was ready for school before she set up her boarding house and expanded her speculations in real estate. Tom was not quite six in the fall of 1906 when he entered the first grade at the Orange Street Public School. The boy's grammar school education was quite ordinary, but he soon

distinguished himself as an avid reader. Driven in upon himself, he
began to spend more and more time with books as the grade school
years passed.

Besides looking at the comic strips of the *Asheville Citizen* and at
the *Saturday Evening Post,* for which brother Fred was the local
agent, he was getting what he could out of the books in the Woodfin
Street house ("Papa's books," they were always called). Like Eugene
Gant, he dreamed of far-off places as he browsed through the leather
volumes of Ridpath's *History of the World* and other illustrated
books—*Beautiful Bible Stories for Boys and Girls,* the Doré Milton,
With Stanley in Africa. As he grew older, he gradually worked his
way through the heterogeneous collection, which is a remarkable
one for a tradesman's home: P. F. Collier editions of Thackeray,
Bulwer, and Scott, *Around the World with Captain Parker,* Stod-
dard's *Lectures,* editions of Shakespeare, Tennyson, Longfellow, and
Whittier, *The Palaces of Sin or the Devil in Society,* The Book of
Common Prayer (W. O. Wolfe had been an Episcopalian),[32] two
family Bibles (one with a temperance pledge signed by W. O.
Wolfe, Julia, and the two girls), an 1858 edition of Noah Webster's
An American Dictionary of the English Language, Melville's *Omoo,*
odd volumes of Dickens and Dumas, Zane Grey novels, *The Motor
Boys on the St. Lawrence,* Grimm's Fairy Tales, Chambers' Encyclopedia, Stoddard's *Golden Treasury of Poetry and Prose,* and so on.[33]
During the winter months, young Tom spent many happy hours at
the Woodfin Street house by the fireplace in the "library," which was
the principal living room of the Wolfe home, and during the summer
he found a retreat, book in hand, in the playhouse or in the "parlor"
(which was only opened when visitors called) until his mother
sought him out by telephone to run an errand.

When the boy began to go outside the family bookshelves for
his reading, he divided his time between dime novels (*Young Wild
West, The Liberty Boys of '76,* etc.) and the varied selection at the
public library: "Those drunken days at the library—9:00 to 6:00
—first, all the children's books, Alger, Optic, the Swifts, Cooper,
Henty, Froissart, Malory—The fiction shelves—Tracy, Hough, Locke,
Churchill, McCutcheon, Porter, Wright (That Printer of Udell's),
O. Henry—At School—what [?]—as yet, little or nothing save poems
from The New England writers." [34]

With his great appetite for reading, the boy was certain to rise above the humdrum routine of the Orange Street School, but he needed guidance badly. Mr. J. M. Roberts, the principal of the school, was made aware of his qualities one day when the sixth grade students were asked to restate in their own words the ideas in a paper that had been read aloud. That night when he and his wife, Margaret Roberts, who also taught at the school, read young Wolfe's paper, they recognized that it stood out above all the others. Roberts praised the paper at school the next day, and the following year, when he opened the North State Fitting School in a house on Buxton Hill in Asheville, he persuaded W. O. Wolfe to send Tom for private schooling.[35] There could not have been much reluctance; the privilege must have been welcomed by the socially ambitious parents. Thus after the sixth grade Thomas Wolfe's young mind developed rapidly under careful supervision and with more concentrated work. In four years he was ready for college.

Mr. and Mrs. Roberts had met while at Vanderbilt University and had married shortly thereafter, before Margaret, who had been ill, completed the work for her degree. When they established the North State Fitting School, J. M. Roberts gave instruction in Latin and Greek, Margaret Roberts in English and history, and Mr. Roberts' sister, Mrs. Hortense Pattison, in mathematics and German. From the Roberts family Thomas Wolfe received good preparatory school training. In the four years of Latin study he went through the usual grammar and composition, Caesar, Cicero, and some Nepos and Ovid.[36] His work in Greek covered grammar and elementary composition, a Greek reader, and Xenophon's *Anabasis*.[37] His three years of German covered grammar and composition exercises, Hillern's *Höher als die Kirche*, Storm's *Immensee*, Schiller's *Wilhelm Tell*, and other common school-readings.[38]

Much as he needed the discipline of language study, it seemed mechanical. His study of literature was what delighted him, and his response to the sensitivity and quiet enthusiasm of Mrs. Roberts made him a favorite. She became more than just a teacher, as his inscription in her copy of *Look Homeward, Angel* shows:

> To Margaret Roberts, Who was the Mother of my
> Spirit, I present this copy of my first book,
> with hope and with devotion.
> Thomas Wolfe, Oct. 15, 1929 [39]

Guided by the new admissions standards of the University of North Carolina,[40] she took him through English and American literature. Only a few of the textbooks in Wolfe's library, selections from the Old Testament, Gummere's book of old English Ballads, Burke's speech on *Conciliation with America*, Shakespeare's *Midsummer Night's Dream, Henry V*, and *King Lear*,[41] can be placed definitely in the years at the Roberts' school, but from his notes and from his autobiographical account in *Look Homeward, Angel*, we can judge that Wolfe read widely. At first Mrs. Roberts guided his taste for fiction away from Emerson Hough and Harold Bell Wright to such books as *Lorna Doone* and *The Cloister and the Hearth*. Later, as the haphazard notes from his Autobiographical Outline show, he ran through a variety of schoolroom classics, from *The Lay of the Last Minstrel* to *Henry IV, Part I*:

Did I take any great delight in poetry? Will O' the Mill. Markheim. All of Stevenson—Dickens—The Newcomes—Vanity Fair—the Independent—Purington's Efficiency Talks—Tom Brown's School Days—Description of the marvellous breakfast—also Quentin Durward—"Breathes there the man"—*The Lady of the Lake*—the contest between the two warriors.... The Water Baby (Water Babies)—"a long hour by Shrewsbury Clock"—"larding the earth as he went."

We read in *Look Homeward, Angel*, "By the beginning of his fifteenth year Eugene knew almost every major lyric in the language." Although the accuracy of this statement seems questionable alongside Wolfe's note in the Outline, "Favorite poems—Lowell's 'Once to every man and nation'—thrilled by its swinging obvious gallop," we can be sure that by the time he left the North State Fitting School he had read every lyric in Palgrave's *Golden Treasury* (the poetry text recommended by the University of North Carolina), he had read much of Shakespeare, and he had browsed through Dr. Eliot's Harvard Classics.[42]

More and more he began to look upon the Roberts' school as his place of security, especially after he had boarded there two winters while Julia Wolfe was in Florida buying and selling real estate. Generally Mrs. Roberts tried to look after him, for, unwashed, his hair uncut, and his appearance unkempt, he obviously lacked a mother's care. Tom came to love Mrs. Roberts deeply, and years later, while he was still moved from having written about her as

Margaret Leonard in *Look Homeward, Angel,* he told her what she had meant to him in those homeless years:

I was. . .groping like a blind sea-thing with no eyes and a thousand feelers toward light, toward life, toward beauty and order, out of the hell of chaos, greed, and cheap ugliness—and then I found you, when else I should have died, you mother of my spirit who fed me with light. Do you think that I have forgotten? [43]

During his four years at the North State Fitting School, Thomas Wolfe distinguished himself, from the first year, when he won the city-wide spelling contest at the local high school, until graduation, when he carried off prizes for public speaking. His parents were proud that Tom was judged best speaker in the debate on the proposition "That the U. S. Should Greatly Enlarge Its Navy" and won the declamation contest, using "Shakespeare the Man," the piece with which he had triumphed in the Asheville essay competition.[44] W. O. Wolfe was especially elated at this display of oratorical powers, for he cherished the hope that one of his sons might be a lawyer. ("Thing to do in the South," Wolfe comments, "every man his own attorney—Way to politics and public fame.") [45] Because of Tom's outstanding work at school it was agreed that he should go to college —the first one of the Wolfes to do so. He wanted to go to the University of Virginia, but his father's ambitions for him to be a lawyer, later judge, and ultimately perhaps, governor of the state, required that he attend the state university. Pleased at the opportunity to continue his education, yet reluctant to go to Chapel Hill ("I arrived at my decision to attend our State University last Wednesday night. Perhaps I should say *forced* instead of arrived"),[46] Thomas Wolfe formally enrolled at the University of North Carolina in September, 1916. The hill-rimmed life was over.

What can be seen in the boyhood of Thomas Wolfe is both the sharpening of a sensibility and the storing of a young mind with lore and with impressions. Because his emotional props were unsteady or changing, he became aware and observant—and tender rather than tough. Because he read widely, he not only developed linguistic skill but lived through a diversity of vicarious emotional adventures. The solid academic grounding he received at the North State School was only a part of his education. Of great importance for the future author of *Look Homeward, Angel* was the immense variety of experience that his boyhood witnessed right in his home town. At the center was the vigorous family life, with its tears and laughter, its quarrels and loyalties, and its rich flood of talk. Then came the world of Asheville. He first saw the life of the town through the eyes of a child selling the *Saturday Evening Post,* and later he saw the nighttime life of both Negro and white through the eyes of a boy delivering papers for the *Asheville Citizen.* More than that, since Asheville was a resort town, a provincial fair to which strangers came from all parts of the eastern United States, he watched part of the crowd coming and going across the threshold of the Old Kentucky Home. For young Wolfe's observation of human behavior, Asheville offered a shifting display, from poor-white mountaineer to New York sophisticate.

NOTES

1. AO.
2. Elizabeth Patton, sister of Wolfe's great-great-grandfather, George Patton, was the second wife of David Crockett. Records and letter sent by Wendell Patton to Elizabeth Nowell, April 13, 1951, now in Pack Memorial Library, Asheville.
3. F. A. Sondley, *Asheville and Buncombe County* (Asheville, 1922).
4. Martha N. Meade, in *Asheville in the Land of the Sky* (Richmond, 1942), gives a glowing description of Vanderbilt's contributions to "Greater Asheville."
5. Passage cut from LHA. See HCL*45M-156F, "O Lost," typescript, p. 467.
6. In *Tar Heels* (New York, 1941), Jonathan Daniels gives an excellent account of the Asheville real estate hysteria, pp. 218-35.
7. For details of W. O. Wolfe's ancestry and early life, see Nowell, pp. 21-23, and Wheaton, pp. 18-38.
8. Hayden Norwood, *The Marble Man's Wife: Thomas Wolfe's Mother* (New York, 1947), p. 77.
9. AO.
10. This probably accounts, too, for Thomas Wolfe's preoccupation with death in his writing. For W. O. Wolfe's dislike of the tombstone business, see Wheaton, p. 97.
11. Frank A. Dickson's newspaper articles entitled "Look Homeward, Angel" in the *Anderson [South Carolina] Independent,* which ran every Sunday, July 9, 1948, through September 4, 1948. The articles were based principally on interviews with Wolfe's sisters, Mrs. Mabel Wolfe Wheaton and Mrs. Effie Wolfe Gambrell. The articles will henceforth be cited as *Anderson [South Carolina] Independent.*
12. Although Mabel Wheaton has told me, "He could act out the whole of *Macbeth* and *Othello,*" this is probably an exaggeration.
13. SN, p. 564.
14. Norwood, *The Marble Man's Wife,* pp. 100-2.
15. According to Fred Wolfe, it was two years at Judson College in Hendersonville (*New York Times Book Review,* July 31, 1960, p. 18); according to Mabel, it was both Judson and the Asheville Female College (Wheaton, p. 85).

16. The line is underscored in Wolfe's copy of George Beaumont's *Book of English Poetry*, HCL*47A-105.

17. Later transferred to the conclusion of YCGHA.

18. AO.

19. The house was torn down in 1954 to make room for a superhighway. Presumably Mr. Wolfe did the stonework for the foundation of the house. Carpenters built the structure (Wheaton, p. 62).

20. HCL*46AM-7(61), Late Notes and Sketches. This repeating of well-memorized rhymes and stories is the source of Mrs. Wolfe's boast that "Tom could read when he was two."

21. AO.

22. *Anderson [South Carolina] Independent*, August 14, 1948. See also Wheaton, pp. 63-66, for a description of the family Christmas festivities.

23. AO.

24. In 1954, this was in the possession of Mabel Wolfe Wheaton.

25. LTM, p. xxii.

26. *Anderson [South Carolina] Independent*, July 17, 1948.

27. LHA, p. 52.

28. Floyd Watkins in *Thomas Wolfe's Characters* (Norman, Okla., 1957) offers an excellent study of the degree of fictional coloring in parts of LHA and other novels.

29. Wolfe himself was uncertain of the date. AO reads: "1907 (or 1908)—Mama buys the O. K. H. Is it this year or the year after that he is stricken with inflammatory rheumatism [?] it is in winter at the dead of night. Mama is already at the O. K. H., because Mabel telephones for her. . . . Effie married 1908—in June—wedding was at O. K. H.—therefore Mama got O. K. H. in Fall 1907 [.]"

30. AO.

31. HCL*53M-113F. If we hold by the criteria set down in Joseph Kahl's *American Class Structure* (New York, 1957), which are prestige, occupation, possessions, social interaction, class consciousness, and value orientations, then it seems clear that the Wolfe family moved in one generation from the working class, through the lower middle class, to the middle class. For the period of Thomas Wolfe's boyhood, lower middle class seems the best label. According to Kahl, the lower middle class is a grouping, not sharply defined, which shades off into the working class. It is made up of the less successful business and professional men and the more successful manual workers, who live in small houses or multiple-family dwellings, who have been graduated from high school, and who maintain firmly a code of respectability.

The insecurity that the family felt about its class position is evident in the almost hysterical reaction which the second generation of the Wolfe family (except for Tom) displayed to such terms as "working man" or "lower middle class." Mabel usually cried, "Why, Papa was a business man!" See also Fred Wolfe's letter to the *New York Times Book Review*, July 31, 1960, p. 18, about the educational attainments of the family members.

These remarks about class are worth making because some attention has recently been paid to Thomas Wolfe's class orientation. William F. Kennedy, in "Economic Ideas in Contemporary Literature—The Novels of Thomas Wolfe," *Southern Economic Journal*, XX (July, 1953), 35-50, uses as evidence Wolfe's assertion in LHA that the Gants were worth $100,000 in 1912. He then calculates the Wolfe family income and estimates that economically they were among the top 1 or 2 per cent of the Asheville community. Kennedy does not take into account Wolfe's tendency to exaggerate or the fact that fictional coloring has affected the picture of the family in the novel.

Walter F. Taylor in "Thomas Wolfe and the Middle-Class Tradition," *South Atlantic Quarterly*, LII (October, 1953), 543-54, argues the thesis that "the life of the young Thomas Wolfe was nurtured, enclosed, and saturated by a middle-class civilization." Taylor's argument is weakened by his failure to make clear his definition of "middle class"—which he associates with the humanistic tradition, nineteenth-century liberalism, the views of the founding fathers, and antagonism to intellectual circles in art and theater. The article only serves to remind the reader of the common saying that America is one great middle class.

32. There is some confusion about this. Mabel Wheaton said in 1954, while I was examining the family copy of The Book of Common Prayer, that her father had been an Episcopalian before his marriage. In her book, however, she states that he had been a Baptist (p. 97). This may only indicate the fluidity of church membership in the Wolfe family, for later they all went to the First Presbyterian Church in Asheville.

33. These and others may be found in the bookcases of the Thomas Wolfe Memorial at 48 Spruce Street in Asheville—although Mabel Wheaton reports that a number of books vanished in the hands of tourists before the bookcases were finally locked. The Woodfin Street furnishings had been moved to the Old Kentucky Home in the winter of 1919-20, when the family home was sold.

34. AO. Wolfe's grammar school textbooks indicate what reading he lumps together as "poems from The New England writers." *Classics Old and New, A Third Reader*, ed. Edwin A. Alderman (New York, 1906) (HCL*46A-763), contains selections from Whittier, Tennyson, Longfellow, Lowell, and others. There is also a children's illustrated text of *Hiawatha* (HCL*46A-792), with notes and exercises.

35. James K. Hutsell, "As They Recall Thomas Wolfe," *Southern Packet*, IV (April, 1948), 4.

36. Of his Latin textbooks only two remain in his library, Nepos, *Greek Lives*, I, ed. H. Wilkinson (London, 1902) (HCL*46A-801), and *Easy Selections from Ovid*, ed. H. Wilkinson (London, 1907) (HCL*46A-802).

37. Wolfe recorded the sale of some texbooks at Chapel Hill in the endpapers of a book of Freshman essays, Le Baron Briggs's *College Life* (Boston, 1904) (HCL*47A-195): "Xeno Anab —25, Moss Reader —30, Latin Grammar —50."

38. Letter from J. M. Roberts in the Harvard Registrar's Office folder, Harvard University Archives, UAV 101.201.10.

39. James K. Hutsell, "Thomas Wolfe and 'Altamont,'" *Southern Packet*, IV (April, 1948), 7.

40. See the detailed admissions requirements in the University of North Carolina Catalogues after Edwin Greenlaw became chairman of the English Department in 1913.

41. HCL*46A-767, 783, 770, 811, 810, 809.

42. "What contact yet with the extraordinary in mind?" he wrote of this period in AO. "None—a great deal with the extraordinary in feeling—Dr. Eliot's Five Foot Shelf."

43. *Letters*, p. 123.

44. *Asheville Citizen*, June 1 and 2, 1916. The manuscript of Wolfe's essay on Shakespeare, together with the judge's comments, is in HCL*53M-113F.

45. AO.

46. *Letters*, p. 2.

3

CHAPEL HILL: STUDY AND WRITING

Both Agatha Boyd Adams in her *Thomas Wolfe: Carolina Student* [1] and Don Bishop in his "Thomas Wolfe as a Student" [2] have shown that the gangling, effusive, clowning, club-joining, pipe-smoking Tom Wolfe at Chapel Hill was nothing like the melancholy undergraduate Eugene Gant in *Look Homeward, Angel.* Elizabeth Nowell's researches have added further details.[3] But there has been no attempt to reconstruct Thomas Wolfe's intellectual surroundings during his college years, and there has been no close look at his studies and his teachers—which were the features of college life that contributed to growth and pointed direction in his literary career.

At the time Thomas Wolfe entered the University of North Carolina, it was, under President Edward Kidder Graham, beginning its expansion and rise to its present position as a leading university in the South. One important event in the history of the university which is pertinent to a consideration of Wolfe's background is the arrival in 1913 of Edwin Greenlaw, who had been invited to Chapel Hill to reorganize the English Department. The new department chairman not only brought with him the research standards of Professor G. L. Kittredge, under whom he had worked as a medievalist at Harvard, and of Professor J. M. Manly, with whom he had taught at the University of Chicago, but he also came with a zeal for good teaching. Greenlaw's influence on the department, which included during Wolfe's stay such men as James Holly Hanford and Norman Foerster, was marked by a raising of standards, a more generous spread of courses over the range of English literature, an increase in graduate study, and an emphasis on literature as learning rather than entertainment. After his appointment as Dean in 1920, Greenlaw reorganized the graduate school and brought its level of studies up to that of the great universities of the United States. His organizational ability and intellectual standards are perhaps most directly revealed by his achievement as managing editor of *Studies in Philology*. He transformed this journal from an occasional publication used to air the research endeavors of department members into a scholarly quarterly of national standing.

By the time Thomas Wolfe came to Chapel Hill as a freshman, the educational aims of the Liberal Arts College were admirable, for the administrators had set down a required program of studies for the first two years that allowed the student no foolish choices. The lower classmen could concentrate in classics, languages, or sciences. Wolfe chose the first, and besides his English and his mathematics, he continued the work in Latin and Greek that he had begun under Mr. Roberts. With Professor George K. G. Henry he went through Cicero's *De Senectute* and *De Amicitia*, part of Livy, Horace's Odes, Epistles, and Satires, Tacitus' *Agricola* and *Germania*, Plautus' *Menaechmi* and Terence's *Phormio*. The well-thumbed and interlined texts of many of these readings still remain in his library to testify to his industry. But for Wolfe these particular selections of Roman literature had little appeal because they lacked emotional power. Perhaps Cicero and Horace acquainted him with a classical view of life, but on the whole his Latin studies served only as an exercise in language. However, he loved Ovid, both the *Amores* and the *Metamorphoses*, and the lyrics of that other lad from the provinces like himself, Catullus (whom he read independently), and he continued to return to them in later years.

Thomas Wolfe's Greek studies, fired by the enthusiasm of Professor W. S. ("Bully") Bernard, a colorful teacher whose "stern charm" [4] and incisive tongue Wolfe never forgot, left a stronger impression on his mind and heart. Professor Bernard, who sat for the portrait of "Buck" Benson in *Look Homeward, Angel*, guided Wolfe through literature which became imbedded in his mind and colored much of his later writing. They began with Homer, whom Wolfe continued to read in later years, after most of his Greek was forgotten. The life of action, the "vast seasurge" of Homer's rhythm, fell on his ears as a new kind of storytelling by a voice that spoke for the world of his time. When, in Bernard's class the next year, Wolfe made his first acquaintance with Plato, he translated the *Apology* and the *Crito*, which developed his great reverence for Socrates. Although the character of Socrates interested him more than the ideas of Plato in these readings, the parts of the *Phaedo* that he translated spurred him to read other Platonic dialogues in English. These glimpses of the Platonic view of man and the soul provided one of the principal ideas that animate *Look Homeward, Angel,* the yearning of the soul for the former state. Years later in New York, he would often read aloud in English the poetic flights of Plato, the myths of Socrates. Other works for classroom translation were Xenophon's *Symposium,* Aeschylus' *Prometheus Bound,* which Wolfe admired as a celebration of rebelliousness, and Euripides' *Alcestis,* which he used as a background myth for the death of Ben in *Look Homeward, Angel* ("Like Apollo, who did his penance to the high god in the sad house of King Admetus, he came, a god with broken feet, into the gray hovel of this world").

Professor Bernard by his lectures on Greek literature also encouraged Wolfe to read Gilbert Murray's translations of the Greek drama. The plays lived in his memory as great emotional peaks of literature, and Murray's style became a model for rhetorical statement. Even Gilbert Murray's words crop up occasionally in Wolfe's writing—for example, Wolfe's symbolic phrase for ecstatic happiness, "the apple tree, the singing, and the gold."

In later years Wolfe virtually lost his knowledge of Greek and Latin. "I can still read my Homer after a fashion," he told Julian Meade in 1932, "and I do believe I could put up some sort of battle with Xenophon and I can still read Caesar[;] I can do fairly well with Catullus, but I regret to say that whatever modest accomplishment I may have once had with the ancient languages I have let slip away." [5] He turned his attention, instead, to French and German. He could, in his middle years, read and speak French, but his German was always very poor. Although nearly half of the books in Wolfe's personal library are French or German, the pages of many of them are uncut. The titles represent a striving after European culture rather than a capture of it.

The other courses at Chapel Hill seemed to interest young Wolfe very little—Archibald Henderson's algebra and trigonometry, ex-President Venable's chemistry (which Wolfe remembered chiefly as a series of demonstrations that never quite came off), physics, European history, and so forth—with the exception of English. He got off to a bad start with freshman composition. His satirical revenge on Professor Turlington, the Oxonian, in *Look Homeward, Angel* [6] was probably based on his own distaste for careful exposition and argument. At midyear, however, he changed professors and found James Holly Hanford and the literary study of the second term more congenial.

In his second year he made his acquaintance with Edwin Greenlaw, "the grim Ironist," as Wolfe called him, "one of the great creative forces in my life." [7] In a classroom in Old East, the first building on the Carolina campus, Greenlaw led Wolfe over the whole expanse of English literature. Since Greenlaw emphasized ideas in literature, it is easy to recognize his stamp on the survey course as the department offered it: "The course aims to develop in the student a sense of the meaning and value of literature in its relation to life. Certain leading ideas—political, social, and religious—rather than matters of literary technique are made the basis of the discussions. The chief authors studied are Shakespere, Bacon, Herrick, Milton, Pope, Addison, Johnson, Burke, Burns, Wordsworth, Shelley, Carlyle, Tennyson, Browning." [8] One may get the best idea of the particular selections emphasized by looking at a copy of the textbook which Greenlaw and Hanford were compiling, *The Great Tradition.*[9] In Greenlaw's course Wolfe first fell under the spell of Carlyle's thunderous rhetoric, finding his anti-democratic ironies attractive. More significant, in this class Wolfe was first introduced to Greenlaw's theory of literature as a transcript of life.

Besides a general survey of English literature, Greenlaw also gave Wolfe a solid undergraduate background in the English Renaissance. In his junior year, Wolfe studied the Elizabethan Drama under Greenlaw, a course which emphasized Shakespeare, Marlowe, and Jonson and in which was born Wolfe's life-long love of Jonson's comedies (which he thought superior to Shakespeare's) for their realism and gusto.[10] In his senior year, he took Greenlaw's course in the non-dramatic literature of the Renaissance, emphasizing the poetry and Spenser in the first quarter and Renaissance ideas and Bacon in the second quarter. In that course Wolfe first looked into the *Faerie Queen* and responded to the great Renaissance theme of mutability,[11] which he later echoed constantly in his own books. In Greenlaw's hands *Paradise Lost* took on new meanings, "the cold sublimity of Milton began to burgeon with life and opulent color." [12]

Also in this course, Greenlaw implanted in Wolfe a great respect for Bacon, as his well-marked copies of *The Advancement of Learning* and the *Essays* show.[13] Later at Harvard one of the first papers he wrote, entitled "For the Relief of Man's Estate," was a treatment of Ben Franklin as a man who put Bacon's ideas into practice.

Although Greenlaw stressed scholarly investigation and criticism of ideas, he also encouraged Wolfe's writing. To his class in advanced composition Greenlaw first read Galsworthy's *Strife* ("How his grim mouth loved it," Wolfe noted) [14] and then organized a writing project in which the whole class collaborated on a novel about a strike. Wolfe jotted this remembrance of the experiment: "My part the breaking of the strike and the two men on the verandah high above town—Greenlaw said I had achieved 'style'—what most men don't get till forty." [15]

Greenlaw's theory of literature as a "transcript of life" is set forth in his book, *The Province of Literary History*. The phrase "transcript of life" itself did not mean mere reporting— "[It] is by no means to be identified with what we commonly call realism," he states. What it did embrace comes out in his statement of the proper aim of literary history:

Such a history takes into account literature as reflecting not the externals of contemporary manners alone, but the spiritual conflicts of an age; an epoch is rarely to be explained in terms of a simple proposition, since its life is very complex and is filled with cross currents; and finally, the "life" of an age or of a representative major intellect of that age is not a matter of household economy, daily experience, party warfare, but includes the intellectual sources, the influence of a past time, transformed or translated in terms of the age or of the writer's genius.[16]

His was a solid, comprehensive approach to literary study. He felt that, in an age of science, humanistic study was suffering from a lack of intellectual strength, and, moreover, it needed to attempt concrete demonstration ("Get the facts. Get the facts and order them," [17] he told his students at the first meeting of a class) in order to take its place beside scientific study. His book is a defense of the scholarly study of imaginative literature, for he regarded poetry along with rhetorical and philosophical literature as a branch of learning.

That Greenlaw preached his theory as early as Wolfe's time

at Chapel Hill is attested by a question found on his examination sheet for English 37 (the Elizabethan Drama course):

> II Transcript and Criticism (Literature is both a transcript and a criticism of life)
>
> 1. Give the substance of Marlowe's view of University education as contained in the opening lines of *Faustus*. Does *Faustus* suggest any improvement? What is the significance, then, of the close of the tragedy? In your answer to this question see that you show how the tragedy, as a whole, is representative of both medieval and Renaissance thought about life.[18]

Greenlaw's view of literature and his continual emphasis on the relation of literature to life (even his series of school textbooks edited for Scott, Foresman and Company is entitled *Literature and Life*) were firmly impressed on Wolfe's mind during his years of study at Chapel Hill. When Wolfe, with his inner necessity for self-expression and his desire to put a world of detail on paper, decided on his course as an autobiographical writer, Greenlaw's critical tenets were exactly the kind of authority he could point to for support. "I intend to wreak out my soul on paper and express it all," he wrote in the long manifesto to his mother.[19] His later obsession to chronicle his life fully, to tell all, to load his narrative with a burden of irrelevant detail, was encouraged by his misconception of Greenlaw's approach to literature. On the other hand, since Wolfe in his writing never overlooked the relation between literature and life, he profited from Greenlaw's teaching and gave his work a vitality that Greenlaw himself admired.

The discipline of Edwin Greenlaw was a fortunate influence on Wolfe's young mind. As a scholar, Greenlaw was learned and intellectually solid; as a teacher he was vigorous, firm-willed, demanding, persuasive—a man who could present ideas in a way that led his students to accept them and believe in them. But Wolfe's temperament did not allow him to follow Greenlaw all the way. He hated scholarship. He thought Greenlaw was too scientific and methodical: "He is a thoroughgoing teutonized scholar and swears by the Ph.D." [20] He thought Greenlaw's mind was too restricted—"his mind under the regulation of formal scholarship—devouring hunger but formalized." [21] In his portrait of Greenlaw in *The Web and the Rock,* Wolfe characterizes Monk Webber's teacher, "Randolph Ware," as a man who wasted great imaginative powers by his search for facts. " 'What do you do with them after you get them?' said Monk. 'I put salt on their tails and get some more,' said Professor Randolph Ware." [22]

Greenlaw was never the kind of campus figure who would be called a "popular professor"; his vast learning made him somewhat forbidding. But he had warmth and spoke with friendly irony. In the morning when Wolfe and others waited for him to come down the walk, he greeted them all by name as "Brother." Wolfe remembered him always with affection and respect, and he acknowledged Greenlaw to be the greatest teacher of literature he ever had.

Greenlaw thought well of Wolfe, too. Remembering the young man's undergraduate years, he wrote this appraisal of him for the Harvard Appointment Office: "I have an extremely high regard for Mr. Wolfe, both as a student and as a man. He is an exceedingly able writer, a hard worker, and a man of interesting personality." [23] When *Look Homeward, Angel* was published, Greenlaw was among the first to write a letter of praise to the author. Had he known that the portrait of Randolph Ware was included in the first manuscript of the book, he would have been amused. Nor did he ever read Wolfe's characterization of him. Edwin Greenlaw died in 1931, eight years before *The Web and the Rock* was published.

II

Thomas Wolfe's activities outside the classroom were scattered. He debated, he wrote, he pursued the amusements of a college boy. Wolfe, hopeful of a career in law, noticed immediately the campus interest in public speaking. Formal debate was popular, campus politics were full of forensic display, and the old Dialectic and Philanthropic Societies were centers for oratorical contests between students from the western and eastern parts of the state. The administration encouraged this interest in speaking (President Graham himself was an accomplished rhetorician) and required every freshman to take one hour in elementary public speaking. Wolfe fitted very easily into this tradition. In his first year he joined the Di Society, as it was called, and by his junior year he was one of the campus politicians.

In his sophomore year, Wolfe joined the staff of the *Tar Heel*, the college paper, and during his senior year he was the editor-in-chief. For the *Carolina Magazine*, he wrote stories, poems, and plays, all of them conforming to the general standards of the magazine, which were execrable. When Milton Abernethy threatened in later years to reprint some of these pieces in *Contempo*, a little magazine published in Chapel Hill, Wolfe earnestly pleaded against it.[24]

When he arrived on the campus, Wolfe began to read widely, but as his outside activities increased, he spent less time with books. Aside from classwork, his reading after his junior year was scant. Frederick Koch spoke of his interest in Shaw.[25] In his own notes Wolfe mentions only Defoe, Smollett, Galsworthy, and the poetry of Hardy—but he no doubt turned to the library shelves for other authors who were discussed by fellow members of Sigma Upsilon, the literary fraternity.

Wolfe's campus life was not unusual, but it seemed, to a boy from Buncombe county, new and exciting. He cheered at football games, tried out for track, entered into dormitory bull sessions, discovered the red-light district in Durham, joined a social fraternity, spoke at initiation dinners, and attended the college dances. As editor of the *Tar Heel*, he felt he was a political spokesman for the student body. He met the outgoing governor, Locke Craig. He editorialized on the 1920 political campaign, addressing his remarks ("Handbook of Useful Information to Those Gubernatorially Inclined Who Will Speak in Chapel Hill") [26] to the contenders, Max Gardner and Cameron Morrison; and he saw with pride that newspapers all over the state praised his editorial, quoting or copying it. In his junior year, he was awarded the Worth Prize in Philosophy for his essay, "The Crisis in Industry." [27] By his senior year, he imagined himself a superior campus figure—"Enlarged opinions of our greatness—'The Big Men' and the feeling of greatness and importance all around us," he recalled in later years.[28] At graduation time he was pleased to see the long list of activities beside his name in the college yearbook. But among the various organizations to which he belonged, only one had a direct bearing on his career, The Carolina Playmakers, supervised by Professor Frederick Koch.

Frederick Koch had been one of Professor George Pierce Baker's students in the 47 Workshop at Harvard. Inspired by Baker, this enthusiastic disciple had first organized the Dakota Playmakers and had then come to the University of North Carolina, where he set up a workshop in folk drama. When Koch formed the Carolina Playmakers at Chapel Hill in 1918, Wolfe, then in his junior year, became a charter member of the group.[29] In "O Lost," the original version of *Look Homeward, Angel,* Wolfe drew a brief sketch of Koch as Professor Hutch, "The Little Man with the Urge." Although Hutch knew very little about plays, Wolfe wrote, his inexhaustible enthusiasm fired his students to turn out abundant work. But the drama seemed only an accidental channel for his boundless energy. "His value to a business corporation would have been incalculable. If he could have convinced himself that the salvation of the earth's children lay in the use of Porter's Pickles—and he could have done this easily—he could have carried the Pickle to the Poles." [30] This caricature of the professor who intoxicated Wolfe with the dream of becoming a playwright was written with bitterness. It shows not only Wolfe's regret that he wasted time trying to fit his talents to the drama but also his resentment that Broadway rejected his work.

Wolfe enrolled in Koch's courses in dramatic composition for two years, but apparently he never worked very hard at his writing. Paul Green recalls that Wolfe would always wait until the night before an assignment was due, stay up all night writing his one-act play, and come to class hollow-eyed and unshaven to read the result.[31] His mountaineer play, "The Return of Buck Gavin," which was enacted in the first Playmakers program, spring, 1919, was composed in this fashion. Wolfe dashed off the play in three hours one rainy evening after seeing a newspaper item in the *Grand Forks [North Dakota] Herald* reporting the capture of Patrick Lavein, a Texas outlaw, in a Chicago tenement. His gift for mimicry made the mountain dialogue an easy matter, but the play was poor, even for a student effort. Nor did the presentation come off well, Archibald Henderson reports; the most interesting feature was the appearance of the author himself as the outlaw.[32]

Although the aim of the Carolina Playmakers was to encourage students to use the materials around them to achieve a vigorous realism and although Paul Green as the best representative of the early group did succeed admirably in converting native themes into drama, most of the folk plays were, like Wolfe's, sub-literary. In later years Wolfe realized the principal difficulty—that the student playwrights (and Professor Koch) did not know what a folk play was.

"A folk play is a play in which the people say 'Hit ain't' and 'that air,'" he quipped in "O Lost" and then proceeded to parody his own play as Eugene Gant's "The Return of Jed Sevier." The curtain line as Jed is captured reflects his mock definition of the folk play: "Hit's the law. Ye cain't buck hit. Hit'll get ye in the end."[33]

His satire on the Playmakers in "O Lost" includes a mock "tragedy of the soil," which is, in fact, a burlesque of the second act of his own play, "The Mountains," written at Harvard in 1922.

> SAL: (*with harsh embarrassed sympathy*) Ain't ye feel no better, Jim?
>
> JIM: (*looking with disgust at the greasy mess before him*) No, an' I don't reckon I'll ever get no better as long as I got to eat this belly-bustin' swill. (*passionately*) Hit's a-killin' me! So help me God this hog wash is a-killin' me. Hit's eatin' my guts out.
>
> SAL: (*with weary despair*) Hit's all the like of us kin afford, I reckon, Jim. I knowed hit weren't doin' ye no good. The doctor said ye were gettin' gassier and gassier, but we ain't got nothin' to buy grub with. Mebbe ye can get old Jarvis to fix another loan.
>
> JIM: (*sullenly*) He said he ain't a-goin' to let me have no more. An' he won't give me no more time on that note. He says he's a-goin' to foreclose this time if we don't make the payment.
>
> DICK: (*he is a sensitive intelligent looking boy of 15, but already bent and worn by hard work and hunger*) Paw, Perfessor Jenkins said I cain't come back to school no more 'less I git some books.
>
> JIM: (*with a sudden outburst of blind rage slapping the boy across the mouth*) I ain't got no money to waste on books, ye little bastard.
>
> SAL: (*slowly*) I reckon them things ain't for the like o' us. . . .Whut's hit all about Jim?
>
> JIM: (*wearily*) God knows.[34]

For Wolfe, two important results came out of his two years with the Playmakers. First, he was introduced to a writing method that he later used in his significant work. Frederick Koch (who had adopted the idea from Professor Baker) urged all his students to use the materials of their own experience in their writing. Later, Wolfe realized that his plays at Chapel Hill were bad because they were false. As he said, he knew all about boarding houses, but he wrote about bootlegging mountaineers. He did not turn to his real experience until his later years at Harvard. The second result came about through the very feature of Koch's personality which Wolfe ridiculed. Although Wolfe's Chapel Hill plays were trivial, Koch's uncritical enthusiasm convinced him they were great. It is one of the fortunate ironies of Thomas Wolfe's life that undiscriminating encouragement launched him on a writing career that was to become the center of his existence for the rest of his life.

Thomas Wolfe often remarked that the two teachers who were most important in his life were the two Chapel Hill professors, Edwin Greenlaw and Horace Williams. Readers of *Look Homeward, Angel* are already familiar with Horace Williams, who appears as Eugene Gant's philosophy professor, Virgil Weldon.[35] A closer look at Williams' personality and teaching will explain Wolfe's attitude, both sympathetic and critical, in this character sketch.

In the courses Wolfe took under "the magnificent twister," [36] as he called Williams, he received a full exposure to Williams' philosophical system with all its adjuncts. As seen in Williams' books, *The Evolution of Logic* and *Modern Logic*,[37] his paraphrase of Hegelianism exhibits two main features, first, a view of life as a process of syntheses ("moments of negation," he called them) of thesis and antithesis, and, second, an idealistic and monistic view of the universe in which Reality only exists in the union of an object with its opposite (the *Begriff* which results at the moment of negation). Ultimate reality, the Absolute, can only exist after the process of continual union of opposites is complete. Evolution, civilization, history, all are a series of unfolding resolutions of conflicts. In illustration of his two principles, Williams' books cite interminably, and without regard for meaning or consistency, the merging of various pairs of opposites. His terminology is a hopeless jargon that became quite familiar to the Carolina students. Any paragraph chosen at random will serve as an example of the occult style of Hegel further obscured by a man who cannot write:

The infinite negates the finite and the finite negates the infinite: the *begriff* negates its own negation and is reality. The *begriff* is the concrete, one of its moments being the negation of the infinite. It is a definite, a particular, one of its moments being the negation of the first negation. The *begriff* being the unity of the infinite and finite has absorbed the moment of negation and is therefore permanent, real. The concrete, the particular as *begriff*, becomes permanent in itself and we have being-in-and-for-itself.[38]

With his framework of Hegelian dialectic he combined a loose Unitarian theology and personal insights on immortality and the supernatural. He had no difficulty forcing a synthesis between Hegelianism and Christianity: "The Hegelian philosophy, which is nothing but a translation of Jesus' life into thought, is the effort to find the unity." [39]

In his junior year Wolfe enrolled in Williams' course, "A Study of the Forces That Shape Life," apparently a series of lectures and discussions that mixed Berkeley, Hume, Kant, Hegel, and Spencer into Williams' own special brew. In his last year Wolfe took Williams' course in Logic, which was not a study of logic in the usual sense; it was a rehash of Hegel's *Science of Logic* and certain parts of the *Phenomenology of Mind*, in which Williams illustrated that Thought and Absolute Idea was Totality.[40] In his classes no books were read and a prejudice against learning was encouraged. Wolfe said in his Autobiographical Outline: "We read nothing—we began to feel a certain contempt for people who did read—Science got facts—not principles—unable to solve its own problems—a monster unable to stop its own work—Had raised questions, but was unable to answer them."

Student opinion polls usually rated Horace Williams as Chapel Hill's most popular professor. In his lectures he impressed the undergraduate mind with his combination of high-sounding abstractions and homely illustrations. As an earthy man from farm country who kept his own cow and distrusted modern plumbing, he adopted the role of cracker-barrel philosopher. Anything was likely to come up in Williams' lectures—that a pig was the negation of beauty or that Christ might be present in Virginia and Georgia at the same time.[41] The moral problem about the sale of a mule which Wolfe used for "The Men of Old Catawba" came from Williams' classroom. Students looked on Williams as an intellectual champion, for he encouraged skepticism toward long-established prejudices and he was actively opposed to the strong forces of Fundamentalism in North Carolina.[42] He took an energetic part in student affairs, coaching debate and aiding in the establishment of an athletic program. More than anything else, his personal contact with his students made him a popular figure. They came to his home as to a confessional, and

Horace, putting his wife out "with the cat," turned a fatherly ear their way. Wolfe recalled the student seekers in his Autobiographical Outline: "The soul struggles of the original thinkers. Up the path to Horace's house—but never about sex—about rather a union with God —or soul wrestling—the Man who went to the woods and fought it out—What Horace called 'the Wilderness Experience.'"[43]

This mixture of kindliness and charlatanism appealed to Thomas Wolfe as a student. His mind was attracted to Williams' teachings in the same way that it later was drawn by the mistiness of Coleridge's speculations. When he turned from the rigors of Greenlaw's discipline, he relaxed in Williams' class, learning "a fascinating system with unending mind-seducing involution—like Royce's picture of a map within a map and so on." He felt "a Liberating Breath."[44] Indeed, Williams seemed at the time a great thinker dealing with life's important problems while other professors concerned themselves with minutiae. Although Wolfe was only a somewhat better than average scholar at Chapel Hill, he had a great interest in primary questions, and to his untrained mind, which delighted in undergraduate discussions of being and essence, the one and the many, truth and goodness, time and immortality, Williams' intellectual nostrums seemed to supply final answers. Moreover, for Wolfe, Williams' personal appeal was strong. Here was a manly man who smelled of the earth, even if it was of the barnyard, and who played the role of the village Socrates. Further, he was paternal. And when one of the members of the faculty spends more time with students than with his colleagues, he is usually worshipped.

It was perhaps unfortunate for Carolina students that Williams set up as a university teacher. Although Wolfe became, as Williams wrote, "one of the six remarkable students in [his] thirty year's experience,"[45] this achievement is really evidence that he left Chapel Hill in some intellectual confusion.

Powerful forces among the university faculty were opposed to Williams and his obscurantism, but it was difficult to get rid of him. In spite of his personal and academic eccentricities[46] and in spite of his "genius for occasional and conscious malignity,"[47] Williams was firmly established. He had been a member of the faculty since 1890, he was the third-ranking professor in the university, and he had a large following among the alumni, many of whom were grateful to a professor who had opened their eyes to the existence of philosophical questions. He was even honored by being appointed a Kenan professor after members of the Kenan family brought pressure to bear on President Harry Woodburn Chase and the Trustees. But the faculty group which was interested in building a great university (and Greenlaw was in the forefront) realized that there could never be a respectable Department of Philosophy as long as Williams was the senior professor.

A few years later, at Harvard, Wolfe began to write a play about the clash of forces that he thought these men represented—Williams, the fiery idealist, and Greenlaw, the representative of scientific method. From the fragments of the play that remain, it is clear that Professor Weldon, the philosophy teacher, was to have been the more sympathetic character.[48]

Wolfe went to Harvard under the influence of Williams' ideas, but a first draft of a letter to Greenlaw in March or April, 1922, shows that by the close of the second year at Harvard he was doubtful of the Hegelian monism that Williams had preached to his college classes: "If I'm ever to be a dramatist I must believe in struggle. I've got to believe in dualism, in a definite spirit of evil, and in a Satan who is tired from walking up and down upon the earth. These are things I can visualize. When we erase the struggle, our power of visualization seems to fade. I have the utmost difficulty in bringing into my mind the picture of Professor Williams absorbing a negation (confidential)." Life as he was now living it and writing as he wished to practice it made him feel that the doctrine of the *Begriff* was only classroom theory that he could forget with no great loss: "I'm beginning to know the kind of thing I want to do now. And it calls for a grasp on the facts of life. When I attended philosophy lectures (and I rate those lectures very highly) I was told that there was no reality in a wheelbarrow, that reality rested in the *concept* or plan of that whee[l]barrow. But the wheelbarrow is the thing you show on the stage. . . ." [49] Yet Wolfe never forgot Horace Williams' kindly attention to him, and he continued to value him as a friend. In *Look Homeward, Angel* he wrote of Virgil Weldon: "To me, you were the sufficient negation to all your teachings." [50]

What permanent influence Williams had on Wolfe's thinking and writing is difficult to discern.[51] Possibly Williams' reiteration of the Socratic "Know thyself" and his emphasis upon this dictum as the purpose of philosophy ("The study of philosophy is, as I understand it, the study of yourself," he told his class in logic) [52] suggested the final decision of Eugene Gant in *Look Homeward, Angel* to search "in the city of myself, upon the continent of my soul." But the passage is a natural one for an autobiographical writer—Proust, for example, concludes *Remembrance of Things Past* in the same way. More probably, Williams' doctrine of individualism lay partly behind Wolfe's attempt to determine his own experience after he went to Harvard. One thing is certain, however: Williams', that is to say Hegel's, concept of life as process, reality as process, prepared Wolfe's mind for the acceptance of the doctrine of vitalism. The world-view that Wolfe later formulated out of Shaw, Wells, and probably Bergson, had its beginnings in Williams' classroom. This is the more evident because of Williams' frequent illustrations of the Hegelian dialectic in Nature in this fashion:

A grain of wheat, for example. When you plant it, it disappears out of your sight. . . .Not only is that true, but the next time you see that grain of wheat it is not a grain of wheat. It is a little green plant, and it has no mark in common with the grain of wheat you planted. You say that little green sprig came out of the grain, although it has nothing in common with the grain so far as you can see. It is green; the grain is yellow. It is long, and the grain is very small. It is different in shape; it is quite different in make-up. When the grain of wheat sprouts—cracks, swells, and dies— it ceases to be a grain of wheat. . . .The negative is just as important as the positive. Would you ever have a process—of life, of wheat growing— without negation? [53]

It is also certain that Williams' teaching accentuated the Westall tendency in Wolfe's mind, the twist of irrationality. This disregard of logic and fact led Wolfe as a man into much loose thinking and many bad judgments. On the other hand, since Wolfe's own approach to problems was intuitive rather than analytically logical, he may have been right as an artist when, speaking of Williams, he made this judgment in 1926: "What I needed was a spirit that knew no reason." [54]

After graduation in June, 1920, Thomas Wolfe returned to Asheville uncertain of his next step. There was little permanent attraction to his home. His father, stricken with cancer, was no longer the dominating figure of the family. His favorite brother, Ben, had died during the "influenza" epidemic of 1918, bringing Wolfe the greatest grief of his early life. Having once left the Asheville fastness and the Old Kentucky Home bedlam, he wanted now to escape for good. Further study seemed to be the answer for both literary and personal needs. Wolfe applied in August for admission to the Harvard Graduate School and was accepted.

During his four years at Chapel Hill, the gawky young man from western North Carolina who had come with expectations of a future in law had met men and circumstances that altered his course. Edwin Greenlaw had praised his writing and encouraged his further study. Frederick Koch had greeted his trivial efforts at playwriting with acclaim. Faculty and student opinion had commended his writing for the *Tar Heel,* the *Carolina Magazine,* and the Playmakers; the yearbook had tagged him a "genius." He wanted to be a writer. Although his student writing, with the exception of the lecture-platform style of "The Crisis in Industry," showed no glimmer of the force that was to come, his presence apparently gave a hint of the creative turbulence that was latent in him. As Paul Green describes it, the spark of promise was there:

The tumult and lyric seething which later become his glowing life began in him I think toward the end of his stay at Chapel Hill. Up to that time his emotionalism was the normal adolescence of any boy. Toward the end of his college career, as I knew him and talked with him now and then in the old Sigma Upsilon writing fraternity and elsewhere, there was beginning that terrific ache and hunger and impetuous reach. And always associated with it in his last college days. . .was the desire to be a playwright.[55]

NOTES

1. Chapel Hill, 1950.
2. Walser, pp. 8-17.
3. Nowell, pp. 33-49.
4. AO.
5. *Letters,* p. 342.
6. See the picture of the lisping Mr. Torrington (Pulpit Hill and Merton, '14) pp. 397-99.
7. AO.
8. *University of North Carolina Record: The Catalogue, 1916-17,* p. 61.
9. Chicago, 1919.
10. At Harvard, Wolfe began a play modeled on *Bartholomew Fair* (*Letters,* p. 39). In the late 1920's, he spent most of an evening at William Tindall's apartment looking at a copy of the 1616 Folio.

11. Wolfe returned often to the *Cantos of Mutability;* in his favorite anthology, George Beaumont's *A Book of English Poetry* (HCL*46A-105), a page is turned down to mark it.

12. From Wolfe's description of George Webber's study under Professor Randolph Ware, a character based on Edwin Greenlaw (W&R, p. 217).

13. HCL*46A-166 and 765.

14. AO.

15. AO. This material probably went into the making of the one-act play, "The Strikers," which Wolfe wrote at Chapel Hill, HCL*46AM-7(15).

16. (Baltimore, 1931) pp. 84-85.

17. HCL*46AM-7(21).

18. HCL*46AM-8(14).

19. LTM, p. 52.

20. HCL*46AM-7(21).

21. AO.

22. W&R, p. 216.

23. Harvard University Archives, UA III 5.78.10, 1st Series, Appointment Office folder for Wolfe.

24. HCL, unpublished letter to Milton Abernethy, April 15, 1932. Floyd Watkins, in "Thomas Wolfe and the Nashville Agrarians," *Georgia Review,* VII (Winter, 1953), overstated the case when he said of Wolfe and his associates at Chapel Hill: "Here were gathered a group which could have written a Fugitive, but they were fleeing the old South, not the new order" (p. 411).

25. *Carolina Folk-Plays, First, Second, and Third Series,* ed. Frederick Koch (New York, 1941), pp. 127-29.

26. Agatha Boyd Adams, *Thomas Wolfe: Carolina Student* (Chapel Hill, 1950), pp. 45-46.

27. Chapel Hill, 1919. Three hundred copies were printed and distributed.

28. AO.

29. Koch has described the origin of the Carolina Playmakers and has recorded his personal recollections of Wolfe in *Carolina Folk-Plays, First, Second, and Third Series,* pp. 127-31.

30. HCL*45M-156F, pp. 1113-14.

31. James K. Hutsell, "As They Recall Thomas Wolfe," *Southern Packet,* IV (April, 1948), p. 4.

32. *Anderson [South Carolina] Independent,* August 7, 1948.

33. HCL*H5M-156F, p. 1115.

34. *Ibid.,* pp. 1116-17.

35. LHA, pp. 593-96.

36. AO.

37. Both privately printed, Chapel Hill, 1925 and 1927.

38. *The Evolution of Logic,* p. 18.

39. *Logic for Living* (New York, 1951), p. 228.

40. The posthumous publication of Williams' lectures for 1921-22, *Logic for Living,* gives us a fairly accurate picture of the lectures (and classroom discussion) which Wolfe heard two years before. In its main headings, Part III of the Williams book follows the section "The Doctrine of Being" in Hegel's *Science of Logic.*

41. AO.

42. The Christian Fundamentalist movement was vigorous in North Carolina even through the twenties. In 1925, with the support of Governor Cameron Morrison, the

Fundamentalists almost succeeded in persuading the legislature to pass the "Poole Monkey Bill," a measure outlawing the teaching of evolution.

43. AO.

44. AO.

45. Harvard University Archives, UA III 5.78.10, 1st Series, Appointment Office folder for Wolfe. President Edward Kidder Graham was the first of the "six remarkable students."

46. Peculiarities of both the ideas and the personal life of this self-appointed North Carolina Socrates may be discerned through the clouds of sentiment in Robert Winston's popular biography, *Horace Williams, Gadfly of Chapel Hill* (Chapel Hill, 1942).

47. AO.

48. HCL*46AM-7(21).

49. *Letters*, p. 30.

50. P. 603.

51. Holman feels that "Wolfe's tendency to see and to express things in terms of oppositions may have been learned at the feet of Horace Williams" (p. 11).

52. *Logic for Living*, p. 4.

53. *Ibid.*, pp. 32-33.

54. AO.

55. Hutsell, "As They Recall Thomas Wolfe," p. 4.

Part II

THE YEARS OF APPRENTICESHIP

4

THE MODERN HERMIT

AT HARVARD, NOT ONLY DID THOMAS WOLFE SOAK HIMSELF IN the great literature of the world but, during this time, he made the all-important decision to become a professional writer. His prolific writing career began in Professor George Pierce Baker's 47 Workshop, where he turned out *Welcome to Our City,* his first creditable literary production. Moreover, living alone, far from home and familiar surroundings, he began to formulate ideas about writing and about the life of the artist that were to have far-reaching effects on his future.

He worked under some of Harvard's most celebrated faculty members during the time he was enrolled in the graduate school. A list of the courses he took from 1920 to 1923 shows the range and variety of his studies. First and most important, he was registered for three years in G. P. Baker's playwriting course, English 47 and 47a (familiarly called the 47 Workshop). He also chose Baker's course, "The Forms of the Drama," a survey of the great works in the drama from the Greeks to the twentieth century, and Professor A. N. Murray's course, "The Drama in England from 1590 to 1642." Under Professor John Livingston Lowes, he studied "The Poets of the Romantic Period" and worked on "Studies in the Literature of the Renaissance" (the Renaissance literature of Italy, France, the Germanic countries, and England). He took Professor Chester Greenough's survey of American literature (reputed to be deadly dull), and he audited Professor G. L. Kittredge's Shakespeare course. Nor did he stay entirely within the English Department. He took a course in aesthetic theory under Professor Langfield in the Philosophy Department and a summer course in British history under Professor McIlwain, and during his last term at Harvard he audited Irving

Babbitt's famous "Literary Criticism of the Neo-Classic Period." In addition, he got up a reading knowledge of French in order to qualify for the A.M. degree.

He did well in his courses, making almost all A's. Likewise, most of his class reports and term papers, which ran in characteristic Wolfean fashion to seventy or eighty pages, received A grades. They were, however, rambling and of unequal quality throughout, as the following representative comments by his professors indicate. Parts of these apt criticisms might well be applied to some of Wolfe's novels. From Professor Greenough: "An interesting discussion. Your quotations are not always critically related. You are apt to be carried away by your enthusiasm and to keep more than is essential to your point." [1] From Professor Murray: "I like the originality and vigor of your appreciation of Ben Jonson. You show genuine understanding of the man and his work. In writing you are inclined to repeat yourself and the essay could profit by a reordering." [2] And most perceptive of all, from Professor Lowes: "This paper shows both insight and a gift for expression. The last, in particular, needs (as Coleridge says) to be 'curbed and ruddered.' The study sprawls a little—yet you can be terse and telling, as you show again and again." [3]

He did almost all of his formal course work in the first year and a half, allowing more time for the Workshop and for extensive reading during the last half of his residence. Yet even during his busiest terms, Wolfe had more time for reading than ever before. At Chapel Hill his campus activities had taken all his spare time, but at Harvard, among students whom he found restrained and distant, he made few friends at first, and he looked to the books of the Widener Library for companionship.

II

We must examine the records that Wolfe left of the Harvard period, particularly the Autobiographical Outline in 1926, for the closest glimpse of his thinking and especially his feelings during this time. It is difficult to fit the disordered phrases of the Outline into coherent patterns, but in these pages he touched more fully on the problems of his life than he did in the letters, essays, or plays of the period.

Wolfe's self-consciousness and the resulting self-dramatization are dominant characteristics of his life and of his writings. The self-consciousness began to develop during his academic career, and even the self-dramatization began to find expression in the plays at Harvard.[4] His profound loneliness recurs again and again in the mass of opinions and feelings expressed during or about the Harvard period, and this sense of seclusion from social communication accentuated his self-consciousness. In the Autobiographical Outline, he spoke of "the imprint of loneliness—the ineradicable strain of solitude upon my spirit." He saw it all around him as "the homelessness and houselessness of modern life." He had the feeling that among the crowd all means of communication failed him. He said that "the modern hermit carries all within him—His retreat is the populous wilderness of this world."

Arising from Wolfe's self-consciousness are four seemingly inconsistent aspirations that are prominent not only in his feeling and thinking of this period but also in his later writing as he expressed, developed, or solved his emotional problems. They are a desire for fame, a desire for encyclopedic knowledge and experience, a desire for escape from such determining forces of the world as seemed to him oppressive, and a desire for some absolute answer to the problem of life.

The desire for fame manifested itself in his aspiration to be a professional playwright. He continually wrote his mother about his hopes and ambitions for footlight fame: "I believe I'll be able to do real work to be talked about when I'm twenty-five years old," [5] or "If I succeed and it is on that I love to think. . . ." [6] Coupled with this desire and growing with it was his conception of himself as an "artist" (in his fictional treatment of Baker's classes he glosses this word: "or as most of Professor Hatcher's young men spoke the word, 'Ottist' ").[7] According to the Outline, certain members of the playwriting group looked upon themselves as members of an aesthetic aristocracy; they discussed the place of the artist in society and the plight of the artist in America. They demanded for the artist freedom from social responsibility; they complained that mankind destroys its prophets; and they damned that villainous opponent of the arts, the businessman. In his Autobiographical Outline, Wolfe looked back on this posturing with some scorn as the "Artist Myth," but it is plain, from his letters to his mother and to Mrs. Roberts during this time, that he looked upon himself as one of the sanctified. Although later he discarded most of the self-pitying, self-praising attitudes of the poet-priest, he always retained the idea of himself in the role of the artist, and as a consequence he was ever serious about his work (and about himself whom he distilled into his work). Although this personality trait has repelled many of Wolfe's readers, this conception of himself was the drive that later enabled him to pour out his material in unbelievable profusion and, never sparing himself, to labor endless hours trying to shape the resulting mass. It was his duty to himself as an "artist."

The desire for encyclopedic knowledge and experience was expressed in many ways, but most often as an acute longing to read all the books in the world and to know all the people in the world. He told Mrs. Roberts about his reading: "I take great delight in counting the victims of my insatiable bookishness," and after listing a few titles, he continued: "I suppose I make a mistake in trying to eat all the plums at once for instead of peace it has awakened a good-sized volcano in me. I wander throughout the stacks of that great library there like some damned soul; never at rest,—even leaping ahead from the pages I read to thoughts of those I want to read." [8] In the Outline he jotted these notes about his feverish pursuit of information: "The merciless dissection of books, probing the bowels of a man's writing—the table, paper, writing materials—all as good as theirs—the constant quest in bad books for good things—the book shops—religious tracts—with a watch in one hand to scan a page—the Farnsworth Room in the Widener Library—the laying waste of the shelves."

"To know all things and to be all places" was related to his desire for fame, for it was a preparation for the task of the artist. He wished to render himself into an Everyman in order that his own experience might be a touchstone guaranteeing the universal in his future writings. In the Outline, he characterized himself as one who "visualized his life as a vast tapering funnel into which everything must be poured."

At this point, it should be explained that Professor John Livingston Lowes was partly responsible for Wolfe's ranging through books. At the time when Wolfe enrolled in the course in Romantic poetry, Lowes was immersed in his study of the poetic process, using Coleridge's 1795-98 Notebook as his principal document. As readers of Lowes' *The Road to Xanadu* [9] know, he was able to demonstrate that Coleridge's vast reading contributed in an astonishing way to the creation of "The Ancient Mariner" and "Kubla Khan." The contents of myriad books lay for years in Coleridge's "deep well of unconscious cerebration" (Lowes takes this phrase from Henry James); and later, isolated words, phrases, images, and ideas rose from the chaos of twilight memory to be shaped into brilliant poetry. Wolfe, fascinated by Lowes' findings, wanted to put the secret formula into practice. He strove to stock his memory with a prodigious store of bookish turmoil from which great poetry might emerge when the imaginative faculty summoned. This is his explanation in a letter to Greenlaw: "Professor Lowes' book on Coleridge (not published yet I believe) which he read to the class last year, had a great effect on me. In that book, he shows conclusively how retentive of all it reads is the mind and how, at almost any moment that mass of material may be fused and resurrected in new and magic forms. This is wonderful, I think. So I'm reading, not so analytically but voraciously." [10]

In his term paper on Coleridge, Wolfe reveals a close familiarity with Lowes' theory of the deep well. He imitates Lowes' method when he points out examples (and very poor ones, too) of phrases from Coleridge's early poetry which reappear in his mature work. But, more important, he again brings himself into the discussion of Coleridge's habits of mind. He quotes from the *Anima Poetae* to show how Coleridge recalled the entire emotional context of a childhood experience, and he goes on to add his own observations:

It has occurred to me that the marvelous fusing quality of Coleridge's imagination over material that had sunk into that "deep well of unconscious cerebration," might be explained to some extent, by the fact of Coleridge's *conscious* interest and efforts at all times with the association of experiences. It is as if the mind were whetted and keened for its work. My own experience in the last four months has interested me and has some bearing on the point I think.

A constant reader until my junior year at college, interest in campus activities at that time diminished the amount of my reading until recently. During the past four months I have resumed my former habits of heavy reading and, as a result, the ghosts of old, supposedly forgotten books are continually walking forth now, almost as distinct in their detail as when I read them. [11]

From several of such statements, it is clear that Wolfe looked upon himself as a young Coleridge. He even confessed it frankly in the Outline: "And then Coleridge came—Perhaps I was not afraid to read in his experience, in his life, a possible portent of my own. Certainly there was a bond in our common thirst for information." Having in mind his own preying among the shelves in the library stacks, he noted in his term paper Coleridge's boast, "I am and ever have been a great reader, and have read almost everything—a library cormorant"; [12] and later in *Of Time and the River* he used a similar predatory metaphor—his alter ego Eugene Gant in his Faustian fits of reading "pictured himself as tearing the entrails from a book as from a fowl." [13]

When Wolfe began to write his novels, he was still playing Coleridge. The notebooks he kept resemble Coleridge's notebooks, not only in the cryptic style and the introspective manner, but also in the kinds of entries—ideas, judgments, moods, projects, reading notes, and diary passages. More significant, when he dredged back into his memory to bring forth material for his autobiographical fiction, he felt that he was served by "the deep well" in the same way that Coleridge had been. Arguing that as an autobiographical writer he was not the less an artist, he pointed to Lowes' *The Road to Xanadu* as evidence that great writers have made use of autobiographical material for their literary work:

Coleridge. . .was not even conscious of the extent to which his own reading influenced him: he made use of a thousand elements of apparently unrelated experiences to create something that was his own and that was beautiful and real and in the highest sense of the word original. Lowes goes on to attempt to show that the thing that happened when Coleridge wrote this poem happens when the artist creates anything—in other words, that his use of experience which is sunken in the well of unconsciousness, or which is only half remembered, is a typical use of the creative faculty. [14]

The effect of Lowes' teaching on Wolfe is probably the first instance in which a scholar's thesis about the literature of the past has directly influenced the behavior of a contemporary writer.

Wolfe's quest for the fullest knowledge and experience is not inconsistent with the third impulse, the desire to escape from the world about him, especially to escape any forces such as family, custom, or social pressure that might retard his personal or artistic growth. When Wolfe left the South for the first time in order to travel to this Northern university, he exulted, the first night in New York, in "the ecstasy of freedom at last." In later years, his first novel, *Look Homeward, Angel,* was the full expression of this escape from family, school, home town, society. In his Outline, he refers to this escape in terms of a retreat behind a wall. But this freedom, this "wall," is not an exclusive withdrawal from life but is rather a withdrawal into a position from which he can select the "fulness of life" in which he wishes to participate. Wolfe's idea of ordering his own experience came, apparently, from Pater's *Marius the Epicurean* (Chapter VI and elsewhere). In the following jottings from the Outline, he related these three desires and concluded that his solitude was his chosen retreat:

A growing belief and understanding of the selective principle (Marius the Epicurean)—a despair because those events and that knowledge which might mean most might not be ordered to come at the exact moment when it was needed, so that all experience became a perfectly governed stream expanding without wastage or confusion under a constant pressure—the extension of this to all life—to the persons one meets— to all that one sees or does—thus at twenty there was no wall except this enforced and growing solitude.

The last of these yearnings, the desire for some absolute interpretation of the meaning of life, is, perhaps, a demand that was nurtured by the lectures of Horace Williams. Although dissatisfied with Williams' approach to the problem in word-quibbling and paradox, Wolfe's mind was stimulated to look for some absolute solution that would embrace all questions. Early in 1922 he recorded his youthful enthusiasm about this problem in a letter to Horace Williams:

Time after time it has seemed as if mankind was about to come upon the Absolute; to plunge into and discover the ultimate impenetrable mystery; and then they quit, or turn to something else, to baffle and foil themselves anew. I tell you, Mr. Williams, I have become almost fanatically convinced, that if the good and the wise and the great men, would all turn to solving one problem at a time, all working in unison, searching together, and letting the false, misleading things go hang, something might be done.[15]

Later, in his paper on Coleridge, he expressed great admiration for Coleridge's attempt to search out some principle of unity, to "unlock the mystery to the universal riddle." In his novel *Look Homeward, Angel,* this desire became one of the principal themes, for it is one of the meanings behind Wolfe's metaphor of the search for a door.

One passage in the Outline seems to place the first three aspirations alongside the last, the search for a door. The firmest grip on life—the fullest ordered experience—was, so far, the nearest approach to the answer he had been seeking, and more understanding might then grow with further experience. He had been speaking about what he thought and felt in his last year at Chapel Hill:

No Utopias did I have—save one—the world had [brave?] places in which to live—they were *in the world* not out of it—Life then and now a thing to be apprehended—Ultimately I came back to the same blind faith—that life in itself was very full—that what failed in it was our apprehension —Is this not the true romantic feeling—not to desire to escape life, but to prevent life from escaping you—Imperfect apprehension: yet these things which are good are so magnificently good—and usually so Easy of acquisition—that perhaps the rest is only the opening of doors as yet unfound.[16]

III

Wolfe's loneliness resulted partly from his failure to fit into his new surroundings. To many he seemed an odd figure as he made his way about Cambridge with long, quick strides. He was a tall, thin, awkward youth. He did not concern himself with grooming. He dressed so shabbily that his Boston relatives worried about him.

Certainly the young man felt out of place. He was at first overwhelmed by the size and the impersonality of the student population. He wanted to make friends, to enjoy the same informal life that he had known at Chapel Hill. But having been used to a small, closely knit college community, he did not adjust to Harvard for almost two years. Moreover, he often met a barrier of snobbery. One of Professor Baker's assistants has said quite frankly: "Oh yes, I knew Wolfe, but I never liked him. I was introduced to him a couple of times, but whenever I saw him in the yard, I cut him." [17] Although Professor Baker, who took an unusual interest in his graduate students, extended his urbane cordiality to Wolfe, there was a personality difference between the two that could never be bridged.

In the classroom he was extremely shy. Furthermore, the step from the chaotic give-and-take of the Chapel Hill playwriting class to the other extreme of mature criticism (and sometimes a vulgar over-sophistication) made him feel at once hostile and inferior to the other, older members of the class. He wrote to Koch at the beginning of his first term: "When [the other members of English 47] criticize it is as follows: 'Sir Arthur Pinero takes that scene and treats it with *consummate art*' or 'the remarkable literary charm of this play seduces my admiration.' Prof, so help me, God, these are direct quotations. Imagine a raw Tar Heel who with native simplicity has been accustomed to wade into a play (at Chapel Hill) with 'that's great stuff' or 'Rotten'—simple and concise." Although English 47 was conducted informally, Wolfe seldom added to the class discussion, for he was overawed by the "concocted eloquence" of such members as his friend Kenneth Raisbeck.[18] He was very shy with almost everyone: he spoke little, and when he did he stammered out what he had to say in halting phrases. At rehearsals of his plays he scarcely made himself known at all; anything that he had to contribute was spoken in a low tone to Professor Baker, who directed the plays.[19] With friends whom he knew well, however, he talked at great length. He loved to corner a listener to whom he could unburden his feelings, opinions, and remembrances. As one friend expressed it, "He didn't talk to you, he delivered a speech at you." The rhetorical patterns of triple word, phrase, and clause found in Wolfe's writings were also conversational habits. He was fond of hyperbole. In his attempts to express himself, he would repeat himself many times, saying, "I know I'm saying this badly, but what I mean is . . ." The effect was that of a man passionately concerned with communication but not at all sure of his penetration.

He lived in various rooming houses similar to those described in *Of Time and the River.* In his last year, at 21 Trowbridge Street, he lived in the downstairs front room of Mrs. D. J. Casey, whose family became the "Murphys" in *Of Time and the River.* He made himself at home there, spending many hours in the kitchen telling the Caseys about Asheville and about his family or enlarging the vocabulary of Mr. Thong, a Chinese roomer, by teaching him the four-letter words he would not find in books.

His room was generally in a great disorder of books and papers. The floor around his desk was littered with pages (a penciled scrawl on yellow typewriter paper) hurriedly tossed aside during his nightly labors. Piles of manuscript, which Mrs. Casey was forbidden to touch, were scattered about the room. Around his favorite armchair, books were stacked—some stuffed with paper markers, others open to a chosen page and turned face down.

His book-buying astounded the Caseys. As a matter of fact, he bought some of the best titles in his library during this period, picking them up for ten or twenty-five cents at the bookstores in Harvard Square. To list a few is to show how he scattered his interests: the plays of Aeschylus, the plays of Beaumont and Fletcher, Aristotle's *Ethics,* Arnold's *Literature and Dogma, Don Quixote, Cyrano,* R. W. Chambers' *The Beginning of the Middle Ages,* Frederic Seebohm's *The Oxford Reformers,* Carlyle's edition of Cromwell's letters and speeches, De Quincey's *Confessions,* Emerson's *Representative Men,* Lamb's essays, a selection of Ruskin's essays and letters, Leslie Stephen's biographies of Swift and Pope.

His reading was extensive but not careful. However, with his remarkable memory, he was able to retain an enormous amount of his discursive reading. For his classes he tried to read the complete works of every poet or dramatist who was emphasized. Otherwise, his reading was not ordered in any way, nor did it reflect any particular tastes. Although he did absorb some of the sophistication of his fellow students (he adopted the urban and aristocratic attitudes of H. L. Mencken, and he discovered a smuggled copy of Joyce's *Ulysses*), still he did not blindly follow all the aesthetic currents; he did not, for example, join in the adulation of Eliot and Donne. He read what came to hand: books his friends were reading, books in the Farnsworth Room, books that were the chance result of browsing in the library stacks. Professor Lowes was much impressed by Wolfe's ability to cite from this great bulk of reading, and he thought Wolfe would do well in the scholarly life.

But the picture of Wolfe at Harvard is distorted if he is seen only as a lonely, brooding, bookish young man. The other side of his nature, warm, gay, gregarious, was there too. As time went on, he had more companionship—among fellow students in the Workshop and among the Southern boys at the University—and, of course, he often saw his Boston relatives on Sundays or at holiday dinners. In the homes of married Workshop members, Henry Carlton, Frederick Day, or Roscoe Brink, he would strain the endurance of his listeners, recounting his mother's parsimonies or describing his brother Ben's death. He found time for evenings with Wilbur Dunkel at the Copley Players or for late-hour carousing with Kenneth Raisbeck. He came to know Boston well, and he loved its atmosphere, "the musty and delightful brownness over all." [20] He knew the Fenway and the Esplanade, the Boston Museum and the Old Howard, Garden Street and Scollay Square, Beacon Hill and the Fanueil Hall Market, the Village Blacksmith Tearoom and Jake Wirth's. William Polk's description of Wolfe away from his books gives us a more full-blooded man than the self-conscious introvert we find in the Autobiographical Outline:

He was full of mighty laughter and abounding energy, which would cause him to split a door with his fist or fill any scrap of paper lying around with descriptions of icebergs or anything else that came to mind. He had a hunger for life, too, which would clothe him in a borrowed shirt—since he had forgot to send anything of his own to the laundry for a couple of months—send him out to the Parker House basement for a quart of surreptitious Scotch, to Durgin-Park's for a steak and to the Boston Common or to Wellesley for a girl or a young lady.[21]

This is Thomas Wolfe at the outset of his career as a writer. In his loneliness he whetted an appetite for life that became omnivorous. In his exciting and challenging surroundings he developed a driving ambition to be a famous artist.

NOTES

1. HCL*46AM-8(12), a comment on a report about Benjamin Franklin and Francis Bacon entitled "For the Relief of Man's Estate."

2. HCL*46AM-8(8), a comment on "The Theory of Ben Jonson's Literary Art as Applied to the Comedy of Humours."

3. HCL*46AM-8(11), a comment on "Italian Influence in the Prose and Dramatic Writings of Robert Greene."

4. Wolfe felt akin to the leading character in "The Heirs." Also, W. E. Harris of Cambridge, Massachusetts, who was in English 47a with Wolfe in 1922-23, recalls an autobiographical play that Wolfe began at that time about a young man at college. The fragment of a scene, HCL*46AM-7(21), which describes a student named Eugene furiously reading in the library is a part of that unfinished play.

5. LTM, p. 36. The date of this letter is *ca.* December, 1920. Professor Baker's students wrote one-act plays during their first year.

6. LTM, p. 27. This letter is out of sequence because of an error in the dating. The date of this letter (sometime after late March in the spring term, 1922) may be determined from his mention of the application for a teaching position and from his report of the courses for which he had been registered.

7. HCL*46AM-7(46), passages rejected from OT&R.

8. *Letters*, p. 24.

9. Boston, 1927.

10. *Letters,* p. 30.

11. HCL*46AM-8(9), "The Supernatural in the Poetry and Philosophy of Coleridge," pp. 10-11.

12. P. 28.

13. P. 91.

14. *Letters,* p. 321.

15. *Letters,* pp. 27-28.

16. Note the expansion of this part of AO in LHA, p. 589.

17. Interview with Ward Morehouse, January, 1950.

18. *Letters,* p. 10. Kenneth Raisbeck, the author of "Rock Me, Julie," produced in New York in February, 1931, was the model for the character Francis Starwick in OT&R.

19. One exception was a strange outburst when Baker cut a line from *Welcome to Our City* in rehearsal. Philip Barber describes it in "Tom Wolfe Writes a Play," *Harper's Magazine,* CCXVI (May, 1958), 71-76: "Tom sprang to his feet with a tortured yell and rushed out into the night."

20. AO.

21. Quoted in James K. Hutsell, "As They Recall Thomas Wolfe," *Southern Packet,* IV (April, 1948), p. 9.

5

WELCOME TO OUR CITY
AND OTHER PLAYS

GEORGE PIERCE BAKER'S 47 WORKSHOP AT HARVARD HAD BEGUN
as a playwriting class in 1905, but no plays were actually produced
until 1912. Subsequently, it operated as a theatre laboratory until
Baker left Harvard in 1924. Selected plays were produced each year
before private audiences, who submitted criticism of the plays after
they were performed. Thereby, the young authors were able not only
to see their own work brought to life but also to revise it in the light
of criticism from an audience. Baker was an excellent example of
that rare combination of scholar, critic, and teacher; and as a shaper
of theatrical talent, he even succeeded in making Broadway producers respect the academic efforts. Robert Edmund Jones, Eugene
O'Neill, Kenneth MacGowan, Philip Barry, Sidney Howard, and S.
N. Behrman are a few of the distinguished names from his English 47
class lists.

The decade of the twenties was the time of the Provincetown
Players, the Neighborhood Playhouse, and the beginnings of the
Theatre Guild. A new vitality in the American theater and the fame
of Professor Baker's Workshop aroused Wolfe's eagerness to try his
hand at playwriting at Harvard. Although he had told his parents
he was going to graduate school to train himself as a journalist, he
went to Professor Baker as soon as he arrived in Cambridge and was
delighted to be admitted as one of "Baker's Dozen." Still, it was not
until he had absorbed the enthusiasm of the older students that he
thought of becoming a professional playwright. He dared to think
so just after he had written his first play, "The Mountains," a one-
act revision of a script begun in North Carolina: "For the first time,
it occurs to me that writing may be taken seriously—separated from

home I realize that it is not a remote thing for me—that it is a very present thing—Life begins to have [shape?] in spite of the welter of events and reading." [1]

"The Mountains," which Wolfe had begun writing in Chapel Hill, is a folk play in which people say "hit ain't" and "that air," [2] and as a folk play it follows, supposedly, the theory of realism that he began to practice at Harvard and developed further for his autobiographical novels. In a paper written for Professor Greenough in the spring of 1921, Wolfe had this to say about the folk plays of the Chapel Hill group: "The promise of such a movement in which the material is based on the author's own experience and observation and more than that, perhaps grows out of his very life, cannot be under-estimated. From such stuff as this drama is made!" [3]

The plot of "The Mountains," however, does not make use of Wolfe's life but only of the mountain region around Asheville. A young Carolina doctor returns from medical school to take up his father's practice in his native region, for he intends to care for the needs of the poor mountain folk. On the day of his return, a long-standing family feud breaks out, and in spite of his former resolve to hold aloof from old quarrels, he goes out with his rifle to join his kinfolk as the curtain falls. Baker liked the play and promised to include it in the next year's program. It was presented first in a trial performance on January 25, 1921, in the Workshop Rehearsal Room along with three other one-act plays. After revision it was included in the regular program of the Workshop performances, October 21 and 22, 1921, as one of three one-act plays, with John Mason Brown as the old doctor and Dorothy Sands as his daughter. Since the dialogue was over-wordy and there was very little action, the play was a miserable failure. The written comment of the audience seemed even malicious to the self-centered young author. A notation in the Outline recalls his hopes and his disappointment: "The writing of my play—reading it to Ketchum [4]—his generous enthusiasm—Alas the *generous* enthusiasm of Baker—But how they turn on you when it fails—the coldness, the neglect."

Wolfe was so discouraged that he was ready to give up writing forever. Since Professor Lowes had suggested that he continue his graduate studies and plan for a teaching career, Wolfe began to consider this possibility. Years later he gave an account of this dilemma and of his appeal to an older friend for advice:

No one thought [the play] was any good, and most people took pains to tell me so. It was a very desperate occasion for me. It seemed to me that my whole life and future depended upon it, and in this state of mind I went to see a man on whose judgment, honesty and critical ability I relied to the utmost. I asked him what he thought of my abilities as a writer, and if he thought I would ever succeed in doing the thing I most wanted to do; and although he tried at first, out of the kindness of his heart, to evade the issue, he finally told me point blank that he did not think I would ever become a writer and that he thought my abilities were critical rather than creative and therefore advised me to devote my time to graduate study in the University, leading to a Ph.D. degree and a position in the teaching profession. . . .I will never forget the almost inconceivable anguish and despair that his words caused me.[5]

Wolfe went ahead with his studies, and by February of this second year he had completed his residence for the A.M. degree and needed only to fulfill the language requirements in French and German. In March he registered with the Harvard Appointment Office to teach English at a college or preparatory school the following September. Meanwhile, he was continuing to work on his playwriting. In spite of his failure with "The Mountains," he must have received some encouragement from Professor Baker with this play, for he had decided to enlarge it to three acts. For Act I, he made use of his Greenlaw-Williams play, which became a rather confusing conflict of ideas between two doctors; Act II was entirely new, and Act III was an improved version of the former one-act play. The Prologue and Act II were the best writing Wolfe had done thus far.[6] They each involved a simple dramatic conflict presented through realistic dialogue cast in the mountain speech with which he was familiar.

During these two years he scribbled at other plays, two of which deserve mention. The first, begun in the spring of 1921 and entitled "The Heirs" or "The Wasters," became the play *Mannerhouse*, which he did not finish until January, 1925.[7] The second play, of which only a disordered mass of fragments remains, was entitled in one of its versions "The Old School." Based on the conflict between Horace Williams and the forces seeking to oust him from the University of North Carolina, the play centers on Professor Job Weldon, his cancer condition, and his three malicious comforters. The clash in the play sets Job Weldon's ideas of religion and philosophy against the narrow views of "a fact-getting group of faculty members. . .of whom Professor X [Edwin Greenlaw] is the finest illustration." [8] Although, as we have seen, Wolfe rejected the Hegelian monism of Horace Williams after he left Chapel Hill, he never forgot the old man's kindness, and in the lonely days at Harvard his cherished remembrance of Williams' fatherly attention grew to inspire this character. But it must be explained that it was only Williams, the man, who found his way into Wolfe's play, for Professor Job Weldon's ideas had their origin elsewhere.

The play itself has no importance, but since it is the first indication that Wolfe was beginning to adopt the world-view which underlies his novels, a comment on the source of the play seems necessary. For "The Old School," Wolfe had taken over the plot of H. G. Wells's modernized Job story, *The Undying Fire*.[9] Although Wolfe had a respect for Wells's novels in general ("one of the few moderns I have had time for," he told Mrs. Roberts),[10] his special enthusiasm for *The Undying Fire* [11] reveals his intense interest in the theory of vitalism and creative evolution preached by Wells's character, Job Huss, while he entertains three visitors on the eve of his cancer operation. Besides the numerous statements about the purposive force that guides Man ("To me it seems that the creative desire that burns in me is a thing different in its nature from the blind Process of matter, is a force running contrariwise to the power of confusion"),[12] Wells even has passages that could be called Wolfean in their style, in their optimism, and in their zest for life:

Has not your life had laughter in it? Has the freshness of the summer morning never poured joy through your being? Do you know nothing of the embrace of the lover, cheek to cheek or lip to lip? Have you never swum out into the sunlit sea or shouted on a mountain slope? Is there no joy in a handclasp?. . .Dare you deny the joy of your appetites: the first mouthful of roast red beef on the frosty day and the deep draught of good ale? Do you know nothing of the task well done, nor of sleep after a day of toil? Is there no joy for the farmer in the red ploughed fields, and the fields shooting with green blades? When the great prows smite the waves and the aeroplane hums in the sky, is man still a hopeless creature? Can you watch the beat and swing of machinery and still despair? [13]

Although Wolfe probably encountered vitalism and creative evolution while reading Shaw at Chapel Hill,[14] he became thoroughly conversant with these ideas through his careful study of Wells's *The Undying Fire* when he sought to imitate it. And in his novels, even to the end of his career, he continued to echo the doubts and affirmations of Wells's Job Huss.

Despite the hopes for his enlargement of "The Mountains," Wolfe was still sensitive about the bad reception of the one-act play and could take no joking on the subject. When he noted in the Outline, "The way the workshop crowd could be swept away at the moment by a bad play, inherit the damnation of the audience, swiftly change over and make mirth with it," Wolfe was referring to the productions called "The 47 Varieties" which were presented at the end of each college year. Songs and parody skits burlesqued all the plays of the season. In May, 1922, one song number entitled "The Maountains" entertained the Workshop audience with this chorus:

> O the Maountains, the Maountains,
> They styarve a man, they styarve a man.
> They grin, like sin,
> They pin you in,
> Till you go out and kyarve a man.[15]

The most encouraging event of the spring was Professor Baker's request that Wolfe return for another year of study in the Workshop.

In June, when his plans were still unsettled and he had just had an offer from Northwestern of an instructorship in English, he suddenly received news that his father was dying. He left immediately for Asheville.

II

In August, 1922, Miss McRady of the Harvard Appointment Office received a letter from Thomas Wolfe about the teaching position for which he had applied the previous spring. He had decided not to take the job:

Matters at home were in an extremely unsettled condition following the death of my father, and it was not until very recently that I knew absolutely whether I should stay at home with my mother, accept the offer from Northwestern, or return to Harvard for another year with Professor Baker. My finances are now in such condition as will permit me to return for another year at Harvard. Professor Baker has been so unfailingly kind and encouraging that I believe this extra year which is now made possible, will be of the utmost importance to me.[16]

Since he had by this time earned his A.M. degree, Wolfe registered in September for only one course, the Workshop. He could now devote all his time to writing. Some of the fragments of plays still extant among the Wolfe papers no doubt belong to this period. The most important of these, entitled "The House of Bateson," foreshadows the Gant family in *Look Homeward, Angel;* here the characters who later emerged as Old Man Gant, Helen, and Ben may be seen in their early condition of development. Since stage directions for one scene describe an undertaking parlor, it seems that the death of Ben was to be the climax of the play. Although Wolfe probably began work on "The House of Bateson" sometime after the death of his father in June, 1922, he had been considering the story of his family as possible literary material ever since his first summer in Cambridge. In his history notebook, there appear preliminary plans for a play about the conflicts of a family surnamed variously Broody, Groody, or Benton, which begins: "The Broody's were a strange family. They never saw each other's good points till one of their number died." [17]

In other fragments he attempts satire and farce. The mummy of Mycerinus comes to life in the Boston Museum for commentary on the twentieth century in one unfinished episode, a witty Satan struts through other pages, a number of scraps contain satiric thrusts at literary pretense in Boston. Nor was "The Old School" his only attempt at imitation. There is evidence that he ventured upon modern versions of Ibsen's *An Enemy of the People* [18] and Jonson's *Bartholomew Fair.*[19]

At the beginning of the term, he brought to class first acts of six different plays within a two-week period. His head was full of ideas, and he was experimenting with assorted techniques. Professor Baker withheld praise for his efforts, merely requesting that Wolfe concentrate on one project and bring in a second act to any one of the plays. This little discipline was evidently the bridle Wolfe needed, and during the term the play "Niggertown" began to emerge, presumably from one of the first-act experiments. As his material grew, the question arose whether it might not be handled more effectively in a series of scenes rather than in the conventional three acts. Indeed, as parts of the play were read in the class, the broad nature of his idea seemed to demand a sequence of scenes, so Wolfe worked out a long script in this way and had a mass of material by January.

In this play Wolfe was attempting what he felt was the "transcript of life" that Greenlaw saw in great literature. In a paper written the previous year for Professor Murray on "The Theory of Ben Jonson's Literary Art as Applied to the Comedy of Humours," he had pondered to what extent realism was possible in literature, but his remarks show that he did not distinguish carefully enough between the two forms, the novel and the drama. In the paper he compares life and art, recognizing that art demands selection, but he fails to acknowledge the limits upon the drama. He defends realism, "a presentment of life as it is," as a desirable goal in art, and he discusses the value of a close approach to actuality within the scope of words. After conceding that it is beyond human power to reproduce actuality, he continues: "Even the camera fails in the attempt. For it can only reproduce a scene upon plane surfaces. The effort is not to be held in contempt. Art and photography are not positive and negative poles as has been asserted. They can merge one into the other and often do. The effect may be artistic even if it goes no farther than plane surface." [20] It was as literary photography, then, that Ben Jonson's art pleased Wolfe; in his four or five great contributions to realistic comedy "he produced human nature upon plane surfaces." With this kind of literary theorizing, Wolfe was certain to extend his efforts beyond the bounds of dramatic form. The "plane surface" of what he wanted to represent was immensely broader than a play of ordinary size could accommodate and called for longer plays than an audience could endure.

Wolfe had come upon the idea for his new play about a year previous to its final production. In June, 1922, when he had gone home for the first time in two years, he found that Asheville had changed. The boom years had come. In a letter to Mrs. Roberts that fall, he thundered out his complaint:

Coming home this last time I have gathered enough additional material to write a new play,—the second fusillade of the battle. This thing I had thought naive and simple is as old and as evil as hell; there is a spirit of world-old evil that broods about us, with all the subtle sophistication of Satan. Greed, greed, greed,—deliberate, crafty, motivated—masking under the guise of civic associations for municipal betterment. The disgusting spectacle of thousands of industrious and accomplished liars, engaged in the mutual and systematic pursuit of their profession, salting their editorials and sermons and advertisements with the religious and philosophic platitudes of Dr. Frank Crane, Edgar A. Guest, and the American Magazine.[21]

This was the situation that set him writing "Niggertown," the play in ten scenes which was produced by the Workshop on May 11 and 12, 1923, under the title *Welcome to Our City*.[22] This work, covering the life of a Southern town, tells the story of a real-estate group who, together with civic authorities, contrive to buy up all the property in the centrally located Negro district of the town. They plan, after evicting all the tenants, to tear down the old property in order to build a new white residential section. When the Negro group resists eviction, a minor race riot breaks out, and the militia comes to restore order. Since Wolfe tries to picture a cross section of the town life, much of the dialogue does not pertain to the central action, but with the exception of the last scene the play reads very well.

Wolfe employs a variety of techniques (even including stylized pantomime) as the play ranges in mood from broad comedy to the tragedy of the death of the Negro leader. His characters include all classes and ages, both colored and white. Here, too, he brings in for the first time some of the "humourous" characters, in the Jonson-Smollett-Dickens tradition, that he was to draw with such success in his novels. His satire has many targets: Southern politics, backward universities, evangelical preachers, small-town boosters, provincial little theatre groups, and even short-sighted humanitarians. Yet for production, such scope and variety presented problems. Professor Baker had always urged students to make use of materials which they could handle, characters and situations of a class or a region well known to them. But he also taught that dramatic presentation was based upon careful selection among the parts of a particular action. When Wolfe wrote out a synopsis for *Welcome to Our City*, he included the youth and background of certain characters, problems that had arisen in the city in recent years, his own ideas on the race question, and so forth. But when he began to turn the synopsis into scenes, even a selection still included too many characters, a number of side issues, and a couple of scenes not pertinent to the action. His plan was, however, to present a complexity of life surrounding his main problem.

Although Baker approved of the idea of providing a context for the dramatic conflict, he pointed out that Wolfe must give his audience a more compressed story so that they would not be distracted from the central problem by the threads of undeveloped action. Wolfe, on the other hand, maintained that if the materials were true to life an audience would continue to give their attention, no matter how long the play or how full the list of characters.

At the root of this disagreement was the distinction between the two forms, the novel and the drama. The problem had often arisen for Wolfe's consideration since he had been working under Professor Baker. The lectures in the course, "Forms of the Drama," had stressed the differences; a question in a mid-term examination had forced Wolfe to write about it; and Baker had called it directly to his attention at least once, in a penciled note beside an elaborate stage direction and character description in Act I of "The Mountains": "Aren't you anticipating your text and writing as a novelist?" Baker recognized Wolfe's potentialities in narrative, his zest for detail, and his interest in the full development of minor characters; and he pointed out to him that his aims in *Welcome to Our City* suggested the novel form rather than the drama. But the "Artist Myth" interfered: at this point Wolfe conceived of himself in the role of the artist as playwright, not the artist as novelist, and he was sure his play would be a theatrical success. And, though he was already pushing the limits of the drama form, he indicated future plans of even larger scope in a note to Baker (when he submitted his script for production): "I have written this play with 30 odd *named* characters because it required it, not because I don't know how to save paint. Some day I'm going to write a play with 50, 80, 100 people— a whole town, a whole race, a whole epoch—for my *souls* ease and comfort."[23] He wished to write something on the scale of *The Dynasts,* but he also counted on stage production.

Welcome to Our City was marked for production in the spring, and Wolfe worked hard to put his scenes into shape for performance. He tried to cut his material and at the same time to retain as much of his own conception of the play as he could. But the play was still too long and still contained some portions that were far below the quality of the whole. It was Professor Baker's policy to refrain from editing scripts that were to be produced for his private audience. Let professional producers deal with scripts as they must, this was the one opportunity for a young playwright to see his play produced exactly as he had written it. Of course, Baker offered criticisms to the young writers, and in most cases his suggestions were adopted. But now he was dealing with a young man who felt that the truth of his realism would balance any dramatic shortcomings.

Wolfe would not cut the play further, and after successive confer-
ences Baker had to do some cutting himself in order to reduce the
excessive running time. Although Wolfe even lost his temper a couple of times during the shaping of the final script and was ready to
withdraw the play, in the end he submitted to Baker's cutting because he wished to get his play produced. Not much substance was
removed, but the concluding scene was considerably shortened.

Welcome to Our City, as produced in Agassiz Theater in May,
1923, was one of the most spectacular productions ever undertaken
by the Workshop. It made use of seven different arrangements of a
unit set and had a cast of forty-four people, with thirty-one speaking
parts (Wolfe himself put on blackface to take part in the crowd
scenes). The performances were very exciting; yet the play was not
a complete success. It was original in its presentation of several strata
of town life and in its forthright treatment of race relations; but
some of the scenes extraneous to the main action were far too lengthy
for their purpose. The chief fault, however, was that the moral positions of the antagonists—Rutledge, the white leader, and Johnson, the
Negro leader—were not clear, probably because Wolfe's views on
the race question were not clear in his own mind. Since the play was
long and the set changes were not made with the necessary speed,
the performances, which began at eight, did not end until midnight.
Most of the written criticisms from the audience remarked on the
unnecessary length, and some were critical of Wolfe's boldness in
putting the realities and brutalities of race conflict on the stage, but
on the whole the audience comment was favorable. As a piece of
writing, the play was the best work Wolfe had done: the characters
were the first life-like creatures he had ever drawn. But he had also
used real-life models for the first time. One of the guests in the audience, Miss Laura Plonk from Asheville, was astounded as the plot
unfolded. After the show, she rushed backstage to Dorothy Sands
to exclaim with horror, "I know every person in the play!"

Wolfe would not state his opinion of the production even to his
mother ("I won't say whether my play was good or bad"),[24] but he
was angry that part of the audience failed to give his work its de-
served acclaim. However, the productions were supposed to be laboratory experiments, and the young playwrights could profit by the
criticism. Bearing in mind the staging of their scripts, they might be
better able to revise their plays to make them worthy of sale to

Broadway producers. Baker saw that Wolfe's play had excellent possibilities if it were judiciously tightened. He told Wolfe that he thought it had a better chance for commercial success than Elmer Rice's *The Adding Machine,* which was just closing a three months' run in New York, and he asked the Theatre Guild to give *Welcome to Our City* a reading.

Quite naturally, Wolfe was excited. Now he really began to conceive of himself as an artist and as a successful one. Already he was planning a trip to Europe with the money he would make on his play. He wrote to his mother, "I know this now: I am inevitable. I sincerely believe that the only thing that can stop me now is insanity, disease, or death," [25] and further, "I will go everywhere and see everything. I will meet all the people I can. I will think all the thoughts, feel all the emotions I am able, and will write, write, write." [26] But this faith in himself, which provided the necessary power and energy to carry out his later literary projects, brought about his downfall, at this point, as a playwright. Not even close friends could convince him that the play had to be cut. When Wolfe visited Henry Carlton in Madison, New Hampshire, Carlton outlined for him the number of plot threads he had introduced and pleaded with him to throw out two or three that were undeveloped. Wolfe would solemnly agree, and after the Carlton family had retired, he would work late into the night. By morning he would have a whole new sequence to insert. He was convinced that his play with the scope of a novel would prove acceptable to a New York audience. Instead of applying the blue pencil, he restored all the cuts that had been made in rehearsal and, late in the summer, set off for New York with great hopes.[27] In September he submitted his play to the Theatre Guild, and after waiting for a month without news, he returned once more to Asheville.

Wolfe's troubles with the drama as a form did not end at Harvard. Three years were to pass before he wrote Mrs. Roberts that he had begun a new project—"a novel, to which I may give the title *The Building of a Wall.*" [28] But the Harvard years had contributed much. At Harvard he found a world in which he could reasonably seek to become an artist, and he began to govern his life in preparation for a writing career. At Harvard he first put into practice his own conception of Edwin Greenlaw's theory of "literature as a transcript of life." As a result he met problems that ultimately forced him to write prose fiction, although it was in the drama workshop that, spurred by the encouragement and discipline of Baker, he did his first mature writing. Wolfe never acknowledged what the University meant to him except as an atmosphere of learning and of books. He felt bitter about his failure to be a playwright. But during these three years he fed his mind with books, and this is the happy remembrance of Harvard that he kept. Even in the arrogant tone of the Autobiographical Outline this is his summary:

What can I say of Harvard? A deficient enough place but for three years I wallowed in books there, performing as prodigious a feat of reading as has ever been performed by a living mortal before or since—having no elections to win, no popular favor to court, no particular student tabu to obey—I found it as free a place for thinking as I have ever found in America—God knows, I went around slovenly enough,—unbarbered, untailored....I lived in a kind of dream—at first a species of nightmare—at last (particularly during the last year)—in a radiance—drunken with joy and with power—To me it was only vaguely a "University"—to me it was a place heavy with the noble enchantment of books—all the beauty, all the power, all the wonder was there for me—the centre of the place now, the first picture that comes to me, is the Farnsworth room—the luxurious couch—and the books....was not a university for me a wall....

NOTES

1. AO.
2. A happily discarded title for this play was "Hell for Women and Mules."
3. HCL*46AM-8(5), "The Beginning of a Native American Drama Since 1890," p. 74.
4. The Reverend Arthur Ketchum of Bedford, New York, who was enrolled in Professor Baker's English 47 during 1920-21, had his one-act play, "The Other One," produced on the same program with "The Mountains."
5. *Letters*, pp. 427-28.
6. According to Wolfe's report, Baker said the prologue was the best that had ever been written in English 47, and the whole class praised it when it was read aloud. LTM, p. 25 (the letter should be dated spring, 1922).
7. See LTM, pp. 14-19, for Wolfe's description of the original idea for this play. The date of the letter is *ca.* March, 1921.
8. HCL*46AM-7(21).
9. London, 1919.
10. *Letters*, p. 24.
11. Reflected in two letters of January or February, 1922, one to Horace Williams, *Letters*, p. 27, and one to Mrs. Roberts, *Letters*, p. 24 ("rarely have I been more stimulated").
12. P. 196.

13. P. 209. The series of questions and the parallelism indicate that Wells was imitating the style of *Job*.

14. Koch remembers that Shaw was Wolfe's favorite playwright in his senior year at Chapel Hill (*Carolina Folk Plays, First, Second, and Third Series*, ed. Frederick Koch [New York, 1941], pp. 127-29).

15. I am indebted to the author of this lyric, Miss Doris Halman, for the text of this bit of Wolfeana.

16. *Letters*, pp. 32-33.

17. HCL*46AM-8(2), History S9, Notebook 2. The fragments of the play are found in HCL*46AM-7(19) and HCL*53M-113F.

18. HCL*46AM-8(3), Comparative Literature 22, Notebook 1.

19. HCL*46AM-15, an undated note to Professor Baker.

20. HCL*46AM-8(8), pp. 21-22.

21. *Letters*, p. 33.

22. First published in *Esquire*, XLVIII (October, 1957), 57-83.

23. *Letters*, p. 41.

24. LTM, p. 53.

25. LTM, p. 49.

26. LTM, p. 53.

27. The Wisdom Collection in the Harvard Library has two versions of the play, one which was used as a basis for the Harvard production and one which was the final version, dating sometime after his first European trip in 1924-25. The text of the play submitted to the Theatre Guild in September, 1923, may be conjectured from the final version.

28. *Letters*, p. 111.

6

MANNERHOUSE

As a playwright, Wolfe served his apprenticeship but never got his papers as a journeyman. What remains to be told is the story of his troubles trying to market *Welcome to Our City* and of his next try for success with a more conventional play, *Mannerhouse*.[1]

In the fall of 1923, Wolfe, back in New York again, inquired at the Theatre Guild for a final word on *Welcome to Our City*. Courtenay Lemon, one of the principal Guild play readers, returned Wolfe's play, pointing out the diffuseness of the several themes and the ambiguity of the moral positions on the race question. He had a word of encouragement, however; the Guild was still interested in Wolfe's work and thought him "the best man the Workshop had yet turned out."[2] Most encouraging of all was the interest of Lawrence Langner, a member of the Theatre Guild board of directors and a man of taste whose patronage has been important in the history of the American stage. Always ready to help a promising young playwright, he now talked to Wolfe about a revision of *Welcome to Our City* that would have more plot unity. On condition that Wolfe reduce the list of characters and chop the number of scenes to eight, cutting the running time about thirty minutes, Langner agreed to put his influence behind the play. If the Guild would not take the play, Langner said he would find another producer for it. Even in the face of this generosity Wolfe protested. "Of course this would mean a more conventional type of play," he wrote Mrs. Roberts. "I told him I had deliberately tried to avoid writing such a play; that I had written a play with a plot which centered about the life and destiny of an entire civilization, not about a few people."[3] However, Wolfe promised to do what he could, for he badly wanted a produc-

84

tion. Still he did not follow Langner's advice. Nor was his stubborn attachment to a theory of presenting life on the stage entirely to blame; he was really unable to select his material and cut the play. As he said later, "This I tried to do, but made it longer." [4] Wolfe's failure to make *Welcome to Our City* acceptable for Langner is another early instance of his need for a persuasive critic like Maxwell Perkins.

It is ironical that Wolfe received the first published notice of his work just at the time his play was rejected and he was in need of a job. Oliver Sayler, who had been in the audience for a performance of *Welcome to Our City*, singled out Wolfe's play for comment in his chapter on "The Theatre in the College" in *Our American Theatre*.[5] Wolfe reflected with some bitterness on Sayler's comment that his play was the first really experimental achievement to come out of the 47 Workshop, "a play as radical in form and treatment as the contemporary stage has yet acquired."

During the next year, Wolfe tried through old friends and new acquaintances to find a producer for his play. The passing months saw only a rejection by the Provincetown Playhouse and a short-lived interest in publication by D. Appleton and Company. Although Wolfe could not sell his work, his efforts set in motion a chain of circumstances that led ultimately to one of the turning points in his life, his meeting with Aline Bernstein. Mr. S. R. Real, the manager of the Hotel Albert, where Wolfe was living in New York, knew that the young man was trying to sell a play. He suggested to Miss Anne MacDonald, a friend connected with the Neighborhood Playhouse, that she bring the play to the attention of Alice and Irene Lewisohn, the chief directors of the Playhouse.[6] Wolfe turned over both copies of his play to Miss MacDonald and then worried through the summer about the outcome. After a careful consideration of *Welcome to Our City*, the board of directors differed in their estimate of its possibilities. Irene Lewisohn and Aline Bernstein approved the play, four others voted against it. Finally they decided that during the summer Mrs. Bernstein should take the play to Europe to get an opinion from Alice Lewisohn, whose decision was the most important.

At the end of August, Wolfe received news of his manuscript. He reported to his mother that the "wealthy woman producer" who had taken his play to Europe "wrote back very enthusiastically, saying it was 'unusually fine,' 'promised well for young America,' and did I have another with not so many characters." [7] He still had only verbal encouragement for his playwriting.

There was one exception. Professor Frederick Koch asked Wolfe's permission to include "The Return of Buck Gavin" in the forthcoming volume of *Carolina Folk Plays*. Although Wolfe knew the play was worthless ("I should hate to see my name attached now," he wrote Mrs. Roberts), he wanted to break into print. After deliberating two months and after protesting that such a juvenile effort should never see light, he finally gave his consent. Now, after his three years in the 47 Workshop, the sole offering he could make to fame was a piece of undergraduate work that had been tossed off in careless haste.

II

While marking time waiting for glory, Wolfe still had to support himself. Eager to stay near the world of the theater in New York, he had resolved to try through the Harvard Appointment Office to get a teaching position at New York University. His last talk with Professor Baker at Christmas time in 1923 had convinced him that Baker would do nothing for him. As he talked to Baker about his future, Wolfe vaguely hoped that his old teacher would offer him some financial opportunity to continue writing (an assistantship, a fellowship, a loan), for he knew that Baker had helped many students —sometimes from his own pocket. When Wolfe told him he was considering teaching, Baker strongly urged against it. Teaching would take all his time from his writing and might even injure his talent, Baker told him, but he made no suggestion how he should support himself. Clearly disappointed that Wolfe had failed to cut the play before submitting it to the Theatre Guild, Baker merely remonstrated with him to make better use of the next four months than he had of the last. He even intimated that Wolfe might never be a playwright—"your gift is not selection, but profusion," [8] he told him, but he encouraged him to go on writing. Wolfe had come to Baker for help and advice. When he realized that Baker could not solve his problems and that he must make his own decisions, he left with his mind made up to teach.

While Wolfe was in Cambridge, he renewed his application papers in the Harvard Appointment Office, for he had heard through a

Harvard friend, Robert Bruce Dow, who taught at the Bronx campus of New York University, about new openings in the expanded program of Washington Square College. This downtown branch of the University had recently created a February-through-September freshman course for mid-year graduates of the city high schools. As this off-schedule enrollment increased, more teachers were needed to handle the multiplying sections of freshman composition. When Wolfe sent a letter of application to Professor Homer Watt, the genial chairman of the English department, he made clear that he had no teaching experience, that he did not plan to make college teaching his profession, and that he intended to devote his life to creative work.[9] Professor Watt liked Wolfe's earnest, naive manner; and since the teaching load was entirely freshman composition, he thought Wolfe's interest in writing was a good qualification. Wolfe was appointed instructor at a salary of $1800 a year and started teaching in February, 1924. Thus began an association that was to continue intermittently until January, 1930, when he decided he could support himself by writing.[10]

New York City frightened and exhilarated him much more than Boston. He regarded the city throngs with intense curiosity and sought a knowledge of the city in its every corner, sure that he would "get material in [his] seven months' stay that may prove invaluable." [11] Although he had chosen to teach in New York because it was the theatrical center of America, he was more unknown and alone here than ever before. He stood out above every crowd, an awkward stranger; as he passed the parochial school playground to meet his class at Washington Square, the school children called after him, "Giant! Giant!" [12] He was xenophobic enough to fear and dislike the immigrant population of New York, which he thought detrimental to the nation: "Yearly we are bringing hundreds of thousands of inferior people, the Latin races, undeveloped physically, dwarfed mentally, into this country. From them we grow the American of tomorrow—'the hope of the world.' It is impossible to regard them without a sinking of the heart," he wrote his mother in a burst of anti-democratic despair.[13]

In 1924 the downtown college of New York University had not been long established in its large, factory-like structure facing Washington Square. Parts of the buildings that the college was soon to occupy still housed drug companies, optical companies, and other com-

mercial offices. In these surroundings, Wolfe was depressed by the
atmosphere of the classrooms and by the thought of teaching English in a crowded, badly lighted office building. Moreover, his anti-
Semitism burgeoned in his new job. "I teach! I teach! Jews! Jews!," [14]
he wrote his Chapel Hill friend, Albert Coates. At first he spoke of
mass education for New York's poorer sons with a patronizing air.
"The students. . .mainly Jewish and Italian, have come up from the
East Side; many are making sacrifices of a very considerable nature
in order to get an education. They are, accordingly, not at all the conventional type of college student." [15] But Wolfe began to change,
for students who struggle to educate themselves prize every word of
instruction they receive, and their curiosity endears them to their instructors. When they hounded him down the corridors asking questions, his ego was touched. When he found himself sought out, cited
as an authority, valued, he began to like it very much. "Really I'm
having a wonderful experience," he wrote Mrs. Roberts in May.
"This place—particularly the University—swarms with life, Jewish,
Italian, Polish. My little devils like me. I tell them every week that
I'm no teacher. I suppose they can see that for themselves; and perhaps that is why they like me." [16]

Wolfe's tireless enthusiasm and his stream of shy, rhythmic speech
delighted the students. His voluminous comments on their weekly
themes (which brought surprise and amusement to his colleagues) [17]
gave the students a sense of special attention from their instructor.
At the end of the year, Wolfe felt justified as a teacher when one
of his classes presented him with a Dunhill pipe as a token of affection. But the story of Wolfe's change in attitude from an uneasy
aversion to a genuine fondness for his students is best told in *Of
Time and the River,* in the episode of Eugene's friendship with Abe
Jones, a Jewish student who goads his teacher into understanding
him. The character of Abe Jones was modeled on Abe Smith, a student of Wolfe's during the first teaching year. After the two became
friends, Smith undertook the typing of the manuscript (over 1100
pages) for the first version of *Look Homeward, Angel.*[18]

Despite his teaching, with its weekly burden of more than a hundred themes to correct, Wolfe continued his voracious reading. Although there is very little record of his first year at New York University, an occasional remark in a letter gives a sample of the books
he took in hand. For example, he wrote to his friend from the Har-

vard Law School, Billy Polk, that he had been reading Greene's *A Short History of the English People,* one of Galsworthy's Forsyte novels, Flaubert's *Salammbô* ("a marvelous thing if you've a taste for horrible detail"),[19] Wells's *Research Magnificent,* and Balzac's *Cousin Pons.* What other books he kept before him during the year may be seen in the notations in his class roll books.[20] For student book reports and group discussions, he listed mostly classics of fiction, old and new, such as *Tom Jones, Anna Karenina,* several of Hardy, several of George Eliot, *The Ordeal of Richard Feverel, Crime and Punishment,* Kingsley's *Westward Ho,* Hugo's *Notre Dame, The Way of All Flesh,* Conrad's *Victory, Nostromo,* and *Lord Jim,* James's *Daisy Miller,* Howells' *The Rise of Silas Lapham,* Crane's *The Red Badge of Courage,* Cather's *My Antonia,* Wells's *Tono Bungay,* Dreiser's *The "Genius,"* Galsworthy's *The Man of Property.* A few non-fiction books dear to Wolfe's heart were scattered among the others—Lamb's *Essays,* Cellini's *Autobiography,* De Quincey's *Opium Eater,* Cowper's *Letters,* and Pepys's *Diary.*

It is amusing that Wolfe expected to devote a good amount of time to writing during his first teaching year. "The men here at the University assure me," he wrote innocently at the beginning of the year, "that I should easily complete my work, in and out of class, with three hours a day." [21] Soon he found out that a conscientious teacher must give all his time and energy to a teaching schedule of eight hours a week in the classroom. In April he wrote his mother,

Just a few lines are all my time allows. I must go back to the interminable work of correcting papers—like the brook, *that* goes on forever. On three days a week—or four—I can sleep late, and generally do, because on my teaching days I am so worn by night fall that I sleep as though drugged. I don't know how to conserve nervous energy; I burn it extravagantly. However, I am not unhappy. I believe I am learning much, although I am doing no writing....Hereafter, I believe, I shall be able to do my work more quickly—I yet strain my Presbyterian conscience; and I believe I do too much.[22]

What he really wanted to do was to find time for his principal creative interest of this year, his play, *Mannerhouse.*

III

The new play already had a long history. He had begun work on the basic plot during his first year in the 47 Workshop, when he was required to submit the synopsis of a three-act play. In a long letter to his mother he described its origin: "I heard Papa tell one time about a family of aristocrats in W. N. Carolina who owned a vast quantity of Mountain land. Major Love, I think he said was the man's name. They owned 500,000 acres and sold it for 20¢ an acre to lumber people simply because they were impoverished by the war. They died in want. I am using this as the basis for my story." [23] He went on to relate the plot in great detail, telling of the defeated efforts of the one good son, Eugene, to save the land. "The Heirs" or "The Wasters," as he titled the play, was an attack on Southern aristocrats who fail to face reality and responsibility.

During the next two years, characters were developed, names were changed, new ideas were introduced, scenes were written, altered, discarded, rewritten. By 1923 the chronology had been moved back to embrace the Civil War. Act I of the new play had been completed during the spring, for Wolfe was able to boast to his mother, "Baker has heard the first act of my second play and says it has an 'epic touch.'" [24] During the summer, while he "revised" *Welcome to Our City,* he completed another act, and the new play remained in this state during the next year, for he made very little progress while at New York University.

To sum up the complications that attended the completion of *Mannerhouse:* After Wolfe had carried the incomplete play to Europe in the fall of 1924, he lost the manuscript when his luggage was stolen from a Paris hotel. Although he complained bitterly in letters to friends and family, he was able to do now what he had been wanting to do all year. He sat down and rewrote the entire play during December, declaring in the end that it was "bigger and better." [25] The mishap brought Wolfe the first money he had ever received for anything he wrote—five hundred francs for the stolen valise and its contents.

Whereas *Welcome to Our City* is a happy product of Professor Baker's training and Wolfe's keen observation of life in his home town, *Mannerhouse* is a combination of all the unfortunate influences of the 47 Workshop and Wolfe's own faults in judgment. As a piece of dramaturgy, it illustrates what can happen to a young writer with great natural powers, who, having studied world drama and having been impressed by professorial commentary, tries to imitate modes of drama he is unfitted to write. It also illustrates

Wolfe's tendency to throw everything in the pot together, thinking that if a few added ingredients improve the dish, a whole cupboardful will make an even better mixture. In later years Wolfe himself criticized the derivative quality of *Mannerhouse* in the discussion of the play which Eugene Gant read to Joel and Rosalind Pierce.[26] But he still maintained that "in spite of this, there was good stuff in the play."

In its final version *Mannerhouse* presents the conflicting loyalties of a young man, Eugene Ramsay, during the Civil War, the decline of an aristocratic Southern family, and the passing of a romantic way of life. Wolfe's own description conveys the mawkish tone of the work:

This theme [the decline of the family and its estate]—which in its general form and implications was probably influenced a good deal by *The Cherry Orchard* of Checkov—was written in a somewhat mixed mood of romantic sentiment, Byronic irony, and sardonic realism. The hero was a rather Byronic character, a fellow who concealed his dark and tender poetry under the mask of a sardonic humor; the love story was colored by defeat and error and departure, and the hero's final return "years later"...was tempered by the romantic gallantry of Cyrano. The final meeting with the girl—the woman that he loved—their ultimate gallant resignation to fate and age and destiny—was wholly Cyranoic; and the final scene, in which the gigantic faithful negro slave—now an old man, almost blind, but with savage loyalty and majesty of a race of African kings from whom he is descended—wraps his great arms around the rotting central column of the old ruined house, snaps it in two with a last convulsion of his dying strength, and brings the whole ruined temple down to bury his beloved master, his hated "poor white" enemy the new owner, and himself, beneath its ruins—was obviously a product of the Samson legend.[27]

There are other classroom sources that Wolfe does not mention. He gives Eugene dark mutterings in the manner of the Elizabethan malcontent, continually stripping away appearances ("...just as all wars are the most terrible, so are all nations the greatest and most powerful; all armies the bravest; and all women the most beautiful and virtuous. Major, everything has grown so great we must prepare for changes").[28] Besides innumerable Shakespearean allusions, he includes a scene in which Eugene, Hamlet-like, harshly rejects his Ophelia. He employs Ibsen's device of giving symbolic significance to a phrase which, early in the play, has been tossed out innocently (for example, the punch line to Eugene's fish story, "The rivers are flowing backward").[29] Of course, Wolfe's use of the techniques or the ideas of other dramatists does not in itself make the play faulty. But when they are tumbled together, when they are introduced inappropriately, or when they contribute a false, contrived color to the action, belief in the author's sincerity is inevitably impaired.

But the chief difficulty with the play came about because Wolfe altered the theme while the writing was in progress. He had begun with an attack on Southern aristocracy,[30] then changed to a preachment of "a sincere belief in men and masters,"[31] and finally arrived at a compromise position; as he told Alice Lewisohn when he submitted the play to the Neighborhood Playhouse, "even in its fierce burlesquing of old romanticism, it defends the thing it attacks."[32] As a result, the gross improbability of Eugene's abrupt shifts in attitude are more disturbing than his mouthing of meaningless paradoxes ("I have lost something in the sun. I cannot find it—there is no moon").[33] It is desirable to have complexity in character, but here is only confusion. Wolfe had become absorbed with Eugene's dilemma, but he still retained the early plot about the sale of the land.

Yet there is, as Wolfe said, good stuff in it. The prologue, the building of the house in colonial times, is thrilling and significant. Later, peeping out of the rubbish of romantic posturing, there are occasional scenes that bring the play to life. The opening of Act II after the war, for example, shows us Bynum, one of General Ramsay's slaves who has taken his freedom, returned, gaudily dressed, to the house where he had been a slave. After a short exchange between Bynum and the house servant who has remained faithful, the scene is climaxed by the entrance of his former mistress. The mixed feelings of the freed Negroes are powerfully summed up in a few simple words as the scene ends:

> *She looks after him, striving hard to control her wounded*
> *pride and curiosity.*
> *Recalling him with an impulsive cry.*
> MRS. RAMSAY: Bynum!
> BYNUM (*returning*): Yas'm.
> MRS. RAMSAY: Why did you go?
> BYNUM (*slowly*): Why, I don' know, Mis' Mary. I reckon
>   it was 'case we knowed we could.[34]

Artistically, *Mannerhouse* is not a step forward from the achievement of *Welcome to Our City*. Although Wolfe never felt the play was a total failure, he returned to the successful method of the earlier play, a reshuffling of characters and events in the life that he knew from close observation, when he began to write prose narrative. However, if we examine *Mannerhouse* for marks of Wolfe's development from 1923 to 1925, there are features that merit comment. First of all, it offers another criticism of urban and industrial civilization, a theme which recurs continually in Wolfe's work. Second, in this play Wolfe makes his first attempt to deal with the problem of reality ("Then, which of us is the ghost? Perhaps we live when we believe, we dream," says Eugene),[35] a problem he later would treat in *Look Homeward, Angel,* using Plato's idea of the prenatal life. Finally, *Mannerhouse* contains the first real manifestations of Wolfe's later prose eloquence. Although the linguistic calisthenics throughout the work occur, for the most part, at the expense of appropriateness, they are replaced occasionally by a highly charged rhythmic style, full of the devices of poetry. An example is the concluding stage direction of the prologue: "A wind blows through the pines. All the million-noted little creatures of the night have come to life and are singing now in a vast, low chorus: a weird ululation which seems to continue and prolong the deep chant of the savages; which seems to hold in it the myriad voices of their demons." [36]

In the realm of social ideas, Wolfe was still under the influence of the anti-democratic writings of Carlyle and Mencken. He expresses these ideas through the character of General Ramsay, who in the end wins Eugene to his own belief in the established order of the South. His social credo is "I believe. . .in my House; in a great ladder of things on which it rests. I believe in heroes and hero worship; in men and masters; in the inequality of all things and all people. I believe. . .in the preservation of my order of things, and in a society which has for its purpose the preservation of ladies and gentlemen. . . ." [37] Human rights were doomed by the necessary inequality of men; democracy was mobocracy; "slavery is eternal, slavery of field and house may go down to slavery of mill and wheel. And that in turn may go down to slavery of another baser sort—the slavery of the mob to itself. . . ." [38]

This, then, was the play Wolfe was chafing to complete while he was crushed under the load of freshman themes in 1924. "Never have

I wanted to write as I do now," he told Billy Polk. "It is a crude hunger of the spirit. And never have I had less time for writing." [39] As a remedy, he determined to go to Europe in September with the remainder of his year's pay, hoping he could accomplish enough work to support himself without teaching. He had resolved, as he did each year for the next five years, never to teach again. "I may conceivably tap on the sidewalk with a cane next season, having bought a pair of smoked glasses. I may shout 'Times, Woild, Joinal'—in a raucous bellow. But—I shall not teach." [40] Since both the Theatre Guild and the Neighborhood Playhouse had expressed interest in his second play, he felt that finishing *Mannerhouse* was his best chance to break into the theater.

Despite his statements that it would be cheaper for him to live in Europe, he had other reasons for his decision to take *Mannerhouse* across the Atlantic. This was the time young Americans were settling in Paris to write, and Wolfe was convinced that going to Europe was the necessary thing for a young writer to do. More than this, he still had in mind his search for experience in order to stock his memory with potential literary material. Wolfe wanted the grand tour, he wanted to extend his observation to the European continent; then perhaps new work would shape itself.

NOTES

1. Published by Harper and Brothers in 1948.
2. LTM, p. 60.
3. *Letters*, p. 58.
4. From a draft of Wolfe's application for a Guggenheim fellowship, reprinted in *Letters*, pp. 210-12.
5. New York, 1923.
6. This is the story Madeleine Boyd has told me. Wolfe refers to Miss MacDonald in a letter to George Wallace, *Letters*, p. 69. Since Mr. Real is no longer living I could not confirm that part of the story.
7. LTM, p. 86.
8. These are his words as Mrs. Baker remembers them.
9. *Letters*, pp. 56-57.
10. Oscar Cargill in his *Thomas Wolfe at Washington Square* (New York, 1954) has devoted a small book to this period of Wolfe's life and included many important documents and memoirs. It was published as part of a two-volume set, the other volume of which was *The Correspondence of Thomas Wolfe and Homer Andrew Watt*. Although Thomas Clark Pollock's name is also on the title page, the preface indicates that Professor Cargill wrote the long title essay. In his essay, Cargill has combined fact and anecdote to give a full and interesting picture of Wolfe during

these years, although he is frequently too dependent on Wolfe's novels for biographical material when he goes outside Washington Square. The essay supports implicitly a thesis that Wolfe was a poor teacher and did nothing but read aloud in his classes, although Cargill does not get close to Wolfe in the classroom routine. Further, it reflects some of the bitterness which still exists at New York University over Wolfe's fictional treatment of the University in OT&R and elsewhere.

11. *Letters,* pp. 59.

12. John Varney remembers Wolfe's telling him this.

13. LTM, p. 59.

14. HCL, unpublished letter, *ca.* April 7, 1924.

15. *Letters,* p. 59.

16. *Letters,* p. 67.

17. So William Tindall remembers. Batches of corrected themes were kept in pigeonholes in a department office.

18. Elizabeth Nowell identifies the typist as James Mandel, but Mandel did not begin typing for Wolfe until after Scribner's had accepted Wolfe's book for publication. See n. 35, Chapter 10, for further details.

19. UNCL, unpublished letter, spring, 1924.

20. HCL*46AM-8(16).

21. *Letters,* p. 59.

22. LTM, pp. 73-74.

23. LTM, pp. 14-15.

24. LTM, p. 45.

25. For the full details, see LTM, pp. 99-103.

26. OT&R, pp. 544-49.

27. OT&R, pp. 544-45. N. Bryllion Fagin discusses *Mannerhouse* and other plays in his article, "In Search of an American *Cherry Orchard,*" *Texas Quarterly,* I (Summer-Autumn, 1958), 132-41. He assesses the attempts of Southern writers to produce an American *Cherry Orchard,* and he attributes their failure to their mistake of equating the pre-Civil-War South to nineteenth-century Russia. Chekov's play is "the product of liberal Russia on the eve of social revolution."

28. P. 113.

29. Pp. 68 and 139.

30. LTM, p. 16.

31. This is reprinted in *Letters* as part of a letter to Merlin Taylor (p. 45). It comes from a letter fragment to an unidentified correspondent. The phrase "men and masters" is from Carlyle's *Past and Present.*

32. *Letters,* p. 104.

33. *Mannerhouse,* p. 130.

34. *Ibid.,* pp. 91-92.

35. *Ibid.,* p. 134.

36. *Ibid.,* pp. 16-17. The stage directions themselves contributed to the success of Gustav Gründgrens' presentations of *Mannerhouse* in West Germany. They were read by a narrator during the prologue while the actors behind a scrim carried out the building of the house.

37. *Ibid.,* pp. 61-62.

38. *Ibid.,* p. 63. This attitude perhaps accounts for the successful reception of *Mannerhouse* on the German stage in recent years. Horst Frenz, in "A German Home for *Mannerhouse,*" *Theater Arts,* XL (August, 1956), 63, 95-96, has described Gustav Gründgrens' outstanding production of Wolfe's play—translated by Peter Sandberg

under the title *Herrenhaus*—at Hamburg in January, 1956. The article also describes productions in Düsseldorf, Hannover, Bielefeld, Nürnberg, and Berlin, as well as radio production and readings elsewhere in Austria and Germany. Frenz feels, however, that postwar disillusionment and anti-war sentiment are the grounds of the appeal for the German audiences.

Mannerhouse has been produced only once in America, by the Yale Dramatic Association, May 5, 6, and 7, 1949—a wretched experience endured politely by small audiences.

39. UNCL, unpublished letter, spring, 1924.
40. *Ibid.*

7

FIRST ATTEMPT AT PROSE NARRATIVE

AT THE END OF SEPTEMBER, 1924, WOLFE ACTED ON HIS DE-
cision. He corrected his last examination paper, drew the remainder
of his year's salary ($750), and turned his attention once more to his
writing career. On his twenty-fourth birthday he reviewed his
meager achievement since leaving North Carolina, then resolved to
write fifteen hundred words a day during his European trip. Not only
was he determined to finish his play, but he thought vaguely of
grinding out short stories in order to support himself. He had told
everyone he would not teach again. He embarked for England on
the *R. M. S. Lancastria* in late October.[1]

Since Wolfe had now made up his mind to try prose narrative, he
felt he could rely on two kinds of material. The first was the excitement of his year in New York: as he wrote Professor Baker, "I
sponged up a million impressions." [2] The second was his day-to-day
experience in the coming year of travel. He began accumulating
those notes as soon as the ship was underway:

SUNDAY, OCTOBER 26

Today, for the first time in my life, I am beginning a more or less
methodical record of the events which impinge on my own experience. I
do this, I believe, because for the first time in my life I feel an utter isolation from such reality as I have known; because I know that I must live
a good week longer with the people on this ship, and that try as we may,
we cannot get away from one another. The opportunities for observation
are humorously unique.

The weather is magnificent—warm, bright, clear—there is no sea; the
boat is perfectly steady.

There are less than one hundred of us on the cabin list. Let us see

97

how thoroughly we can dislike one another before the voyage is over. Nine days with your companions is a long time. . . .[3]

The uneventful voyage seemed an intoxicating dream to Wolfe. The English ship made him feel part of a cosmopolitan world. He studied his fellow passengers, mostly American tourists from various parts of the United States; he became acquainted with a member of the English embassy staff as well as a London cockney; he worried about the spectacle of the American on tour as he listened to a pompous Cleveland attorney discourse on European travel; he saw another side of the writing profession when he drank with a cynical contributor to the slick magazines. In exploring the entire ship, he stared with awe at the captain and with sympathy at the hands below decks (his expectation of seeing "hairy apes" stoking the furnaces was quashed when he discovered the ship burned oil). Every night before retiring, he recorded the day's impressions in his log.

Hoping for publication, Wolfe had from the beginning planned to convert his notes into a connected narrative. His aim was not high. If the *Asheville Citizen* would print his work, that was as much as he would ask. On arrival in England he wrote his friend, George Mc-Coy, of the *Citizen* staff, promising to send him publishable material immediately. He often mentioned his intention in letters to his mother, but it was March, 1925, before he finally dispatched any work. Instead of sending it directly to the *Citizen*, he sent it in installments to Mrs. Roberts, his old high school teacher, whom he called on to be a combination of editor and agent.

Wolfe's writings during his year in Europe divide into two parts. The first group, "Passage to England," is within the framework of the ocean voyage to Europe. Although the scheme was never completed, there seem to have been eleven installments and a prologue, perhaps 50,000 words altogether.[4] The second batch of material, which for convenience may be called "The 1925 Sketches," consists of episodes based for the most part on his travel notes as he wandered about Europe during the year. Besides the three sketches which are complete, there are fragments of about two dozen others.

In writing "Passage to England," Wolfe made very little change from the diary he kept during the days at sea. Compare, for example, the first passage in the diary quoted above with the opening paragraph of the second installment:

SUNDAY, OCTOBER 26

There are less than one hundred of us in the cabin list, and for nine days, at least, we will not be able to get away from one another. The opportunities for observation are humorously unique. We are one day out; we have seen, yesterday afternoon, New York, far off, bound half way up her thin far spires by a flanking girdle of cloud and mist. . . .

The weather was warm, bright, clear, and golden. The sea was as calm as an inland lake. The ship was perfectly steady. . . .[5]

As a result, Wolfe's first efforts at narrative are poor stuff, indeed. In his laziness or in his ignorance of narrative method, he seemed not to be troubled by his ragbag organization—except that he wished to publish anonymously. He felt that the mere exercise of daily scribbling would serve to train him. Writing as he pleased meant for Wolfe at this time filling in a sketch book. The "Passage to England" episodes are a mixture of passenger characterizations, voyage impressions, and editorial excursions into literature, politics, international relations, and American manners and morals—all hung on a weak narrative line, the few events of shipboard life.

The fifth installment, covering November 1 and 2, is a typical example. It opens with a satirical portrait of "The Man from Dayton." This experienced traveler from the Midwest is presented as an outspoken critic of the attitudes and antics of the average American tourist at the same time as he exhibits them himself. Wolfe then gives a series of passenger descriptions, followed by a discourse on class hatreds among the English. This leads to an observation on the complexity of American life and a refutation of G. Lowes Dickinson's thesis in his essay on the "Divine Average" in America.[6] Yet, says Wolfe, this variety in American life is not enough for the spontaneous emergence of a great literature; even though America is not one vast bourgeoisie, it still has failed to produce any great poetry. The installment concludes with an argument about literary standards between "Cat-Eye," the slick-magazine writer, and a young man (Wolfe himself) who is just beginning to write.

"Passage to England" suffers not only from interrupted narrative but also from weak characterizations. Wolfe failed to supply details of speech, manner, gesture—all the tricks he later employed to make his great characters real and memorable. For example, the second installment contains an early sketch of Abe Jones, but no personality emerges from Wolfe's pages. We are told only that the boy, "ashamed secretly of his own emotion and deriding it in others but capable of fierce and amorous devotion to an idea," has the soul of an artist. In a brief description of dinner at the boy's house, Wolfe stands off from his subject and sees no humanity there; he merely digresses upon the problem of anti-Semitism.

For ideas, the most interesting section of "Passage to England" is the first installment, the prologue, which explains the subtitle, "Log of a Voyage That Was Never Made." In his early work on "Passage to England," Wolfe had not gone beyond a close reporting of passenger life on board the *Lancastria*. Even his two methods of naming characters scarcely disguised the actual personages he traveled with: he gave his characters names recognizably close to their real names—for example, Hugh Tennant, the traveler from the British diplomatic service, is called Wyant [7]—or he chose general descriptive tags—for example, George T. Baunder, a Cleveland attorney, is called "The Man from Dayton." To mitigate the dangers that this kind of fidelity to reality might bring, Wolfe cloaked the voyage in fantasy by means of an elaborate prologue. In the beginning, the narrator, who has planned to leave on a transatlantic trip, learns that the sailing date of his ship has been postponed. Nevertheless, he and his friend, George Scoville, go to the pier on the appointed day, and at sailing time he insists that he is on board the ship. When they return to his hotel room, he begins to feel ill, and after being examined by the hotel physician, he learns that he is suffering from seasickness. This phenomenon leads to a long discussion between the narrator and Scoville on the reality of imagined experience. The voyage log which follows in several installments is then supposed to be a record of an imaginary ocean trip. With this device, Wolfe has constructed a frame for his narrative, and at the same time he has provided himself an opportunity to present, in the discourse on imaginary experience, a literary theory, his notion of the task of the artist.

Wolfe set forth here his theory of the poetic process of the romantic artist, which he had derived from his studies under John Livingston Lowes. As in all of Wolfe's theorizing, his thoughts on this subject are not stated with clarity, but this is what he is trying to say. The role of the artist is first that of observer not only of other men but of his own emotional experience. There is, Wolfe states through his narrator, "a calculation in the experiences of writing people that is at once comic and terrible. They are stricken, subdued, overwhelmed by an emotion, grief, hatred, love, and all the time they are measuring greedily and exultantly the depth and extent of the wound: thus they give their readers minute and elaborate descriptions of their crucifixion. . . ." [8] The world of fact in which the artist lives appears as a chaos. But, as Wolfe said again in the Autobiographical Outline of 1926, the true romanticist does not try to escape life but tries to apprehend it more surely by seeking experience; then, by exercise of the imagination, he may discover an order beneath the welter of these experiences. The artist will become lost, in fact, if he merely reports his observations (gives them "extension in time and space"); therefore, the perfect experiences are those which occur "in the quiet eternity of thought." This is to say that the artist's creative imagination can produce an ordered world which is more real than the chaos around him. [9]

One further idea in the prologue deserves comment. We find from the discussion between the narrator and his friend that Wolfe by this time was forming the view of life that he set forth in *Look Homeward, Angel*. We have seen that Wolfe looks about him to see a disordered world of chance but that he disputes the reality of this world. The real world of order and necessity, which can be perceived by thought, lies behind the chaos. The narrator goes on further to consider man's place in this dual universe. In the chronicle of time, man's course moves along, guided by Necessity. But the "fatality of things" does not totally determine his life. Man's choices, both good and bad, can in some measure control his life within the areas of Necessity: "we must know that our lives are charted by roads which we have walled off ourselves because of our pride, fear, or adhesion to custom." The possibility of self-determination that Wolfe thought about at Harvard was the means, then, to select other roads by the best choices. But within Necessity and beyond control of Will are accidents that further alter man's course. With this last addition we see that the scheme is similar to Melville's warp of Necessity, shuttle of Free Will, and sword of Chance. [10] This is Wolfe's tripartite view of destiny that was to undergo further interpretation when he wrote his first novel.

Since there are significant ideas in "Passage to England," the lack of literary merit in the work is a disappointment. The failure of this series of sketches lay partly in Wolfe's inability to handle narrative at this time and partly, perhaps, in the haste with which he converted his notes into narrative. The experience had not aged long enough in his memory. If it had, he would have remembered the voyage as uneventful, and it would have seemed a meager literary source. Since Wolfe never threw away anything that he wrote and since he later reworked almost everything that had been cut from his first novels, he no doubt recognized the worthlessness of "Passage to England," for he never turned to it again.

II

Wolfe arrived in England on Guy Fawkes Day and went immediately to London. During his month in England, he continued to keep travel notes, for he reported to his mother that he was "writing it all up." [11] Only a sheet or two survive, but some parts of "The 1925 Sketches"—"London Tower," "The Revival" (a scene with some Welsh street-evangelists), and "Prolog to Liliom" (a description of an Oxford Street carnival)—indicate that he visited the common tourist shrines and that he roamed the streets of London at night, watching the Cockney at his pleasures. He "went down almost every back alley in London and into most of the disreputable pubs" [12] with that curiosity which always led him to explore every possible stratum of a city's life. He had no plan for his tour but traveled by impulse. When a guidebook to Bath fell into his hands, he decided suddenly to see western England. A fragment from "The 1925 Sketches" preserves his impressions of Bath as he tried to picture the city's life on history's stage, from the Roman occupation down to the nineteenth century. Another scrap records his delight in the bells of Bristol, where he had gone to shed a tear at the grave of Chatterton.[13]

He spent the next two months in Paris, sometimes with American friends but oftener alone, following a routine of writing and sightseeing, and then set out to explore the region just south of Paris—Chartres, Orléans, Blois, and Tours. He took notes industriously and prepared a harvest he was to reap almost ten years later. Among "The 1925 Sketches" were a story of peasants on the train to Orléans; "a great and compassionate satire" [14] of the Countess Constance Hillyer de Caen; and a story of "an old villain of a Marquise." [15] When in later years Wolfe reworked these sketches, they finally found a place in *Of Time and the River* as adventures in Eugene Gant's aimless wandering in France.

After Paris, Wolfe turned south toward St. Raphael. He was so exhilarated during the journey that in his notes he always referred to this period as "The South and madness." He stayed a lonely two months in St. Raphael, working on "Passage to England" and other sketches. He spent no time in perfecting anything, for he was too overwhelmed by the excitement of his European experiences; he merely let his pencil run on. "What I am doing is to write, write, write—" he told Homer Watt, "it may be the most frightful muck, but I can't help putting it down." [16]

When he settled down next, first for a month in London and later for a month at Ambleside in the Lake Country, he wrote furiously, fancying himself a Coleridge or De Quincey in a London lodging-house or in Dove Cottage at Grasmere. He now worked on a dozen of "The 1925 Sketches" and piled up notes for a score more. He had been pleased to learn that his sketch, "London Tower," had appeared in the *Asheville Citizen's* Sunday edition on July 19. With this encouragement, he packed off more manuscript to Mrs. Roberts.

"The 1925 Sketches" have an extraordinary diversity of subject matter. Besides the vignettes already mentioned, Wolfe wrote a story with an Asheville background, "The Grocer's Daughter," which included a portrait of Sister Theresa, who appears in *Look Homeward, Angel;* [17] a character sketch based on an encounter in Trafalgar Square, "The Dean of St. Rupert's," in which the old dean's theme echoes Goethe's line, "Gib meine Jugend mir zurück"; [18] and a daydream of "John Dempsey Gant," the champion, stepping into the ring to defend the title—the first occurrence of the name Gant in Wolfe's writing. Notes and fragments of other sketches indicate the variety of ideas he was experimenting with. A scene below decks in the Melville manner presents a group of mariners singing an ironic chorus on the roundness of the world. Several pages show work on a satire of Bryan and the Scopes trial. Probably from the same episode are the pages characterizing "Graham," an urbane lawyer, who, in irascible fashion, disqualifies one mountaineer after another from jury duty. Other fragments show work on a mock book review supposedly by Mencken and Lewis; a "Judgment in Heaven" wherein God and Satan try to judge a Unitarian; "The Isle of Quesnay," a satire in imitation of *Penguin Island;* [19] a scene of an enthusiastic prayer meeting in the South; a satiric debate among Oxford men on beauty and the passions. When we remember that these sheets represent only a few of the projects Wolfe had in hand, we get an idea of the great energy with which he undertook his daily writing.

More important, however, are fragments that show Wolfe's mind going back to childhood remembrances of Asheville and his family. Among his papers are notes on the following subjects: the smell of hot tar on the Asheville streets, the spring flowers, the "Jew bread" he ate at his mother's boarding house, the draymen in front of his father's shop, his father's hands, Ben and the newspaper boys in the all-night lunchroom, the prophet Bacchus and Billy Westall—all suggestions, perhaps never developed in 1925, that came to life in *Look Homeward, Angel.*

Among other notes, his explicit statements on style are of greatest interest. In "Passage to England" he had declared, speaking through the narrator, that he would try to model his style on the early nineteenth-century writers; in these later notes he has, in a hastily jotted scribble, narrowed his choice: "Manifestly, the whole course and purport of my intent is to fashion in English prose a personal and distinctive style. If I am to write at all, it is to be in the language of the tongue I speak, and not in Chinese, Italian, or Greek. It is far more to the point, therefore, that I imitate,—aye, in the straight, literal sense,—the prose of Thomas De Quincey, than the prose of Cicero, Renan, or Thucydides." [20] Wolfe's taste for Romantic prose and especially for the most flamboyant of the Romantic group caused the development of a style that is unique in twentieth-century American literature. Although the rhythmical phrases and the emotionally charged diction are not peculiar to De Quincey alone and although other stylistic influences (Shakespeare's rhetorical passages, Biblical poetry, Burton, Urquhart, Whitman, Conrad, and Joyce) may be found in Wolfe's writings, De Quincey is the first among these writers of rich, heavy styles that Wolfe acknowledged as master.

In these 1925 notes, Wolfe's conception of the artist penetrating life's mystery through experience is set forth, and so is the symbolism of the door: "I have not felt the world's imprisonment; I have wanted a key that would let me enter, not a key to set me loose." [21] In order to make life as full as possible, the artist ideally must control the events of his own life as closely as he can. Wolfe's notes, as we might expect, associate this theory with Pater's novel: "*Marius the Epicurean,* that if experience could be selected, so that it might meet the life of a man at the time it would have most meaning, the importance and the quality of the man would be vastly increased. This, says Pater, happened to Marius when a certain book came into his hands at a certain time." [22] A fragment on Shaw and the Life Force shows that Wolfe had not forgotten this idea after he put aside his incomplete play based on Wells's *The Undying Fire.* The passage begins as Wolfe's autobiographical self presses the pulse which is "beating slowly, slowly" in a vein on his neck:

This, then, that he felt was the Life Force about which Bernard Shaw had spoken so frequently, about which so many other writers had spoken solemnly, balefully, portentously, but rarely gaily or exultantly; which penetrated so many religions, was adjudicated by so many customs and constitutions, and was frowned upon at every convention of the Methodist church, unless it was ecclesiastically tethered.[23]

Further, Wolfe's notes on the blind waste of evolution and on the grandeur of unchanging forms—notes found in the same heap of manuscript in which he set down his convictions about fate, free will, and chance—show again that he was ready to combine these speculations into some comprehensive interpretation of life.

By the time Wolfe was preparing to sail to America at the end of August, 1925, he had, despite his vows, accepted an offer from Professor Watt to teach at New York University. He had spent a seemingly fruitless year. He had wandered in Europe only after humiliating requests to his mother for money; he had worked intermittently for ten months, only to produce a sheaf of amateurish sketches. Yet this was an important year in Wolfe's development. He had made contact with other cultures, observing the common characteristics of men beneath their unfamiliar ways. He had the opportunity that falls to all European travelers to look more objectively at American life after his return. He could, in the future, write with the breadth he needed for that work encompassing "a whole race, a whole epoch." Moreover, he had stumbled upon a working method for the novels he was later to write. He had put into practice his habit of conscious observation of all men and women that he met. He had begun accumulating his observations and ideas into notes. He had turned to autobiographical narrative, which would be the means for his interpretation of life. One more experience awaited him that would prove to be a decisive turning point in his career.

III

When Wolfe booked a third-class passage home on the *Olympic* that summer in 1925, he was pleased to have the company of a young man whom he had known at Harvard.[24] During the voyage, his Harvard friend introduced him to two ladies who were traveling first class, Mrs. Aline Bernstein and Miss Mina Kirstein. Ever ready to talk about himself, Wolfe rattled on about his playwriting and his hopes for a production by the Neighborhood Playhouse. His excitement at learning Mrs. Bernstein was a member of the board of directors for the Neighborhood Playhouse turned to astonishment when she pulled *Welcome to Our City* out of her luggage. In their talk about the play, Wolfe stubbornly refused to make any revisions that the Neighborhood Playhouse group suggested, but he talked eagerly about his plans for *Mannerhouse,* which he was bringing back to America. Here, in a discussion of Wolfe's future as a playwright, began one of the most publicized love affairs in modern literary history.

Some men puzzle over the spectacle of couples oddly matched in love or marriage, but the contrasts, physical, economic, and social, between Thomas Wolfe and Aline Bernstein will strike anyone as extraordinary. He was not yet twenty-five years old and she was forty-three. From his height of six and a half feet, he towered over her tiny figure. Yet with his extremely youthful appearance, he must have seemed childlike beside a woman whose hair already had begun to gray. He was poor, still drawing on his mother's money to supplement his salary as an instructor; she had wealth, both through her early marriage to Theodore Bernstein, a successful stock broker, and through her career as a theatrical designer. He was an ill-dressed, awkward outlander from the Southern Appalachians; she was a beautifully gowned, well-graced matron who moved in the most sophisticated circles of the New York theatre. He was a wild, unstable bachelor; she, while by no means a domestic woman, still had long been a wife and was now the mother of two children. Even in their creative work, they presented a contrast: his genius seemed the more erratic alongside her competent craftsmanship.

Despite these differences, they were temperamentally alike. Both were surging with vitality, running after life, seizing and savoring the moment. They laughed heartily, wept easily, acted impulsively, angered quickly, loved deeply. Since each felt he had found a soul like his own, they even shared a belief in extrasensory communication. Drawn together by emotional kinship, they were to find, however, that their passionate natures were the source of clash as well as union.

Because of Mrs. Bernstein's companionship, the next few years of Wolfe's life were the happiest he had ever known. He always spoke of them as a "period of certitude." As he wrote to her from Wiesbaden in 1928, "We are strangers and exiles here. . .and the only home a man ever has on earth, the only moment when he escapes from the prisons of loneliness is when he enters into the heart of another person." [25]

Besides love and companionship, Mrs. Bernstein provided financial help, and her money made possible more than a series of apartments they shared. They traveled to Europe together in the summers of 1926 and 1927, and with her help Wolfe traveled in Europe alone during most of 1928. Through her aid, he was freed of his teaching chores during the fall of 1926 and the spring of 1927, and in this period he was able to write most of *Look Homeward, Angel.*

It is clear that the meeting with Aline Bernstein marks the end of Wolfe's apprenticeship. It had been a period of trial and failure, through which writers who attempt much must pass. During this time, travel and new associations not only broadened him but increased his thirst for experience. Intellectual ferment, first at Harvard and later among his colleagues at New York University, stimulated him. Experiment with a variety of literary forms gave him practice in his chosen profession. He was ready to move toward mature achievement. And he was able to attain it sooner now because of the love and encouragement of a beautiful and wealthy patroness.

NOTES

1. Wolfe was accompanied to the dock only by two of his freshman students—an indication of the friendless life of his first year at New York University.

2. *Letters*, p. 70.

3. HCL*46AM-7(23), Box 1. This is from one of the few remaining sheets of the diary Wolfe kept aboard ship.

4. Manuscript copies of the prologue and installments one to five and eight and eleven, and typescript copies of the prologue and the sixth installment, are still extant.

5. HCL*46AM-7(23), Box 1, Second Installment.

6. The essay was included in the freshman textbook Wolfe used at New York University—Harold Bruce and Guy Montgomery, *The New World* (New York, 1920). Wolfe's copy is HCL*46A-102.

7. For Wolfe's continued practice of naming his characters this way, see Floyd Watkins' discussion in *Thomas Wolfe's Characters* (Norman, Okla., 1957), p. 8 and elsewhere.

8. HCL*46AM-7(23), Box 1, First Installment.

9. F. David Martin, in "The Artist, Autobiography, and Thomas Wolfe," *Bucknell Review*, V (March, 1955), pp. 15-28, outlines an aesthetic theory about autobiographical literature that he applies to Wolfe. He begins with the assertion that good art is dependent upon form and insight and asks how autobiographical material can be transformed into art. The answer is, by means of "insight into a hierarchical relationship of values"—that is, an insight into a value system outside of oneself. A "comprehensive insight" is a *Weltanschauung* or philosophy of life which is necessary for the artistic fulfillment of epical intentions such as Wolfe's. Martin, who finds Wolfe "an inductionist who would have beaten Francis Bacon at his own game," feels that Wolfe's artistic failures arose from his "belief that he had to learn everything for himself." Finally, Martin feels that "as Wolfe matured, he began to recognize that what he needed was a more comprehensive insight, that he had to have a vision of order that would enable him to transcend the momentary and the particular by placing them in relation to the universal."

Wolfe's prologue to "Passage to England" is evidence that he understood the need for "comprehensive insight" very early in his career. Indeed, a few years later, in LHA, he demonstrated that he could achieve it.

10. *Moby Dick*, Chapter XLVII, "The Mat Maker."

11. LTM, p. 96 and p. 97.

12. *Letters*, p. 73.

13. HCL*46AM-7(23), Box 2.

14. *Letters*, p. 91.

15. *Letters*, p. 95.

16. *Letters*, p. 98.

17. Pp. 186-87.

18. *Faust*, "Vorspiel auf dem Theater."

19. For further discussion, see Daniel L. Delakas, "Thomas Wolfe and Anatole France: A Study of Some Unfinished Experiments," *Comparative Literature*, XV (Winter, 1957), 33-50.

20. *Ibid.*

21. *Ibid.*

22. *Ibid.*

23. *Ibid.*

24. So Mrs. Bernstein reported in an interview with me in January, 1950. Search and inquiry have not been able to identify him.

25. HCL, unpublished letter, August 27, 1928.

Part III

THE SHAPING OF *LOOK HOMEWARD, ANGEL*

8

EXPLORING THE BURIED LIFE

DURING THE WINTER OF 1925-26, WOLFE HAD A LITTLE MORE time for writing, because he was repeating his chores as an instructor of freshman composition. He worked over some of his European sketches—especially his favorites, the story of the Countess, the episode of the peasants on the train to Orléans, and the Bryan satire —and he often read them to friends. After sending off *Mannerhouse* to the Theatre Guild, he began work on *Welcome to Our City* once again, but with dubious results. Pleased with his recent labors on *Mannerhouse,* he unfortunately persuaded himself that a few more pages of urbane and irrelevant dialogue would round out the character of Rutledge, the real estate entrepreneur, and enlarge the significance of Jordan, the writer. Although this sequence only added further length to the play, other revisions did make the positions of the antagonists, Rutledge and Johnson, clearer. Wolfe inserted speeches making Johnson, the Negro, less sympathetic so that the characterization of Rutledge would be more acceptable to the audience.[1]

But Wolfe had no more success with the marketing of his plays now than he had had before. *Welcome to Our City* went to the Provincetown Playhouse for reconsideration but again was rejected.[2] The Theatre Guild kept *Mannerhouse* for months but then returned it without encouragement. He had hoped that Mrs. Bernstein, through her many associations in the theater, could help him to get his plays produced. But when he gave her *Mannerhouse* to read, she only made him furious by telling him how bad it was. Nevertheless, she agreed to pass it on to Alice Lewisohn, who also rejected it and commented, as Wolfe later discovered, that he was "the most arrogant young man she had ever known."[3] About the same time, Wolfe asked his friend, Henry Carlton, whose play, *Up the Line,* was being produced during the current season, if he could help him sell *Mannerhouse.* Carlton turned it over to Harold McGee of the Provincetown Players, but McGee thought it so poor that he returned it (although Wolfe never knew) without ever sending it to the board of directors.

His habits of life changed but little after he met Mrs. Bernstein. Although he read less omnivorously than before, he still spent hours browsing through his poetry anthologies or reading aloud to Mrs. Bernstein. In addition to his desultory play revision, he worked at prose narrative, either materials begun on the European trip or new projects prompted by childhood memories. He had told J. M. Roberts, Jr., the previous September that he was determined to write a novel with an Asheville setting.[4] But he felt disorganized. He had already accumulated a trunkful of manuscript which he continued aimlessly to pile higher. When his plays did not sell, an inner compulsion still drove his pencil across the page, but he no longer had purpose. He later described his despair and lethargic productiveness to Henry Allen Moe of the Guggenheim Foundation: "I was quite unhappy about my writing—nothing I did ever saw the light of day: I wrote at random but all the time: [I wrote on loose sheets of paper, and lost or got hopelessly confused what I had written.] When I had finished something, a powerful inertia settled on me—I would not show what I had written to anyone, I would not send it out for publication, I did not know what to do, or how to go about it."[5] Along with this sense of defeat, he had begun to feel that he could never be a playwright:

Two or three years had passed since I came to New York and the conviction was growing on me that I would never write plays. I had begun quite by accident at North Carolina, and continued by chance at Harvard. I loved the theatre, but I began to see I had to find a medium where I could satisfy my desire for fulness, intensity, and completeness. I could never do this in the theatre, and my creative sense was troubled further by knowing what I did would be touched and reshaped by a hundred different people—directors, actors, designers, carpenters, electricians. I did not like this; what I did had to be my own.[6]

Always pettish about the success of others, he began to swell with envy at the attainments of his contemporaries. He looked grimly at the publications of New York University colleagues. In spite of his admiration for John Varney's volume of verse, *First Wounds,* it may be supposed that he was full of resentment even as he introduced Varney at a public reading of the poems in the Greenwich Village Theater. Ill will gnawed at him as he contemplated the play productions of 47 Workshop classmates Philip Barry and Henry Carlton. But when his fellow playmaker at Chapel Hill, Paul Green, won the Pulitzer Prize for *In Abraham's Bosom,* he became so furious that he was drunk for three days.[7]

Out of this Eugene Gantian pit of despair he was drawn by the aid of Aline Bernstein, who gave him "companionship, affection, and the inestimable comfort of human belief." [8] Sometime in the winter of 1925-26, Wolfe left the Hotel Albert and moved to grim Greenwich Village quarters (a large bare loft, without plumbing, at 13 East Eighth Street) for which he and Mrs. Bernstein shared the rent.[9] In this room, scantily furnished, the walls lined with Mrs. Bernstein's theatrical sketches and the floor littered with Wolfe's uncorrected student themes, they spent many hours together. Since both were great talkers, they poured out detailed accounts of their lives to each other, recalling forgotten years in their childhood. In this way, during the spring of 1926, Wolfe began to reassemble the accumulated moments of his life, along with the flood of feeling that surrounded them. His mind was filled with memories which he now viewed afresh; from his new position of clarity and certainty, he saw his past as a whole.

During the spring he decided to go ahead on the novel, and Mrs. Bernstein stood behind him financially, offering him an opportunity to go to Europe to write as soon as the college year was over. A report to Olin Dows shows his renewed interest in life and even revived hope that one of his plays might see production: "There's little about me to tell you—little that *can* be told. Make the most of that. It seems a theatre here may do one of my plays next season. Meanwhile, I seethe with the finest ideas I've ever had, and little time for writing. It's England in June, and the continent for the next year or two." [10]

Having followed Wolfe's troubled career in the drama, anyone can see why he turned to the novel. Probably shame at his failure prevented Wolfe himself from saying much about the reasons for his decision. Besides the brief statement to the Guggenheim Foundation, he made only one other reference to his problem. In a few notes for a speech, in 1929, he summarized his struggle to write plays that would give the broad prospect of life that he wished to present: "Had tried to write plays—plays didn't succeed—too long—thought if I wrote a book I should at last find something long enough to fit."[11] He said nothing about his inability to excise inappropriate or dramatically irrelevant material.

Why he, like other fledgling novelists, chose to write an autobiographical work must also seem obvious. His self-consciousness points certainly in this direction. Further, he had never lost sight of his intention to write about his family, ever since the abortive "House of Bateson" and the synopses about the "Broody" family in his Harvard notebook. Then, too, he had examples before him in many of his favorite authors who had shaped great literature from autobiographical material—Wordsworth, Coleridge, Byron, De Quincey, Carlyle, Dickens, and in his own century Conrad, Maugham, and Joyce. However, *Look Homeward, Angel* is unusually introspective because Wolfe was strongly influenced by psychoanalysis at the time he decided to write his first novel. He consciously undertook to write fictional autobiography with a vague notion that he was plumbing the depths of his inner self in the same way the psychoanalyst's patient unwinds the wrappings of time to discover himself.

Perhaps it may seem pointless to raise this matter, since it is commonly recognized that depth psychology has made a powerful impact on both the subject matter and technique of modern literature in general. But the influence of depth psychology upon Wolfe's novel demands comment because he himself often scoffed at psychoanalysis. His earliest reference to Freud, in a letter to Frederick Koch, hoots at the pretentious statement of one of his peers in the 47 Workshop: "Why, one man the other day made a criticism of a play as follows: 'That situation seems to be a perfect illustration of the Freudian complex' and it gladdened me much when Mr. Baker, the most courteous of men under very trying conditions, replied 'I don't know about the Freudian complex; what we are discussing now are the simple human values of this play.'"[12] In his 1925 notes, he attributed a great deal of the popularity of Joyce's *Ulysses* to adulation of "the dunces" who "waited at the feet of the Man from Vienna."[13] Later, in a letter to Henry Volkening, he scored psychoanalysts and their pathetic patients "suffering from nothing but too much money and too little to do, without the sense to know that it is all in Plato, in understandable language not especially manufactured for the trade." [14] Further, his library contains, of Freud's works, only *The Problem of Lay-Analysis*,[15] and nothing of Jung or Adler. Since Wolfe hated fashionable cults, it is easy to see why he snorted at psychoanalysis. Even so, he did take a considerable interest in psychoanalytic theories of human nature and human motivation during the time he knew Aline Bernstein.

It was easy for Wolfe, living in New York and moving among people who followed the intellectual currents and eddies of their day, to absorb a knowledge of psychoanalytic theory without making a study of Freud or Jung. Max Eastman had begun to popularize Freudian theory in *Everybody's Magazine* as early as 1915; [16] such groups as Mabel Dodge's circle began to cultivate the study of Freud even before 1920, and by the early 1920's Greenwich Village was said to be the center of popular Freudianism in America. Besides living in the Village and visiting the Village bookshops, Wolfe was in daily contact with New York University instructors and their discussions of new ideas. Since he was preoccupied with the theater when he first came to New York, he no doubt saw one of the many performances of Susan Glaspell's *Suppressed Desires*, a play which, in spite of its satire, served to familiarize its audiences with psychoanalytic jargon.

After Wolfe met Aline Bernstein, however, he became acquainted for the first time with people who could afford to be psychoanalyzed. Mrs. Bernstein has told a story of her own adventure in psychoanalysis.[17] One day when she was in Brentano's, she picked up a copy of Beatrice M. Hinkle's translation of Jung's *Wandlungen und Symbole der Libido*.[18] The introduction, setting forth Jung's whole body of thought and distinguishing it from Freud's, fascinated her to the extent that she looked up Dr. Hinkle and asked to be psychoanalyzed. Although Dr. Hinkle was reluctant to accept the merely curious as patients, she finally consented to undertake a series of investigatory sessions with Mrs. Bernstein, which, in the end, lasted two years. Many of Mrs. Bernstein's friends were equally concerned about their psyches. Alice Lewisohn went to Zurich to be psychoanalyzed by Dr. Jung, and another friend went to England for treatment by Ernest Jones ("He was a Freudian," Wolfe quotes her mockingly in one of his notebooks, "Wasn't that déclassé").[19] Indeed, as one of Mrs. Bernstein's close friends reports, "The people Wolfe met through Mrs. Bernstein were, I think, largely Jungians but there may have been Freudians too." [20] In this environment Wolfe became intensely curious about the search into the unconscious, and he begged Mrs. Bernstein to tell him about every detail of her visits to Dr. Hinkle. He even promised to be psychoanalyzed himself if he should ever get enough money to pay for it.

Wolfe's knowledge of psychoanalytic theory was neither deep nor extensive. He did not distinguish accurately between the differing schools of psychoanalysis: it was mostly Freud to him. But his association with the followers of Jung deserves emphasis because Jung's theory of the libido does not clash with Wolfe's vitalistic ideas. Jung does not give the term, libido, the dominant sexual character that it has in Freud's writing; his term, in fact, resembles Bergson's "élan vital," for he conceives of it as a cosmic urge, an energy that includes a will to live, a will to reproduce, and a will to create. Further, Wolfe seems to have absorbed some of the ideas about racial memory which Jung stressed in his work. As Mrs. Bernstein put it, "Tom believed that people knew more than they knew—that is, what their ancestors had known." Some passages in the later Wolfe novels reflect this notion of the racial memory traces in the unconscious.

We have seen Wolfe's excitement over the "deep well of unconscious cerebration" in Coleridge, and we have seen his striving to follow Coleridge's example in tumultuous reading—even going beyond it to seek variety of experience. Now the life with Aline Bernstein led him to seek a new kind of experience, an examination of his inner life, and to find perhaps some understanding of life through a scrutiny of his own accumulated experience. One of the concluding paragraphs of *Look Homeward, Angel* records this decision in Eugene Gant's life. When the ghost of Ben tells him, "*You* are your world," Eugene replies that he will no longer seek his answers abroad in the world but in the lost land of himself:

O sudden and impalpable faun, lost in the thickets of myself, I will hunt you down until you cease to haunt my eyes with hunger. I heard your foot-falls in the desert, I saw your shadow in old buried cities, I heard your laughter running down a million streets, but I did not find you there. And no leaf hangs for me in the forest; I shall lift no stone upon the hills; I shall find no door in any city. But in the city of myself, upon the continent of my soul, I shall find the forgotten language, the lost world, a door where I may enter, and music strange as any ever sounded.[21]

The decision that Wolfe so records in his book was prompted by his recently acquired knowledge of psychoanalytic theory, for an earlier draft of this passage (quite different in tone) reads:

We have haunted ourself across the desert, we have looked for our self among the crowd, we have fled from that which we sought and now, weary of all other voyages, we face the only one that matters. We stand on the shores of that dark sunken sea, hearing only its mighty and secret whisper, the terrible and insistent evil of its music beating below the little [sugar?] bank of our defenses, the awful rhythm that unites us to eternity. The sad family of this world is damned all together, and joined, from its birth in an unspoken and grievous kinship in the incestuous loves of sons and mothers; in Lesbic hungers and parricidal hatreds; in the terrible shames of sons and fathers, and the uneasy shifting of their eyes; in the insatiate sexuality of infancy, in our wild hunger for ourself, the dear love of our excrement, the great obsession of Narcissus, and in the strange first love of every boy which is for a man.
And as we stand in the crowd, lonely, silent, and abashed before the mockery of the fool or the thrust of the coward, which of us has not felt a [hard?] shame because of his silence? Which of us has not felt a secret unspeakable joy at the thought of this voyage into a newer stranger land than Magellan dreamed of, a world more golden than Columbus thought to find? We stand upon the shore of the magic world, unable yet to see it save for the bare appalling flashes that the great wizard of Vienna has thrown upon it. But he has spoken a century too soon: we need tougher sinews, greater hearts. We will fight desperately yet awhile to save our fudge, we will dilute terror and beauty with milk and water, and as long as we can we will proclaim the idiot health of the animal, and deny the epic disease that makes us men. So until daybreak, long live Tom Sawyer! Long live Penrod and the Rollo Boys. God's in his heaven and the wicked shall be punished.[22]

Eugene Gant's outburst in the conclusion of *Look Homeward, Angel* may be interpreted biographically as Wolfe's revelation of a major decision in his career, his intention to write autobiographical fiction. Still, even though Aline Bernstein's familiarity with depth psychology affected Wolfe's approach to his novel, it was her actual presence that made possible his serenity for self-scrutiny. Wolfe's whole experience in writing the book and the circumstances that sharpened his perception may best be described by a quotation from Matthew Arnold's "The Buried Life"—the poem that Wolfe marked freely in his New York University textbook and to which he then alluded in the subtitle of *Look Homeward, Angel:*

> When a beloved hand is laid in ours,
> When, jaded with the rush and glare
> Of the interminable hours,
> Our eyes can in another's eyes read clear,
> When our world-deafened ear
> Is by the tones of a loved voice caressed—
>   A bolt is shot back somewhere in our breast
> And a lost pulse of feeling stirs again.
> The eye sinks inward, and the heart lies plain,
> And what we mean, we say, and what we would, we know.
> A man becomes aware of his life's flow,
> And hears its winding murmur; and he sees
> The meadows where it glides, the sun, the breeze.
>
> . . . .
>
>   And then he thinks he knows
>   The hills where his life rose,
>   And the sea where it goes.

Sometime during the spring of 1926, Wolfe jotted down a few ideas for the projected work. One loose sheet among his papers, perhaps only one of several such notations, preserves for us the earliest germ of the theme: "The Book shall have this unity—it shall represent the struggle of a man to stand alone and apart—Such a man as would be forced to stand alone by his physical and spiritual structure." [23] Later he expanded this statement into his first plan. The fragments that remain begin in this fashion: "The book shall represent the emergence of an individual but rather towards Creative independence and an inner solitude, of freedom from certain forces, and of bondage toward others. The three time elements shall be as follows—1) Infancy, 2) Childhood 3) Young Man-hood—but there shall be another time element which shall select and combine events before the first." [24] Even at this early stage, Wolfe wanted to have the history of the Gant family precede the birth of Eugene. This earlier "time element" refers not only to the Gant-Eliza marriage but also to the fictional counterparts of the early Wolfe ancestors, for the last page of this fragmentary plan contains these notes:

CHRONOLOGY

Richard Wellington—Born 1813—London, England
A gambler and a barkeeper—origins unknown—died
Gettysburg Pa. 1859.
Mary Augusta Reez—Born 1818
Near Gettysburg Pa.—Died there 1914—Aged 96 years
(cause—fracture of the hip) [25]

With some definite plans and with new determination, Wolfe sailed for Europe as soon as his classes were finished. This expedition would not be another *Wanderjahr:* he was determined to return with a completed novel.

II

The compelling itch to do a piece of work which mirrored his own life and set down the family annals had been with Wolfe for years. In the summer of 1921, he had prepared notes for the play or short story about the Broodys. It seems that Wolfe had planned to deal with recent family history. In these notes, the father is already sixty-five years old, "with a great long rack of a frame that still told of a once powerful physique. . . .Now he was wasted by a disease, a slow creeping, unstoppable thing, that would someday destroy him." [26] His death was perhaps to be the central event of the work, but the bickering and quarreling, the conflict between family groups that results in disintegration, was the principal subject of the passages that Wolfe set down. Yet the following year the fragmentary play, "The House of Bateson," reflects an amiable and loyal household: Bateson teaches his son, Jim, to recite "To be or not to be"; the boy, Henry, receives a new watch on his birthday; and Helen spoons soup into her drunken father.[27] After the death of W. O. Wolfe, Tom, grasping at the memory of his father, had resolved to fashion a great literary figure of the powerful stonecutter. In March, 1923, he wrote:

"Mama, in the name of God, guard Papa's letters to me with your life. . . . He is headed straight not for one of my plays, but for a series. He dramatized his emotions to a greater extent than anyone I have ever known—consider his expression of "merciful God"—his habit of talking to himself *at* or *against* an imaginary opponent. Save those letters. They are written in his exact conversational tone: I won't have to create imaginary language out of my own brain—I verily believe I can re-create a character that will knock the hearts out of people by its reality." [28]

In May of that year, during the excitement of the Harvard production of *Welcome to Our City* and the possibilities of a Broadway production, Wolfe spoke as if the story of his family were to be his next project. But only the childhood remembrances scattered among his 1924-25 notes indicate that he had not forgotten his fervent intentions. Not until the spring of 1926 was he ready to handle his material, having at last turned to the novel, the only form that could enclose the jumble of particulars that swirled in his brain. In the first, hastily drawn plan he began to formulate his ideas about the escape theme more clearly:

The Family—His connection with the family must not be broken completely at the beginning of the book; it must rather be shown as in a state of gradual severance throughout. *But,* the period of infancy and childhood, the myriad sensations, Even with monstrous exaggerations of their importance, the entire impact of a distrait, nervous, powerful family group upon a child, and the hideousness of the first wounds, for the cause or defense of which he had no knowledge or means of protection must be spoken of fully.

But he then lapsed into a series of hurriedly phrased reminiscences:

Speak of Walter Krause, the long-limbed German boy, with the large nose, and soft white hair on his face, the first grade—the miraculous writing. Pictures—the enormous budding intelligence of childhood—dare to speak of this:—how even an infant in the cradle gets majestic pictures of the brooding world: the capacity, even then, for unlimited thought, without the capacity for articulation. . . .[29]

In July, 1926, when Wolfe arrived in Europe to join Mrs. Bernstein for a six-week tour through France and England, he began an expanded outline of his novel in this same fashion, allowing his mind to rove freely, dredging up memories as if he were on the psychoanalyst's couch. He bought a paper tablet in Paris and began to fill its hundred leaves with a chronological series of remembered impressions, extending from his cradle days to 1923. Although a few pages are lost, the first extant page of this "Autobiographical Outline" begins early in the narrative:

Over the fence, near Britt's is a cow. I imitate its sound. "Moo" First articulate speech. Father delighted. Tells story over and over getting me to repeat the sound all afternoon for guests and neighbors. The smell, the sound, the day I remember accurately: it was Sunday. (The hot smell of dock weed in the rich rank South) Spring 1902—They kept me in a great wicker laundry basket—I remember climbing to the edge and seeing vast squares of carpet below me; the sitting room was shuttered— the drowsy intermittent crowing of hens outside—a sleepy forenoon. Beyond in the parlor Effie practising at the piano—Paderewski's Minuet— Later this Spring, I saw Effie go back to school. It was the recess hour— she was at Miss Ford's school in the brick house at the top of the hill—I was in the basket at the top of the steps—I watched her go up the hill—the Hazzards and the great house—at two o'clock each afternoon the negro drove up the drive for them.[30]

Having scribbled his tablet full, Wolfe went with Mrs. Bernstein to London; he purchased a second notebook to use while he moved from place to place in early July. The highlight of the London stay was, for Wolfe, a brief glimpse of his idol, James Joyce. Unfortunately, when Wolfe was introduced to his hero, he was very shy and Joyce was very tired from a day-long conversation with Mrs. Bernstein, so the meeting was only an exchange of polite remarks.[31] Still, the mere handshake was inspiring to the young man about to draw his own portrait of the artist.

At length Wolfe arrived at York, where Mrs. Bernstein had business to discuss with Sidney Smith, the grandson of the famous clerical wit of Edinburgh. When Smith learned that Wolfe was eager to begin writing a book, he recommended the little resort town of Ilkley as a quiet place to work. In Ilkley, then, on a hill outside the village, while Mrs. Bernstein sat making sketches of the landscape, Wolfe at last made a start in a huge, red accounting ledger that Mrs. Bernstein had bought him.

Twenty months of work later, in New York City, Wolfe declared he had reached the end, and in March, 1928, he packed his manuscript off to publishing houses with hopes of sale. This novel, which Wolfe entitled "O Lost," was finally accepted for publication by Charles Scribner's Sons in January, 1929, and published under the title, *Look Homeward, Angel* in October of that year. But before following Wolfe in the shaping of this novel, it is necessary to look at the final product, especially its structure and meaning.

NOTES

1. HCL*46AM-7(13), Scene III. This material is not in the published version.
2. The play apparently made little impression. Kenneth McGowan, who had

asked to see it, remembers that the play was sent, but he does not remember reading it.

3. *Letters*, p. 122.

4. J. M. Roberts, "Letter to the Editor," *Life*, LXI (October 8, 1956), 22. Roberts apparently saw some of the completed sections of "Passage to England," which his mother was editing, and some sketches about Wolfe's childhood.

5. *Letters*, p. 211. The bracketed statement is crossed out in the original.

6. *Letters*, pp. 210-11.

7. So Mrs. Bernstein reported in an interview with me, August, 1950.

8. *Letters*, p. 113.

9. Miss Nowell (p. 107), who places Wolfe's first establishment in this apartment in January, 1927, is a year off in dating. In some autobiographical notes, Wolfe states, "...I saw her several times before my twenty-fifth birthday (Oct. 3, 1925).... We began to see each other frequently—at first two and three times a week, later every day. I had been living at the little hotel in which my first year in the city had been spent, but during the winter I moved to the sweat shop garret in 8th Street which she was using as a studio." HCL*46AM-7(70-a).

10. *Letters*, p. 105.

11. PN 12, October, 1929, to January, 1930.

12. *Letters*, p. 10.

13. HCL*46AM-7(23), Box 2.

14. Walser, p. 37.

15. HCL*46A-289 (New York, 1927).

16. For an extended account of the spread of psychoanalytic theory in America, see Chapters II and III of Frederick J. Hoffman's *Freudianism and the Literary Mind* (Baton Rouge, 1945).

17. Interview, August, 1950.

18. English title, *Psychology of the Unconscious* (New York, 1916).

19. PN 10, March to June, 1929, *ca.* May 6.

20. Mrs. Mina Curtiss, letter to me, April 19, 1952.

21. LHA, p. 625.

22. HCL MS 326F, IX, 194-96.

23. HCL*46AM-7(21).

24. HCL*46AM-7(24-a).

25. *Ibid.* As an example of Wolfe's desire to make use of all the material he had planned, note the humorous twist he has allowed Eliza Gant to give the arrest of this good woman's triumphant march down the years in *The Web of Earth*:

> Why didn't I see the old woman myself, when we were up there that time, eat a whole chicken and three big hunks of pie—says to Augusta, you know, "Daughter, fill my plate again," she says, and she was in her seventies then—that's exactly how she got her death, sir. "To think of it!" I said when I heard the news—in her ninety-sixth year and fell out of her chair and broke her leg while reachin' for an ear of corn" (FDTM, p. 296).

This is a humorous exaggeration of the circumstances attending the death of Wolfe's paternal grandmother, Eleanor Jane (Hiekus) Wolfe.

26. HCL*46AM-7(8)3, History S9, Notebook 2.

27. HCL*46AM-7(19).

28. LTM, pp. 46-47.

29. HCL*46AM-7(24-a).

30. AO. Two notebooks full of smudged, penciled phrases remain among the Wolfe papers as a record of his working notes for LHA. This is the manuscript referred to as the Autobiographical Outline.

31. This is Mrs. Bernstein's account, interview with me, January, 1950.

9

THE DESIGN OF
LOOK HOMEWARD, ANGEL

Look Homeward, Angel IS THAT WORK WHICH WOLFE ASSURED
Professor Baker he would write "for [his] *souls* ease and comfort." [1]
Stepping far beyond his attempt to present the cross section of a town
in *Welcome to Our City,* he created an elaborate microcosm in which
to place his autobiographical hero, Eugene Gant. He assembled a
throng of characters, ranging from briefly glimpsed citizens, who are
sharply caricatured, to those figures closest to Eugene, who are as
fully alive as any literary creations can be, well-defined, yet containing a mixture of good and evil, strength and weakness, capacity
and limitation. By means of symbol and allusion, he enlarged his
scene beyond the family circle and town life to keep the history of
man before us. More than this, he circumscribed the whole spectacle
with a cosmic view that dominates the book.

Critics have commented extensively on Wolfe's characterizations
in *Look Homeward, Angel,* delivering their just appreciations of
the vigorous Gant, theatrical in his bluster; the patient, grasping
Eliza, her mind a sea of trivia; the impulsive, generous Helen; and
the brooding, nocturnal Ben. They have drawn conclusions about
the author's life from the character of Eugene and from his relations with his family. They have discussed the book as the first
movement in Wolfe's four-novel symphony of life.[2] But of the order
of his little universe in his first work, of the structure and unity of
Look Homeward, Angel, the only long novel that Wolfe brought
to completion himself, nothing has been said. And unless we recognize the three separate planes of statement that Wolfe has fused into
a unified narrative, we not only fail to appreciate the fullness and

the seriousness of his achievement but we even fall short of grasping the full meaning of his book.

The central narrative presents the story of the growth of Eugene Gant toward a freedom from forces deterring him from the best fulfillment of his nature and, more positively, toward a realization of what life means within the world scheme that Wolfe sets up. Wolfe has embedded this central narrative within a family chronicle in which Eugene plays his small part. From the very outset, Wolfe had this much of his plan in mind, as we see from the letter he sent Mrs. Roberts from Bath:

...its unity is simply this: I am telling the story of a powerful creative element trying to work its way toward an essential isolation; a creative solitude—a secret life—its fierce struggles to wall this part of its life away from birth—first against the public and savage glare of an unbalanced, nervous brawling family group; later against school, society, all the barbarous invasions of the world. In a way, the book marks a progression toward freedom; in a way toward bondage....Just subordinate and leading up to this main theme is as desperate and bitter a story of a contest between two people as you ever knew—a man and his wife—the one with an inbred, and also an instinctive, terror and hatred of property; the other with a growing mounting lust for ownership that finally is tinged with mania—a struggle that ends in decay, death, desolation.[3]

As he worked, his plans enlarged. He placed these two narrative elements within a double framework of ideas. The greater presents an all-inclusive view of the universe, and the lesser deals with individual man's place within this universe.

The larger and more general framework is Wolfe's biological interpretation of life—vitalism, emergent evolution, or creative evolution. As we have seen, this philosophy possibly grew from seeds planted by Professor Horace Williams in lectures at Chapel Hill, but it seems more likely to have taken shape from Bernard Shaw and H. G. Wells, especially from Wells's novel, *The Undying Fire*.[4] Wolfe incorporates this view of life in his book, but since he is a novelist, not a philosophical essayist, the creative evolutionary theory is implied rather than expounded in *Look Homeward, Angel*. The theory, based on a distinction between life and matter, may be summed up briefly in this way: Matter existed before organism, but when conditions permitted, life began (no attempt is made to explain how) and undertook its evolutionary climb, making use of matter for sustenance and for body. Organism, guided by Life Force, the essence of life, evolved from a microscopic blob, through an animal without a backbone, to man, and is still moving onward, though its destiny is unknown. Although life moves forward through what seems to be blind-chance struggle, its ruthless and apparently wasteful progress has a certainty of purpose that is beyond our comprehension. Since Life Force, living in matter and with the help of matter, adapts matter to its own ends, it represents a super-will in the universe. Man's role in the evolutionary progress is unspecified. Although man houses a larger share of the energy of life than lower forms of organism, this power is, in Wolfe's eyes, a magnificent but tragic gift.

In tracing the growth of Eugene, Wolfe treats the idea of the Life Urge within the body very much like the Jungian concept of libido, which goes beyond the sexual emphasis of Freud's use of the term to become a kind of life energy. In fact, psychoanalytic concepts color the book throughout. Wolfe probes the psychic recesses of Eugene, of W. O. and Eliza Gant. He employs sea and grotto imagery. Certainly he makes Eugene's Oedipal attachment to his mother an important feature of his narrative. It is clear that he developed a ready familiarity with depth psychology during the time he knew Aline Bernstein.

In *Look Homeward, Angel* Wolfe begins his presentation of the vitalistic world view on the title page. In the motto, "At one time the earth was probably a white-hot sphere like the sun," we have initial matter, the earliest stage of man's known universe before it was invested with life. Then as we begin Chapter I, we are immediately confronted with life and its progress, for the white-hot sphere has long since cooled, thus allowing the Life Principle to enter on the scene and to combine with matter.

But the purposive character of Wolfe's view of life is not explicitly stated at the outset; it is not revealed until the last chapter. In the beginning, Wolfe emphasizes the "waste and loss" that surround life's movement and change; and throughout the narrative, he repeatedly asserts the power that "the dark miracle of chance" exercises upon the course of the Life Urge.

The early statements about chance gradually mingle with reflections on Fate, especially in Eliza's murky observations of the tide of events surrounding her family. At the death of her son Grover, we see her grim acceptance of life's harshness: "...she had looked cleanly, without pretense for the first time, upon the inexorable tides of Necessity, and...she was sorry for all who had lived, were living, or would live, fanning with their prayers the useless altar flames, suppliant with their hopes to an unwitting spirit, casting the tiny rockets of their belief against remote eternity, and hoping for grace, guidance, and delivery upon the spinning and forgotten cinder of this earth." [5] In other places Wolfe introduces phrases reminiscent of Hardy that imply plan in terms of chaos: "blundering destiny," "aimless impulsion of accident," "on the hairline of million-minded impulse, destiny bore down on his life again," and so on.[6] Occasionally when he uses the word Chance, Wolfe might easily have substituted the word Fate—for example, in the child Eugene's earliest interpretation of life: "The fusion of the two strong egotisms, Eliza's inbrooding and Gant's expanding outward, made of him a fanatical zealot in the religion of Chance. Beyond all misuse, waste, pain, tragedy, death, confusion, unswerving necessity was on the rails, not a sparrow fell through the air but that its repercussion acted on his life...." [7]

In combining, and at times confusing, the ideas of Chance and Necessity, Wolfe presents all the appearances of a formidable determinism operating on men's lives. In granting Chance a part to play, he emphasizes man's limited understanding of any purpose that Life Force may be working out.

In the concluding scene of *Look Homeward, Angel,* Wolfe reveals his view of life in the meeting between Eugene and the returned ghost of his brother, Ben. Eugene, seeking an answer to the meaning of life, is raised to a God-like stature,[8] and he sees a vision of life in which only the Life Urge is eternal, striving to fulfill its unnamed purpose over the centuries as civilizations rise and fall:

...he saw the fabulous lost cities, buried in the drifted silt of the earth— Thebes, the seven-gated, and all the temples of the Daulian and Phocian lands, and all Oenotria to the Tyrrhene gulf. Sunk in the burial-urn of earth he saw the vanished cultures: the strange sourceless glory of the Incas, the fragments of lost epics on a broken shard of Gnossic pottery....

He saw the billion living of the earth, the thousand billion dead: seas were withered, deserts flooded, mountains drowned; and gods and demons came out of the South, and ruled above the little rocket-flare of centuries, and sank—came to their Northern Lights of death, the muttering death-flared dusk of the completed gods.

But amid the fumbling march of races to extinction, the giant rhythms of the earth remained. The seasons passed in their majestic processionals, the germinal Spring returned forever on the land,—new crops, new men, new harvests, and new gods.[9]

Wolfe combines other ideas with this basic conception of life. Although his eclecticism does not make for perfect coherence, the sweep of his ideas is impressive and it adds weight to his narrative. Since the concept of a developing universe invites contemplation of the problem of time, three of these ideas center on the time element that accompanies the evolutionary march of the Life Principle: the question of the inheritance from time past, the question of the present existence of past moments, and the question of fixity and change.

Wolfe feels that the individual is a representative of all his forebears and all the experience that has formed their lives: "we are the sum of all the moments of our lives" and "each moment is the fruit of forty thousand years."[10] One of the dilemmas of the boy Eugene is presented by the opposing traits he inherited from his parents. He finds in himself not only his father's desire to wander but his mother's affinity for home, not only the Gant liberality but the Pentland stinginess, not only the Gant realism but the Pentland superstition and mysticism. This conflict is developed more specifically in Wolfe's later books.

The idea that life is an accumulation of moments into one moment goes beyond the question of the inheritance of the past to put before us the question of the present existence of past moments. Eugene first senses the accumulation in his own life when he is twelve years old: "I am, he thought, a part of all that I have touched and that has touched me, which having for me no existence save that which I gave to it, became other than itself by being mixed with what I then was, and is now still otherwise, having fused with what I now am, which is itself a cumulation of what I have been becoming." [11] And throughout the book he yearns to recall a past moment or a forgotten face. In the concluding scene, he is allowed a vision of earlier stages of his own life, all simultaneously "printed in the air." He sees a selection of the moments that made up his life, his comings and goings through the town square. The scene was probably suggested by Bergson's "cinématographique" analogy of time and life: although the analytical intellect perceives separate moments as snapshots, they are actually part of the ever-moving stuff in the cinema of life.[12]

Eugene is also obsessed with the problem of fixity and change: "He did not understand change, he did not understand growth. He stared at his framed baby picture in the parlor, and turned away sick with fear and the effort to touch, retain, grasp himself for only a moment." Wolfe occasionally introduces the grasping of a present moment while time and all activity remain at a standstill. These time-stops, similar to the transcendental moments of the Romantic poets, go beyond the universe of Life Force with its ceaseless change. Wolfe describes the experience when the boy Eugene, passing through Georgia on a train, glances out of the window to see a woman leaning in a cabin door:

It was as if God had lifted his baton sharply above the endless orchestration of the seas, and the eternal movement had stopped, suspended in the timeless architecture of the absolute. Or like those motion pictures that describe the movements of a swimmer making a dive or a horse taking a hedge—movement is petrified suddenly in mid-air, the inexorable completion of an act is arrested. Then, completing its parabola, the suspended body plops down into the pool. Only, these images that burnt in him existed without beginning or ending, without the essential structure of time. Fixed in no-time, the slattern vanished, fixed without a moment of transition.

Here we do not have a moment treated as an accumulation of the past. This phenomenon is a "terrible moment of immobility stamped with eternity in which, passing life at great speed, the observer and the observed seem frozen in time." [13] These time-stops are glimpses into another world.

This brings us to the second framework of ideas that gives *Look Homeward, Angel* additional technical richness and further philosophic depth. In dealing with individual man's place in the universe of Necessity and Chance, Wolfe makes use of the Platonic myth of pre-existence. In the Platonic scheme as set forth in the *Phaedo, Meno, Timaeus,* and other dialogues, man's spirit leaves the real and unchanging world of immortality and enters a mortal body at the time of birth. During its temporary exile in the imperfect world of grief and change, man's spirit yearns to return to the divine world of reality. Wolfe had been familiar with the idea of prenatal life ever since he had translated Plato in his Greek classes at Chapel Hill. In addition, he had heard the doctrine in the classrooms of John Livingston Lowes at Harvard. The idea made its deepest impression upon him, however, in Wordsworth's great ode, "Intimations of Immortality from Recollections of Early Childhood," for *Look Homeward, Angel* abounds with echoes from this poem.[14]

Wolfe introduces the idea of pre-existence when Eugene is brought into the world in Chapter IV. The infant remembers the former life, but he gradually adjusts to the present life as growth and sensation drive out the memory of pre-existence. For Eugene's faint remembrance of the former life, Wolfe usually employs the symbol of undersea sound: "He had been sent from one mystery into another: Somewhere within or without his consciousness he heard a great bell ringing faintly, as if it sounded undersea, and as he listened, the ghost of memory walked through his mind, and for a moment he felt that he had almost recovered what he had lost." [15] Other symbolic sounds are musical, varying from a full orchestration to the notes of far-off horns.

To sum up, Wolfe views man as a creature not only with a body molded by Life Force, activated by Life Force, and bearing the seeds of Life Force but also with a spirit "trailing clouds of glory. . . from God who is our home." Man's physical life is subject to the determinism of Life Force, which threads its way through a world of chance, but his spirit represents a free will operating within these limitations, an individuality which can respond intellectually and emotionally, make choices, and strive to achieve an understanding of life's complexities. This dualism of the physical and spiritual, of the ideas of creative evolution and of pre-existence, sets up an ideological conflict within the book. One group of ideas acknowledges a world of accumulation and change; the other assumes the existence of a timeless, ideal world. The human dilemma between what is and what ought to be, between two kinds of reality, is what Eugene Gant must face. Wolfe introduces this painfully complex problem in the proem which precedes Chapter I, and he develops it throughout his pages.

Within this double framework of ideas, Wolfe presents his central narrative of the boy, Eugene, and his secondary narrative of the Gant family. Like Butler in his treatment of the Pontifex family in *The Way of All Flesh,* Wolfe begins his novel with the early generations of the family from which his hero springs. Since the body of Eugene Gant contains all his ancestral past, we get a brief glimpse of the first Gant who arrived in America, then a more detailed account of Eugene's parents, W. O. Gant and Eliza Pentland. Their fortunes and those of their children weave in and out of Eugene's story, but the family fades into the background as the boy grows up.

The course of the family narrative follows what Wolfe called "the cyclic curve of a family's life—genesis, union, decay, dissolution." [16] Gant and Eliza meet, marry, and have a large family. In the beginning there is strife between the parents because of Gant's periodic sprees, but for the children there is a good family life, roaring fires, groaning tables, and family love. When Eliza buys her boarding house, the family center is split between the two places. As Eliza's wealth grows, there is conflict between her desire for property and Gant's abhorrence of real estate investment. As the children grow older, dissension begins among them. Meanwhile, Gant slowly succumbs to cancer. The family disintegration is complete when the family house is sold and the children quarrel over their dying father's money. Eugene manages to escape from this atmosphere of contention as he prepares to leave for Harvard and the North.

The family relationship is further strained by the attachments and jealousies between the sexes. Wolfe scarcely needed to impose a Freudian interpretation upon his material; he had only to exaggerate the attractions already existing in his own family between daughter and father, son and mother. Helen, the youngest sister, is strongly drawn to W. O. Gant, and she ministers to him, replacing Eliza wherever she can. Since she keeps house and cooks for Gant after Eliza establishes the boarding house, the hostility between mother and daughter increases. More than this, Wolfe, remembering his own entanglement in apron strings, has with autobiographical honesty emphasized Eliza's possessiveness about Eugene, "the last coinage of her flesh." Eugene sleeps in his mother's bed until he is nine years old; he is frequently humiliated when she calls him "my baby" even in his later teens. Eliza's reluctance to relax her hold on the boy intensifies Eugene's struggle to break away from home, and the situation reaches its climax in a moving scene, Eugene's leave-taking, just before the close of the book.

Surrounding the Gant family stand the citizenry of Altamont. As the novel proceeds, Wolfe now and again steps into the streets to view the varied panorama of town life in order to enlarge his scene.

But since his satiric eye sees much of it as banal and brutal, his picture of Altamont has a necessary part in the work as something further that Eugene longs to escape.

Against this background of town and family and within his framework of old and new ideas, Wolfe tells the story of Eugene Gant, a story found in many autobiographical novels. We follow the central character through the usual sequence: childhood experiences, school, the world of books, early sexual curiosity, college life and its freedoms, and the arrival at an awareness that demands a search for the meaning of life. While it is true that Wolfe's urge to dramatize himself placed his principal interest in the central narrative, still his desire to present his view of life led him to interpret the autobiographical events in the light of his ideas whenever possible. As a result, we are always conscious of ideas sweeping across the background of the story, and we usually find them integrated with the action whenever some important incident in Eugene's life takes place. But this is a question of Wolfe's treatment, which needs further examination.

II

In the proem to *Look Homeward, Angel,* Wolfe announces in rhythmic prose a number of the emotional motifs of his work. He voices directly the problem of human isolation: that man is lost in this world, alone and unable to communicate with his neighbor or with his dearest loved ones. They are akin to him in flesh only.

Naked and alone we came into exile. In her dark womb we did not know our mother's face; from the prison of her flesh have we come into the unspeakable and incommunicable prison of this earth.

Which of us has known his brother? Which of us has looked into his father's heart? Which of us has not remained forever prison-pent? Which of us is not forever a stranger and alone? [17]

Introducing his principal symbols, he expresses the longing to return to the former life, to the reality which has been left behind at birth: "Remembering speechlessly we seek the great forgotten language, the lost lane-end into heaven, a stone, a leaf, an unfound door."

The unfound door is a complex symbol: it is the entrance to the former life; it is the escape into illusion, including the imaginative

realm of literature and art; it is the avenue to one's own past life
which exists only in memory; it is the way to life's ultimate secrets;
in short, it is the door to a world of spirit. A number of commentators
have seen the door symbol as the desire to retreat to the security of
the womb, but this interpretation is too limited. The symbol suggests the return to the womb only as a passage back to the world of
pre-existence. Wolfe preferred to merge what he knew of Freudian
concepts into larger schemes—in this case, Platonic theory.[18] The
stone, too, is an entrance symbol, the stone which hides a secret
passage: "I shall lift no stone upon the hills; I shall find no door in
any city." [19] Likewise, the leaf symbolizes the covering of the secret
pathway: "He groped for the doorless land of faery, that illimitable
haunted country that opened somewhere below a leaf or a stone." [20]

Whereas the proem emphasizes the ideal world of pre-existence,
the opening of Chapter I turns to the naturalistic world of change.
Wolfe begins his presentation of life by reflecting on the amazing
network of circumstance which lies behind time's unfolding:

> Each of us is all the sums he has not counted: subtract us into naked-
> ness and night again, and you shall see begin in Crete four thousand years
> ago the love that ended yesterday in Texas.
> The seed of our destruction will blossom in the desert, the alexin of our
> cure grows by a mountain rock, and our lives are haunted by a Georgia
> slattern, because a London cutpurse went unhung. Each moment is the
> fruit of forty thousand years. The minute-winning days, like flies, buzz
> home to death, and every moment is a window on all time.

All life having accumulated to one moment in time, the narrative
begins with the arrival of Gilbert Gant on American shores in 1837.
Wolfe passes swiftly through events as his one specimen family
flowers forth. The introductory chapters serve chiefly to set the family chronicle going; the wanderings of W. O. Gant before his meeting
with Eliza are most prominent.

In Chapter IV, the baby, Eugene, is brought into this new world in
which he gropes for understanding as the strange impressions impinge on his consciousness. Wolfe's use of the infant's point-of-view
here provides entertainment as comic exaggeration while it also
brings out the overwhelming importance of the child's problems.[21]
Eugene is particularly troubled by his ignorance of the language of
his new surroundings. He cannot express his knowledge, for the signs

and symbols of his former state are now a "lost language." Wolfe pictures the baby Eugene puzzling over some alphabet blocks, only dimly aware now of his former state: "Holding them clumsily in his tiny hands, he studied for hours the symbols of speech, knowing that he had here the stones of the temple of language, and striving desperately to find the key that would draw order and intelligence from this anarchy. Great voices soared far above him, vast shapes came and went, lifting him to dizzy heights, depositing him with exhaustless strength. The bell rang under the sea." [22]

With the birth of Eugene, Wolfe can introduce his theme of escape toward independence. The child lying in his crib stirs restlessly, waiting for "physical freedom" so that he can control his body and govern his surroundings through mobility. Then, too, as he strives for attainment of the new speech, he listens "intently day after day, realizing that his first escape must come through language." [23]

During Eugene's earliest years we follow the family narrative. We see Gant's disappointment in Steve, his eldest son, the summer in St. Louis, and the death of the son Grover. The clashes between Gant and Eliza punctuate this narrative until there is a brief moment of tenderness and understanding at the death of Grover. Shortly thereafter, the contest of wills begins again as Eliza's acquisitive hands reach for property. In spite of this mounting conflict, Wolfe's nostalgia colors this early portion of the book. An aura of the good life hangs over the household: holiday times bring the family together in the ritual of Thanksgiving and Christmas feasts; daily life is cheered by laughter, horseplay, and the material abundance of table.

Wolfe now adds depth of background with a survey of Altamont. Through the eyes of Gant, returned from California, we see the familiar landmarks as he rides the trolley car, and in his thought-stream we discover the associations they have with his past life and with townsmen he has known. The sequence ends with a suggestion of the good life he brings with him; he comes home and builds a roaring fire.[24]

When the narrative shifts back to the family, we find Eugene placed between two opposing characters, his brother, Luke, who "lived absolutely in event," [25] and his brother, Ben, the stranger who also sought "some entrance into life, some secret undiscovered door —a stone, a leaf—that might admit him into light and fellowship." [26] Ben emerges as Eugene's good genius in the next chapters, which set forth Eliza's principal business venture, the purchase of Dixieland. For in the neglect and degradation of boarding house life, Eugene loses home and security. With the comings and goings of boarders, he is moved from room to room, he is fed only when the bustle permits.

Part II of *Look Homeward, Angel* is the most satisfactory portion of the novel. Here Wolfe carefully intertwines the two narrative threads of family life and of Eugene's development and employs a good deal of technical dexterity to bring into the pattern the full range of his ideas. Here, too, he delves deeper to uncover the buried life of Eugene Gant. In fact, the opening chapters stand as a particularly pleasing illustration of Wolfe's ability to merge a number of elements into an exciting and fascinating literary complex.

Part II opens with a prose lyric of the passing seasons in which the plum tree symbolizes the eternal resurgence of Life Force:

The plum-tree, black and brittle, rocks stiffly in winter wind. Her million little twigs are frozen in spears of ice. But in the Spring, lithe and heavy, she will bend under her great load of fruit and blossoms. She will grow young again. Red plums will ripen, will be shaken desperately upon the tiny stems. They will fall bursted on the loamy warm wet earth; when the wind blows in the orchard the air will be filled with dropping plums; the night will be filled with the sound of their dropping, and a great tree of birds will sing, burgeoning, blossoming richly, filling the air also with warm-throated plum-dropping bird notes.[27]

As the plum tree burgeons, so spring advances, and this greater passage of time contrasts with the following series of lazily paced sketches which show us Altamont from 4 A.M. to 8 A.M. on an April morning. Wolfe has introduced them (frankly imitating the "Wandering Rocks" episode of Joyce's *Ulysses*) in order to show the variety of life flowing around Eugene. Here we see the waking town from its earliest risers, milkmen, market vendors, doctors returning from nighttime emergencies, and so on until all of Altamont has stirred into activity. The episode has more than a chronological organization. As we shift from scene to scene, we follow, through glimpses, two integral narrative threads. The first is the progress of the newspaper, from the time Ben goes to the pressroom until carrier "Number 3" has folded and thrown his last paper and snuggled into bed with May Corpening (an event which looks forward, by the way, to Eugene's temptations as a paper carrier). The second is the climb of Tom Cline's locomotive bringing train 36 up the grade to Altamont.

Now that the scene has been spread before us, Eugene wakes to this little round, and the narrative focus narrows down to the boy at the age of twelve. We see him puzzling over the problems of fixity and change, and we learn of his attempts to transcend the unreality of the life around him by grasping at moments in the past:

He heard the ghostly ticking of his life: his powerful clairvoyance, the wild Scotch gift of Eliza, burned inward back across the phantom years, plucking out of the ghostly shadows a million gleams of light—a little station by the rails at dawn, the road cleft through the pineland seen at twilight, a smoky cabin-light below the trestles, a boy who ran among the bounding calves, a wisp-haired slattern, with snuff-sticked mouth, framed in a door, floury negroes unloading sacks from freight-cars on a shed, a man who drove the Fair Grounds bus at St. Louis, a cool-lipped lake at dawn.

His life coiled back into the brown murk of the past like a twined filament of electric wire; he gave life, a pattern, and movement to these million sensations that Chance, the loss or gain of a moment, the turn of a head, the enormous and aimless impulsion of accident, had thrust into the blazing heat of him.[28]

We peer into his mind to see his awareness of life as a continual becoming and his naive belief in a predetermined destiny in which Chance is Fate's innocent instrument. We are led to his world of fantasy, his visions that beyond the circle of mountains lie romantic lands, King Solomon's Mines, the ranch house of the Triple Z, the casino at Monte Carlo, the Hanging Gardens of Babylon.

From these illusions, we jump suddenly back to the shabby reality of Eliza's boarding house and her real estate dealings, "Meanwhile business had been fairly good. . .," and we look over a tabulation of lots, prices, shares, investments. The contrast is repeated as we move from Eliza's money-changing to Eugene's fantasies about the luxurious lives of millionaires and then back once more to the boarding house, where Eliza has an insane millionaire and his keepers as tenants. As a final touch, this bedlamite fills Eugene's hands with dimes, adding the counsel, "Always be good to the birds, my boy," which carries us to the closing line of the paean to the passing seasons, "—And the air will be filled with warm-throated plum-dropping bird notes." [29] We have returned once more to the developing child, the orchard, and the spring darkness—the point at which the panorama of town and family life began. Thus within these chapters Wolfe has arranged an elaborate overture of themes and variations comprising the rhythms of earth, the common activities of Altamont, the family business dealings, the growth of Eugene, and the problems of Time, Memory, Chance, and Illusion.

The narrative spins out the next years of Eugene's life in this design: Eugene's rare opportunity to develop the life of the spirit at the Leonards' private school is contrasted with the barren and loveless atmosphere of life at Dixieland. In alternating episodes Margaret Leonard, Eugene's "spiritual mother," is set beside Eliza, the neglectful, money-grubbing mother of the flesh. While Margaret Leonard lavishes affection on Eugene, at home Eliza goads him with reminders of the cost of education and nags him into taking work as a paper carrier. The episode of Eliza's insistence that he wear Ben's castoff shoes, even though they are too small, contrasts with Margaret's anxious concern for Eugene's welfare: "How much sleep have you been getting?. . .See here, 'Gene, you simply can't afford to take chances with your health." [30] At the Altamont Fitting School, Margaret Lenoard opens the world of poetry to the boy. His spirit blossoms with the study of literature; he steps closer to the lost lane-end into heaven as she takes him into the order and reality of the world of art.

Midway along, Gant returns to dominate the scene once more as a prelude to his downfall. First there is an Indian Summer interlude between Gant and "Queen" Elizabeth, a brothel-keeper, who comes to buy a headstone for one of her girls. Beneath the comedy of her pious and sentimental mission lies the revelation of Gant's age and loss of power. As they walk to the porch of the shop absorbed in reminiscence about old times, Gant, looking out over the town, experiences a moment in which time stops and he glimpses the reality beyond life. All activity seems suddenly arrested; even the fountain in the square holds its jet suspended in mid-air. "And Gant felt himself alone move deathward in a world of seemings"; [31] he becomes aware of the downward rush of his life toward its end.

Among the many links between the family narrative and the story of Eugene, the parallels and contrasts between W. O. Gant and Eugene contribute most to narrative pattern. Each is the seeker, the artist, the lover of abundance, the grasper of life. Now, midway through the book, they move together, exuberant youth and advancing old age. A double stream-of-consciousness passage draws out their thoughts as they walk home after an evening at the moving pictures. Gant's musings on the past are placed alongside the elaborate fantasies of Eugene, whose life is before him. Later, after Wolfe reveals Gant's illness, a prostate gland disorder, he takes this character whom he has built up to heroic proportions and reduces him to a whining bundle of human weakness. Meanwhile, Eugene in adolescence is daily increasing in vitality. The Life Force seethes in his body. Exulting in mere existence, he leaps into the air with Bacchic cries. These "animal squeals" are the instincts of his evolutionary forebears whose life impetus he carries forward. While he is working as a paper boy in Niggertown, his mounting natural impulses drive him to seek sexual experience with Ella Corpening, one of his Negro subscribers. But he cannot carry out his bargain; he retreats in terror before her animal passion.

In describing Eugene's job as a paper carrier, Wolfe develops other themes as well. Since Eugene begins work in the darkness of "prenatal dawn," the atmosphere is appropriate for the theme of the former life, for Wolfe has already associated nighttime with the intimations of pre-birth existence ("Night. . . .Heard lapping water of inland seas").[32] Eugene's early waking is set forth as a daily repetition of the birth trauma:

His thin underdeveloped body drank sleep with insatiable thirst, but it was now necessary for him to get up at half-past three in the morning with darkness and silence making an unreal humming in his drugged ears.

Strange aerial music came fluting out of darkness, or over his slow-waking senses swept great waves of symphonic orchestration. Fiend-voices, beautiful and sleep-loud, called down through darkness and light, developing the thread of ancient memory.

Staggering blindly in the whitewashed glare, his eyes, sleep-corded, opened slowly as he was born anew, umbilically cut, from darkness.[33]

As the boy awakes or when he stands in the dark street, voices call to him of the stone, the leaf, the door, and the lost lane-end into heaven. And he cries: "I will remember. When I come to the place, I shall know."

After Wolfe's camera eye has made another satiric sweep through

Altamont, using well-known tags of verse for ironic commentary on the town,[34] we get another close look at Ben. When the Kaiser's army overruns Belgium, Ben, hoping to enlist in the Canadian army, finds he is physically unfit. As Ben questions the doctor, we get a preview of Eugene's questions in the final scene of the book. "Where do we come from? Where do we go to? What are we here for? What the hell is it all about?" Dr. Coker's reply is the answer of science, "I've seen them born, and I've seen them die. What happens before or after I can't say." His ironic assessment of life's values, of "what happens to them in between," implies that an impulse to live is all that he can see.[35]

Part III of *Look Homeward, Angel* includes some of the best of the book and some of the worst. But it differs notably from the earlier parts of the novel in its narrative preoccupation with the character of Eugene. Since Eugene at college is separated from his family much of the time, the reader, missing the fascinating Gant clan, grows tired of the extravagances of the teen-age hero. More than this, personal reminiscence clogs the narrative flow until the later chapters. Wolfe's manuscript shows that numerous chunks of extraneous matter had to be cut from Part III, but it is regrettable that Scribner's editor, Maxwell Perkins, could not persuade Wolfe to trim more of its bulk away.

Some of the episodes of Eugene's college days, however, bring Wolfe's major themes into play. Eugene's first drinking bout further identifies him with his father; "the terrible draught smote him with the speed and power of a man's fist. . . .And suddenly, he knew how completely he was his father's son. . . ." Wolfe also uses the experience as another step in search of the unfound door. The liquor is deceiving; it is "divine," it is "god in a bottle," it brings Eugene almost face to face with his demon: "there lay in him something that could not be seen and could not be touched, which was above and beyond him—an eye within an eye, a brain above a brain, the Stranger that dwelt in him and regarded him and was him and that he did not know." And yet, he finds no solution to the riddle of existence. Eugene's apostrophe to his demon, calling upon him to show his face, gets no reply; "There was nothing but the living silence of the house. No doors were opened." [36]

In the latter portion of Part III, the novel rises again to its earlier level of excellence as the narrative brings Eugene back into the family context with a telegram that Ben is on his deathbed. Because he has included so many pages of family strife, Wolfe is able to achieve a great solemnity and pity in the moment of family union as the Gants gather at Ben's bedside: "They grew quiet and calm. . . they drew together in a superb communion of love, valiance, beyond horror and confusion, beyond death." Standing by his brother's side, Eugene looks back on his own shabby upbringing at Dixieland and sees himself in Ben's place. Ben, the only Gant child besides Eugene who was aware of his demon and who sought in his lifetime the world of reality, the lost world of pre-existence, passes to that world when he reaches the last moment, which contains all that has gone before: "Filled with a terrible vision of all life in the one moment, he seemed to rise forward bodilessly from his pillows without support— a flame, a light, a glory—joined at length in death to the dark spirit who had brooded upon each footstep of his lonely adventure on earth. . . ." [37]

Wolfe has offered almost no answers to the metaphysical questions he has raised throughout the novel; he has maintained an attitude of awe and of stoic acceptance in face of the events Fate and Fortune bring. Now in the concluding chapters, he brings forth his answers about the immortality of both body and spirit. Stricken at the death of Ben, Eugene gropes helplessly for some assurance that Ben has not passed into nothingness. He prays hopelessly and repeatedly to a God in Whom he does not believe. At length, he visits the grave of Ben and there realizes that Ben's body will be immortalized in the continuity of the Life Flow; that Ben will return like the harvest god in spring, "the cruelest and fairest of seasons"; [38] that "in the flower and leaf the strange and buried men will come again." [39] He also finds solace in a Prime Mover, the original impetus of Life Force, who is "over us all." When spring comes, Eugene's belief in the physical immortality of the dead is vindicated. The Life Principle has metamorphosed Ben: "With victorious joy, Eugene thought of the flowers above Ben's grave." [40]

In Eugene's final year at college, he becomes more self-conscious. Absorbed with himself and with questions raised by the death of Ben, he seeks an interpretation of life that will help him make his way. An itch, or in Wolfe's Elizabethan euphemism "a patch of tetter," breaks out on Eugene's neck. It is the Pentland "taint," a skin disease borne by all members of his mother's family upon some part of their bodies. Eugene begins to feel, because of the death of Ben and the appearance of the taint, that death and decay must be a part of the life scheme. Although he has already reconciled the death of Ben's body with the return of the flowers, he now looks upon mere health as a characteristic of a lower order of life. He believes that the intellect has been evolved at the expense of health and that Life Force, which has produced health "in the steady stare of the cats and dogs," [41] has reached a higher point in man, whose brain and sensibility tax his body.

After Eugene's graduation from college, Wolfe gathers his narrative threads together. Already he has brought Eugene to the decision to leave home. The dissolution of family solidarity parallels the mounting impulse of Eugene's flight. Gant has become a feeble invalid, and Eliza's real estate obsession has led her to sell both the family house and Gant's shop. Since Ben's death, the children have bickered among themselves, and after Gant has made his will, their suspicion and conflict break all family unity. Eugene, in a desperate attempt to get economic and physical freedom, pleads with his mother to let him go to Harvard with the money due him at his father's death. She promises to send him for a year. The envious brothers and sisters tempt him to sign a form acknowledging the receipt of a college education in lieu of a share in his father's estate. As he grimly signs his name, Eugene feels the break with the family is complete.

In the final chapter, the fantastic meeting with Ben's ghost in the town square, Wolfe's troubled style clouds what he is trying to say.[42] Some of his statements are humorless imitations of Stephen Dedalus' meditations by the sea: "Inevitable catharsis by the threads of chaos. Unswerving punctuality of chance. Apexical summation, from the billion deaths of possibility, of things done." Others are pretentious word-jugglings, signifying very little: "Who are, who never were, Ben, the seeming of my brain, as I of yours, my ghost, my stranger, who died, who never lived, as I?" [43] Nevertheless, Wolfe tumbles all his ideas together and in this scene provides Eugene with answers.

Through his vision and through questions put to the oracle, Ben, Eugene is able to form an interpretation of life, and he is able to find a way of life for himself. Visiting his father's shop in the deserted, moonlit Square, he finds Ben, as scowling and as contemptuously kind as ever, leaning against the porch rail. Eugene has stepped into a world in which his father's stone angels move about and in which Ben is not dead. Here by the fountain, by the City Hall, by the Greek's lunchroom, within earshot of the bank's chimes, an American ghost walks and brings the power of vision and the power to transcend time. Looking over the Square, Eugene sees the countless moments of the past come alive; he sees himself as a paper boy stride through the "pre-natal" dawn. All the moments of his life are not gone but are accumulated in the present. Thus, at Ben's blunt assertion, "*You* are your world," Eugene realizes that he should no longer seek "through the million streets of life" to find himself but that he must look within: "'I shall save one land unvisited,' said Eugene, *Et ego in Arcadia.*" At last, Eugene has come to terms with the world of change. He can accept life because he is a part of it and it is a part of him. And through self-scrutiny, he can discover the secrets of his nature and can reach whatever sight of reality is possible: ". . .in the city of myself, upon the continent of my soul, I shall find the forgotten language, the lost world, a door were I may enter, and music strange as any ever sounded." [44]

More than this, Wolfe suggests metaphorically that death, as the other gateway to return, is part of the fulfillment of the spirit, that death is not an end but a continuing: "With his feet upon the cliff of darkness, he looked and saw the lights of no cities. It was, he thought, the strong, good medicine of death." Using the imagery of death and darkness and the symbols of the sea and music, Wolfe describes both the "terrible voyage" back through memory and the death voyage: "He stood naked and alone in darkness, far from the lost world of the streets and faces; he stood upon the ramparts of his soul, before the lost land of himself; heard inland murmurs of lost seas, the far interior music of the horns. The last voyage, the longest, the best." [45]

Eugene's vision has swept back to the earliest civilizations, he has seen the timeless presence of the Life Urge—"amid the fumbling march of races to extinction, the giant rhythms of the earth remained." Yet beyond the fateful progress of the Life Principle, beyond the "unswerving punctuality of Chance," he has had intimations of an immortal destiny of spirit that will continue its passage. However, Wolfe makes no conjecture beyond life. He is no Dante, he is no Plato; there is no unfolding of a paradise or a union with the absolute. The reappearance of Ben is as much mythology as he will attempt. When Eugene asks what will come after his life of seeking, the vision ends, and Ben without reply fades away.

When we last glimpse Eugene, at daybreak, he is strengthened in knowledge and belief, looking into the future. But Wolfe's final statement does more than close the narrative with Eugene's act of turning from Altamont and his family to gaze toward new lands of the North; it implies the continuity of the Life Force and the immortality of Eugene's own personality. Thus Wolfe's structure is complete: "Yet, as he stood for the last time by the angels of his father's porch, it seemed as if the Square already were far and lost; or, I should say, he was like a man who stands upon a hill above the town he has left, yet does not say 'The town is near,' but turns his eyes upon the distant soaring ranges." [46] The novel, like the poem from which it took its name, ends on a note of restored vigor after long brooding; the mood is Milton's "Tomorrow to fresh woods, and pastures new."

The very abundance which Wolfe manages to pack into *Look Homeward, Angel* has troubled critics in their assessment of the work. They are ready to see it as the animal a thousand miles long that Aristotle pictured when he warned about proper magnitude. But if they do, they forget the very nature of the novel as the literary form that embraces life so generously: very few novels that have the pulse of life, the jostle of human activity, stay within the restrictions of form. Wolfe's work has this combination of virtue and fault largely because of his autobiographical impulse. In order to be able to create the vigorous life that surges through his novel, he seems to have been compelled to include some events merely because they were part of his experience and not because they had a place in his total scheme. Fortunately, many of these passages were removed from the first version of the novel at the demand of his friend and editor, Maxwell Perkins. Even so, *Look Homeward, Angel* transcends its imperfections because of the general structural unity and because of the intensity, vitality, and grandiose scope with which Wolfe rendered "the vision of life which burned inside of him." [47] Interweaving his themes and ideas with his central narrative, he has transformed an ordinary *Bildungsroman* into a fragment of human history.

NOTES

1. *Letters,* p. 41.

2. With the exception of reviewers, most critics have lumped all of Wolfe's work together, using LHA as a starting point for discussions of his coming to terms with life or of his developing concept of America. Typical are Edwin Berry Burgum, "Thomas Wolfe's Discovery of America," *Virginia Quarterly Review,* XX (Summer, 1946), 421-37; Alfred Kazin, *On Native Grounds* (New York, 1942), pp. 465-84; Maxwell Geismar, *Writers in Crisis* (New York, 1942), pp. 185-236; and Leo Gurko, *The Angry Decade* (New York, 1947), pp. 28-33, 148-70. John Peale Bishop, in "The Sorrows of Thomas Wolfe," *The Collected Essays of John Peale Bishop* (New York, 1948), pp. 129-37, uses the first two novels as the basis of his argument that Wolfe failed because his work had no structure, therefore no meaning. Joseph Warren Beach, in *American Fiction 1920-1940* (New York, 1948), pp. 173-93, comments on the presence of three themes, the search for a father, the search for a door, and the search for the word, as he finds them in the first three novels. Herbert J. Muller, in the best piece of criticism on Wolfe in print, *Thomas Wolfe* (Norfolk, Conn., 1947), discusses LHA along with OT&R as he points out the features of Wolfe's early work. Monroe M. Stearns, when he focuses on this novel in the last part of "The Metaphysics of Thomas Wolfe," *College English,* VI (February, 1945), 193-99, approaches a proper interpretation of Wolfe's ideas, but he does not relate them to the structure or to the narrative. However, the fullest handling of Wolfe's ideas is Karin Pfister's rather uneven *Zeit und Wirklichkeit bei Thomas Wolfe* (Heidelberg, 1954), in which Wolfe's books are not treated as artistic works but as repositories of philosophic reflections. Louis Rubin in his study, *Thomas Wolfe: The Weather of His Youth* (Baton Rouge, 1955), is the only commentator who does not ignore the fact that Wolfe conceived of his first novel and executed it as a unit; however, he is more concerned with Wolfe's creative process than with the literary values of the book. Brief references in F. David Martin, "The Artist, Autobiography, and Thomas Wolfe," *Bucknell Review,* V (March, 1955), 15-28, and in C. Hugh Holman, *Thomas Wolfe* (Minneapolis, 1960), indicate that critics are now beginning to recognize the integrity of LHA. As for Wolfe's art in general, the prevailing opinion has been that his work has no "clear intention or design," as Muller says, or that, as Beach puts it, the form was not apparent until the last novel, YCGHA, brought his cycle to a close.

3. *Letters,* pp. 111-12.

4. The influence of Bergson is also possible. See n. 12.

5. LHA, pp. 59-60.

6. LHA, pp. 59, 192, 212.

7. LHA, pp. 192-93.

8. In the manuscript, before this scene was altered for publication, the passage began: "He seemed to become an enormous lidless Eye, a vast Stare fixed in the brain of heaven above the weary parchment of earth" (HCL, MS 326F, I, 488). In both his published and unpublished writings, Wolfe often referred to the idea of God as a "lidless Stare"; see, for example, LHA, p. 289.

9. LHA, p. 623. The manuscript version includes a vision of life from its primitive evolutionary forms up through fish, reptiles, beasts, and early man.

10. LHA, pp. 1, 3.

11. LHA, p. 192.

12. The time concept in LHA almost certainly has its source in the philosophy of Bergson, although Wolfe made no mention of Bergson in his letters or notebooks until a couple of months after he completed the book. However, he did have an interest in Bergson at about this time. In his library there is a copy of a group of selections from Bergson, *Henri Bergson, choix de texte avec étude du système philosophique,* ed. René Gellouin (Paris, n.d.) and a copy of Bergson's essay *Dreams,* trans. Edwin E. Slosson (New York, 1914), although it is not known when he bought them or whether he ever read them. Also, his pocket notebook records during the summer of 1928 several reminders to get books by or about Julien Benda, the great opponent of Bergson. When he finally bought Constant Bourquin's *Julien Benda, ou le point de vue de Sirius,* he showed his approval of Bergson by a cryptic remark in a letter to Aline Bernstein, July 25, 1928.

Wolfe should not be called a Bergsonian. He only made use of a few of Bergson's ideas in his work, and the ideas may not have come directly from Bergson's writings but from an article or the conversation of a friend. For a comparison of Wolfe's ideas on time with those of Proust, who did follow Bergson closely, see Margaret Church's "Thomas Wolfe: Dark Time," *PMLA,* LXIV (September, 1949), 629-38. Karin Pfister, in *Zeit und Wirklichkeit bei Thomas Wolfe,* discusses Wolfe, Bergson, and Proust at more length, although his commentary is less a critical treatment of the relationships of ideas than a demonstration that quotations from Wolfe on time, memory, perception, and identity show general similarity to points of Bergson's theory.

13. LHA, pp. 191-92.

14. The influence of Wordsworth's "Immortality Ode" on Wolfe's idea of pre-existence was studied first by Monroe M. Stearns in "The Metaphysics of Thomas Wolfe." Louis Rubin in *Thomas Wolfe: The Weather of His Youth,* Chapter III, offers a full discussion of Wolfe and Wordsworth.

One evidence that Wolfe consciously drew inspiration from Wordsworth's ode is the fact that among the quotations he jotted down to consider for his title page and his dedication page are the lines,

> The rainbow comes and goes
> And lovely is the rose,

in PN 11, June 11 to October 15, 1929. For some of the echoes from Wordsworth, see nn. 17, 32, and 45.

15. LHA, p. 38.

16. *Letters,* p. 129.

17. In this dark picture, we see the influence of Wordsworth's ode again with its idea of earthly life as a prison term for "Inmate Man":

> Shades of the prison house begin to close
> Upon the growing Boy.

In his proem and in other places in the novel, Wolfe plays with the word "prison" to signify three states: the imprisonment in the womb, the imprisonment in life, and the solitary confinement within the self. As a gloss upon the first two uses of the figure and upon the whole notion of pre-existence and afterlife, I point out that one other motto which he considered for his title page was a quotation from Donne's Sermon XV, First Friday in Lent (*LXXX Sermons,* 1640):

> Doth not man die even in his birth? The breaking of prison is
> death and what is our birth but the breaking of prison?

PN 11, June 11 to October 15, 1929.

18. Lionel Trilling, commenting on Wordsworth's great ode, reads the whole idea of heavenly pre-existence as the desire to return to "physical prenatality," for "the

womb is the environment which is perfectly adapted to its inmate and compared to it all other conditions of life may well seem like 'exile' to the (very literal) 'outcast'" (*The Liberal Imagination* [New York, 1950], p. 147). But whatever Wolfe's impulse may have been or however it may be interpreted biographically, his intention in the novel was to include a suggestion of an immortal state in terms of the Platonic myth.

19. LHA, p. 625.

20. LHA, p. 277.

21. For comment on Wolfe's comic materials in this book, see B. R. McElderry, Jr., "The Durable Humor of *Look Homeward, Angel*," *Arizona Quarterly*, XI (Summer, 1955), 123-28, and Paschal Reeves, "The Humor of Thomas Wolfe," *Southern Folklore Quarterly*, XXIV (June, 1960), 109-20.

22. LHA, p. 39.

23. LHA, p. 37.

24. Originally this episode was placed near the beginning of Part II. Maxwell Perkins suggested that Wolfe move the scene forward to give variety to the narrative of Eugene's early years. See his article, "Thomas Wolfe," *Harvard Library Bulletin*, I (Autumn, 1947), 272. However, he is not accurate when he says that the passage had been followed by Eugene's jaunt through town with his school-fellows.

25. LHA, p. 115.

26. LHA, p. 113.

27. LHA, p. 165.

28. LHA, pp. 191-92.

29. LHA, p. 200.

30. LHA, p. 231.

31. LHA, p. 269.

32. LHA, p. 200. Note the variation on Wordsworth's beautiful metaphor in the "Immortality Ode":

> Hence in a season of calm weather
> > Though inland far we be,
> Our Souls have sight of that immortal sea
> > Which brought us hither,
> Can in a moment travel thither,
> And see the Children sport upon the shore,
> And hear the mighty waters rolling evermore.

33. LHA, p. 295.

34. That Wolfe clearly intended that this episode should enlarge the scope of his scene is established by his letter to John Hall Wheelock at Scribner's, July 22, 1929: "I do hope people will not look on this section as a mere stunt—I really don't know what to do about cutting it—it is not a stunt, a great deal of the town is presented in short order" (*Letters*, p. 188).

35. LHA, pp. 353-54.

36. LHA, pp. 493-94.

37. LHA, p. 557.

38. Wolfe's echo of Eliot here, taken from "The Burial of the Dead" section of *The Waste Land*, is certainly intentional. Ben is the planted corpse that will sprout and bloom.

39. LHA, p. 582.

40. LHA, p. 584.

41. LHA, p. 587. Note also that the metaphors characterizing Eliza have associated

her with a lower order of nature—all feeling and no brain. And Eliza is in perfect health.

42. I do not know if Wolfe ever read *The Mysterious Stranger*, but some of his statements in this final chapter are remarkably similar to the last colloquoy between Satan and Theodor Fischer in Mark Twain's book. If Wolfe had *The Mysterious Stranger* in mind as he began to write his conclusion, it is quite possible that Mark Twain's pessimism so clashed with his own dearly wrung optimism that we could find here another source of the puzzling quality of this last chapter.

43. LHA, p. 624.

44. LHA, p. 625.

45. LHA, p. 625. "Inland murmurs" is a phrase of Wordsworth's in "Tintern Abbey":

> Five years have past; five summers, with the length
> Of five long winters! and again I hear
> These waters, rolling from their mountain-springs
> With a soft inland murmur.

This is a fascinating example of the merging of Wordsworth's poems in Wolfe's mind, for the phrase "inland murmurs" seems to summon up for him all the associations of the passage cited in n. 32, with its "waters rolling evermore."

46. LHA, p. 627.

47. Wolfe's description of the book in a letter to Mrs. J. M. Roberts, February 2, 1930, published in *Atlantic Monthly*, CLXXIX (February, 1947), 56.

10

FIRST VERSION: "O LOST"

But in Europe in 1926 Wolfe was months of labor and anguish from that final manuscript. After Mrs. Bernstein returned to the United States in August, he went down to London, where he took a two-room flat in Chelsea at 32 Wellington Square. He reported his progress to Henry Carlton, who had struggled unsuccessfully with Wolfe over cutting *Welcome to Our City:* "I have finished a very full and complete outline of my book—the outline itself the length almost of a novel [1] —and at present I am writing about 3000 words a day which I hope to increase to 4000. The novel will be Dickensian or Meredithian in length, but the work of cutting—which means of course adding an additional 50000 words—must come later." [2]

But this outline he boasted of was only a crude series of notes. Wolfe's plan for his novel was still unformed. His principal ideas developed as he wrote the work, and his symbols were not chosen until he was halfway through Part II. Even his attitudes changed as he went along. He began in bitterness against his family, but he ended up celebrating them. He started out to say, O Lost! but he ended with a sense of self-discovery.

Even the chronology was uncertain. At first he planned to divide the book into five sections: Eugene's ancestors and the early history of Gant and Eliza; the birth and childhood of Eugene; Eugene's secondary school years; Eugene at Chapel Hill and later at Harvard; Eugene in New York and in Europe. He wanted to extend the action to the year 1925, for in his pocket notebook he had sketched an outline which followed his own life from 1923 to spring, 1925:

The Last Book
—New York—the Play
—The Month at Home
—Arrest and Capture
—New York again
—Cambridge—The Widow—The Decision
—The Year in New York
—Voyage—The Boat—London—England—France—
    Paris—The Stolen Play—The Passionate Friends—
    The Widow—The World of Women—The Countess—
    The South and Madness—the Two Women.[3]

This outline is followed by the query: "Should the book end abroad or at home?" Later he felt he must limit the book. On one page of the Autobiographical Outline where he had listed "Preface. Childhood. School. College. The World. The Voyage," he indicated his decision by drawing a line between "College" and "The World." But he still planned to include Eugene's years at Harvard, for he cautioned himself in his pocket notebook: "Death of Gant better at end of third book otherwise anti-climax." [4]

The manuscript of "O Lost" is in seventeen tall accounting ledgers of varying thickness, their pages filled with Wolfe's large, penciled scrawl. His working methods seem to have been simple. At first, with the Autobiographical Outline at hand he wrote drafts of episodes on ledger pages he later tore out to set in sequence. Finally he made a fair copy, with revisions, in the ledgers that now contain the whole novel.[5] Later, when he had gathered momentum, he dispensed with first drafts altogether and wrote his final copy as fast as the words came to him. Sometimes he recorded his working time in the margins of his ledgers. The interlude of Gant and "Queen" Elizabeth, for example, seven pages of printed text, was probably done from a few preliminary notes; Wolfe wrote it in four sittings totaling about five and a half hours.[6]

When he began, Wolfe put off writing the introductory portion about Eugene's ancestors and started to work on his childhood. As he searched to uncover "the whole structure and frame of things that had produced me," [7] the book began to write itself. He was an imaginative archaeologist conducting a spiritual "excavation." What he found he did not record as fact. He tried to reach beyond fact to achieve a poetic reality. He could not say what he was doing.

Years later, in attempting to describe what he was after, he called it legend. He theorized this way:

...a legend, considered in one light, is only a condensed and heightened form of reality. With every great legendary book, for instance with the *Odyssey*, with *Don Quixote*, in our own times, in particular with the *Ulysses* of James Joyce, the legend is not a fanciful interpretation of human life but really an intense illumination of that life. . . .It is apparent that the legend attains a superior reality through the clarity and intensity of its vision. . . .I have passed by a certain door a thousand times and always seen that door, yet never saw it as it was. And then one day, when I was far away, years after I'd passed that door, I would suddenly remember it. And instantly I would see that door the way it was. Now, what has happened? Did I see that door as it had looked just once in all those thousand times that I had passed it? No, I think that finally I saw that door as it had looked a thousand times and under a thousand lights and weathers of man's life and spirit. And finally, long afterwards, I saw it, the essential door, the way it was. The final door, therefore, was the legendary door, and yet it was at last the right one.[8]

As Wolfe sat in his rooms in Chelsea, images like that rose up before him—his father's mustache, his mother's brisk nod, the blazing family hearth, the dreary cells in the Old Kentucky Home—and voices floated to his ears—a roaring complaint, a stoical reply, whoops of laughter. His descent into the greater depths of memory was emotionally so draining that he could not stay there constantly but turned from time to time to work on Eugene's years at Harvard too. In spite of this divided approach, he could report by September 22 that "it grows in clarity and structure every day." [9]

After six weeks of living by himself with the specters of memory, he began to suffer from loneliness. As a beery scrawl in his notebook records, he kept on this daily schedule: "I stay in my pajamas till one o'clock, writing, then I dress and go to the Express [.] Four [*sic*] three or four hours I am heavy with lunch and beer, buying books on the Charing Cross Road or walking [.] At five or six I return and work to 8 or 9 [.] Then I eat [.] I return at 11 or 12 and right [*sic*] to 1. The night hours from 7-9, until I have fortified myself with beer, are frightful." [10]

To keep these evening hours from being oppressive, he tried a change of atmosphere and took a trip to Brussels, Antwerp, and Bruges. For the first time, he began to carry pocket notebooks to record sights, thoughts, story ideas, and memoranda of various sorts. During this time he sketched out the characterization of "Uncle Emerson" and his family (which he later developed into the short novel, *A Portrait of Bascom Hawke*); he turned out a characterization of "Sedwick" (who later became Frances Starwick in *Of Time and the River*); he completed most of the episode of Eugene's callous behavior to the Melrose girl and her family. But he devoted by far the most attention to Eugene's feelings about the city, about Harvard, about the library, and to Eugene's fantasies while he was alone in Boston.

Shortly he began to put what he had written into final copy in the "O Lost" ledgers,[11] and by the time he went to Oxford in October he had reached the description of life at Dixieland. He felt he had worked himself into mental exhaustion ("My mind has gone to pieces these last three days. It is scattered and cannot follow either reading or writing"),[12] and when he found he was spending too many nights at the local pub, he decided to travel again. After he crossed to Paris, he was in better spirits and began to make some trial drafts for the introductory part of the book. He set down notes for an imaginary characterization of one of the early Westalls, establishing some of the hereditary gifts that would be passed on to Eugene. Eliza's power of instinct was to be foreshadowed in a portrait of his great-great-grandfather: "The first Westall who came to America in 1796 from England was a Cambridge man:—he had been a year in Italy, he dabbled in paints and did bad pictures after Romney—there are some still of Americans in Baltimore. The soul of this young man was blind—he saw nothing but he felt everything; he was something undersea, groping without eyes, but with a thousand feelers [.] He saw nothing, and he felt everything. He was one of the most complete romantics that ever lived." The Pentland skin disease was to crop up early: "He had a scorbutic hand; on the back of his left hand there was a scaled corruption at which he tore constantly with his stubby fingers; it did not come at all upon my great-grandfather, but my grandfather had it in his thigh, my mother has it on the back of her left hand, my uncle on the back of his right, at which he tears continually with a queer itching smile of delight on his face, finally paring his nails with a blunt knife, and scraping the blade across the flaky scales: I have it on the nape of my neck."[13] Although he began to write about Charles Westall in one of the large ledgers,[14] he abandoned the attempt after a few pages. Nor did Wolfe return to the early Westall ancestors again for his beginning; he turned at length to his father's side of the family.

From Paris, he went to Strasbourg, Stuttgart, and then Munich. His preoccupation with his task had intensified his usual suspiciousness, for he gloated, paranoically, over the addition of a new country to his list as he crossed the Rhine: "Aha, you bastards," he muttered as he recorded it in his notebook, "you can't take this from me." His first glimpse of Germany pleased him immensely, especially the communal spirit of the Hofbrauhaus—"the magnificent beer—the place sloppy and powerful with beer and smoke and the great cheerful dynamic vitality of their 1200 voices." [15] While in Munich he put material together for Book II. He worked first on Gant's return from California, which at this time was part of the opening chapter of Book II. During the week he set down a note that shows he was preparing to write about Eugene's puzzle over time's fleeting and separate moments: "The movement of the men in the street—this moment caught and gone forever." [16] Fascinated by this familiar sight in a strange city, he took a mental snapshot of it.

Perplexed about the future, Wolfe began to prepare for his return to America. He had not finished his novel as he had hoped, and he was unsure what his relationship with Mrs. Bernstein would or should be. His one determination was to get the book done, and on the voyage home he continued work, writing the opening of Book II, the lyric of the plum tree.

As soon as his ship had left Cherbourg, he felt a lift. Reading his penciled notation, "America I come—you are a strong drink," one can almost see him on the prow beating his breast. When he arrived on December 29, the New York air stimulated him "like cold wine," but New York had all the unreality of a dream after the months of Europe and the absorption with his own past. During the week he came back to reality. But meanwhile he had quarreled publicly at a New Year's Eve Ball, and for several days he had behaved strangely amid the crowded New York streets. "Why do I become angry when people stare at me?" he asked himself. "Fear—Fear—like a cold oil around my heart—of what I do not know—Always carry in your heart the war on fear, fear, fear." [17] Even so, he was exultant about his accomplishments of the previous five months, and he read aloud portions of what he had written to Henry Carlton and his family during a three-day period at Croton-on-the-Hudson.

It is difficult not to be amused at Wolfe's eccentricities during a period of creative intensity. But his brain was spinning with the ideas that cram the first chapters of Part II of *Look Homeward, Angel*. The complex pattern and the linguistic opulence in these chapters come out of a new determination that he expressed a few days after his return to America: "I am weary of the old forms— the old language—It has come to me quite simply these last three days that we must mine deeper—find language again in its primitive sinews—like the young man, Conrad—Joyce gets it at times in Ulysses —It is quite simple but terrific—Build the book brick by brick." [18]

He moved back into the old studio on Eighth Street once more, feeling irresolute about the choices ahead of him. He did not have to return to teaching immediately, for Mrs. Bernstein agreed to support him during the spring, while he finished his novel. He was to spend the next seven months in the Eighth Street apartment writing, going out only to eat or to wander the streets at night, going occasionally to the Harvard Club for dinner, a shower, and a couple of hours of letter writing. He seldom saw anyone except Mrs. Bernstein; for the most part he lost touch with his colleagues at New York University or his friends from the South and from Harvard. It was a grim period, during which he lived in a recreated world of the past.

During January, 1927, he finished the first chapter of Part II, the awakening of Altamont, the characterization of the townspeople, and the scene in the lunchroom. The sequence, double the length of the printed version, included a great variety of scene, with frequent changes of tone wrought by parody of one style and then another. The most amusing bit was a parody of Eliot's "Sweeney Among the Nightingales." Wolfe had enjoyed Eliot's Sweeney poems, especially the use of the mock-heroic and the method of ironical juxtaposition. But in the parody his appreciation is mixed with satire upon Eliot's style in general. Unfortunately this piece was later omitted when Maxwell Perkins hewed a big chunk out of Book II of the novel. In the published version of the novel, the reader is shown a panorama of the town of Altamont at dawn. One passage describes Moses Andrews, who has lain drunk all night behind a board fence. His pockets, which had been full of money given him by Saul Stein, the pawn-broker, for some stolen clothes and jewelry, are now empty.

His throat has been cut from ear to ear by Jefferson Flack, his rival for the affections of Molly Fiske.[19] Wolfe's original version added the following description of the murder.

No one knew, no one even suspected, and no one ever got the whole truth out of it except a modern poet and critic who, many years later, celebrated the event in these memorable verses:

MOSE EXTINCT

Defunctive music in the dim
Drugged thickets of the convolutions,
A flying gleam leaps to the rim,
Mose stirs, and thinks of quick ablutions.

Too late: the slack jaw opens wide,
The sloping thighs resist and quiver,
The hasp slides through, the walls divide
Red chasms to a crimson river.

The lids rip open at the seams,
The fat brain dreams, but reads it error,
Buttered on steel the moonlight gleams,
The balls are strung on steel and terror.

Cloud-charioted up the silver beach
The Thracian huntress rolls the disk.
Jeff, keeping loot and loan in reach,
Shelves round the haunch of Molly Fiske.

All day the hungry housecats whine,
The flies grow drunk with blood and loathing,
Day bleeds to death, and Mr. Stein
Puts tickets on the underclothing.[20]

At the end of January Wolfe was working out his description of Eugene's transcendental moment, "the terrible moment of immobility, stamped with eternity," for he jotted this entry into his notebook: "Unreality of things seen in motion—from a train (the striving and dividing sea is very deep)." [21] He was trying to express something about memory and something about time and motion. In order to articulate his ideas, he gathered memories from various blocks of his life—thoughts about the strangeness of circumstance, impressions of train journeys, sights of the movement in crowded streets. In the beginning he had only a note or two scribbled in his ledger: "His enormous grip on detail—station at dawn, things seen

from train window, a road untaken, a woman in a doorway." [22] In
the end he had fused all of his half-grasped feelings into a concrete
expression of a mystical experience, Eugene's glimpse of the "wisp-
haired slattern" "fixed in no-time."

By February he had gone on to Eugene's years at Leonard's school
and Gant's conversation with "Queen" Elizabeth. He enjoyed writing
the verse for the tombstone of the Queen's lady-in-waiting, for he
had the same knack for verse parody that he had for caricature. He
had also begun to think about the ending of the book. In late January,
he had composed stanzas of the poem that he intended for the scene
by Ben's grave. Now he began a trial draft of the meeting with Ben's
ghost. At this stage of the planning, Ben was to appear on the campus
at Pulpit Hill:

Moonlight lay on the earth like silence. It was young spring. There was
a bright murk in the air.

Eugene came in by the west wall of the Campus at the edge of the
class playing fields. Under the moonlight a man was sitting on the wall
smoking a cigarette. It was Ben.

Eugene went slowly toward him and stopped. Ben did not move: He
looked scowling at his brother.

"I thought you were dead, Ben," Eugene said after a moment. "I was
in the room with you the night you died. Do you remember?" [23]

Wolfe kept writing night after night in his bare studio, part of the
time huddled in a blanket after the heat in the building had been
turned off. About five or six hours of actual writing seemed to be all
he could manage on a daily schedule, but his mind was filled with
the book at all times. He even dreamed of it. In one nightmare preserved in his notes, Mrs. Bernstein betrays him with a carnival man:
"I discover [them], I destroy my book tearing it to pieces and feed-
ing it to the fire—I fall senseless." [24] This tension increased his normal
irascibility. He quarreled frequently with Mrs. Bernstein, and at a
party at Phillip Moeller's he behaved intolerably. His description of
the evening is mild and defensive: "Went to one terrible studio party
where I met a man named Van Vechten, novelist, a horrible woman
named Elinor Wylie, who is all the go now—she writes novels and
poetry—and her husband Will Benet—I hated them so that I managed to insult them all." [25] According to Mrs. Bernstein, he arrived
at the party so drunk he could hardly stand, he thought the social
conversation of the group pretentious, he felt the literature they dis-

cussed was milk and water beside the hearty solid fare that he himself was serving up, and he ended by calling them vile names.

To ease his strained nerves, he took short trips out of town. He carried his ledgers with him both to write in and to read aloud to his friends. On one trip to Boston in March to gather up books he had left with his uncle, he brought back *Ulysses.* While riding on the train, he copied down Joycean word combinations that fascinated him. Thereafter, he kept Joyce's book by him and frequently turned to it for refreshment or suggestion.[26]

Sometime during this period he decided to use the door, leaf, and stone as his symbols for search and for entrance to the lost pre-birth world. He had used them as symbols of entrance to the world of imaginative illusion in the interior monologue of Gant and Eugene returning from the moving pictures. Now he used them in the pre-dawn sequence in which Eugene, carrying his papers in Niggertown, hears the voices call to him from the real world.

About the first of May, he filled pages of his notebook with familiar verse quotations and set to work on Eugene's promenade through Altamont. By June, when the summer heat began to grow unbearable in his garret, Wolfe went up to Rhinebeck at the invitation of Olin Dows and stayed in the gatekeeper's lodge for a couple of weeks, still keeping to his schedule. He had written to his mother: "I am very tired but I can see no let up until I get the thing finished: I find that if I stop writing for a day, it is hard to get back into it again."[27] When he felt he was getting stale, restlessness drove him to wandering again. He still maintained that he was close to the end, but he had only started Part III when he began to make plans for a tour through Europe in July and August with Mrs. Bernstein.

Just before he left to spend this summer of 1927 in Europe, Wolfe had a unique experience that made a profound impression on him. One night when he looked up an Asheville friend, Dr. Donald Mc-Crae, at a maternity hospital, he had the opportunity to watch the birth of a baby. Awkwardly clad in a long surgeon's gown, he stood in the delivery room, a man intensely interested in life's processes and keenly aware that life's good is inextricably mixed with pain and evil, seeing in the miracle of birth a symbolic truth. He saw human life emerge out of pain and struggle. No sight could have stirred him more deeply or excited him more. "It was ugly, bloody, messy, horrible—but somehow beautiful," he told his sister; "when I saw the little skull begin to come, and then the little body, and the doctor held him by the heels and spanked him, and he screwed his face up and let out his first yell (a good loud one), I could restrain myself no longer: I gave a yell of my own and said 'Come on, baby! Come on!' That made them laugh: they did not understand why anyone should get so excited. The ugliness, the horror, the pain is gone now: all that remains is that little perfect child, and all the mystery and tragic beauty of life, which now seems greater to me than ever." It was with this experience lingering in his mind that Wolfe wrote the prose poem that begins *Look Homeward, Angel.* The birth of the child renewed his awareness that the lonely, troubled journey of man begins with the birth struggle: ". . .something gathers in my throat and my eyes are wet when I think of all the pain and wonder that little life must come to know; and I hope to God those feet will never walk as lonely a road as mine have walked, and I hope its heart will never beat as mine has at times under a smothering weight of weariness, grief, and horror; nor its brain be damned and haunted by a thousand furies and nightmare shapes that walk through mine. This is no sentiment—but the stark truth, from a very deep place in me." [28]

Although the trip to Europe was for relaxation and change of scene, Wolfe set to work again after a few days on the ocean. On a blank page of his ledger he scribbled an outline of what yet remained to be done:

> Christmas—Home
> Rest of year (War)
> Clara [29] (Mabel at Home)
> Miss Bullard—Miss Smith [30]
> Second Year at Univ (Drill)
> Norfolk and Newport News
> Ben's Death   (war over)
> Third Year at Univ (Playmakers—Koch—Greenlaw)
> Fourth ”   ”   ”   (Parting with Horace)

Although this outline followed his own career closely, Wolfe now planned to place the death of Gant at the end of Eugene's college days, for he noted:

> End of 3rd Book
> Gant's death
> Settlement and Desolation
> New Lands [31]

During the summer he filled in the narrative outline of Eugene's college career. He selected the title "O Lost" [32] and wrote the proem which opens the book. He scribbled the words, "O Lost and by the wind grieved, ghost, return," in the back of his notebook, and after working a rephrasing of it into the proem, he repeated it first in the story of Laura.[33] His progress is marked by one note in a manuscript margin that records this goal: "Get up to Ben's death before going to New York." [34] By this time, he had put aside the materials for Eugene's Harvard years, for he saw that he had an outsize work already. In September he made preparations for the voyage back to America, hoping he could finish by the end of the year.

For more than a year now, his time had been almost completely devoted to his novel, but in the next year he would be writing only in his leisure hours. In the spring he had contracted to return to New York University at the fall term. When he arrived in New York in late September, he was able to arrange a convenient teaching schedule so that he could work on the book. All class time except two hours was in the evening, 6:30-9:00, and it was arranged on four consecutive days of the week, leaving him free from 9:00 P.M. Thursday until Monday evening. His surroundings were to be pleasanter for the next two years. In early October, he and Mrs. Bernstein took a spacious three-room apartment, the upper floor of a house at 263 West 11th Street. The sparsely furnished rooms, light and airy with high ceilings, looked bare. But Wolfe had plenty of space in which to scatter his manuscripts, he could look out on a garden in the rear and a quiet street in front, and at least he did not have to go to the Harvard Club to take a bath.

When he decided that the typewriting of the manuscript should get underway, he was lucky to get Abe Smith, his former student and devoted disciple, for the job.[35] Wolfe worked four or five hours a day reading aloud to Smith from his ledgers and making some revisions as he went along. During the fall, Smith typed from Chapter III, the year 1900, to Chapter XXXVII, the scene by the grave of Ben. Wolfe had yet to write only the introductory portion and this concluding sequence that he blocked out in his pocket notebook: "Three teachers [36]—after that last night on campus—Graduation—Departure—Old Man at window—Bell ringing—Last summer at home—dentist's wife —squabble over property—Eugene signs a release—Gant lost and indifferent—Final scene." [37]

While the book was being typed, Wolfe began the early history of the Gants. After a brief exposition about Grandfather Gilbert Gaunt, the opening scene described W. O. Gant as a little boy watching the rebels march by on their way to Gettysburg. Wolfe was wasting his time; both this episode and the subsequent material about Gant's youth and early marriages were to be cut out of the book before publication.

In early December he worked furiously, trying to complete Eugene's college career, and by Christmas he wrote his mother: "I am almost at the end of my book (and of my strength!). If I hold out I should finish by Jan 1, or a little later. I am writing the 'big scene' at the end now. I haven't wasted my time by sleeping. I work until five or six o'clock in the morning." [38] But it was the end of March before the book was in final form, over eleven hundred typewritten pages. Wolfe immediately sent a copy to James B. Munn, the young dean of Washington Square College who had encouraged him with *Mannerhouse*, asking him his opinion:

Now I give you a book on which I have wrought out my brain and my heart for twenty months. There are places in it which are foul, obscene, and repulsive. Most of those will come out in revision. But please, Dr. Munn, believe that this book was honestly and innocently written. Forgive me the bad parts, and remember me for the beauty and passion I have tried to put in it. It is not *immoral*, it is not *dirty*—it simply represents an enormous excavation in my spirit. Saying that, I feel better[.]

My energy is completely exhausted—I felt as if I should drop dead when I came to the last comma. I feel as if my life were beginning again, and what I shall do for a year or two, or where I shall be, I don't know....

Here it is—my heart is in it[.] [39]

Wolfe had no idea whether the book was publishable, for he had written it to satisfy himself, with no eye to publishing standards. Now he was ready to alter it to conform to publishers' demands if necessary, and he addressed a note to the "Publisher's Reader" to accompany his manuscript: "There are some pages here which were compelled by a need for fulness of expression and which had importance when the book was written not because they made part of its essential substance, but because, by setting them forth, the mind was released for its basic work of creation. These pages have done their work of catharsis, and may now be excised." [40] He was more willing to compromise now than he had been with Professor Baker and with the Theatre Guild.

NOTES

1. A typical exaggeration. It would scarcely amount to 100 typed pages.

2. *Letters*, p. 113.

3. PN 1, September 8 to November, 1926.

4. PN 2, November, 1926, to September, 1927.

5. Scarcely any first-draft pages are extant. However, William Tindall remembers that Wolfe had loose sheets for the novel lying around his apartment, and Henry Carlton recalls that Wolfe visited him carrying a sheaf of papers from which he read passages aloud.

6. HCL MS 326F, IX, 176-235.

7. HCL*49M-209, The Purdue Speech.

8. HCL*46AM-7(56) "The World, The Oktoberfest," p. 1, dictated in the fall of 1936.

9. HCL*46AM-13, unpublished letter to Aline Bernstein. For other early reports on his progress, see Nowell, pp. 106-7.

10. PN 1, September 8 to November, 1926. Notes for a letter to Aline Bernstein.

11. Three red ledgers purchased in Ilkley and one purchased in Brussels are in the Harvard Library, HCL*46AM-7(30). All their pages but a few are torn out, although some loose sheets that belong to them are extant, HCL*46AM-7(39). These loose sheets and a typed recapitulation on the cover of each ledger (probably added in 1930) indicate that much of the material concerned Eugene at Harvard.

Volume II of the "O Lost" manuscript begins the present Chapter III of LHA. This ledger, which was purchased in England, was the first one of the final autograph copy to be filled and was originally marked as Volume I. The ledger which is Volume I of the present manuscript, containing the early history of Gant and Eliza, was purchased in New York and was filled sometime after October 3, 1927.

12. Nowell, p. 106.

13. PN 2, November, 1926, to September, 1927.

14. HCL MS 326F, XVI.

15. PN 2, November, 1926, to September, 1927.

16. The only date in the entire seventeen volumes of the "O Lost" manuscript is on a page with the draft of Gant's return: "Munich, Dec. 15," XVI, 27.

17. PN 2, November, 1926, to September, 1927.

18. *Ibid.*, quoted in Nowell, p. 108.

19. LHA, pp. 184-85.

20. HCL*45M-156F, p. 268.

21. PN 2, November, 1926, to September, 1927.

22. HCL MS 326F, IX, 76.

23. *Ibid.*, X, 70.

24. PN 2, November, 1926, to September, 1927.

25. *Letters*, p. 121. Here is the germ that grew into Chapter 30 of W&R.

26. PN 2, November, 1926, to September, 1927, *ca.* March 6: "Jingle-Jangle-Jaunted-Jigley," "Jogjaunty," "ardentbold," "nobkerry," and so forth, mostly from the "Bronze by Gold" passage. HCL MS 326F, XII, 378: "Lemonyellow," "stone-

horned," "dogsbody," "poxybowsy," and so on. Volume XIII, 152, lists references to Joyce's episodes. This listing, by the way, is near Eugene's saunter through town.

27. LTM, pp. 141-42.

28. *Letters,* pp. 126-27.

29. This note refers to Clara Paul, Wolfe's first love. In the novel he changed her name to Laura James.

30. Miss Mallard and Miss Brown, LHA, Chapter XXXI.

31. HCL MS 326F, XV, 312.

32. This is probably another reverberation from Wolfe's study of the Romantic movement. In Scott's *Lay of the Last Minstrel,* the wild and mysterious dwarf runs through the forest crying, "Oh Lost! Lost! Lost!"

33. LHA, p. 456. Wolfe later inserted the phrase into appropriate places in earlier chapters. He likewise sprinkled the word "Lost" liberally through the early pages.

34. HCL MS 326F, XVII, 154.

35. Miss Nowell (p. 110) identifies the student as James Mandel. But Mandel did not begin typing for Wolfe until 1929, when Wolfe was making revisions required by his publisher. (See Mandel's memoir in Oscar Cargill and Thomas Clark Pollock, *Thomas Wolfe at Washington Square* [New York, 1954], p. 93). According to Mrs. Bernstein, Abe Smith typed Wolfe's manuscript. Mrs. Bernstein, always uneasy when questioned about her helping Wolfe with money, declined to say whether or not she paid for the typing (interview with me, January, 1950).

36. The "O Lost" manuscript contains episodes about Professor Hutch (Frederick Koch), Randolph Ware (Edwin Greenlaw), and Virgil Weldon (Horace Williams). Only the last remained in the published version.

37. PN 3, Fall, 1927, to September, 1928.

38. LTM, p. 153.

39. *Letters,* pp. 131-32.

40. *Letters,* p. 129.

11 〰〰〰〰〰〰〰〰〰〰〰〰〰〰〰

THE WRONG RIVER
AND THE WRONG PEOPLE

NOW THAT THE BOOK WAS READY TO GO TO A PUBLISHER, WOLFE
gave the typescript to Mrs. Bernstein with relief. He had done all
he could do, he said; now she must do the rest. Mrs. Bernstein
turned first to her friend, T. R. Smith, an editor at Boni and Liveright, and asked him for a reading. The waiting period was a terrible
one for Wolfe. Although he continued his teaching, at home he
paced the length of the large apartment on Eleventh Street and
grew more nervous every day. After five weeks, Smith sent out
letters of rejection to Wolfe and to Mrs. Bernstein. Wolfe was furious
not only about the rejection but about the weary, bored tone
of the letter. Years later, he showed his resentment in the parody
he included in *The Web and the Rock* as George Webber's reply
from the publishers, Rawng and Wright.

Meanwhile, Mrs. Bernstein had also arranged through her friend,
Thomas Beer, to have Ernest Boyd read the book. Boyd, who was a
literary agent and a scout for Little, Brown, and Company as well as
a critic, was at the height of his influence and held an eminence in
New York literary circles alongside Mencken and Nathan. If anyone
could place the book, Mrs. Bernstein felt, Boyd could. But there was
one difficulty with Boyd as an agent. Because he looked down on
novels, he never read them; he turned all novel manuscripts over to
his wife for reading. Since Ernest and Madeleine Boyd were in the
midst of a quarrel at this time, Wolfe's manuscript lay unread for
about three weeks. As a result of their domestic trouble, Madeleine
Boyd set up a literary agency of her own and asked Mrs. Bernstein if
she could have Wolfe's novel and act as Wolfe's agent.

Madame Boyd, a high-spirited Frenchwoman, was an ideal person to take over Wolfe's novel, for she brought great enthusiasm to her work. Because it was her first manuscript in her new venture, she felt a little apprehensive when she saw its size. But she sat down to read in mid-afternoon and buried herself, fascinated, in the life of the Gant family until 3 A.M. Coming to one of Gant's performances at the table, heaping up smoking platters of food, she suddenly realized she had not eaten for twelve hours. Her surprise rose to a shout loud enough to disturb the neighbors across the hall. "I have discovered a genius!" She continued reading the next day, wept over the death of Ben, and was deeply moved by Eugene's story. On May 20 she asked Mrs. Bernstein to send Wolfe over to talk about the book. This odd pair had an immediate dislike for each other. Wolfe recoiled from Madame Boyd's volatile behavior and her fiery temper, whereas she was irritated by his suspicious nature and his volubility. Nevertheless, she was the first person in the publishing world to have confidence in his book, and he yearned for publication. He agreed to let her handle the sale of the manuscript.

But publishers' readers were not overwhelmed by Wolfe's genius. Mrs. Boyd sent the manuscript to Pascal Covici, whose Chicago publishing house had a hard-won fame for its courage in publishing new authors. Covici had just formed with Donald Friede the new firm of Covici-Friede. But Wolfe's manuscript got only a hasty reading there.[1] It was turned down with the usual publisher's request for an option on Wolfe's second novel.

Mrs. Boyd next attempted to work through others. Although she could not persuade Ernest to recommend the book to Little, Brown, her friend, Cleveland Chase, of Longmans, Green, and Company, took the manuscript in. William Sloane, who was at that time a Longmans reader, has reported its fate in the Longmans office: "My fellow reader and I jockeyed about for a good while before I managed to stick him with its reading. . . .He read 50,000 words of that tome, some of them aloud to me. What I heard of it was terrible. Finally we sent the manuscript back, presumably in a truck." [2]

Wolfe's state of mind rocked at these rebuffs. Although he drew encouragement from what little praise was offered, he sank in despair at the rejections and rose in rage at the neglect of his talent. He took heart, however, when he thought of Dean Munn's advice, "I would

not change a word." [3] The only worthwhile outcome of the readers'
criticisms was that Wolfe began thinking about a second novel.

II

Wolfe's first impulse was to write anything, to do some kind of
hack work that would bring in money. Any unrecognized writer can
become cynical when his worth goes unacknowledged, but a dedicated artist cannot carry through an intention to gain mere success
in the market place. An embittered Faulkner sat down to write something sensational in order to shock the public and create sales, but
when he finished *Sanctuary,* he still had an artistic product. Wolfe's
second attempt at a novel began in the wrong spirit, but his artistic
conscience would not permit him to continue in this way. Gradually his plans changed, until he was working on chapters of such
caliber that they could eventually find a place in the middle of *Of
Time and the River.*

The record in Wolfe's notebook shows that at first he seriously
considered writing popular fiction. One entry even shows him exploring the possibilities in pulp fiction: "Magazines—Adventure, Popular Sea Stories, Western Stories, Mexican Stories, Stories of mining
interests everywhere—War and Marine stories." In another entry
he sketched out a plot for a slick-magazine piece, and in still another
he stooped to "true confession" heart-throb:

STORY

Scene: a crack Atlantic Liner—New York to Cherbourg
People: A Beautiful American girl, a handsome rich
　　young American man, a third woman—beautiful but in-
　　triguing—an international Jewel thief for whom the
　　police of two continents are searching; a humorous
　　cockney steward, who turns out to be Inspector Fortes-
　　cue of Scotland Yard.

STORY (I confess)

Girl in Southern town—prominent socially—Daughter of
a Judge—Mother love—Mother dies (?)—Judge wants her
to marry young rake, son of his deceased partner, distinguished man (formerly Governor of State)—But she
loves honest young fellow—Stigma over his name—no
great social prestige [—] Finally gives in to her father. [4]

At length—and for Wolfe it seems incredible—he chose to write a novel with a background as far removed from "O Lost" as he could get. When from time to time Wolfe had been invited up to Rhinebeck by Olin Dows, he had met or heard friendly gossip about the Delanos, the Astors, the Vanderbilts, and other great families from nearby estates. Awed by their wealth and property and fascinated by their lavish ease, he had hoped some day to write about it. Now, he turned his plebeian gaze upon the moneyed gods for a romance which he called "The River People." Although his aim, both in plot structure and subject matter, was for popular appeal, his artistic conscience began to trouble him. He revealed his dilemma as he described his plans to Dean Munn:

I've got a *new* book in mind. I thought I should not write again for several centuries, but there's no cure for my own kind of lunacy. I don't see how this one can fail—it has everything: rich people, swank, a poor but beautiful girl, romance, adventure, Vienna, New York, a big country house, and so on. Also, after a careful examination of 4,362 novels, I have decided to make it exactly 79,427 words long. . . .In spite of my summary I've got stuff for a good and moving book—also, perhaps stuff for a bad and trashy, but possibly successful book. Now, what's a poor young guy to do, Dean Munn? I've got to do it one way or the other—straddling the fence is no good.[5]

Outlines in his notebook show that "The River People" was based on his experiences in Boston, New York, Rhinebeck, and various European cities. But the narrative thread probably came from a story he had heard first or second hand from a friend. He had further indecision about the treatment of the plot: how many of his own experiences should he include? how closely should he follow the central narrative? These were problems that haunted him for the remainder of his literary career.

Roughly the story seems to have been this: While at Harvard, Oliver Weston [6] meets Joel Pierce, a young painter who asks him to pose for a picture. The two become friends, and Joel invites Oliver to his father's estate on the Hudson River. When Oliver gets to Europe, he meets Greta Weinberg, an Austrian girl who nurses him when he is ill. After his recovery, he wanders over Europe, then returns to America. Later that year, Greta and her husband visit America, Oliver meets her again, and he introduces her to Joel. The two fall in love, but certain problems must be faced before they can marry—first, a divorce for Greta and, second, the heated objection of Joel's cousin, John. The couple travel to Vienna, where Oliver finds an apartment for them and divorce proceedings are begun. Back in America once more, they plan a marriage when final divorce papers are granted. In a last scene on the Hudson River, Greta meets a violent death at the hands of cousin John, and the grief-stricken Joel is left with only his memories and a single magnificent painting of her. At the conclusion the two friends, Oliver and Joel, part, and each has something to say about love, life, and art. This was the book that Wolfe planned in May, worked on sporadically the rest of the year, but never finished.[7]

As spring came to an end in 1928, Wolfe's personal life grew more and more disorganized and distraught. His teaching was a day-to-day routine, but his anxiety about the success or failure of his first novel led to quarrels with Mrs. Bernstein that made both of their lives unbearable. The period of happiness and certainty in Wolfe's life had not lasted long. Mrs. Bernstein led a very full life in which Wolfe had only a small part; she had her family, her social affairs, her theatrical career—all aspects of her life which Wolfe could not or refused to share. He had lost his heart to a woman who did not have enough time for him. "I used to feel," he wrote Mrs. Bernstein in 1928, "that love was part of my life and all these thousand things that swarmed through my mind was a part of love; I have never been able to cut them apart, as you have, your life, your many activities, and your feeling for me. And I think a great deal of our trouble has come from that." [8]

Both Wolfe in *The Web and the Rock* and Aline Bernstein in *The Journey Down* have given fictional accounts of their breakup, which led tragically to the near-suicide of Mrs. Bernstein in 1931. Each assumed the blame for their violent quarrels. Wolfe himself called George Webber's jealousy psychotic—"a madness which was compounded of many elements took possession of him. . . .And in the tortured, twisted crevices of his brain, he felt, with a wave of desolating self-pity and despair, that Esther had contrived ruin against him." [9] In *The Journey Down*, Mrs. Bernstein allowed her heroine to speak of herself as a divided being—consciously she watched her external self, "a nagging, tearful, self-centered woman," fray the bonds of love: "I saw my immortal soul sitting inside of me like

Buddha, calm, immobile, allowing this vulgar fishwife to have her say." [10] Though both Wolfe and Mrs. Bernstein were emotional tinderboxes, it is probable that Wolfe, with his moodiness, with his black anger that could cloud reason, was chiefly at fault.

"The anatomy of jealousy," Wolfe wrote to Perkins, "is the most complicated and tortuous anatomy on earth: to find its causes, to explore its sources, is more difficult and mysterious than it was for the ancients to probe the sources of the Nile." [11] But some of the springs are discernible. Both in his letters to Perkins and in *The Web and the Rock*, Wolfe indicates clearly that he detested Aline Bernstein's friends in the Neighborhood Playhouse and the Theatre Guild because they reflected the vulgar over-sophistication of the gilded twenties. But he does not admit that because of his failure in the theater he resented their success. In his hatred, he grew to think that all theater people were intellectually shallow and morally corrupt. And if Aline Bernstein was one of them, she could not escape his calumny. Besides, he was envious of her own successful career, and as her reputation grew, he brooded about her fame, remembering that his own work was yet unpublished. Actually, their worst quarrels began in the spring of 1928, when he could not find a publisher willing to take his book.

In addition, Wolfe had some old wounds that were still tender. Since Aline Bernstein played the maternal role in her cooking and housekeeping and in her attempts to look after Wolfe's clothes, to send out his laundry, and generally to supervise the routine details of his daily existence, she repeated Julia Wolfe's pattern of treatment of her son, the inexplicable alternating between neglect and fierce possessiveness. Aline's commitments to family and career were like Julia Wolfe's duties as a boarding-house keeper. Aline tapped all the reservoir of love that Wolfe had in him to give to a woman, but she also re-created all the pain of his boyhood years because of her part-time attention to the young man whose company she enjoyed.

Wolfe's anti-Semitism was the final ingredient in the explosive mixture. He was brought up in a family and a social class which expressed this prejudice blatantly. Even with his love for Aline Bernstein, it did not vanish, for he was ever conscious of her background. His pet name for her was "my dear Jew," and he felt that many things that endeared her to him were part of her Jewish heritage: her emotional enthusiasms, her delight in life, her expansiveness, her cookery, her strong family loyalties to her blood relations, father, sister, children. This identification lay ready-made, then, for him to attach to it the irrationalities that grew from his neurotic anguish. At first he thought her life the happiest he had ever known. Gradually, however, as her glittering world of wealth and of the theater grew distasteful to him, he began to characterize it as a Jewish world, and all the mindless hates of anti-Semitism returned to batten on his jealousy and his disappointments.

This neurotic indulgence is an unblinkable blot on Wolfe's character. And the anti-Semitism spread from his own life into his work, giving an offensive tone to such passages as those describing Eugene Gant's struggles as a teacher in "the brawling and ugly corridors of the university, which drowned one, body and soul, with their swarming, shrieking, shouting tides of dark amber Jewish flesh," [12] or George Webber's abhorrence of Esther Jack's world "inhabited by rich, powerful, and cynical people—great, proud and potent beak-nosed Jews." [13] The harpy of his prejudice returned from these flights to roost, justly, on his own rafters, for in his lifetime letters from irate readers denounced him for his back-alley attitude toward the Jews, and after his death reviewers such as Malcolm Cowley did not spare their castigation of his "middle-class prejudice and naive but offensive anti-Semitism." [14] It is unfortunate that he did not live a little longer so that he could have revealed more fully his own later realization, after a second trip to Hitler's Germany, of the inhuman dangers in his prejudice.

The mounting tension drained him of his energy to do creative work. He decided that another trip to Europe, with his whereabouts kept secret, would solve all his problems: he would break with Mrs. Bernstein, and he would be able to get his new book underway. By the time he sailed, he had been given very little encouragement from any of the publishing houses. He had been told that his writing was good but that "O Lost" was too long and diffuse. But since they had asked to see a second novel "of reasonable length," Wolfe went away determined to please them. He had characterized his new book to his mother only in terms of length: "A short one this time." In spite of his chagrin about the first novel, he left for Europe full of zeal to work on "The River People"—to build from this first outline set down in his pocket notebook:

THE RIVER PEOPLE

Wolfe carried along a large ledger and a great deal of determination, for he felt he had to prove to himself that he could make a living by writing. If he could break into print with "The River People," perhaps then publishers would clamor for his first novel. If all went awry, however, he still had some financial security. Dean Munn, who had always stood behind his creative work, held out the offer of a teaching job. "Professor Watt says you are away next year writing. Go to it. The latchstring will be out for your return," and again, "Don't mind the criticism. Follow your soul or spirit or whatever guides you. I believe in your work implicitly." [16]

During the year Wolfe wandered in Paris, Brussels, Antwerp, Cologne, Bonn, Wiesbaden, Frankfort, and finally Munich, where he spent three days in a hospital recovering from head wounds got in a brawl at the Munich Oktoberfest. Roaming restlessly, despondent about the fate of "O Lost," in a mental jangle about his voluntary breach with Aline Bernstein, he hunted furiously through bookshops and art museums, joined *Rundfahrten,* visited shrines, attended festivals. His pocket journals became crammed with comments on art and literary criticism, comparisons between European and American literature, lists of French and German books and authors, paintings viewed, cities toured. In a new upsurge of world-devouring hunger, he was maddened by the knowledge that his reading could only be "a spoonful of the ocean of print." But this was to be the last time his seeking would rise to such a frenzied height. He could see the senselessness of this saturation: "I am overpowered by number, not by quality." [17] Late in the year, he began to exercise control. The time spent in the Munich hospital gave him opportunity to re-evaluate his life and to recognize the folly of intellectual greed: "But I am tired," he wrote in November, "the desire for it *all* comes from an evil gluttony in me—a weakness, a lack of belief." [18] A statement to Mrs. Roberts about his injuries and his hospital meditations reveals the calmness and attendant self-assessment that follow violent agitation: "for the first time I went to the bottom of my soul, and saw how much power for evil and insanity lies in all of us." He found himself "crying out inside me not because of my body's loss, but because of my soul's waste and loss." [19] Some reorientation of Wolfe as a social being had taken place: "I have, I think, now that my spiritual torment regarding the Oktoberfest has died down, on the whole, a feeling of increased confidence. Before that a certain fear of people —my "crowd neurosis" caused me to bristle up, and be pugnacious [.] This comes from a sense of fear than otherwise—but now that I have shed blood and have got a scar—a new confidence and balance seems to have come to me. I feel kindlier toward people." [20]

During these unhappy months, he had accomplished very little on the second novel, for he had abandoned the idea of popular treatment. His days spent pawing through bookstalls were only an escape, and he knew it. "There is always the moment when we must begin to write," he acknowledged. "There are always the hundreds, the thousands of hours of struggle, of getting up, of pacing about, of sitting down, of laborious uneven accomplishment. During the time of actual work, what else besides ourselves can help us? Can we call to mind then the contents of 20000 books? Can we depend on anything other than ourselves for help?" [21] He had written a few episodes for "The River People," but the drive that carried "O Lost" to its conclusion was not there.

In mid-November in Vienna, he received a letter from Maxwell Perkins of Charles Scribner's Sons expressing interest in "O Lost." Although the letter offered promise, Wolfe's previous experience with publishers' replies (which usually held out hopes that "if your second book is shorter, we might consider it") prevented him from celebrating a triumph. Nor was he optimistic enough to rush home.

He continued his tour, going to Vienna, Salzburg, Budapest, Florence, Rome, and finally, in December, Naples, where he came to the end of his money.

As usual, the European trip had made Wolfe conscious of his native land. During the summer he was repelled by the materialism and weariness of European civilization and defensively indignant at the patronizing attitudes of the European citizens. By mid-November, the urge to do more than a piece of popular fiction had grown stronger. He wrote Mrs. Bernstein:

I am coming home. I am an American and I must try to take hold somewhere. I am not burning with indignation or revolt or anything. I am tired of struggle and should like to fall in step if only I knew how. But how? I have no genuine conviction that any other nation cares more for the good and the beautiful than it does for money. They are all so far as I can see, an ugly grasping greedy lot—if anything a great deal grosser in their desires than we are—and their cry against us comes from a dirty money-envy and money-hatred, and from nothing better. This goes for everyone I have seen this time except the Austrians; and the Austrians are a gentle indifferent lot who want to dream—who live in a world of images ....I am a citizen of the most powerful and interesting nation of modern times—and I wish to God I knew how to make something of it.[22]

When could he make something of it? Certainly his conception of "The River People" was a move in the wrong direction. What he needed was encouragement through publication of the book he had put his heart in. Then he would be ready for the bigger venture.

NOTES

1. See the reader's report in Donald Friede's *The Mechanical Angel* (New York, 1948), pp. 88-89, which indicates a careful perusal of the "Notice for the Publisher's Reader" and a partial reading of the manuscript.

2. "Literary Prospecting," *Saturday Review of Literature,* XIII (December 3, 1938), 4. Sloane himself claims to have read about one-third of it. It was not to his taste; twenty years later the only thing he could remember was "the evidently bad quality of the book." Letter to me, August 1, 1950.

3. HCL*46AM-12(4), April 3, 1928.

4. PN 3, Fall, 1927, to September, 1928.

5. *Letters,* p. 135.

6. During the months Wolfe was at work, he changed the names of his characters several times.

7. The opening chapters and scraps of other parts here and there are still extant.

8. PN 3, Fall, 1927, to September, 1929, letter draft *ca.* July 28, 1928.

9. W&R, p. 539.

10. (New York, 1938) pp. 159-60.

11. Unpublished letter, January 19, 1931, in the files of CSS.

12. OT&R, p. 419.

13. W&R, p. 539.

14. "Thomas Wolfe's Legacy," *New Republic*, XXXIX (July 19, 1939), 311-12.

15. PN 3, Fall, 1927, to September, 1928. Joel calls his father "Pups."

16. HCL*46AM-12(4), April 3, 1928, and May 24, 1928.

17. PN 4, September to October, 1928.

18. PN 5, October 24 to November, 1928.

19. HCL*48M-211, January 12, 1929, published in the *Atlantic Monthly*, CLXXIX (January, 1947), 40-41.

20. PN 7, December, 1928.

21. PN 6, November to December, 1928.

22. HCL*46AM-13, unpublished letter, November 17, 1928.

12

THE HAND OF AN EDITOR

In the late summer of 1928, Madeleine Boyd had made an appointment with Maxwell Perkins of Scribner's to talk over a translation of André Chamson's *Le Puits des Miracles*. She had not thought to send Wolfe's novel to Scribner's, but now she remembered Maxwell Perkins' careful attention to manuscripts. As she chatted with him about the translation, she could not refrain from bursting out about her new discovery. Her enthusiasm interested him, but she realized when he asked to see the book that the impact of "O Lost" was cumulative, and she was afraid that he might bog down in the earlier section of the novel before the story of Eugene began. Max Perkins gave one of his quiet smiles as she made him promise "on his word of honor as a Harvard man" to read it all the way through himself.[1]

When the Scribner's delivery truck brought the "O Lost" manuscript to Perkins, he soon tired of the early narrative of the Gant and Pentland families, so he sacrificed the honor of Harvard and turned the manuscript over to a reader for completion. Wallace Meyer of the editorial department read the manuscript carefully and called Perkins' attention to several impressive passages in the book. From this moment, Wolfe's manuscript had its great opportunity in the hands of a sympathetic and discerning editor.

In early October, Perkins told Mrs. Boyd that Scribner's would like to see the author of "O Lost" to discuss possible publication. Mrs. Boyd employed a detective agency to find Wolfe in Europe, and on October 22 Perkins wrote Wolfe, letting his real excitement about the book slip through the jargon of the business letter.[2] Most important, he asked Wolfe to come in for an interview to discuss the book when he returned to New York.

Whatever changes had come over Wolfe during the autumn of 1928, the great change of his life began on January 2, when he went to the Scribner's office to see Maxwell Perkins. He poured out a detailed account of the interview to Mrs. Roberts. Gone was the pride that made him balk at the cutting of *Welcome to Our City*. "When I saw now that [Mr. Perkins] was really interested I burst out wildly saying that I would throw out this, that, and the other." As they began to discuss the book scene by scene, Wolfe gradually realized that at last his manuscript had had a careful reading: "I saw now that Perkins had a great batch of notes in his hand and that on the desk was a great stack of handwritten paper—a complete summary of my whole enormous book."

This interview was not like the polite but weary encounters with other publishing houses. The Scribner's staff had perceived the form of the book, and they had not allowed the faults in technique or taste to obscure its real value.

For the first time in my life I was getting criticism I could really use— the scenes he wanted cut or changed were invariably the least essential and the least interesting; all the scenes that I had thought too coarse, vulgar, profane, or obscene for publication he forbade me to touch save for a word or two. . . .He said the book was new and original, and because of its form could have no formal and orthodox unity, but that what unity it did have came from the strange wild people—the family—it wrote about as seen through the eyes of a strange wild boy. These people, with relatives, friends, townspeople, he said were "magnificent"—as real as any people he had ever read of. He wanted me to keep the people and the boy at all times foremost—other business such as courses at the state university, etc., to be shortened and subordinated.[3]

Wolfe began at once to plan his revision of the manuscript according to the suggestions Perkins had made.[4] Perkins was pleased, not only with the book, but with Wolfe's cooperative attitude, and he gave him an unofficial acceptance of the manuscript. Wolfe rushed to tell Aline Bernstein. In the fashion of a boy carving a record on a tree, Wolfe placed in his notebook the initials "TW" and "AB" and under them: "January 7, 1929. On this day Charles Scribner and Son, Pub. accepted the *MSS* of my first book."[5] His boyish delight in having his first novel published carried sanguine hopes for a fortune in royalties. "If I get rich," he told Mrs. Boyd, "nothing would please me more than to see you get prosperous (This is a kind of joke, but I wish it would come true.)" [6] Scribner's was willing to give him a small advance payment, but Wolfe had to lift Dean Munn's ever-ready latchstring at New York University in order to eat. He had only one class to teach, however, and he could announce to his colleagues that glory awaited him as he set to work on his revision.

II

As Wolfe had predicted in his "Notice for the Publisher's Reader," there was almost no rewriting to be done at all. To shorten the book, the cutting was done in large blocks: pages and paragraphs were dropped out, and minute revision was not necessary. The principal changes reduced the manuscript from eleven hundred pages to about eight hundred. The first fifty pages, which concerned the Gant ancestors, the battle of Gettysburg, and the early life of Gant, were reduced to three; several pages at the beginning and many scattered throughout the narrative that were devoted to the Pentland kin were thrown out; the backgrounds and personal histories that introduced most of the minor characters in the book were thinned out; digressions in which the author addressed the reader with his opinions on politics, economics, morals, and religion were cut out; irrelevant changes of place, such as Eugene's trips to Florida with his mother, were cut out; the material about Eugene's life at the state university was considerably reduced; and the two lengthy scenes which gave a panorama of the town were pared to half their former size.

A single transposition was made, the best of Perkins' suggestions: the stream-of-consciousness passage, Gant's tour of the town, which had been more or less buried in the "Awakening of Altamont" scene in Part II was fitted more appropriately into Part I, because it was more effective standing alone, because it represented Gant at an earlier period of his life, and because it made a transition between Eugene's early childhood and his starting to school.

Some word changes occurred. Gutter words that appeared here and there were replaced by more acceptable ones, and a few passages were toned down by removing a phrase or two. Names had to be changed. Perkins had read Wolfe's statement in the "Notice for the Publisher's Reader" about the autobiographical nature of the novel, but he did not realize how many living persons were in the book until the cutting began. Here were characters with the same first names as the real parents, brothers, sisters, aunts, and uncles that Wolfe chatted about—Julia, Helen, Fred, Frank, and so on. Other names were chosen for family members as well as for many identifiable minor characters.

The only addition to the entire manuscript, probably made at the suggestion of Perkins, was the parting of Eugene and his mother the night before the journey to the North. This scene was the climax to many lesser breaks from Eliza, and since Wolfe wrote the scene a year after he had finished "O Lost," he was able to complete his portrait of Eliza by adding a touch of sympathy and understanding.

Perkins had brought critical powers to bear on the manuscript in a way that Wolfe could never have done. The cuts he suggested made the difference between a loose, uneven piece of work that sacrificed effectiveness to digression, and a full, varied representation of life that gathered power as Eugene and the Gants lived out their days. For in making the revision, Wolfe quickened the narrative flow and centered attention on the main characters. He was forced to curb his tendency to step before the curtain with distracting comment. The most important single change, however, came as a result of Wolfe's rewriting the opening pages of the book. He was able to begin his story on a philosophical note with his speculations on Time and Chance.

Not all the changes were improvements. Some of the passages that were dropped had been additional variations on Wolfe's themes. For example, glimpses of the infant Eugene groping his way in a new world as the growth of sensation blotted out the memory of a former world were lost. And the first description of Eugene's "gray-lipped" demon, which forced him to speak with "savage honesty," went into the waste basket. But the scene that suffered most in the cutting was the final scene in the square with the ghost of Ben. Perkins was right in calling for a more swiftly paced close to the book. But the scene as it now stands contains references that do not make sense in the present context; it has some abrupt transitions that leave a wish for further explanation in the reader's mind; and all in all, its meaning is not easily perceptible. Wolfe's problem was probably this: he had, in the first place, had difficulty expressing his ideas clearly; then when parts of the scene had to be removed, he felt he could not supply transitions without writing as much as had to be cut. Thus he added almost nothing to connect the passages that remained.

As Wolfe went to work on the manuscript in January, he was more at peace than he had been since 1925. With tensions banished, he and Mrs. Bernstein were happy together for the next eight months. Since Mrs. Bernstein was currently working with the Civic Repertory Theater, he moved to a new apartment at 27 West 15th Street in order to be near her. Into this apartment he brought what furniture he had, including an ugly, heavy dining table on which he had finished "O Lost." The principal feature of the place was a large, barn-like room, where he worked blissfully, surrounded by heaps of socks and stacks of dirty dishes.

When Scribner's requested that Wolfe retitle his novel, he filled page after page of his notebook with phrases. After rejecting such possibilities as "Alone Alone," "Prison of Earth," "The Lost Language," and others just as unsatisfactory as "O Lost," he finally thought of *Look Homeward, Angel* from Milton's "Lycidas." He recorded his choice with a double underscoring in the textbook he was using at New York University.[7] He entered in his notebook a reminder which he never heeded: "Put into final scene of book 'Look Homeward, Angel, now, and melt with ruth.'"[8]

By April he had completed the revision that he had outlined in January, but he had grown reluctant to give up material that had cost him so much labor. As a result, the manuscript was still too long. For the next couple of weeks, Perkins went over the book with Wolfe, making swift, telling slices in the text. At this time most of the patent irrelevancies were weeded out, but along with them went a number of amusing parodies, dropped in order to reduce the bulk or avoid repetition. Among them were Eugene's fantasies written in pulp-fiction style (General Gant, the Scourge of the Greasers; Marshal Gant of the Foreign Legion; Young Gant, the best fullback Yale ever had; and Eugene Gant, the matinee idol of the cinema), a Joycean whimsey of "high society fiction," a parody of Elizabethan low comedy, a mock catalogue from a Christian Fundamentalist prep school, a burlesque letter from an English war hero, and so on.

Wolfe took these last cuts with great pain and protest. He felt that if one parody was good, more were better. In the same way, he fought to retain all his prose lyrics, many of which were vague, bombastic outpourings. He complained loudly to his colleagues and his students at New York University, and to his literary agent he abused Perkins and Wheelock and roared: "Those sons of bitches, they are taking the balls off me!" He was persuaded, however, when Maxwell Perkins suggested that he could use some of these passages in later work.

Perkins wished to give the young author some advance publicity, and he arranged to have one unified piece out of the manuscript published as a story in *Scribner's Magazine*. He had Wolfe send the editor "An Angel on the Porch" (the scene between Gant and "Queen" Elizabeth extended by a little introductory matter), which was scheduled for the August issue. Wolfe also hoped that the editor would take some other stories, but four episodes taken from the manuscript and peddled as separate stories were not accepted by *Scribner's Magazine*. Mrs. Boyd also tried these with the *Bookman* and the *American Mercury* but without success.

By June, Scribner's was putting the revised manuscript into print, and Wolfe decided to correct proofs at Boothbay Harbor on the Maine Coast. Here, during July, he and Mrs. Bernstein went over the galleys together, making so many changes in words and phrases for the final printed version that he ran up a printer's bill of $700 for author's corrections. Scribner's, always lenient with Wolfe, bore the expense for him.

Wolfe was apprehensive about the reception of his book in Asheville. In June he had written to his mother: "I hope you will not talk too much about my book—I really meant it several months ago when I begged you all not to. I don't think you understand my feelings in the matter very well—I certainly am grateful for the interest you all take—but I know that more things are hurt by too much talk than by too little." [9] He got his first blast of the heat that was to come when "An Angel on the Porch" was published in late July and he received a sizzling letter from Mrs. Roberts. He tried to defend himself, but his heart sank as he realized the truth of his statement to her: "I hope you may be wrong in thinking what I have written may distress members of my family, or anyone else. . . .I am afraid, however, that if anyone is distressed by what seemed to me a very simple and unoffending story, their feeling when the book comes out will be much stronger." [10]

In September, just before the publication date, Wolfe made one last trip home to visit his family. He said almost nothing about the subject matter of the book; he only muttered to his sister, Mabel, as he boarded the train, that he might have to wear dark glasses and a false beard the next time he came back.[11] When he bade them goodbye this time, he was not to return again for almost eight years.

When pre-publication copies were available, Wolfe sent a few home to Asheville, but the first copy went to Mrs. Bernstein with the following inscription on the dedication page:

TO

ALINE BERNSTEIN

> On my 29th birthday, I present her with this, the first copy of my first book. This book was written because of her and is dedicated to her. At a time when my life seemed desolate, and when I had little faith in myself I met her. She brought me friendship, material and spiritual relief, and love such as I never had before. I hope therefore that readers of my book will find at least part of it worthy of such a woman.[12]

Look Homeward, Angel was published on October 18, 1929.

NOTES

1. These details were supplied by Mrs. Boyd, interview with me, January, 1950. See also Maxwell Perkins' account in "Thomas Wolfe," *Harvard Library Bulletin*, I (Autumn, 1947), 270.

2. The letter is published in *Editor to Author, The Letters of Maxwell Perkins*, ed. John Hall Wheelock (New York, 1950), p. 61.

3. *Letters*, p. 169.

4. See his notes in Nowell, pp. 133-34.

5. PN 8, December, 1928, to January, 1929.

6. *Letters*, p. 161.

7. HCL*46A-148, Homer Watt and James Munn, *Ideas and Forms in English and American Literature* (New York, 1925).

8. PN 10, March to June, 1929.

9. LTM, p. 176.

10. *Letters*, p. 197.

11. Mabel Wolfe Wheaton, interview with me, September, 1954. See also Wheaton, p. 215.

12. HCL*AC9 W8327 9291(B).

13.

DONNING THE MANTLE

THE DEMAND FOR *Look Homeward, Angel* HAS NEVER SLACK-
ened since its publication. Because reprints by the Modern Library
and by Grosset and Dunlap have continued to pass over the counters
of book stores and because copies in public libraries have frequently
been worn out with reading, one might assume that Wolfe achieved
his much-desired fame overnight. But his reputation grew much
more gradually. Leo Gurko's assertion that the book "was the nearest
thing to a literary thunderbolt in the twentieth century" [1] must be
interpreted as a retrospective glance, for in 1929 most of the reviewers found it merely "a promising first novel." The most widely
circulated reviews, the *New York Herald-Tribune Books,* the *New
York Times Book Review,* and the *Saturday Review of Literature,*
supplied some of the usual blurb material: "robust sensitiveness," [2]
"a book of drive and vigor, of profound originality, of rich and variant color," [3] "mammoth appreciation of experience and of living." [4]
Yet the praise was qualified. For example, Basil Davenport, observing that all things seemed to take on a great significance for the
author, wryly added: "It must be confessed that he has just missed
the greatest of gifts, that of being able to convey his interest to the
reader."

Even so, the glowing terms in these commonplace review sheets
sent Wolfe into a flurry of excitement that mounted all during the
next year as the more considered judgments of later reviewers returned sound appreciations. As a result, Wolfe felt a heightened sense
of responsibility about his career, while a statement like this by
Stringfellow Barr made his spirits rise to a fervor of self-dedication:

I should call "Look Homeward, Angel" a work of genius but that word is somewhat overworn of late. In any case I believe it is the South's first contribution to world literature....A lesser artist looking on that scene, would have become excitedly denunciatory or triumphantly analytical and would have discovered in it no more than another Zenith City or another Winesburg Ohio. What Mr. Wolfe beheld was the travail of the human spirit, blind to its own stupidities, its cowardice, its lusts. His novel is of epic proportions, physically and spiritually.[5]

With the newly won fame, Wolfe felt like a new member of a rather exclusive club. He lunched with Carl Van Doren and Van Wyck Brooks; he went to parties given by leading citizens of the publishing world. In January he was able to boast of his literary social-climbing in this fashion:

The literary life—I know these 'uns:

Dubose Heyward	Hugh Walpole	Ernest Boyd
W. Rose Benet	Jim Boyd	R. Nathan
Lyle Saxon	Tom Beer	Van Dine
Bromfield	Struthers Burt [6]	

As the months passed, Wolfe watched the sale of his book as a father watches the growth of his child. Although he felt some temporary excitement over the possibility that Carl Van Doren might choose *Look Homeward, Angel* for the Literary Guild, his book lost out because the Guild had recently sent its members an autobiographical novel. He had even hoped the frankness of statement in *Look Homeward, Angel* would provoke Boston into banning his book, an event that usually boosted sales figures. He wrote to his friend George Wallace, who now worked for the *Boston Evening Transcript*, hinting that any publicity that might bring down the Watch and Ward Society on his head would be welcome.

As *Look Homeward, Angel* continued to sell steadily, Wolfe discovered to his surprise that his public was not a column of figures in the Scribner's bookkeeping department but was a varied group of real people: he got fan mail. From then on he would receive a flow of comment and praise both for his books and his magazine fiction. Most letters were from ordinary readers. Many were from teachers, librarians, and club members, many from future acquaintances in the literary world—Clifton Fadiman, Henry Seidel Canby, Sherwood Anderson, and Marjorie Kinnan Rawlings. There were a few from distinguished persons who did not know Wolfe at all—of these the most important to Wolfe was Percy MacKaye, who had been one of his early idols. Wolfe saved most of his correspondence over the years, and it remains a fascinating record of a writer's impact upon his diverse audience. The first letter that arrived, a few days after the publication of *Look Homeward, Angel,* came from Mark Schorer, who was then an undergraduate at Harvard. Enthusiastic response like this, ". . .it is the most magnificent book I know. This is the sort of book I have always wanted to write," [7] made Wolfe realize he had spoken for the young men of his generation.

But not all the response to the book brought happiness: it is well known what a storm of abuse issued from his native region.[8] Since Wolfe's practice of drawing characters from real life even extended to giving them almost-recognizable names (for example, Mr. Armstead, the school principal, was called Armstrong, and Wolfe's schoolmate, "Daddy" Hildebrand, was called "Pap" Rheinhart), [9] the book caused a bigger sensation in Asheville than the bank failure the following year. The reverberations began when the Wolfe family received advance copies. They had some suspicion that the book would be controversial, for they had heard about *Welcome to Our City* and its handling of Negro and white relations, but they were totally unprepared for a family chronicle.

The family reaction was only a small flutter amidst the general uproar in Asheville; the Wolfes even felt that, if Tom had treated the family more generously, the whole town would have turned against them. When the *Asheville Times* reviewed the book playing up the "local angle," [10] people rushed for copies. The book stores were soon sold out, and the rental libraries began charging their customers fifty cents a day. Since readers looked upon the book as a journalistic exposé, their curiosity was at the tabloid-newspaper level, and they filled the margins of rental library copies with character identification and comment, much of which was spurious and vulgar. To prevent this kind of scandal-mongering, the public library refused to carry the book.[11] The members of the Wolfe family themselves suffered greatly from crank telephone calls and, much more offensive, from words of sympathy offered by well-meaning friends. They sensed a current of resentment from the townspeople in general. Mabel, the only younger member of the immediate family then living in Asheville, felt her social standing sink when she arose before an unsmiling group at the next meeting of the ladies' club to read her Secretary's Report.

Wolfe's reports of the abusive and even threatening letters that he received are well-known from his fictional account in *You Can't Go Home Again* and from *The Story of a Novel,* where he describes the gem of the lot: "One venerable old lady, whom I had known all my life, wrote me that although she had never believed in lynch law, she would do nothing to prevent a mob from dragging my 'big overgrown karkus' across the public square." [12] But the indignation was not merely local. The book was regarded in many quarters of the South as a "bitter attack" on the whole region. Jonathan Daniels in the *Raleigh News and Observer* at the state capital denounced it: North Carolina and the South had been "spat upon." [13]

Although some of the consequences of the appearance of *Look Homeward, Angel* in Asheville were amusing and some were trivial, others were serious, even cruel. Wolfe wounded his beloved teacher, Mrs. Roberts, by portraying her husband as a bully and a pedant. Mrs. Roberts' first letter to Wolfe about the book closed with the accusation, "You have crucified your family and devastated mine." [14] Many blows fell on persons outside the circle of Wolfe's immediate attachments. One letter, written as late as 1935, shows the far-reaching effect of *Look Homeward, Angel* on the reputation of the woman Wolfe had portrayed as W. O. Gant's mistress, Mrs. Selbourne:

Dear Tom

I'm honest in saying your Look Homeward Angel is breaking my heart and those who are dearest to me, and I'm appealing to you to use that unusual brain and mind of yours to correct or undo some of the damage that has been done, for contrary to your assertion that I am not the Mrs. Selbourne portrayed in your book, people think I am, and I'm being crucified daily. To show you how insidious and far reaching the hurt is, two weeks ago a very dear friend of our family was sitting in the lobby of the Ponce de Leon hotel in Roanoke, Va. and overheard two men talking about your book and my supposed important part in it. The man who was doing the talking. . .said *you* had told him positively that I was the character referred to in your book and that you told him also what a notorious woman I'd been and why you used me for this character in your book.[15]

Many people whose feelings were pricked by a word or a brief description perhaps felt a momentary thrill of notoriety and then forgot about the book, for, despite the talk exchanged among Asheville citizens about law suits, no one pressed a case. The only immediate consequence was that Wolfe went into voluntary exile from his home for the next seven years. His family, who stood by him, saw him only occasionally in New York or Washington.

Whatever his apprehensions, Wolfe certainly had not foreseen that his book would create a sensation. His first concern was for his family: he telegraphed his assurance that "Great figures in novel are Eliza, Helen, Gant, and Ben. Everyone thinks they are grand people." [16] Later he wrote that "the people are like people everywhere all over the world—and it seems to me, and to Scribner's, and people who have read the book up here that on the whole they are pretty fine." [17] He pleaded his innocent intentions again and again. He wrote Mrs. Roberts with great excitement, "Will you please believe me when I tell you sincerely and earnestly that when I began this book in London, and finished it in New York, I shaped and created its reality from within: my *own* world, my *own* figures, my *own* events shaped themselves into my *own* fable there on the page before me, and that I spent no time in thinking of actual Smiths, Joneses, or Browns; nor do I see yet how such a thing is possible." [18]

In spite of his protests, Wolfe was not telling the whole truth. He had admitted in his "Notice for the Publisher's Reader" that parts of the book had been for him a catharsis. Applied to his satiric sketches, that word is a euphemism—he was really settling old scores. When Wolfe read portions of the manuscript to close friends, he would sometimes stop in the midst of a section and say with great gusto: "His real name is so-and-so. Do you know what that son of a bitch did to me once? Well, now, wait till he sees this!" [19] There is some evidence that he realized his novel contained explosive material. When he was in Europe in 1928, he cautioned Mrs. Bernstein not to allow the Robertses to see his manuscript when they called at his apartment in New York. After the novel was accepted, he began to worry about the hometown resentment so much that he removed certain vigorous thrusts here and there. He even added one paragraph (beginning "Leonard was not a bad man...") to offset his treatment of Mr. Roberts.[20] Since all his life Wolfe dealt with his enemies, real and imagined, by means of harsh satire, it is gratifying to note that he apparently achieved a purgation of hate and rancor. In an unguarded moment, he jotted down this reflection on personal satire: "One may begin by hating them, when he writes about them but as he goes on he comes to have a kind of loving tenderness for them: 'Ah, you bastard, ['] he will whisper tenderly at length, 'you bastard! What a beautiful, complete, and perfect specimen you were!'—and from the moment that he feels this, he can never hate that man again." [21]

Most of the time, however, the concern with personalities must have been unconscious—even when Wolfe revealed resentments—for there is no other answer to his protest made in a letter to Mabel: "Does anyone seriously think that a man is going to sweat blood, lose flesh, go cold and dirty, work all night, and live in a sweatshop garret for almost two years as I did, if his sole purpose is to say something mean about Smith and Jones and Brown?" [22] Thus Wolfe was more innocent than much of the evidence seems to show. Further, he had no idea that his little blaze could grow to prairie-fire proportions; he thought his book might be read by a dozen Asheville citizens, and he hoped that his family and close friends would offer understanding. His life was soured when one of his old friends from Asheville and Chapel Hill revealed cheerfully the way the book was being read: "I read 'Look Homeward Angel' with a great deal of pleasure because you certainly gave the real low down on some of the birds around here. Honestly your description of them and their true make-ups fits like a glove. I was rather uneasy, while reading it, that you were going to hop on me. . . ." [23]

The Asheville uproar provoked Wolfe into a hair-splitting defense of his method. In his letter to Mrs. Roberts he tried to articulate how it differed from close reporting (although he failed to answer her charge of needless wounding). He described his creative process— his impressions, selected and altered by time, are reshaped in his mind just before they take on new life in a fictional world:

. . .here it is indicated in outline: that all creation is to me fabulous, that the world of my creation is a fabulous world, that experience comes into me from all points, is digested and absorbed into me until it becomes a part of me, and that the world I create is *always inside* me, and never *outside* me, and that what reality I can give to what I create comes only from *within*. Its relation to actual experience I have never denied, but every thinking person knows that such a relation is inevitable, and could not be avoided unless men lived in a vacuum. [24]

Thus such a character as Eugene Gant at Pulpit Hill is quite different from the happy-go-lucky Tom Wolfe at Chapel Hill, and Ben, the dark, brooding, tortured brother of Eugene, is a fictional interpretation of Ben Wolfe, the quiet, kindly brother of Tom. But if characters and events took on a poetic reality for him that was quite distinct from the original characters and events, another trouble arose for unlucky Ashevillians. Wolfe introduced fictional elements into the lives of his characters but still allowed recognizable traits of real persons to remain.

For the rest of his career, Wolfe continued to answer attacks on his use of autobiographical material. He defended himself in lectures, in prefaces, in letters, and in his long essay, *The Story of a Novel*. He knew that most good writers of the previous hundred years made use of their experience in their work, but he failed to make distinctions between literal transcription and imaginative fusion of facts. In one statement in a letter to Julian Meade (a young man preparing articles about Wolfe and other contemporary writers), he pointed back to his "Studies in the Romantic Poets" at Harvard, where Professor Lowes demonstrated Coleridge's poetic process and gave Wolfe theoretical backing as an autobiographical writer:

But I want to repeat that nowhere can you escape autobiography whenever you come to anything that has any real or lasting value in letters. For example, as I walk around my room in the act of dictating this letter the first book my eye falls on is called "The Road to Xanadu" . . . . Professor Lowes has managed to track down almost all of the obscure and bewilderingly manifold elements which had gone into the making of "The Ancient Mariner." He knew . . . that Coleridge was an enormous reader, that he literally read almost everything, and Lowes, by plowing through ten thousand forgotten and obscure books, has managed to show where almost every line, every image, every sentence in "The Ancient Mariner" comes from. . . .

Now what is this, Meade, except the most direct and natural use of autobiography, and how could Coleridge have written differently from the way he did write, and how could Joyce have written differently from the way he wrote, and how could Proust have written differently from the way he wrote: Coleridge's experiences came mainly from the pages of books and Joseph Conrad's experiences came mainly from the decks of ships, but can anyone tell you that one form of experience is less real and less personal than another. . . ? [25]

By the time he wrote *The Story of a Novel,* Wolfe admitted that his zeal for confessional reality had limited him. When an author bases a character on a living person, the external details are unimportant, he told his audience, but "the young writer chained to fact and to his own inexperience, as yet unliberated by maturity, is likely to argue, 'She must be described as coming from Kentucky because that is where she actually did come from.' " [26] Until 1936, then, there are almost no instances in which Wolfe did not put recognizable tags on a character, whether all the character's actions were true to the original or not. Only gradually did he begin to disguise his models or to create figures of his own designing.

II

During the months following publication, Wolfe was the victim of the badgering that often harries new authors. Women's clubs invited him to speak; and despite his dread of club-woman chatter, he accepted because he was told it would help the sale of his book. Smaller, more intimate groups invited him to dinner, and after hours of social chit-chat, he was expected to autograph books for the company. At other, more sophisticated gatherings where prohibition gin flowed freely, he did his best to oblige young New York socialites who wished to add one more author to their list of conquests. A few private invitations to dinner ended in bed. His notes for a fictional episode indicate that during one discussion of his book a wealthy matron cried, "I wept over it and I wanted to be some part of it," and then flung herself into his arms.[27] Wolfe began to feel more like a well-advertised product than a man. He complained to Mabel, "People have almost driven me mad—the telephone rings twenty times a day, and it's someone I don't know, or don't want to know, or met once, or who knows someone who knows me. In addition, I get dozens of letters—invitations to speak, dine, write." [28]

At literary parties, amid guests from the world of writing, publishing, and theatrical producing, he was not forced to be the center of attention, of course, but he was irked by the literary shop talk and repelled by the pretentious name-dropping, " 'Alfred Lunt was telling me' (O casually)." [29] Though his shy nature sometimes kept him in the background, at other times drink made him dogmatic and voluble. If he were insulted by some polite jibe, his bull-like bellow in reply was anything but apt. On one such occasion when the drawing-room criticism was annoying Wolfe, an acquaintance asserted that he could write better than either Wolfe or Hemingway. In his notebook (which contains a synopsis of the whole evening in a drunken scrawl) Wolfe recorded his pitiful retort: "You could do nothing—you're nothing but a dirty little [— —?] fellow—I know what you are." [30]

Wolfe soon found that he did not fit into New York literary life, and his brief career as a celebrity seemed to him very cheap indeed. He began to refuse invitations and to resume his old routine of teaching and writing. As he recovered from the fevered excitement of his ride on the literary skyrocket, he recorded in his notebook in January: "I notice during the last week or two that I have quit coughing. The terrific nervous tension has quieted since Christmas—I am probably smoking far less." [31] He now broke free of his teaching load at New York University in order to get more work done on his second novel. He corrected his final batch of freshman themes and resigned his instructorship permanently. Mr. Perkins aided him in applying for a Guggenheim fellowship, and in March the Guggenheim Foundation awarded him a fellowship of $2500.

Wolfe planned to go abroad not only to escape the New York literary scene but also to make another determined effort to sever his relations with Mrs. Bernstein. He had tried to break away when he had finished "O Lost" in 1928. After their frequent quarrels that spring, he had gone to Europe, but his long, tortured letters confessed his continuing attachment. This time he felt more certain he could end the jealousy and heartache that attended his life with her and, most important, could achieve a more self-centered freedom that would allow him to work. The urgency that Wolfe felt about his next book, the whirl of new excitement as a fledging author, and the struggles, the emotional tensions created in leaving Mrs. Bernstein, often put him into a state of nervousness he could scarcely control: "I am now in such a mood that the littlest things possess and harrow my soul—the small imbecile triumphs of other people give me pain, and my own no pleasure at all." [32] Grateful for deliverance, he fled to Europe in May with his ledgers under his arm, hoping to bring to order the ideas that had been tumbling in his brain for a year.

III

During the previous seven months, Wolfe's literary outlook had taken on new dimensions. His friends, the Scribner's staff, and the Scribner's authors had been lavish with their praise; and a few reviewers had compared his work with that of Balzac and Dostoevsky, of Melville and Whitman.[33] Although Wolfe had been eager to merit his newly won place, this generosity now prompted him to aspire beyond it. He hoped to enlarge his scope and to attempt an interpretation of the American spirit. As soon as he sensed this inner urgency to speak for his nation and for his whole generation, he began to think in terms of "The Great American Novel." The sale of his book to an English publisher particularly encouraged him because, during the negotiations with the representative of William Heinemann, Hugh Walpole was sending reports from New York to the English newspapers that *Look Homeward, Angel* was the brightest gleam on the American literary skyline.

Still not certain of the scheme of his second novel, Wolfe thought he might adapt the American theme to work that he had already projected—"The River People," especially one newly planned section of it entitled "The Fast Express." Nor did he intend to abandon the autobiographical method: "What I want to write now and I imagine for some time to come," he told a lecture audience in November, "comes pretty directly from direct experience—from what I have seen, felt, thought." [34] He remembered the profuse notes that he made during the European trip of 1928. When he placed his prospectus on the desk of Henry Allen Moe of the Guggenheim Foundation, he tried to articulate a theme for his material. His statement calls to mind what Robert Frost said about the conception of a poem, that "it begins with a lump in the throat, a sense of wrong, a homesickness, a loneliness. It is never a thought to begin with. It is at its best when it is a tantalizing vagueness." Wolfe wrote:

...the book has a great many things in it, but its dominant theme is again related to the theme of [*Look Homeward, Angel*]: it tries to find out why Americans are a nomad race (as this writer believes); why they are touched with a powerful and obscure homesickness wherever they go, both at home and abroad; why thousands of the young men, like this writer have prowled over Europe, looking for a door, a happy land, a home, seeking for something they have lost, perhaps racial and forgotten, and why they return here, or if they do not, carry on them the mark of exile and obscure longing. This is a hasty statement, but I hope it indicates a theme, or an emotion and experience which this writer believes in passionately because he has felt and experienced it with all his heart.[35]

Wolfe's hankering to accent things American had grown in proportion as he accumulated phrases and scenes in his pocket notebooks. Early in 1929, his idea for "The Fast Express" was only a frame around Eugene's (or Oliver's) journey North to Harvard; the train ride home after the death of his father was to conclude the section. Later that year, the train ride began to take on more significance. When Wolfe traveled to Asheville in August, he filled his notebook with descriptive phrases and crude line drawings of mountains, ravines, streams, houses, and main-street fronts of small towns. One sketch of a ramshackle house that had seen more prosperous days he entitled "This is the South." The return trip likewise supplied him with notes, but the attempts to pin down his impressions of the American landscape are then mixed with misgivings about his isolation, "Shall I ever come back to my home ever again?" [36]

On the night boat going to Boston in January, 1930, he jotted the phrase, "Of wandering forever and the earth again," which was to epitomize the theme he outlined to the Guggenheim Foundation, of men divided in their yearning to roam and to return home. He had begun to make extensive notes for a panorama of the American night scene, "from the tide winds and waters of our sleep on which a few stars sparely look" (lifting another phrase from Milton's "Lycidas"). His glance would take in "all-night lunchrooms—the taxi men—the cops—the crooks—those who wait wearily for morning trains—workmen with steel cutters and goggles—the late subways—women cleaning up office buildings," [37] sailors, police courts (he planned to use a night court story that a Harvard friend, Rollo Wayne, had recounted). More generally, he planned to stress the power and immensity of America at night as seen in night trains, newspaper printing rooms, ships at sea, waterfront cargo platforms, and river traffic, then to move from the activity of harbor and city to the stillness and silence of the American landscape, "America by Moonlight."

On his return from Boston by train, he recorded fleeting observations of the New England landscape and of passengers briefly met.

During the next few months, he filled his notebook with conversations overheard in the city, descriptions of commonplace scenes and people, impressions of spring in New York, and remembrances of the American scene viewed from train windows. He even traveled in the engineer's cab of the Boardwalk Flyer for the most immediate experience of that ever-changing phenomenon of American speed, "the fastest train in America."

Even though Wolfe sought to interpret America through his own eyes, he also began to consider the American literary tradition more closely. In January he was reading *Moby Dick*,[38] in February he lectured at New York University on "The American Novel," and before he left the country he wrote out in his notebook lists of books that he considered typical national products of Germany, of England, and of America. His American list includes "Moby Dick, Memoirs of Davy Crockett,[39] Mark Twain, Young Wild West,[40] The Scarlet Letter, Whitman, Franklin, Edwards, Mather." [41]

This American self-consciousness reached its peak during his stay in Europe in 1930. It was sometime during this year that he bought a Tauchnitz edition of *A Portrait of the Artist as a Young Man* and marked and underlined the conclusion, "I go to encounter for the millionth time the reality of experience and to forge in the smithy of my soul the uncreated conscience of my race." [42] Wolfe's preoccupation with the American theme during this year was not merely a convenient means for aggrandizing his narrative; he felt a real identification with his native land. He wrote to Perkins from Paris, "I have missed America more this time than ever: maybe it's because all my conviction, the tone and conviction of my new book is filled with this feeling, which once I would have been ashamed to admit." [43]

At Harvard, where he had adopted the attitudes of Mencken and the *Smart Set*, Wolfe once "would have been ashamed to admit" this resurgence of feeling for America. The change in position that had occurred in the meantime can be traced in his writings. Although *Welcome to Our City* and all the "Passage to England" sketches were conceived in the anti-booboisie frame of mind, Wolfe began to change his views when he revised *Welcome to Our City* in late 1925. His numerous trips to Europe over the years contributed to the change, but it was very gradual. *Look Homeward, Angel* was still in the

Mencken-Lewis vein, but much of the criticism reflected his personal revulsion at the changes wrought by "Progress" on an American town. By the time he was revising the book in 1929, he toned down one strong anti-democratic passage [44] by removing references to Eugene's hatred for "the great mongrel nation of which he was a part," "the federated Half Breeds of the world." [45] Shortly after the publication of *Look Homeword, Angel,* he told a lecture audience that he wished to celebrate the variety of America, and he directly faced up to the type of criticism being launched at American life by the *American Mercury:* "I do not believe for example that all small towns are alike. I do not believe that most business men, clergymen, and realtors are alike. I have not found what life I have known through the country standardized." [46] By now the recognition accorded his work by friends and reviewers completed the about-face he was making.

This year of Wolfe's self-dedication to the office of novelist, American style, was climaxed ironically by a tribute from one of his early literary heroes. When Sinclair Lewis, America's first Nobel prize winner, was interviewed about the award and was questioned about American writers, he told the world that Wolfe "may have a chance to be the greatest American writer. In fact, I don't see why he should not be one of the greatest world writers. His first book is so deep and spacious that it deals with the whole of American life." Later in his acceptance speech at Stockholm, as Lewis discussed the future of American literature, his catalogue of writers on whom the continuity of American letters depended included "Thomas Wolfe, a child I believe of thirty years or younger, whose one and only novel, *Look Homeward, Angel* is worthy to be compared with the *best* in our literary production, a Gargantuan creature with great gusto of life." [47] Wolfe's emergence into fame was now complete: he had been honored at America's literary triumph of the year.

During these months, then, the gradual recognition of his talents fired Wolfe's ambition to strike high. This young American, who had never in his adult life been west of the Appalachians, who had spent twenty years in North Carolina, three in Boston, and four in New York City, who yet had managed by means of his memory and a conscious quest for experience to grasp the variety of American life, now strove to celebrate his nation in these expansive rhythms:

Trains cross the continent in a swirl of dust and thunder, the leaves fly down the tracks behind them: the great trains cleave through gulch and gulley, they rumble with spoked thunder on the bridges over the powerful brown wash of mighty rivers, they toil through hills, they skirt the rough brown stubble of shorn fields, they whip past empty stations in the little towns and their great stride pounds its even pulse across America. Field and hill and lift and gulch and hollow, mountain and plain and river, a wilderness with fallen trees across it, a thicket of bedded brown and twisted undergrowth, a plain, a desert, and a plantation, a mighty landscape with no fenced niceness, an immensity of fold and convolution that can never be remembered, that can never be forgotten, that has never been described—weary with harvest, potent with every fruit and ore, the immeasurable richness embrowned with autumn, rank, crude, unharnessed, careless of scars or beauty, everlasting and magnificent, a cry, a space, an ecstasy!—American earth in old October.[48]

NOTES

1. *The Angry Decade* (New York, 1947), p. 29.

2. Basil Davenport in *Saturday Review of Literature*, VI (December 21, 1929), 584.

3. Margaret Wallace in *New York Times Book Review*, October 27, 1929, p. 7.

4. Margery Latimer in *New York Herald-Tribune Books*, November 3, 1929, p. 20.

5. "The Dandridges and the Gants," *Virginia Quarterly Review*, VI (April, 1930), 310-13.

6. PN 12, October, 1929, to January, 1930. He had met Ernest Boyd, Thomas Beer, William Rose Benét, and Robert Nathan earlier through Mrs. Bernstein.

7. HCL*46AM-12(4).

8. The story has been told many times, with a varying amount of detail. See Wolfe, SN; George W. McCoy, "Asheville and Thomas Wolfe," *North Carolina Historical Review*, XXX (April, 1953), 200-17; Nowell, pp. 150-55; Wheaton, pp. 215-29; Floyd Watkins, *Thomas Wolfe's Characters* (Norman, Okla., 1957), pp. 38-45.

9. See Watkins, *Thomas Wolfe's Characters*, pp. 7-8, for a discussion of the names of Wolfe's characters.

10. One of Wolfe's supporters in the town, George McCoy, wrote him that his fiancée, Miss Love, had reviewed the book for the *Asheville Citizen* and had adopted an objective point of view, but the *Asheville Times* had emphasized the "local application" in both the daily paper and a special Sunday spread. HCL*46AM-12(4), letter dated November 1, 1929.

11. HCL*46AM-12(4), letter dated November 1, 1929, and HCL*48A-1, a recorded interview at the Library of Congress with Mrs. Mabel Wheaton. Miss Myra Champion, reference librarian and now curator of the Thomas Wolfe collection at the Pack Memorial Library, tells a story which is part of the Wolfe tradition in Asheville. About 1936 or 1937, Scott Fitzgerald asked for a copy of LHA at the library and was told, "We don't keep trash." He went out and bought a couple of

copies and persuaded the chief librarian to catalogue the book and keep it on the shelves. See also McCoy, "Asheville and Thomas Wolfe," p. 211.

12. SN, p. 571.

13. October 10, 1929.

14. HCL*46AM-11. From a fragment of Mrs. Roberts' commentary on her Wolfe letters. Her letter to Wolfe is no longer extant.

15. HCL*46AM-12(4), April 21, 1935. Since this was just after OT&R had become a best seller, it is possible that this plea was for financial reparation. Wolfe wrote a long reply in which he expressed regret for her predicament but explained that the character was really based on another woman he had known years later, and he denied even knowing the man who quoted him as authority for the statement. Still, he never mailed the letter.

16. *Letters*, p. 207.

17. LTM, p. 170.

18. *Letters*, p. 220.

19. An anecdote supplied by Henry Carlton.

20. LHA, p. 232. This is the insertion he refers to in the letter to John Hall Wheelock, July 19, 1929 (*Letters*, p. 186).

21. HCL*46AM-12(10), fragments found among correspondence.

22. *Letters*, p. 216.

23. HCL*53M-113F. Letter from S. B., November 12, 1930.

24. *Letters*, p. 220.

25. *Letters*, p. 321.

26. SN, p. 573.

27. HCL*46AM-7(30), Box 2, "October Fair" ledger.

28. *Letters*, p. 214. Wolfe fictionalized some incidents of this period in "The Lion Hunters," YCGHA, Chapter 23.

29. HCL*46AM-7(30), Box 2, "October Fair" ledger.

30. PN 12, October, 1929, to January, 1930.

31. *Ibid.*

32. PN 13, February, 1930, to May, 1930, *ca.* March 22.

33. In fact, Wolfe's friendship with Robert Raynolds began after the glowing review in *Scribner's Magazine*, LXXXVI (December, 1929), 2, in which Raynolds associated him with Melville and Whitman.

34. PN 12, October, 1929, to January, 1930, from notes for a talk at the [Carl?] Club, *ca.* November 19.

35. *Letters*, p. 212.

36. PN 11, June 11 to October 15, 1929.

37. PN 12, October, 1929, to January, 1930.

38. *Ibid.*, notebook entry: "Melville—there is an island in every man's soul—let him beware, etc.," a reference to the conclusion of Chapter 58.

39. A reference to *A Narrative of the Life of David Crockett of the State of Tennessee* and other Crockett narratives edited by Hamlin Garland for Scribner's Modern Student's Library. A well-thumbed copy is in Wolfe's personal library, HCL*46A-234. He was interested in the Crockett legends, of course, because Crockett was his great-great-great uncle by marriage.

40. The dime-novel series by that name.

41. PN 13, February to May, 1930.

42. HCL*46A-352.

43. *Letters*, p. 238.

44. LHA, p. 516.

45. HCL*45M-156F, p. 848.

46. PN 12, October, 1929, to January, 1930, Notes for a lecture at the [Carl?] Club, *ca.* November 19, 1929.

47. *Addresses by Erik Axel Karlfeldt and Sinclair Lewis on the occasion of the award of the Nobel Prize* (New York, n.d.).

48. OT&R, p. 331.

Part IV

THE ACCUMULATION OF A SECOND NOVEL

14.

SEED TIME

WHEN *Of Time and the River* WAS PUBLISHED IN 1935, IT CAR-
ried a publisher's notice that it formed part of a larger work:

This novel is the second in a series of six of which the first four have
now been written and the first two published. The title of the whole work,
when complete, will be the same as that of the present book, "Of Time
and the River." The titles of the six books, in the order of their appearance,
together with the time plan which each follows, are:

> Look Homeward, Angel (1884-1920)
> Of Time and the River (1920-1925)
> The October Fair (1925-1928)
> The Hills Beyond Pentland (1838-1926)
> The Death of the Enemy (1928-1933)
> Pacific End (1791-1884)

This hexology, which was to depict American life from the early
Federalist days to the twentieth-century-depression years, would
present a family chronicle, a personal narrative, and the history of
an artist's development, as well as an interpretation of American life
and an anthology of dithyrambic statements about man and his
destiny. Wolfe planned to end on a note of triumph—the artist overcoming his problems and America looking to a hopeful future, both
artist and country vigorous because of an active spirit that would not
cease to struggle against defeat.

After the publication of the second volume, Wolfe abandoned the
scheme for a complication of reasons. But every reader of Wolfe's
posthumously published books realizes that the story of George
Webber's love affair with Esther Jack in *The Web and the Rock* is
reworked from his proposed Volume III, "The October Fair," and
the same reader may guess that portions of George Webber's re-

orientation about life, love, fame, creative activity, suffering, and social justice in *You Can't Go Home Again* were originally planned for Volume V, "The Death of the Enemy." In Volume IV, "The Hills Beyond Pentland," Wolfe planned to include not only some stories about Eugene's forebears but also Eugene's further memories of his boyhood. Most of what he had written went into *The Web of Earth*, into "The Four Lost Men," and into the first half of *The Web and the Rock*. Volume VI, "Pacific End," [1] was probably to open with the arrival of the first Pentland in America and was to continue the Pentland story, including the early history of Eugene's paternal ancestors, up through the early life of W. O. Gant. Thus literary historians have not been wrong to discuss the later adventures of Eugene Gant and George Webber as one continuous narrative (in spite of the unfinished state of the posthumous volumes), for they developed from the plans for one book.

This gigantic scheme was projected between May, 1930, when Wolfe went abroad on the Guggenheim fellowship, and March, 1935, when the publisher's notice appeared. What Wolfe tentatively called "The October Fair" in his application to the Guggenheim foundation gradually took on the proportions of five huge volumes. Thus, to follow Wolfe's work on his second novel will be to watch the development of not only *Of Time and the River* but the whole proposed series of books.

When Wolfe arrived in Europe in 1930, he settled in Paris and began to go over the manuscript sheets, ledgers, and pocket notebooks that were the repositories of his ideas during the previous year or two. As the scope of his work expanded, outlines and notes multiplied. On May 28 he jotted down three narrative themes that later were more or less divided among three parts of his proposed series, *Of Time and the River*, "The October Fair," and "Death of the Enemy," themes of hunger for knowledge and experience, of love, and of affirmation:

Man is a measure, *the* measure, not of all things but of himself. He may quest far, and the scope of his apprehension, the amount of his foreknowledge can be enormous. But he can not know all nor see all. The only infinite, the only insatiable thing in man is hunger and desire, that is unending and everlasting and it steeps him in his deepest hell. But it is also the greatest thing in him: it is the demon that can possess him, and that may destroy him [.]

Love is the only triumph over life and death and living; over hunger and desire. Love begins as madness and disease: it can end as health and beauty.

The eternal coward is with us yet, is with us always. It is necessary to affirm rather than to deny, and love is the supreme belief, the final affirmation.[2]

These themes were added to his general intention to celebrate America and to represent the opposing impulses of "wandering and return" that he found characteristic of Americans. Further, he planned to insert one central theme: the search for certainty and authority as expressed by a symbolic search for a father, an idea inadvertently suggested by Maxwell Perkins.[3] Although this theme runs intermittently through *Of Time and the River*, it is uncertain whether the quest would have had an ending on more than one level—that is, whether the outcome for Eugene would have been the discovery of a father substitute, a Perkins-like editor, or whether the answer would have been found only in death, as the death of W. O. Gant in *Of Time and the River* seems to indicate. In reality, Wolfe did look upon Perkins as a sort of spiritual father. Even before he began to call Perkins by his first name, he wrote this tribute in a 1929 Christmas Eve letter: "Young men sometimes believe in the existence of heroic figures, stronger and wiser than themselves, to whom they can turn for an answer to all their vexations and grief. Later, they must discover that such answers have to come out of their own hearts; but the powerful desire to believe in such figures persists. You are for me such a figure: you are one of the rocks to which my life is anchored." [4]

Numerous other motifs are introduced here and there by means of symbols as well as situations. In *Of Time and the River*, Wolfe's vitalistic view of the world, which runs as a current through all his work, is represented by many references to the seasons, to plant growth, and to the power and goodness of life itself. Opposing this view is the city, which represents the materialistic strangulation of life, and the Harvard Playshop and the American expatriates, both of which represent the retreat from vigorous art into an empty aestheticism. A few other symbols are dominant: the river stands for the flow of time, while the sea and the earth represent the opposition of wandering and return as well as male and female forces. "By 'the earth again,'" he wrote Perkins, "I mean simply the everlasting earth, a home, a place for the heart to come to, and earthly mortal love, the love of a woman, who, it seems to me [,] belongs to the earth and is a force opposed to that other great force that makes men wander, that makes them search, that makes them lonely, and that makes them both hate and love their loneliness." [5]

Note how many of his themes Wolfe is able to blend into the proem to *Of Time and the River,* a lyrical preface which he began to compose in the summer of 1930. Here the tones of Ecclesiastes are given a triumphal ring as Wolfe assesses man's participation in the immortal vitality of the Life Principle. "Love" in this statement represents not only communication and passion but the Life Urge itself.

. . .of wandering forever and the earth again. . .of seed-time, bloom, and the mellow-dropping harvest. And of the big flowers, the rich flowers, the strange unknown flowers.

Where shall the weary rest? When shall the lonely of heart come home? What doors are open for the wanderer? And which of us shall find his father, know his face, and in what place, and in what time, and in what land? Where? Where the weary of heart can abide forever, where the weary of wandering can find peace, where the tumult, the fever, and the fret shall be forever stilled.

Who owns the earth? Did we want the earth that we should wander on it? Did we need the earth that we were never still upon it? Whoever needs the earth shall have the earth: he shall be still upon it, he shall rest within a little place, he shall dwell in one small room forever.

Did he feel the need of a thousand tongues that he sought thus through the moil and horror of a thousand furious streets? He shall need a tongue no longer, he shall need no tongue for silence and the earth: he shall speak no word through the rooted lips, the snake's cold eye will peer for him through sockets of the brain, there will be no cry out of the heart where wells the vine.

The tarantula is crawling through the rotted oak, the adder lisps against the breast, cups fall: but the earth will endure forever. The flower of love is living in the wilderness, and the elmroot threads the bones of buried lovers.

The dead tongue withers and the dead heart rots, blind mouths crawl tunnels through the buried flesh, but the earth will endure forever; hair grows like April on the buried breast and from the sockets of the brain the death flowers grow and will not perish.

O flower of love whose strong lips drink us downward into death, in all things far and fleeting, enchantress of our twenty thousand days, the brain will madden and the heart be twisted, broken by her kiss, but glory, glory, glory, she remains: Immortal love, alone and aching in the wilderness, we cried to you: You were not absent from our loneliness.

For the basic narrative stuff of his novel series, Wolfe clung to the material of his own life and observation, but at the outset he hoped his future work would be far less self-centered than his first effort. Although he partially achieved this aim, his plan for the work went through innumerable changes before he returned at last to a continuation of Eugene Gant's life story. As he worried through these many alterations in plan, he generated almost all the remaining work of his career.

Once before Wolfe had struggled without success to produce a second novel; he had wandered around Europe filling his notebook but, for the most part, writing little ordered narrative. In the spring of 1929, he had begun to think about "The River People" again and, led somewhat astray by the autobiographical character who played a part in the story, he planned the section called "The Fast Express." In his outline at this time he included several episodes he had written earlier for Eugene Gant's years in Boston:

THE FAST EXPRESS

Make it (this whole section) about 60000-80000 words long—end it with the talk between the two women (Helen and Eliza)

Outline

1. Meeting at Twilight [6]
2. Eugene's fantasies and life in Boston [7]
3. Emerson Pentland, and all the other Pentlands.
4. The Girl in Medford
5. Promenade of Mr. E. G. Faust
6. Gant's Death
7. The Fast Express
8. The Two Women [8]

For his train episode he not only made the profuse notes on the American scene but he occasionally jotted down passenger sketches, lines from old American songs to be sung on the train, and rhythmic chants of his own to represent the pounding train wheels.

In May he began to make notes for the story of his love affair with Mrs. Bernstein, a book he proposed to call "Faust and Helen." According to one note, the train material was apparently transferred to this book:

FAUST AND HELEN

Book I   The "Story"
Book II   Faust and Helen
Book III   The Fast Express [9]

In June he considered a book about his wanderings in Europe, to be titled "Oktoberfest" or "The October Fair," and later he toyed with the idea of a book about Mrs. Bernstein's early life, based on the thousand stories she had told him about her childhood and her fabulous father, the actor Joseph Frankau. At the end of his notebook, he made this optimistic summary of his projects:

Books written or Planned
Look Homeward Angel   Pub when I was 28
29 The Oktoberfest
30 Faust and Helen
31 The River People
33 A Woman's Life [10]

Wolfe's numerous changes in plan during the summer can best be summarized by noting that by August, 1929, he had made two decisions: he had abandoned Joel Pierce's love story as the main plot of "The River People" and he had decided to lump together all his various projects into one book, "The October Fair." He listed, in a great many scenes, some of his memories from the previous nine years that he wished to include:

Narrative episodes in The October Fair (each must be made as good as possible)
1 Nearing land (invocation to Earth) Mrs. Kerr and the land—Plymouth harbour—"Well, here we are"— the sea gulls—Eugene and the Cockney embrace each other in their joy.[11]
2 On the train—the race outside of Elizabeth—all the train scene.[12]
3 The hospital—child-birth.
4 Joel Pierce on Mrs. Annster's water closet.
5 The German girl.[13]

6 Meeting Irene on the boat.[14]
7 The woman in the 6th Avenue market.[15]
8 The tubercular—Diabetic—the night scene in the 11th St.[16]
9 The visit of Abraham Jones to 11th Street.
10 The party in 11th St. (the instructors and the girls).[17]
11 Building Irene's house—Mr. Milesend (Landsend).[18]
12 The literary party at P. Moeller's.
13 The week-end at Chartres.[19]
14 The New Year's Dance at Webster Hall.[20]
15 The summer in Maine.
16 The cottage in the Lake District.[21]
17 Wertheim's lunch at Ye Olde Cocke Taverne.[22]
18 Irene and Gene in Philadelphia—in Boston.
19 A walk, a talk, a visit from Varney.[23]
20 McKee his French mistress and Dorothy.
21 Luke and the girl he loved too late. (the New York visit, etc) [24]

This notation shows the scattered fashion in which Wolfe was to work from 1930 through 1931. In writing most of *Look Homeward, Angel* he had maintained a steady chronological progression, but for his second book he took up episodes, first from one area of his work, then another, as they interested him; he moved from one characterization to another and then back again as new ideas struck his fancy; he partially developed one group of notes, then dropped it for another, as the pressure of time seemed to direct him. This indecision gripped Wolfe because the experience he was drawing upon was fresh in his memory and almost beyond his selective powers. Furthermore, while this list of narrative episodes is one example of the diversity of scene and character that he hoped to synthesize, his pocket notebooks teem with others. His memory-aids thus complicated his difficulty.

In his attempt to control the mass of material, Wolfe deliberated carefully over the simplest technical devices. One of his first problems was choice of a central character. He wished to employ an autobiographical character whose experience, like his own, could provide some commentary on life as he moved amidst the great variety of the American scene to tell his story, yet Wolfe also wished to smother reviewers' charges that what he had again produced was a simple autobiographical record. As a result, he relinquished Eugene Gant in favor of a character who was more indirectly a fictional self, a new creation named David Hawke. "I have made him out of the *inside* of me," he wrote Perkins, "of what I believed the inside was like: he is about five feet nine, with the long arms and prowl of an ape, and a little angel in his face—he is part beast, part spirit— a mixture of the ape and the angel. There is a touch of the monster in him. But no matter about this—at first he is the bard and, I pray God, that is what I can be." [25]

Later in the year Wolfe, giving him the nickname "Monkey" Hawke, conceived a whole characteristic childhood for him, including acrobatic adeptness and the desire to join a circus. During the process of this development, Wolfe accumulated myriad notes about David. Some were to be used; others, such as this list of David's fantasies of wealth and fame, were meant merely to surround David with so much detail that Wolfe himself could feel he was real:

The Real Things You Wanted

To Be a Great Athlete (Baseball, Football,
    Boxing, etc.)
To Rescue Beautiful Women
To Be Desired by Rich Men's Wives
To Be an Engineer
To Be a Soldier
To Be Famous
To Discover Gold
To Lie with Miss Lindquist
To Be a Hobo
To Save People from Fires
To Run a Restaurant ("Monkey" Hawke's Place)
To Go with a circus
To Make Money out of hot dogs, etc.[26]

Readers of Wolfe's posthumous books will recognize that, although David Hawke never made his way into *Of Time and the River,* he appeared under the name George Webber in the huge manuscript Wolfe was working on at the time of his death.

What narrative point of view should govern the new book was another important question, though Wolfe considered it only briefly. He flirted with the idea of the "interested observer" ("I knew David. We were both born in Altamont and we had known each other from childhood"),[27] but he cast aside this, his best opportunity to exploit the divided self he described to Perkins, taking instead the first-person point of view. Although the notes and drafts which had accumulated in the preceding two years are, like *Look Homeward, Angel,* in the third person, all the materials for the next three-year period are written in the first person. Only late in 1933, when Wolfe and Perkins revived Eugene Gant and his family, did the chronicle assume the third-person point of view again.

Wolfe also tried to use myth and legend to give shape and meaning to his narrative. He had not experimented with this method on such large scale since his Harvard days, when he had worked with H. G. Wells's Job story, *The Undying Fire.* His reference to the Faust legend now, in titles and chapter headings, carried an intense personal meaning for him. As far back as his furious European trip of 1928, Wolfe had recognized in Faust the symbol of his own youthful spirit seeking to devour the whole of culture and experience. When he wrote back to Mrs. Bernstein that he had seen *Faust* at the Burg-theater in Vienna, he reported the effect the performance had upon him: "Faust's own problem touches me more than Hamlet's—his problem is mine, it is the problem of modern life. He wants to know everything, to be a God—and he is caught in the terrible net of human incapacity." [28] From this time on he alluded to Faust when he wished to refer to the inordinate desire to see all and know all. For example, on November 28, 1928, after an exhausting day in Vienna fumbling through bookshops and scrambling through museums, he recorded: "Faust business again today—too much to see—we learn restraint too slowly." [29] When *Of Time and the River* was written, the allusions to Faust in the story of Eugene Gant at Harvard made possible another dimension in characterization: Eugene took on heroic proportions.

He felt that he might suggest the story of Antaeus in the same way that Joyce made use of the wanderings of Ulysses. In one of the most enthusiastic letters he ever wrote, he explained to Perkins that he wished to preface his book with an argument in terms of the Antaeus myth:

Argument: of the Libyan giant, the brother of Polyphemus, the one-eyed, and the son of Gaea and Poseidon, whom he hath never seen, and through his father, the grandson of Cronos and Rhea whom he remembereth. He contendeth with all who seek to pass him by, he searcheth alway for his father, he crieth out: "Art thou my father? Is it thou?" And he wrestleth with that man and he riseth from each fall with strength redoubled, for his strength cometh up out of the earth, which is his mother. Then cometh against him Heracles, who contendeth with him, who discovereth the secret of his strength, who lifteth him from the earth whence his might ariseth, and subdueth him. But from afar now, in his agony, he heareth the sound of his father's foot: he will be saved for his father cometh!

Now don't get alarmed at all this and think I'm writing a Greek myth. All of this is never mentioned once the story gets underway, but it is a magnificent fable, and I have soaked myself in it over a year now: it says what I want to say, and it gives the most magnificent plot and unity to my book. The only other way in which the Antaeus legend is mentioned directly is in the titles to the various parts which are tentatively at present 1) Antaeus, 2) Heracles, (or Faust and Helen), 3) Poseidon.

To give you the key to all these symbols and the people—Antaeus, of course, is a real person, he is in me but he is *not* me as the fellow in the first book was supposed to be—he is to me what Hamlet or Faust may have been to their authors—thank God, I have begun to create in the way I want to—it is more completely *autobiographic* than anything I ever thought of, much *more* than the first one—but it is also completely *fictitious* —nobody can identify me with Antaeus—whose real name is David Hawke, but who is called Monkey Hawke—except to say, "He has put himself into this character." It is a magnificent story, it makes use of all the things I have seen and known about, and it is like a fable—the other symbols are: Heracles, who is the City; Poseidon, who is the Sea, eternal wandering, eternal change, eternal movement—but who is also a real person (*never* called Poseidon) of course, the father of Monkey Hawke, whom he has never seen and whom, I have decided, he shall never see, but who is near him at the end of the book, and who saves him (the idea that hangs over the book from the first to last is that every man is searching for his father)....[30]

In spite of the ingenuous tone of this outburst, this was one of the best solutions Wolfe ever devised for his problem of organization. Almost none of his works have plot in the conventional sense of a limited sequence of incidents, having a definite center of interest, developed through conflict to climax and denouement. When they do achieve form, they have a thematic pattern which, consciously or unconsciously, Wolfe has been able to arrange. In adopting a myth or legend he would not only have gained in meaning, in complexity, and in richness of association but he would have found the ordinary sequence of a plot line already ordered for him. For this book, the Antaeus myth itself would have provided, besides plot organization and conflict, many appropriate possibilities for symbolism: the central character, displaying the power and appetite of a giant, reflecting his heritage of continual wandering, regaining his strength with each return home, corresponds to Antaeus; his opposition to the city constitutes the struggle with Heracles; and his friend and enemy, Starwick, represents one of the aspects of Polyphemus, "the principle of sterility that hates life—i.e. wastelanderism, futilityism, one-eyedism." [31] But Wolfe abandoned the idea. In so doing he let slip an unequaled opportunity to control the burden of detail that his experience and memory thrust upon him.

In the end, however, Wolfe did make some haphazard use of mythical allusion in *Of Time and the River*. The titles of the eight sections ask us to compare Eugene with Orestes, Faust, Telemachus, Antaeus, and other heroic figures. A few of the titles had their place in Wolfe's plans for later volumes, one or two were vestiges of earlier ideas, some were merely last-minute labels. As a consequence, the success of the device varies. Wolfe's characterization of Eugene as Telemachus or Faust draws strength from the truths of ancient myth and modern legend, but his attempt to give Eugene's adventures with the countess some association with the Antaeus myth becomes only academic pretense.

During the first months of concentrated work on his second novel, Wolfe thus fattened a book which was very little like the published volume of 1935. But these glimpses of some of the shifts in plan not only dramatize Wolfe's creative problem but they also explain some of the features of *Of Time and the River* as it was finally published.

II

This year of the Guggenheim fellowship proved to be the most fertile of Wolfe's entire career. While at this time he cultivated the growth of the main stem (which so flourished that pruning and trimming occupied the remainder of his days), he also developed among his notebooks and ledgers an incredible profusion of seedlings for future episodes and stories. Since he felt some responsibility to attempt a distinctly "American" novel, he also conceived during this year an idea that gave him some feeling of surety about his capabilities, a feeling that his own experience was adequate to provide material for the task. He told Perkins:

My conviction is that a native has the whole consciousness of his people and nation in him—that he knows everything about it—every sight and sound and memory of the people—don't get worried: I think this is going to be all right—you see, I *know* now past any denial, that *that* is what being an American or being anything means: it is not a government, or the Revolutionary War or the Monroe Doctrine—it is the ten million seconds and moments of your life—the shapes you see, the sounds you hear, the food you eat, the colour and texture of the earth you live on.[32]

He would probably have qualified his statement to say that only a very few, himself included, could ever communicate this sense of being an American because only a few could look within themselves carefully enough. This idea of "racial memory" that Wolfe blurted to Perkins, a further development of his notion that life is an accumulation of moments, is not scientifically sound, or even original, but for Wolfe an instinctive assumption such as this was important because he held it with an emotional conviction strong enough to lend force to his rendering of the American scene.

During this time abroad, Wolfe's emotional state was so keyed that most of his flights of prose-poetry come from that year. Having dashed phrases into his notebook, he reworked them into prose lyrics during the summer, employing Biblical phrasing and parallelism on a large scale. The style grew out of his Bible reading. He was "soaking in it," he told Perkins. "...it is the most magnificent book that was ever written....It is richer and grander than Shakespeare even, and everything else looks sick beside it: in the last three days I have read Ecclesiastes and the Song of Solomon several times: they belong to the mightiest poetry that was ever written—and the narrative passages in the Old Testament—stories like the life of King David, Ruth and Boaz, Esther and Ahasuerus, etc.—make the narrative style of any modern novelist look puny." [33] These notebook phrases grew into the passages, "He wakes at morning in a foreign land," "Long, long, into the night I lay, thinking how I should tell my story" (Esther Jack's theme), "October is the richest of the seasons" (Wolfe's Ode to Autumn), "Play us a tune on an unbroken spinet" (a consideration of the unchanging minutiae of human life), "The time that is lovely" (a celebration of an earlier America),

"Whoever builds a bridge across this earth," and many others. Of the scores of other phrases, outlines, and digressions in notebooks large and small which grew later into scenes and characterizations scattered through his later work, we can only glance at a few as we follow Wolfe's progress on his book.

When Wolfe arrived in Paris on May 19, 1930, he began his task immediately by buying the same kind of accounting ledgers that contained the final draft of *Look Homeward, Angel.* By June he was jogging along at a pace of five or six hours of writing a day. After some preliminary fussing with his notes and plans, he began a new ledger with a statement of self-dedication:

This book started in Paris June 6, 1930, from notes and fragments which have been collecting for two years. Now I hope with all my heart for courage and strength enough to see it through to its end, on paper as it is in my spirit, to make it as good as I can, and to do it day by day no matter where I am, no matter what despair or loneliness I may feel and at no matter what cost of flesh or blood or spirit.[34]

Having played all spring at titles, section headings, chapter names, and quotations (a game he never tired of), he now set up one of his title pages:

The October Fair
by
Thomas Wolfe

"I am a little world made cunningly
Of elements and an angelike sprite"

To

Maxwell Evarts Perkins

"I pass like night from land to land
I have strange power of speech
The moment that his face I see,
I know the man that must hear me
To him my tale I teach."[35]

"The October Fair," as Wolfe planned it at the time, seems to have this narrative sequence: David Hawke on board ship contemplates his return to America in a series of visions demonstrating the variety and movement of American life; he meets Esther Jacobs[36] on board ship and falls in love. After they arrive in New York, he takes a long train ride home on the Fast Express and sees "America by moonlight." He returns to New York for a long, tempestuous love affair with Esther, and following their quarrel, he wanders in Europe, has his head broken at the October Fair in Germany, and finally returns to his native land to discover a father-like character (presumably a Maxwell Perkins).

By the middle of June, Wolfe's pencil was scratching industriously. He wrote to John Hall Wheelock at Scribner's to report enthusiastically on his progress.

. . .I've just finished the first section of the first part—it is called *Antaeus*, and it is as if I had become a voice for the experience of a race: It begins, "Of wandering forever and the earth again". . .the two things that haunt us and hurt us—the eternal wandering, moving, questing, loneliness, homesickness, and the desire of the soul for home, peace, fixity, repose. . . . Well there are these scenes [of movement]—a woman talking of the river —the ever-moving river—coming through the levee at night, and of the crippled girl clinging to the limb of the oak, and of how she feels the house break loose and go with the tide, then of living on the roof top with [her man?] and the children, and of other houses and people— tragedy, pity, humor, bravery, and the great wild savagery of American nature; then the pioneer telling of "the perty little gal" he liked, but moving on because the wilderness was getting too crowded; then the hoboes waiting quietly at evening by the water tower for the coming of the fast express; then a rich American girl moving on from husband to husband, from drink to dope to opium, from white lovers to black ones, from New York to Paris to California; then the engineer at the throttle of the fast train; then a modest poor little couple from 123rd St— the woman earning [a] living by painting lampshades, the man an impractical good-for-nothing temporarily employed in a filling station— cruising in their cheap little car through Virginia and Kentucky in autumn —all filled with details of motor camps, where you can get a shack for $1.00 a night, and of the "lovely meals" out of cans—whole cost $0.36— etc.; then a schoolteacher from Ohio taking University Art Pilgrimage No. 35 writing back home "—didn't get your letter till we got to Florence. . . stayed in Prague 3 days but rained whole time we were there, so didn't get to see much, etc." Then Lee coming through Virginia in the night on his great white horse; then the skull of a pioneer in the desert, a rusted gun stock and a horse's skull; then a Harry's New York Bar American saying, "Jesus! What a country! I been back one time in seven years. That was enough. . . .Me, I'm a Frenchman. See?" But talking, talking, cursing, until he drinks himself into a stupor—then a bum, a natural wanderer who has been everywhere; then a Boston woman and her husband who have come to France to live—"Francis always felt he wanted to do a little writing....we felt the atmosphere is so much better here for that kind of thing"; then a Jew named Greenberg, who made his pile in New York and who now lives in France having changed his name to Montvert, and of course feels no homesickness at all, save what is natural to 4000 years of wandering—and more, and more, and more! [37]

This montage of the American people and the American continent that Wolfe described to Wheelock marks his first real performance in his role of American bard. The *Smart Set* attitude, critical of his native culture, which had reached its satirical peak in his castigation of Asheville in *Look Homeward, Angel*, he now rejected completely. The conversion came with powerful emotional sweep. "I am writing a book," he told Wheelock, "so filled with the most unspeakable desire, longing, and love for my own country and ten thousand things in it— that I have to laugh at times to think what the Mencken crowd and all the other crowds are going to say about it. But I can't help it—if I have ever written anything with utter conviction it is this." [38]

Wolfe did not lay aside this intention to render the qualities peculiar to America, as he had so many of his other ideas, because on this European trip he was more afflicted with nostalgia, more conscious of his American heritage, more belligerently defensive of his nation than ever before. Even though he had left New York because of "the ballyhoo, the gush, the trickery, the intrigue," he remembered the "enormous beauty" and vitality of the city as soon as he sailed.[39] On his arrival in Europe he was "one great ache of homesickness"; [40] in the drowsy air of Rouen he missed the "sharp burning oxygen of America"; [41] in Paris cafés he contended with expatriates and continentals about the virtues of his native land. During the first month, Wolfe had two literary encounters that provoked discussion of America. When Wolfe met James Boyd, one of America's finest regional and historical novelists, "we went to a nice café and drank beer[,] talked over the American soil and what we were going to do for literature." But Wolfe found an opposite attitude toward America in Scott Fitzgerald, who was revisiting Babylon this summer. He derided Wolfe's statement that Americans "were a homesick people and belonged to the earth and land we come from as much or more as any country." Francis Scott Key Fitzgerald's remark that America was not a country and that "he had no feeling for the land he came from" provided Wolfe with grounds for suspicion about him. The Americans in Paris, Wolfe wrote Perkins, "are all homesick, or past having any feeling about anything." [42]

Maxwell Perkins had asked Wolfe to look up Fitzgerald, for Perkins liked Scribner's authors to encourage one another. But the temperaments of the two American provincials differed so markedly that Fitzgerald was probably bored by Wolfe's interminable talk of himself, his loneliness, and his book, while on the other hand, Wolfe certainly felt no veneration for Fitzgerald. Wolfe sensed sham and pose in Fitzgerald, and as this description of his last glimpse of Fitzgerald in Paris indicates, he shied away from him with his customary suspicion: "I finally departed from his company at ten that night in the Ritz Bar where he was entirely surrounded by Princeton boys, all 19 years old, all drunk and all half-raw; he was carrying on a spirited conversation with them about why Joe Zinzendorff did not get taken into the triple-Gazzaza Club: I heard one of the lads say 'Joe's a good guy, Scotty, but you know he is a fellow that ain't got much background—' I thought it was time for Wolfe to depart and I did." [43] After this summer the two were never friendly but maintained only the polite acquaintance that might have been expected between two writers associated with the same publishing house.

This meeting between Fitzgerald and Wolfe came just at the time when it could represent the clash in attitude between the writers of the twenties and those of the thirties. Wolfe, who had cried "O Lost" in his first novel, was just donning his robes as American bard when he met a real spokesman of the lost generation. And Fitzgerald, distraught and struggling because of his family tragedy and his special propensity for burying himself in debt, was one member of the lost generation who never did get over the twenties. Wolfe's argument with Fitzgerald went into his mental file to be brought out again just before he died as the background for part of George Webber's statement of belief to his editor: "I do not feel that I belong to a Lost Generation, and I have never felt so. Indeed I doubt very much the existence of a Lost Generation, except insofar as every generation, groping, must be lost. Recently, however, it has occurred to me that if there is such a thing as a Lost Generation in this country, it is probably made up of those men of advanced middle age who still speak the language that was spoken before 1929, and who know no other. These men indubitably *are* lost. But I am not one of them." [44]

Although the work progressed, life in Paris presented some of the same troubles that Wolfe had left New York to avoid. His English publisher, A. S. Frere-Reeves, of Heinemann, came over to the continent to introduce Wolfe to some of the literary folk then in Paris. In this way Wolfe met Richard Aldington, Michael Arlen, and "some Left Bank People." Since he had carried his skittishness with him from New York, Wolfe must have stirred up some social discord, for the Frere-Reeves entertainment was followed by the usual Wolfe epilogue, a note of apology. Dramatizing his personal tension, Wolfe scribbled out a highly charged first draft of the apology in his notebook, complaining that "fools and cowards sense this and rush in to triumph over me." [45]

Wolfe was not served up as a tea-table celebrity as often as he had been in New York, but one encounter with a jaded New Yorker whom he had met through Mrs. Bernstein is noteworthy because it provided material for one of George Webber's experiences with the "Lion Hunters" in *You Can't Go Home Again*. Wolfe was impressed by this New York woman's invitations because of her connection by a first marriage to one of America's famous families, but he soon looked at her hospitality as a personal affront.[46] As he later wrote to Henry Volkening, "[I] went to her apt. for lunch, returned once or twice, and found that I was being paraded before a crowd of worthless people, palmed off as someone who was madly in love with her, and exhibited with a young French soda-jerker with greased hair who was on her payroll and [,] she boasted to me [,] slept with her every night (I like his bod-dy, she hoarsely whispered, I must have somebod-dy whose bod-dy I like to sleep with, etc.)." [47]

Finding life in Paris a little too much like the literary life he had fled in America, Wolfe moved on to Montreux shortly after the first of July and settled in a quiet hotel to continue his work. Distractions came here, too, in the person of Fitzgerald, who chided him for hiding himself away and who badgered him for an introduction to the shop-worn New York divorcee. After news of the ensuing complications had reverberated to America and had given Aline Bernstein knowledge of his whereabouts, Wolfe went on one of his drunken romps, which ended in his being kicked out of the hotel. Angry and disconcerted, he went to Geneva, hoping he could keep himself from diversion and from drink long enough to accomplish something worthwhile.

As he continued to write and plan, he realized more and more what an enormous task he had in hand. He received some encouragement from reading Perkins' favorite book, *War and Peace*, for there he found a largeness of scale he might adopt for his own book—scores of characters, length and variety of scene. By about the first of July he had sketched out a tentative outline of the whole book with the knowledge that each part might run to hundreds of thousands of words.

THE OCTOBER FAIR

Part I   The Fast Express
18 mos.   Book One   Antaeus
Book Two   Heracles
Book Three   The Train
Part II   Faust and Helen
Part III   The October Fair
18 mos.   Book One   The Voyage Out
Book Two   In the Dark Forest
Book Three   Oktoberfest
Book Four   Telemachus
Part IV   Telemachus
Book One   Return, Return
Book Two [48]

"I think the seething process," he wrote Perkins in mid-July, "the final set of combinations has been reached. I regret to report to you that the book will be very long, probably longer than the first one, but I think that each of its four parts makes a story in itself, and if good enough, might be printed as such." [49]

Although he was generally sure of what he wanted to do, the magnitude of his task frightened him. It is pathetic to see how much he looked to Perkins for support; in his letters he discloses plans, then either pleads for help ("Please write me and tell me if all this has meant anything to you and what you think of it") or offers concessions ("All these names are tentative and if you don't like them will get others"). If the prospect of the years and volumes ahead of him was not enough to shake the confidence of this novice to the craft of fiction, three external problems harassed him further: the torment caused by his parting from Aline Bernstein, the annoyance caused by certain English reviews of *Look Homeward, Angel,* and the worry caused by financial setbacks of members of the Wolfe family.

III

Since Wolfe complained constantly of unhappiness, loneliness, and homesickness, he seems, if he did not enjoy it, at least to have relished telling his correspondents about it. But this was his way. His distress was genuine and, at the same time, self-dramatization helped to alleviate it.

His decision to break away from Aline Bernstein was one of the most trying he had ever faced in his life. In spite of the misery her presence had recently brought him in quarrels and jealousy, his attachment to her was still strong, and he loved her more than he allowed himself to know. He wrote her only once after his arrival in Europe and then refused to answer her letters in an effort to forget her. "...I sweat and work," he told Wheelock, "it's the only cure I've found for the bloody hurting inside me." [50] After his years of companionship with Mrs. Bernstein, he felt his loneliness more acutely than ever before. But since the decision had been his, he would "choke loneliness down and eat it and make it sit easy on [his] stomach" [51] in order to accomplish the amount of work that made isolation necessary.

The second set of disturbing influences began about the same time. Bastille Day in 1930 set off no giddier behavior than Wolfe's own frenzied antics resulting from the English publication of *Look Homeward, Angel* on that day. He was always oversensitive to criticism, and he knew it. "You don't read reviews, do you?" Hemingway once asked him. "You bet I do!" was Wolfe's answer. "And if Miss Suzy Stross was writing a piece about me in the Skunktown, Ohio, Busy Bee, I'd stay up all night to get the first copy off the press." [52] Since he remembered the tension he had been under while waiting for reviews in New York, he told Frere-Reeves not to send him any reviews of the English publication. Not realizing the extent of his sensitivity, Frere-Reeves gradually sent him dozens of reviews. At first Wolfe was elated over the reception accorded his book: the sale was brisk in spite of its high price, and the reviews were very favorable. He was especially delighted by the review in the *Times Literary*

Supplement, and he forwarded it along with other clippings to Scribner's, suggesting that some quotes be used in their advertising. But the calm did not last long. His belligerence at harmless qualifications in the praise the reviewers gave him ("About these people, both in England and America, who say 'This is not a great book' or 'great art' or 'a work of genius'—I have never said it was") grew to fury when he received a bad review from Frank Swinnerton.[53] In Geneva when he received two more reviews which he interpreted as "cruel, unfair, bitterly personal," [54] all the pressure of the summer exploded. He told Perkins that he had decided to give up writing. "The English edition has been a catastrophe," he pronounced in a lengthy letter to John Hall Wheelock. "Life is not worth the pounding I have taken from both public and private sources these last two years." [55] But instead of throwing himself from an Alpine pass, he packed his gear and, going immediately to the airfield, took the first plane that was scheduled out. The thrill of his first airplane ride overcame some of his vexation of spirit, and he landed at Lyons to set to work once more.

In the last month his attempt to work methodically on his book had been a failure. He jumped from episode to episode, writing about aspects of the American scene, his diabetic friend at New York University, Esther Jacobs, the construction of Bergdorf-Goodman's, Asheville, the maternity case, Esther's father, a death in the subway, and a host of other diverse subjects. He was sick with the realization that outside concerns were preventing his control of his work. In his notebook he confided, "I am all broken up into fragments myself and all I can write is fragments. The man is his work: if the work is whole, the man must be whole." [56]

As Wolfe continued to travel in order to quell the tumult within, he moved to Marseilles, then on to Arles, then back to Geneva, and finally settled in Freiburg in the Black Forest for the last three weeks of September. Gradually he had left behind much of his distress: he could write humorously to friends about his strange conduct; he could cable Perkins "Working again excuse letter." [57]

As he had traveled, Wolfe had been able to channel his writing in more orderly fashion. It is clear that three main narratives received most of his attention during this time: the love affair of David Hawke and Esther Jacobs; Esther's early life (to which he gave the title "The Good Child's River"); and the trip on the express train (which he began to call "K 19," the number of a pullman car that ran between Asheville and New York). In Marseilles he examined his progress, trying to narrow himself to one subject: "I have started three books and written twenty or thirty thousand words on each—I *must* finish one. Which?" [58] By the time he reached Freiburg, he had decided; he set to work once again on the story of David and Esther.

At the invitation of Frere-Reeves, who said he could find Wolfe a quiet place for work, Wolfe went to England in time for his thirtieth birthday in October, and he remained there through the winter. In the weeks before and after his arrival in London, Wolfe never ceased toying with the frame of the David and Esther love story, making sure always to include David's search for his father. In one such plan David was to be an illegitimate child in search of his father. This is his chapter outline:

Chapter I   The Ship — Here the desire to find his father just beginning
Chapter II   The Native Earth (Old Catawba?) — find his father just beginning
Chapter III   Youth of Monkey Hawke — beginning
Chapter IV   The Circus— } Here begins search
Chapter V   Bitter Boston— } Father's relatives here—expediency
Chapter VI   The City— } necessity
Chapter VII   The First Voyage— } Desire— } here his father is abroad
Chapter VIII   Another Ship— } chance
Chapter IX   Capture
Chapter X   Flight } Remembers his mother, how
Chapter XI   Return } faithless she was, etc.
Chapter XII   Faust and Helen
Chapter XIII   Antaeus — In all these episodes contest
Chapter XIV   K 19 — between Esther and Father
Chapter XV   The October Fair — going on.
Chapter XVI   Telemachus [59]

In another outline, the scene is shifted back to Civil War days. Monkey Hawke seeks his father, who disappeared after the Battle of Antietam. Later he marries a Jewish woman who presents him with a beautiful daughter named Esther. But in spite of Wolfe's fanciful ideas, he always returned to the chronology of his own life whenever he did any actual writing.

Wolfe was living at this time in a lodging house at 75 Ebury Street in London. He had chosen it because of its literary association with George Moore.[60] Wolfe, well at home in a rooming house, found his surroundings, as literary material, more than he could resist. Since his narrative had developed backward into Esther's early life, as well as forward into her love affair, he digressed to make use of the residents as characters in the episodes in which Esther's aunt runs a boarding house. Two of the Ebury Street figures in particular struck his fancy. One was a Russian abortionist who, when he was not gabbling about the private lives of his patients, wrote Christmas stories; the other was the charwoman who cooked and cleaned for Wolfe while she confided to him her interests and those of her relatives. Although Dr. Bunine, as Wolfe called him, made only a brief, anonymous appearance in Wolfe's published work,[61] the charwoman who at first was intended for Esther's story became the Daisy Purvis of *You Can't Go Home Again*. It was through her that Wolfe gathered much of his information for his satire on the English class system, for as he told Perkins, he learned "her whole philosophy, which is most curious and [,] I think [,] the same as that of the poor people all over England." [62]

The depression was beginning to show its effects in England, and about the time Wolfe was beginning to hear of bread lines in America, he slowly became aware of the suffering of the English poor. ". . .I saw half naked wretches," he wrote his mother, "sitting on park benches at three in the morning in a freezing rain and sleet: often I saw a man and a woman huddled together with their arms around each other for warmth, and with sodden newspapers, rags, or anything they could find over their shoulders." [63] It was at this time that his observations swept into his memory the image of the "little gnome" of *You Can't Go Home Again*.[64] Wolfe's compassionate treatment of this boy, a modern version of Dickens' Jo, the crossing sweep, demonstrates how moved he was. As he pursued his romantic odyssey, he had scarcely ever been touched by social conditions; now his eyes began to perceive the plight of the impoverished and the unemployed all around him.

News from home brought the effect of the world-wide economic slump closer to his own life and presented him with one more worry to fret him while he struggled with his book. In November, Asheville's biggest bank, rotten with political intrigue, failed. Both city funds and individual savings were lost. This catastrophe was the climax in a series of financial reverses in the Wolfe family. Wolfe described the situation to Perkins in December:

. . .my family have suffered the most terrible calamities—they have simply been wiped out. Mabel and Ralph (that is my sister) have been sold out in Asheville, they have lost everything they had, every piece of property, every cent of money, and he has lost his job: they are at present living in Washington where he is trying to earn a $50 a week commission salary; my other sister's big family have been for the most part out of work, and my brother Fred has been struggling to keep them up. In addition he has had to quit his job because there is no business—things in the South are in a horrible hell of a shape.[65]

Wolfe did what he thought best by borrowing five hundred dollars from Scribner's to send to Fred, but he had so little knowledge of his own finances that he could do no more.

When we consider these distractions, we must admire Wolfe's progress with his book, for during most of this period he toiled along with solid day-after-day application. Probably his homesickness, after four or five months away, provided the proper emotional state for his work, because during this siege of "sodden weather" in England he wrote some of the most eloquent catalogues of the American scene that are found in *Of Time and the River.* In one letter written to Perkins in December, Wolfe gives evidence of the Whitmanesque sweep that he was attempting. After presenting his idea for the Antaeus myth, he goes on to describe an experiment he has just completed, a chant which he later published separately under the title, "The Names of the Nation": [66]

"Cronos and Rhea" occurs on board an Atlantic liner—all the Americans returning home—and the whole intolerable memory of exile and nostalgia comes with it: it begins like a chant—first the smashing enormous music of the American names—first the names of the States—California, Texas, Oregon, Nebraska, Idaho, and the two Dakotas—then the names of the Indian tribes—the Pawnees, the Cherokees, the Seminoles, the Penobscots, the Tuscaroras, etc.—then the names of the railways—the Pennsylvania, the Baltimore and Ohio, the Great Northwestern, the Rock Island, the Santa Fe, etc.—then the names of the railway millionaires—the Vanderbilts, the Astors, the Harrimans; then the names of the great hoboes—Oakland Red, Fargo Pete, Dixie Joe, Iron Mike, Nigger Dick, the Jersey Dutchman, etc. (the names of some of the great wanderers i.e.)—then the great names of the rivers (the rivers and the sea standing for movement and wandering against the fixity of the earth):—the Monongahela, the Rappahannock, the Colorado, the Tennessee, the Rio Grande, the Missouri—when I get to the Mississippi I start the first of the stories of wandering and return—the woman floating down the river with her husband in flood time tells it. It is good—the whole thing is this pattern of memory and nostalgia...[Goes on about the Antaeus myth].

I don't know whether you can make anything out of this or not—it is 10:30 o'clock, I have worked all night. As I finish this in the morning of Tues. Dec. 9, there is a fog outside that you can cut, you can't see across the street, I am dog tired—I want to come home when I have this thing by the well known balls—write me if you think it's a good idea, but say nothing to anyone.[67]

If Wolfe wished to remain in Europe until he had the proper grip on his book, he might have stayed there until 1935, for although he worked steadily, he digressed often. Finally, toward the end of winter, he gathered his ledgers together and returned to America to talk over his problems with Perkins. Maxwell Perkins was decidedly pleased with the advance in power evident in some of the material Wolfe showed him, but he was apprehensive of the way Wolfe had scattered his energies during the year. As usual, Perkins encouraged Wolfe, and his advice cut some of the cords that Wolfe had knotted around himself. They agreed optimistically that the job could be finished with another six months of work.

In order to proceed with his writing undisturbed and in order to avoid seeing Mrs. Bernstein, Wolfe established himself in rooms in a quiet section of Brooklyn—at 40 Verandah Place, one of two rooming houses owned by Marjorie Dorman, a young woman who had formerly been a reporter for the *Brooklyn Eagle*. Soon, however, Mrs. Bernstein sought him out, and she confronted him several times in his Brooklyn apartment. Because Wolfe was determined to remain free of entanglement, there were violent scenes, with a painful amount of shouting and weeping. If Wolfe thought that Aline Bernstein was only playing with her emotions when she threatened to kill herself, he found out she meant what she said. One night in March, after talking with Wolfe and Perkins, she tried to commit suicide and very nearly succeeded.[68] Her fictional account of her recovery of the will to live is in the final chapter of her novel, *The Journey Down*. Naturally, Wolfe was horrified and remorseful at the catastrophic results of his decision. He visited her in the hospital, where she remained for some time, but they did not return to their old relationship after her recovery. The near-tragic turn of events was probably responsible for Wolfe's going back once more, in a gesture of expiation, to his story of Esther Jacobs' early life, the part of "The October Fair" called "The Good Child's River." From the source of his happiness and his misery, he wrought the most vigorous character in his later writing. Esther became the child, the woman, the mother, "the bringer of hope, the teller of good news," with her flowerlike face, with her "rich, full-throated woman's yell of laughter." As the material developed she became the good genius of Eugene Gant-George Webber.

Since the narrative concerned Joseph Frankau [69] as well as his daughter Aline, Wolfe became very much interested in him. She had given Wolfe a picture of her father dressed for the role of Met in Steel MacKaye's *Hazel Kirke*. Wolfe, who soon felt that he knew him as well as his own father, used to keep the picture pinned on the wall over his writing table. Wolfe had heard Aline recount her life adventures many times, and he had asked her to write to him daily about her life. This was now the stuff of his narrative. In the same way that he arranged his own remembrances, Wolfe compiled many long outlines of this material, such as this one from his pocket notebook:

Chapters to Follow

1 The Three Sisters
2 My Father's Family
3 Bella (Dr. Bunine—His Day—His Women Patients—His Xmas Stories, etc—How E drank Morphine, etc.)
4 The Trip abroad—England—My Aunt—Wilkie Collins [70]—Mrs. Daisy Pace [71]
5 Home Again—My Grandfather etc
6 Aunt Mary's Boarding House (the doctor has died—killed himself on a trip abroad)—The people there (Father was starting immediately on tour—we went there)
7 Difficulties—Poverty—Grandfather, etc
8 The Street and Our Neighbors—My Friends
9 School—Miss Lavina Brill, etc
10 The Library
11 The Mother's Death
12 The Bridge [72]
13 Bella's Pink Tea [73]
14 Uncle John and Uncle Fred—Bella's second Marriage
15 Mrs. Daisy Pace—Her Story [74]

Since Wolfe had not experienced the life of the 1890's and early 1900's, he spent some time in the public library absorbing what authenticity he could from files of the *New York Times, Life,* and *Leslie's.* He took notes from them in the same way that he filled his pocket notebooks with direct observations. To get the feel of the times, he jotted down comments on the faces and dress of the people in photographs and drawings; he copied down restaurant names, theater programs, news items, advertisements, jokes; and he made his own crude cartoons of Times Square, lamp posts, hansom cabs, and costumes. To acquire some knowledge of Aline's own surroundings, he looked in the City Directory for the residences of Joseph Frankau from about 1873 to 1900 and of Theodore Bernstein from about 1900 to 1924, and he went to inspect those he could find.

Because Wolfe believed so strongly that there must be experience at the core of every properly rendered literary achievement, for "The Good Child's River" he was depending on his intimacy with Aline Bernstein to carry his experience back about nineteen years and also to carry it to New York years before he ever saw that city himself. The recapture of the past through Mrs. Bernstein had an importance beyond its function in Esther's story, for it gave Wolfe a refreshing as well as solid historical sense of the American recent past that he used to good advantage throughout his work.

Besides the Esther story, Wolfe also worked on other parts of his manuscript during the summer—especially scenes of the lovers' quarrels—in a vain attempt to complete his main narrative. But his efforts were so sporadic that he began to lose confidence in his power to complete the book at all. Wolfe had another problem besides making an ending; he had extreme difficulty in settling on a beginning. From his main story, the love affair of David and Esther, he was forever turning back to what had gone before: not only was there Esther's life story, but her father's life story; not only her sister's, but her aunt's and uncle's; not only David's study at Harvard and his first year in New York, but his childhood and his memories of uncles and aunts; not only the affairs of these relatives, but those of his paternal and maternal ancestors. Wolfe's theory of the consciousness of an American (as being composed of all the moments that formed the national history) wound him back beyond his own experience to the Appalachians that had sheltered the Westall family and to the Pennsylvania farm land that had surrounded the Wolfes.

The result would be, four years hence, that Wolfe's attempt to write the story of his love affair with Aline Bernstein had expanded in both directions until his plans embraced a chronicle running from 1791 to 1933.

By the end of the summer he had reached a point of despair to which he had never descended before. Since Scribner's were eager for the book and since they continued to press Wolfe for some definite news about its completion, Wolfe was actually glad when Perkins sent him a note asking for the manuscript. He could now state plainly to his publishers what had happened to his original plan.

You say you think I ought to make every conceivable effort to have the manuscript completely finished by the end of September. I know you are not joking and that you mean this September, and not September four, five or fifteen years from now. Well, there is no remote or possible chance that I will have a completed [manuscript] of anything that resembles a book this September, and whether I have anything that I would be willing to show to anyone next September, or any succeeding one for the next 150 years is at present a matter of the extremest and most painful doubt to me....

I want to tell you finally that I am not in *despair* over the book I have worked on—I am in *doubt* about it—and I am not sure about anything.... I had an immense book and I wanted to say it all at once; it can't be done—now I am doing it part by part, and hope and believe the part I am doing will be a complete story, a unity, and part of the whole plan. This part itself has now become a big book; it is for the first time straight in my head to the smallest detail, and much of it is written—it is a part of my whole scheme of books as a smaller river flows into a big one.[75]

From this point of doubt, one can look back briefly over the fifteen-month period to see that for Wolfe most of it had been, in fact, a period of great accomplishment. The year abroad had been a time of conception for a whole scheme of novels, it had been the seed time for most of the details that would enrich them, it had been the beginning of two or three powerful themes to strengthen them. During these months, Wolfe had unlocked his tongue about America, he had set up a comprehensive symbolism, he had extended his power in prose lyrics, he had sketched a host of living characters, he had begun innumerable episodes that in revision would be energetic scenes. But the most important feat of the year was Wolfe's success in expanding his self-consciousness into national consciousness. Wolfe as a self-crowned American laureate began his career in Europe in 1930.

NOTES

1. In all of Wolfe's manuscript materials in the Harvard Library, there is no indication of his plans for "Pacific End," with the exception of one page of notes dated, in an unidentified hand, "1935," HCL*46AM-7(24-v):

What Have I to Complete and Write about

Hills Beyond Pentland	I
	II
	III
The October Fair	I
Death of the Enemy	II
Completion	III
Pacific End	I (The Story of the Swan Girl, the Englishman, Bill Pentland and his children, etc.)

2. PN 14, May to August, 1930.

3. UNCL, unpublished letter, Maxwell Perkins to John Terry, October 29, 1945. Perkins describes the walks he and Wolfe used to take through Central Park in 1929. "It was on one of those walks that I told Tom I had always thought a wonderful novel could be written (but I was thinking of a sort of picaresque novel where the wanderings are toward a goal) about a young man who for some reason has never known his father and goes in search of him. Tom seemed to consider this as if it were a serious matter and finally said, 'I think I could use that, Max.' . . . He was taking the search for a father in a profound sense. . . ."

4. *Letters,* p. 213.

5. *Letters,* p. 239.

6. This was the title of the first chapter of "The River People."

7. This item and the next three items represent material that Wolfe had worked over in the summer of 1926.

8. PN 9, February to March, 1929, *ca.* March 20.

9. PN 10, March to May, 1929, *ca.* May 7.

10. *Ibid.*

11. This arrival in England had been part of the Eleventh Installment of "Passage to England."

12. This episode was later developed for "The Train and the City" and was included in OT&R, pp. 407-19.

13. This is probably Wolfe's last reference to the love story planned for "The River People."

14. One of the several names used during the development of the character Esther Jack.

15. See W&R, pp. 457-58.

16. A sequence, never completed, based on the life of Wolfe's friend, Desmond Powell, an instructor at New York University, who was stricken with tuberculosis. See below, under the title "Early Sorrow."

17. Two of the New York University instructors, William Tindall and Emmet Glore, visited Wolfe's apartment at 263 West 11th Street with two girls one evening for a steak dinner. Mrs. Bernstein passing the apartment saw a woman's shadow at the window, and suspecting Wolfe was up to no good, rushed upstairs for an immediate investigation. Finding a whole group in the apartment, she left without creating a scene, after Wolfe made a reassuring explanation.

18. A reference to the Bernstein country house at Armonk Village and its architect, Mr. Woodsend.

19. Wolfe and Mrs. Bernstein had visited Chartres in July, 1926.

20. The Fine Arts Ball, December 31, 1926, when Wolfe had just returned from Europe. He quarreled with a young man who put his arm around Mrs. Bernstein.

21. Midsummer, 1926, when Wolfe, beginning his first novel, stayed at Ambleside with Mrs. Bernstein. For a fictional description of Wolfe at this time, see *The Journey Down*, Chapter 2.

22. This episode became Eugene's first meeting with Francis Starwick, OT&R, pp. 93-102.

23. John Varney, one of the New York University instructors.

24. This series of episodes is quoted from PN 11, June 11 to October 15, 1929.

25. *Letters*, p. 245.

26. PN 15, August 14, 1930, to February, 1931. The entry is in September, 1930.

27. PN 14, May to August, 1930.

28. HCL*46AM-13, unpublished letter to Aline Bernstein, November 18, 1928.

29. PN 6, November to December, 1928.

30. *Letters*, pp. 278-79.

31. *Letters*, p. 281.

32. *Letters*, pp. 279-80.

33. *Letters*, p. 247.

34. HCL*46AM-7(30), Box 1, black ledger labeled "The City, the Voyage, and the River."

35. *Ibid.* The quotation from "The Ancient Mariner" replaces Chaucer's lines describing the "verray, parfit, gentil knyght," which are crossed out.

36. Esther's name remained Jacobs even into the proof sheets for OT&R. A meeting between Esther and Eugene was cut out after the book was in proof.

37. *Letters*, pp. 234-35. Most of the detailed interpretation of America described here was later used in Books I and VII of OT&R, as well as in the short stories "One of the Girls in Our Party," "The Bums at Sunset," and "The Far and the Near."

38. *Letters*, p. 234.

39. *Letters*, p. 227.

40. HCL, unpublished letter to Henry Volkening, June 10, 1930.

41. PN 14, May to August, 1930.

42. *Letters*, pp. 237-38.

43. *Letters*, p. 263.

44. YCGHA, p. 715. Scott Fitzgerald is given the fictional name, Hunt Conroy.

45. PN 14, May to August, 1930.

46. Wolfe immediately planned his literary vengeance and recorded a formal reminder in his pocket notebook: "On May 31 in Paris on Saturday after mailing letters to me, Mrs. ——— conspired that I be insulted at her ap't 6 Rue Montaliset." Her first portrait in one of the Antaeus vignettes, the "rich American girl moving on from husband to husband, from drink to dope to opium," was much harsher than her final appearance in YCGHA, pp. 346-48.

47. *Letters*, p. 263. Cf. YCGHA, pp. 346-48.

48. PN 14, May to August, 1930. Part IV is crossed out.

49. *Letters*, p. 242. In Wolfe's various outlines, the four parts differ.

50. *Letters*, p. 234.

51. HCL, unpublished letter to Henry Volkening, June 10, 1930.

52. An anecdote Wolfe told to a class at the University of North Carolina in January, 1937 (George Stoney, "Eugene Returns to Pulpit Hill," *Carolina Magazine* [October, 1938], pp. 11-14).

53. *Letters*, p. 248. The review appeared in the *London Evening News*, August 8, 1930.

54. *Letters*, p. 264. One review by Gerald Gould in the *London Observer*, August 17, 1930, parodied Wolfe's style. The second may have been the Swinnerton review already cited.

55. *Letters*, pp. 257-58.

56. PN 15, August 14, 1930, to February, 1931.

57. *Letters*, p. 261.

58. PN 15, August 14, 1930, to February, 1931.

59. HCL*46AM-7(30), Box 2, black ledger.

60. HCL, an undated, unfinished letter to Messrs. Roy and Cheyney gives this address and the information that Wolfe moved on October 11, 1930. Nowell gives the address as 15 Ebury St.

61. YCGHA, pp. 518-19.

62. Unpublished letter, January 19, 1930, in the files of CSS.

63. LTM, p. 210.

64. YCGHA, pp. 529-31.

65. *Letters*, pp. 276.

66. *Modern Monthly*, December, 1934. It finally took its place in OT&R, pp. 861-70.

67. *Letters*, p. 280. This material was used in Book I and Book VII ("The Names of the Nation" section), OT&R.

68. HCL*49M-209, Edward Aswell's notes of an interview with Mrs. Bernstein. Nowell states that Mrs. Bernstein took sleeping pills (p. 195).

69. In all of Wolfe's manuscripts, Joseph Frankau is given the name Joe Lindau. Wolfe's second editor, Edward Aswell, altered the name to Linder.

70. W&R, p. 409, and *The Journey Down*, pp. 119-20.

71. Cf. Aline Bernstein, *An Actor's Daughter* (New York: Alfred A. Knopf, 1941), pp. 38-40. Wolfe intended to use the London Charwoman as the basis for this character. Later she became the Daisy Purvis of YCGHA.

72. Cf. W&R, pp. 409-11.

73. Cf. "Nana's Party," Chapter 3 in *The Journey Down*.

74. PN 16, February to July, 1931. Most of this material appeared in Aline Bernstein's *An Actor's Daughter*. "Have you read *An Actor's Daughter?*" she once asked me. "That was Tom's book. He was going to write my life, you know."

75. *Letters*, pp. 304-7.

15

MEMBERS OF THE HAWKE FAMILY

WOLFE'S ENTIRE CAREER WAS MARKED BY BURSTS OF CREATIVITY followed by periods of plodding and lack of certainty. He finished *Welcome to Our City* in three months, then spent almost two years on *Mannerhouse;* he finished "O Lost" in twenty months, then failed even to get a good start on "The River People" in almost a year; in 1930 he had erected a suitable scaffold for his second novel, but when he returned home he could not progress toward a finished structure. By the fall of 1931, he was so far from completing any one of his planned sections that he did not know what the future held. On this account he was glad he had not signed a contract with Scribner's, even though he had accepted $1000 from them the previous spring.[1] What obligations he did feel were personal ones, to Perkins and other members of the staff. When he began to run low on money again, he still did not sign a contract for his book. Instead, he began to look for some immediate means of making shorter pieces pay his way, hoping not only to ease the pinch on himself but also to be of more help to his family in the South. This is how it happened that toward the end of his first Brooklyn year (the period from March, 1931, to March, 1932, in which he seemed to be accomplishing so little) Wolfe turned out for ready cash two hastily assembled but brilliant short novels.

When Wolfe had returned from Europe seeking an out-of-the-way place to live, a friend from the South, Beverly Smith, suggested Marjorie Dorman's rather Bohemian house at 40 Verandah Place, Brooklyn. Marjorie Dorman, who was excited at the prospect of housing the author of *Look Homeward, Angel,* was stunned when he first appeared. Wolfe was unshaven, wearing a grimy, shapeless coat and a hat with a broken rim. He brought few furnishings with him, chiefly a heap of books, a packing case full of manuscript, a bed long enough to accommodate his frame, his huge, heavy writing table, and his assortment of oddly matched dishes.

He rented an apartment with two rooms, one in the basement and one on the first floor opening on a little courtyard. Always painting the darker picture, he referred to the place as a basement apartment, but the rooms were not as depressing as the "cellar depths" he pictured in "No Door" [2] and in "The Locusts Have No King" [3]—where the walls "sweat continuously with clammy drops of water," "more like a dungeon than a room." But Wolfe soon cluttered the apartment with his customary accumulation of scattered papers and books, unwashed coffee cups, and saucers foul with cigarette stubs. Verandah Place (the Balcony Square of "No Door," "called so because there was neither square nor balconies") was more of an alley than a street, and Wolfe's front door faced a tall board fence running behind the houses of the next street. As for the neighborhood, the scenes of violence described in "No Door" were true to the locale but isolated. Sharing the community life of the two adjoining rooming houses, Wolfe really felt happier than he had any time since he had lived on 11th Street with Mrs. Bernstein.

Wolfe enjoyed Brooklyn as a place to work. He lived there for the next four years. "I came here," he wrote George McCoy, "because I knew that my friends in New York would come to see me if they wanted to see me and that the other people would not bother, and that is the way exactly it has worked out." [4] As it was for George Webber, South Brooklyn became for Wolfe a universe. And in spite of the darker coloring he gave it in his fiction, he never forgot the little moments that brought his sympathies into harmony.

[Brooklyn's]got power and richness—sure enough! As to the beauty— that's a different matter. You are not so sure of that—but even as you say this you remember many things. You remember a powerful big horse, slow-footed, shaggy in the hoof, with big dappled spots of iron gray upon it that stood one brutal day in August by the curb. Its driver had unhitched it from the wagon and it stood there with its great patient head bent down in an infinite and quiet sorrow, and a little boy with black eyes and a dark face was standing by it holding some sugar in his hand, and its driver, a man who had the tough seamed face of the city, stepped in on the horse with a bucket full of water, which he threw against the horse's side. For a second, the great flanks shuddered gratefully and began to smoke, the man stepped back onto the curb and began to look the animal over with a keen deliberate glance, and the boy stood there, rubbing his hand quietly into the horse's muzzle, and talking softly to it all the time.[5]

As a result of living in Brooklyn, Wolfe began to write about the American scene with more social sympathy. Besides the catalogues of place names and besides the general symbols of the nation's power, he began to bring the common man into his vision of America. Since his daily walks around Brooklyn took place during the depths of the Great Depression, he was moved from his restricted concern for himself toward a deep sense of human brotherhood.

Everywhere around me during these years, I saw the evidence of an incalculable ruin and suffering. . . .
And the staggering impact of this black picture of man's inhumanity to his fellow man, the unending repercussions of these scenes of suffering, violence, oppression, hunger, cold, and filth and poverty going on unheeded in a world in which the rich were still rotten with their wealth left a scar upon my life, a conviction in my soul which I shall never lose.
And from it all, there has come as the final deposit, a burning memory, a certain evidence of the fortitude of man, his ability to suffer and somehow survive. And it is for this reason now that I think I shall always remember this black period with a kind of joy that I could not at that time have believed possible, for it was during this time that I lived my life through to a first completion, and through the suffering and labor of my own life came to share those qualities in the lives of people all around me.[6]

As in England, he was brought closer to suffering humanity, and the Brooklyn years awakened a social compassion that was to appear in *You Can't Go Home Again.*

Wolfe had begun to make a habit of walking across the Brooklyn Bridge once a week to draw money out of his account at Scribner's and to talk to Perkins and other friends in the office. As the amount on the Scribner's books began to shrink away, he went to Perkins for advice on turning some of his work into money for running expenses. Since the Scribner's editors made use of *Scribner's Magazine* both for providing additional money for their authors and for getting them before the public more often, Perkins had only to speak to Alfred Dashiell, the editor of *Scribner's Magazine,* who arranged that Wolfe should submit something of suitable length. When Wolfe turned to the new task his spirits lifted, as he told George McCoy:

When I came back from Europe about a year ago, I was really in a
state of despair about my book, not because I could not write it but because I could do nothing else but write it. I had written until I had
hundreds of thousands of words; it was reaching a staggering length and
I did not know what I could do to cut it or get it within some reasonable
reading compass. The plan and the material, every incident of it, had
been clear in my mind for months; I saw the whole thing through to its
end, down to the minutest detail, and the more I thought about it the
longer it got: Then because I needed money and had a feeling of despair over the book I stopped suddenly, worked furiously for a month on a
short novel and completed it.[7]

This short novel was *A Portrait of Bascom Hawke,* Wolfe's second
published work, which appeared in *Scribner's Magazine* for April,
1932. By August, it had brought him, in addition to the $500 selling
price, a $2500 prize, when it tied for first place in the *Scribner's
Magazine* short novel contest. *Bascom Hawke* as one of Wolfe's best
and most characteristic pieces is not as well known as it should be,
for Wolfe later buried it in the midst of Book II of *Of Time and the
River,* destroying its organization.

When Wolfe gave the manuscript of this short novel to Perkins for
his inspection, he spoke only generally about the unifying scheme:
"Part of this was written some time ago, and part very recently—and
some of it quite rapidly. I've simply tried to give you a man—as for
a plot, there's not any, but there's this idea which I believe is pretty
plain—I've always wanted to say something about *old men* and *young
men* and that's what I've tried to do here." [8] The something that he
wanted to say made *Bascom Hawke* a study in the contrast of youth
and age, of vitality and disintegration, of youthful hope and elderly
indifference. The narrative alternates between David Hawke, at
Harvard and in the rush of the metropolis, and his uncle Bascom, in
his real estate office and in his home. David is twenty, alone in Boston, and torn with the urgency to read all the books in the Harvard
Library and to encompass all the places and people in Boston. His
seeking to devour learning and life in bulk is the epitome of youthful
extravagance. Uncle Bascom, representing a vitality that has waned,
is seen as a parsimonious and eccentric remnant of his former self,
who occasionally looks back only to say, "I'm an old man. I have lived
a long time. I have seen so many things. Sometimes everything seems
so long ago." As usual in Wolfe's writing, the pattern is not perfect;

there is a disturbing digression—a comic anecdote about Bascom and a widow. Still, the pattern comes through clearly enough to fulfill Wolfe's intention.

After an extensive characterization of Uncle Bascom which goes back to the man's own eager youth, the concluding scene brings the contrast to a climax in the mind of David as he sits beside his uncle one spring day. For David spring had come that year "like a triumph and like a prophecy." "My hunger and thirst had been immense; I was caught up for the first time in the midst of the Faustian web. . . .I wanted to know all, have all, be all—to be one and many, to have the whole riddle of this vast and swarming earth as legible, as tangible in my hand as a coin of minted gold." [9] Two things are juxtaposed to bring the story to its climax. When, on the way to visit his uncle's office, David had passed through the Boston market with its store of meat, its profusion of fruit and greenery, it had seemed a symbol of the earth's abundance in spring. Now, as he sits by his uncle's desk, the sight of the quiet, brooding old man brings him a vision of a group of old people seated at a table, their life past and even their memory "gone lifeless."

David, then feeling a necessity to deny this spiritual dryness, senses a "union with the past" and yearns to revive the vigorous years of the old man, who has come up "from the wilderness, from derbied men and bustled women, from all of the memories of lavish brown. . . ." "Suddenly it seemed to me that if I could put my hand upon my uncle, if I could grip my fingers in his stringy arm, my strength and youth would go into him, and I could rekindle memory like a living flame in him, I could animate for an hour his ancient heart with the exultancy, the power, the joy that pulsed in me; I could make the old man speak." Uncle Bascom, lost in his own world, unable to communicate, only murmurs, "So long ago." And David, rising, leaves his uncle to go back into the world of spring, into life:

. . .into the streets where the singing and lyrical air, the man-swarm passing in its million-footed weft, the glorious women and the girls compacted in a single music of belly and breasts and thighs, the sea, the earth, the proud, potent, clamorous city, all of the voices of time fused to a unity that was like a song, a token and a cry. Victoriously, I trod the neck of doubt as if it were a serpent: I was joined to the earth, a part of it, and I possessed it; I would be wasted and consumed, filled and renewed eternally; I would feel unceasingly alternate tides of life and dark oblivion; I would be emptied without weariness, replenished forever with strong joy. I had a tongue for agony, a food for hunger, a door for exile and a surfeit for insatiate desire: exultant certainty welled up in me, I thought I could possess it all, and I cried: "Yes! It will be mine!" [10]

With this naive cry Wolfe ended *Bascom Hawke*. The irony of expressing the youthful exuberance of 1921 at a time when he sat in Brooklyn struggling to get enough money to keep his pencil pushing was not lost on him. Still, this was part of the general view of life he wished to set forth. He disdained a man who, having lived an abundant life, refused to remember it and value it and, above all, who failed to make his past life a living and present reality. Alongside such lack of fulfillment, the foolish aspirations of youth, Wolfe thought, seem momentous. This concluding scene completes the pattern of the story. It carries not only a judgment about looking at the past but also an implication of the continuing life cycle with the return of spring and the renewal of the old man's energies in his nephew.

The characterization of Uncle Bascom himself gives the simple pattern color and variety. He is one of the foremost in Wolfe's gallery of extended caricatures—that is, sharply defined characters filled in with enough detail to make them seem living beings, a mixture of wisdom and folly, dignity and contemptibility. He is sketched as long, lean, and slightly stooped, wearing a buttoned sweater, never an overcoat, shod with brogans, clothed with old, awkwardly fitting garments, quoting Scripture or howling an old man's invective at motorists. As a former minister, he has an evangelical preacher's rant, full of repetition, stress, and exaggeration, rich with enjoyed Latinate words: "Can you *imagine*, can you ever *dream* of such a state of affairs if he had possessed an atom, a *scintilla* of delicacy and good breeding!" His peculiar speech, his snuffling laugh (Phuh! Phuh! Phuh! Phuh!), his scornful denunciations (Oh vile! vile! vile!), are matched by oddities of habit—he eats only raw vegetables, does his own laundry, cobbles his own shoes, practices a hundred subterfuges because of his parsimony.

Emphasizing these eccentricities, Wolfe begins his portrait as a comic one. We get such a picture as Bascom's response to Mr. Brill's morning joke when he arrives at the real estate office: "... if he was really in a good humor, he might snuffle with nosey laughter, bend double at his meager waist, clutching his big hands together, and stamp at the floor violently several times with one stringy leg; he might even go so far as to take a random ecstatic kick at objects, still stamping and snuffling with laughter, and prod Miss Brill stiffly with two enormous bony fingers, as if he did not wish the full point and flavor of the jest to be lost on her." [11] Gradually, however, details are added that temper the comic effect. Bascom is the scholar of the family, having left the South to work his way through Harvard College and Divinity School; he has a prominent brow that "in its profound and lonely earnestness, bore an astonishing resemblance to that of Emerson"; he quotes the Old Testament and Carlyle; and he writes poems modeled on those of his favorite, Matthew Arnold. More than that, Wolfe manages to convey to us a sense of Bascom's fiery, energetic past: his struggles, his travels, his sermons (a Father Mapple in a Midwest pulpit) on "Ruth, the Girl in the Corn" or "Potiphar's Wife," his prayers, which were "fierce solicitations of God so mad with fervor that his audiences felt uncomfortably they came close to blasphemy," his wrestling with conscience that led him from churches "Episcopal, Presbyterian, Unitarian, searching through the whole roaring confusion of Protestantism for a body of doctrine with which he could agree." Finally, as in the last scene, we see the meditative Bascom—a noble, mortal, dignified, pitiful creature,

staring straight before him, with his great hands folded in a bony arch, his powerful gaunt face composed in a rapt tranquility of thought. At these times he seemed to have escaped from every particular and degrading thing in life—from the excess of absurd and eccentric speech and gesture, from all demeaning parsimonies, from niggling irascibilities, from everything that contorted his face and spirit away from its calmness and unity of thought. . . .

One day I went there and found him thus; after a few moments he lowered his great hands and, without turning toward me, sat for some time in an attitude of quiet relaxation. At length he said:

"What is man that thou art mindful of him?" [12]

It is this kind of fully proportioned sculpture that Wolfe chisels when he allows a character a generous amount of space in one of his books.

Although Wolfe told George McCoy that he "worked furiously for a month on a short novel and completed it," the history of *A Portrait of Bascom Hawke* is a long and tangled one, going back to Wolfe's days at Harvard. Here Wolfe came to know the original of Uncle Bascom, his mother's brother, Henry Westall, whose life in its external details corresponds closely to the old man's life in the story. Often visiting his uncle at home or at his office, Wolfe became fascinated with his oddities of character and even then thought of exploiting him for literary material. He wrote Fred from Cambridge: "You should hear our Uncle Henry curse Yankee weather, Yankee honesty, and everything Yankee in general. He and Aunt Laura are a great pair; they are giving me materials for a great play which I shall write some day." [13]

The growth of *Bascom Hawke* from this declaration gives an excellent illustration of the method of composition—from notes, through preliminary sketches, to final versions—that Wolfe followed for almost every good piece of work he turned out. When he began "O Lost" in 1926, he jotted down a series of notes on the life of "Uncle Emerson," beginning, "He went occasionally on Sunday to visit his Uncle Emerson and his Aunt Louise. Emerson Westall had been the scholar of the family—." [14] Then in one of the big red ledgers he had bought in Ilkley he scribbled hurriedly through long rambling episodes entitled "Boston Kin," in which he characterized Uncle Emerson, Aunt Louise, their two daughters and two sons. Wolfe tumbled this out in a hasty conversational style, full of shifts and digressions, much as if he had been talking aloud. Since Wolfe never threw anything away, this ledger went into his packing case when he decided to end "O Lost" with Eugene still in the South.[15] In 1928 Wolfe thought he could use "Uncle Emerson" and his family at the beginning of "The River People," and after this project disintegrated, he planned to incorporate them somewhere in whatever second novel he would write. Accordingly, during the year in Europe on the Guggenheim fellowship, Wolfe decided to adapt this material to his current purposes. He outlined a new section and wrote a whole ledger full of Uncle Bascom's life at the office with Mr. Brill and the office staff, again allowing himself to be digressive and anecdotal.[16] Finally, when he was casting around for a piece to give to *Scribner's Magazine,* he rewrote the Uncle Bascom episodes, selecting parts from his earlier attempts and adding new portions to form a unified short novel. After considerable revising and scratching over, this version was typed and submitted to *Scribner's.* Although some chunks were removed from this typescript, it represents Wolfe's final version of the story he had been accumulating for six years.

The most important fact in the development of this story lies behind the concluding scene, with its affirmation of purpose and love in modern man's life. This belief turned the episodes about Uncle Bascom from a mere portrait into a unified, meaningful piece of work. Although Wolfe's view here is his usual one, the particular statement of David's dilemma as he thinks about his uncle was provoked by T. S. Eliot and his admirers. Wolfe had first heard of Eliot at Harvard and no doubt was repelled by the adulation of a special group there.[17] He did read Eliot's work, however, and he admired him, as he said in his 1928 notebook, as "the critic with the greatest subtlety." [18] Although Wolfe scorned as pretense the elliptical style of much contemporary poetry, he had a sensitive ear for Eliot's prosody; he echoed his "I do not hope to turn again" phrases in one passage of "K 19" and even thought to imitate the haunting first paragraph of *The Waste Land* in the beginning of "April, Late April." Other lines of Eliot's that he brought into his workshop to play with would make a good-sized list. But Eliot's attitudes were a different matter. Although Wolfe later demonstrated strong antagonism toward some of Eliot's ideas [19] and especially toward his expatriation,[20] *A Portrait of Bascom Hawke* is his first direct opposition to what he thought *The Waste Land* represented. Along with a great many other people, Wolfe interpreted the work as an expression of complete nihilism. While he was at New York University, Wolfe heard a great deal of literary chit-chat about Eliot's poetry from Eda Lou Walton, Edwin Berry Burgum, and other colleagues interested in modern literature. Since he felt that they held values that ran counter to those he felt most deeply, the discussion produced a reaction that began to appear in pocket notebook phrases about "the barren earth" and "dry bones" [21] during the months just before he left for the Guggenheim year in Europe. The idea that these phrases represented in Wolfe's mind brought about the conclusion to David's vision in *A Portrait of Bascom Hawke*.

David's vision presents a group of old people seated around a table, their strength and hope gone, the memory of their past lives faded or banished. They represent Man defeated by modern life, indifferent to passion and vitality. Wolfe jumps off from an Eliot phrase in the concluding comment on the vision: "Words echoed in their throat but they were tongueless. For them the past was dead: they poured into our hands a handful of dust and ashes." Then in a series of rhetorical questions, he denies that life is sterile and that *The Waste Land* is an acceptable symbol:

The dry bones, the bitter dust? The living wilderness, the silent waste? The barren land?

Have no lips trembled in the wilderness? No eyes sought seaward from the rock's sharp edge for men returning home? Has no pulse beat more hot with love or hate upon the river's edge? Or where the old wheel and the rusted stock lie stogged in desert sand: by the horsehead a woman's skull. No love?

No lonely footfalls in a million streets, no heart that beat its best and bloodiest cry out against the steel and stone, no aching brain, caught in its iron ring, groping among the labryinthine canyons? Nought in that immense and lonely land but incessant growth and ripeness and pollution, the emptiness of forests and deserts, the unhearted, harsh and metal jangle of a million tongues, crying the belly-cry for bread, or the great cat's snarl for meat and honey? All, then, all? Birth and the twenty thousand days of snarl and jangle—and no love, no love? Was no love crying in the wilderness?

It was not true. The lovers lay below the lilac bush; the laurel leaves were trembling in the wood.[22]

David Hawke's triumphant belief in a meaningful course to man's life is a legitimate assertion that life, though full of anguish, is good, that the struggle itself is good, and that man's life, though enclosed by the "canyons" of urbanization, has value through human passion. But Wolfe's symbol at the end of his quizzing seems a little silly. Coupling in the shrubbery is a limited answer when placed alongside the Give, Sympathize, Control that the Thunder said. Wolfe, then, took a pot shot at the aged eagle and missed. But though Wolfe's shot went wide, he had another kind of success: his belief gave organization to his novel.

This optimism of Wolfe's, this passionate denial of forces that obstruct life, was a deep strain in his emotional life, for on the surface he seemed to engage in endless contention with the world around him. Again and again in his letters and notebooks he lashes out at the world of men; in fits of temper or self-indulgent egoism he sees mankind as a mob of fools and knaves, and he finds modern life full of ugliness and brutality. He clung to the optimism, then, in spite of his opinion that modern life, and especially American life, failed to make good its possibilities. With the wide-eyed longing of a mountain boy, he felt as keenly as any of his literary contemporaries the shortcomings of a nation full of power and richness that too often brought forth waste and sham. But the faith in life remained to be asserted many times. It is part of this paradox that he turned on Eliot when he himself grieved at the spiritual debility in so much of life around him. Even at the time he was finishing *Bascom Hawke,* he could describe life in the 1930's as the same pageant of living dead that Eliot had pictured in *The Waste Land* ten years before:

Jan 1, 1932

Yesterday was the last day of one of the unhappiest, dreariest years in the nation's history. The "depression" so-called, has a strong and oppressive physical quality. Just how one feels this I do not know, but we breathe it in the air, and we get it in a harrassed and weary feeling which people have: the terrible thing in America now, however, is not the material bankruptcy but the spiritual one. Instead of revolution—which is a co-herent and living act of the spirit—one feels the presence of something worse—a mindless chaos, and millions of people blundering about without a belief in anything, without hope, with apathy and cynicism.[23]

II

During October, 1931, Wolfe had moved to 111 Columbia Heights, for he had originally wanted to be near the river when he thought of living in Brooklyn. Much pleasanter than the alleyway of Verandah Place, Columbia Heights ran along a high embankment above New York Harbor. Here Wolfe had a whole third floor of a brownstone apartment, which he furnished scantily but soon had well-strewn with manuscript leaves, books, socks, shirts, and whatever else he pulled out for use and then put aside. Here alongside the harbor, he heard the ships at night, blowing in the channel. Here he drudged on this kind of schedule:

...I begin to work about midnight and keep at it until four or five o'clock in the morning, then I go to bed and sleep till about eleven, get up, make coffee, of which I drink a pot or two every day, and then work on my manuscript until about one or two o'clock in the afternoon when the young man who is typing my book comes. We work together until six or six-thirty, when he goes, and then if I have any energy left in me, I take a bath, get shaved and dressed, and go out to eat. I have a few friends here in New York of whom I am very fond and who have been wonderfully kind and decent to me: occasionally I spend the evening with them but most often I spend it alone. Sometimes I go over to town—by town I mean Manhattan—and eat late and then go to the Harvard Club and read for an hour or two before it closes at one o'clock; then I come home and, if I can, get to work again.[24]

His work sheets during these years show about four or five hours of writing in steady, day-after-day industry. Wolfe never wrote for ten, twelve, fourteen hours a day as he is reputed to have done—except occasionally when he was trying to meet a deadline.

As one of "those Noctambuloes and nightwalkers," [25] Wolfe continued his habit of wandering around the streets of New York and Brooklyn at night, occasionally making his notes "The Diary of a Brooklyn Pepys" which placed the "and so to bed" about 4:00 A.M. He had grown quite heavy since his return from Europe, and he presented a huge silhouette as he loomed beneath the street lights. Since his apartment was only a few blocks from the Brooklyn Bridge, he made the crossing to Manhattan one of his favorite walks. William Tindall remembers Wolfe on one occasion striding across the bridge reciting his rhythmic passage about the horses of the night.[26]

He saw no literary people at all except the staff at Scribner's; he saw some of his old friends from Harvard, from New York University, or from Chapel Hill; and occasionally he looked up an old telephone number in his notebook to call one of his various girl friends. In spite of this apparent withdrawal, he talked to a host of people every week, for he always made friends where he lived, and in his night walks he soon got to know waiters, countermen, bartenders, policemen, taxi-drivers, and other familiar bit-players in the city scene.

His mother visited him in January, 1932, while Wolfe was living at 111 Columbia Heights. Julia Wolfe's second trip to New York was the occasion for Wolfe's writing *The Web of Earth*, his next short novel, which was published in *Scribner's Magazine* in July, 1932. As far back as September, 1929, Wolfe had jotted down a few notes on a story of his mother's that had become legendary in the Wolfe family: she had heard two voices speak to her in the night, whispering, "Two, two. Twenty, twenty." As Elizabeth Nowell says, Julia Wolfe's stories were like phonograph records, available for almost exact repetition, and she told Tom this story again on her latest visit.[27] Her rambling talk during her short stay with him set him to work on the novel in January, and in spite of an injury to his arm, he completed it by the end of March.

Wolfe declared that *The Web of Earth* was really a part of his extensive narrative plan. The story of the Westalls, done perhaps in the manner of Glenway Wescott's *The Grandmothers* (a book Wolfe had listed among a dozen modern novels for his students to read at New York University), had long been in his mind. The notes and outlines he had written for the early history of his mother's family made him aware that the pioneer heritage of his central character could be stressed to enhance his American theme. As a result, he decided to change the name of his central character to John Crockett Hawke, a name he bore until the total work was assembled for Max Perkins late in 1933. Creating the atmosphere of an earlier America, Wolfe worked rapidly on *The Web of Earth*, gathering together countless stories of his maternal relatives. Yet he turned out a piece of work that had no artistic flaws. Digressions that he had been powerless to control in earlier work were not only made appropriate to the narrator but were each fitted into the design of the whole. Moreover, a single point of view gave the story a tightness of plot that Wolfe had not achieved before.

The point of view is given to Delia Hawke, who is speaking to her son, John. A few lines of conversation open the story, the rest is a monologue. Taking his mother's stories and making use of her conversational habit of digression by association, Wolfe imposed a coherent pattern on an impossible array of material to bring forth the whole life surrounding the Hawke family. The central narrative is simple. Delia explains how she heard two ghostly voices one night and how she tried to interpret their eerie message, "Two, two. Twenty, twenty." Attempts to solve the riddle of the voices bring in false evidence that gives the narrative a running plot about two murderers escaped from the town jail. As she unfolds the story, she digresses, weaving in other narrative threads, which in turn produce other associations and therefore other narratives. In the middle of the story, she finishes the inmost narratives one by one, and she returns over the sequence of her associations, closing each narrative until in conclusion she relates the birth of her twins and her interpretation of the ghostly message. In the meantime, we have met a parade of characters, including a troop of her brothers and sisters, and have been taken through Mr. Hawke's three marriages.[28]

The narrative is only a skeleton upon which Wolfe hangs the rich and varied life of the Hawke family. In the folksy speech of Delia, Mr. Hawke (again a heroic rendering of Wolfe's own father) is pictured as someone especially vigorous. We see him at times as the Far Wanderer and again as a kind of harvest god, storing the house with food, forty dozen eggs, a wagon load of melons, loads of "roastin' ears and termaters and string beans and sweet pertaters and onions and radishes and beets and turnips and all kinds of garden vegetables and all sorts of fruit, peaches and pears and apples and plums." [29] To his wife's bewilderment, he buys animals at market and butchers them himself:

"Why, man alive!" I said, "What ever persuaded you to go and do a thing like that!" Here we were with hams and bacon in the pantry that he'd bought, six smoked hams, if you please, and here he comes with this whole hog. "Why, man, you'll kill us with all this hog meat!" I said—yes! with lots of chicken of our own and a twelve-pound roast he'd sent down from the market—"Why we'll get down sick," I said, "you'll have the childern all in bed! So much meat isn't good for people." [30]

Delia Hawke herself is the Earth Mother. Her life has been full, close to the earth, and concerned with the essentials of life's continuity. Self-sufficient, she is proud of her power in the struggle for existence. She rejoices as she carries the burden of life and triumphs over obstacles: "...don't I remember it all, yes! every minute of it like it was today, the men marchin', and the women cryin', the way the dust rose, the times we went through and the way we had to work, the wool, the flax, the wheel, the things we grew and the things we had to make, and a thousand things you never dreamed or heard of, boy, the summertime, the river and the singin', the poverty, the sorrow, and the pain—we saw and had to do it all." [31]

Differing from Wolfe's usual practice, the characterization of Delia Hawke is entirely dramatic; he supplies no commentary whatever. Her character develops slowly, becoming in the end a full-blooded creation. She is at first a confused old lady who cannot tell from which direction the ships' whistle blasts come, then a garrulous visitor who jumps from one subject to the next, then a mother weaving a family chronicle, and finally eternal woman bearing her children, guarding her household, preaching a homily that the life struggle is never lost.

"And Miller," I said, "the banks haven't got everything," I said. "They may think they have, but now," I said winkin' at him, "I've got a secret that I'm goin' to tell you. I've still got a little patch of land out in the country that no one knows about and if the worst comes to the worst," I said, "I won't starve. I'll go out there and grow my food and I'll have plenty. And if you go broke you can come on out," I said. "You won't go hungry, I can make things grow." "Oh, but Delia," he said, "it's too late, too late. We're both too old to start again, and we've lost everything." "No," I said, "not everything. There's something left." "What is it?" he said. "We've got the earth," I said. "We've always got the earth. We'll stand upon it and it will save us. It's never gone back on nobody yet." [32]

Wolfe brings his story to a conclusion with a skillful juxtaposition: Delia plans for spring, describing her garden and orchard, while the ships, eager for voyages, blow out in the harbor. *The Web of Earth* is the first and best realization of Wolfe's theme of "wandering forever and the earth again."

Because Wolfe kept himself out of the story, there is none of the startling over-emotionalism characteristic of Eugene Gant in it. He proved to his critics that he could be dramatic if he wished and let his story make its own impact. Moreover, in the writing of it he did not agonize about structure or completion, nor was he dependent on Perkins for criticism. He was in full command of his powers. He was proud to have Perkins' comment, "Not one word of this should be changed." [33] However, because of its excessive length for magazine publication, it had to be cut slightly. Even so, when published, *The Web of Earth* was still the longest piece *Scribner's Magazine* had ever printed in a single issue—a quantitative record that pleased Wolfe immensely.

These two publications in 1932 demonstrate clearly that the short-novel form was well suited to Wolfe's talents. He liked to develop a situation with full detail, and it was almost impossible for him to write a short story. Many of the parts of his novels were written as separate chunks over a two- or three-month period, during times when he seemed to be unable to proceed with his novel as a whole. Some of these, like the death of Gant in *Of Time and the River*, the quarrel with Esther in *The Web and the Rock*, "Penelope's

Web," and "I Have a Thing to Tell You," have their own set of characters, their own beginning, climax, and conclusion.

If Wolfe had not had the compulsive urge to write a several-volume work of epic proportions, he could, by writing only short novels, have spared himself the heartache of his unceasing toil, the chaos of changes in plan, and the despair of goals never reached. His literary accomplishment would have been neater and would have been brightened by more artistic finish. But it would have been as much a waste of talent as if Joyce had continued to turn out Dubliners stories, or Virginia Woolf had confined herself to minute critical sketches. Nor was it in Wolfe's nature to avoid striving.

He kept to his larger task, and thereby achieved a scope that rose above the carelessness of loose-knit narrative and outweighed the tediousness of uninspired passages. We have the sprawl and the jerky transitions, but we also have the teeming fictional world common to great works in the novel form. As a result, Wolfe's reputation stands secure above the reputations of many successful practitioners of shorter forms who exhibit nicety and limitation.

Although Wolfe had demonstrated his ability at the short novel, he turned back to his original task now that he once more had money to carry on. He no longer had any illusions of a quick and easy completion for his projected work. There is a new, mature note in the statement he made to George McCoy early this year, after he had become resigned to patient labor: "I have found out that the man who hopes to create anything in this world of any enduring value, or beauty, must be willing to wreak it out of his spirit at the cost of unbelievable pain and labor; I know of no other way it can be done, he must work in the solitude and loneliness of art, no one can do it for him, and all of his childish dreams of a various and golden life, in which he has time to do everything and triumph in all of them, are out of the question." [34]

NOTES

1. This sum represents four payments of $250 made before March, 1930, when Wolfe was awarded the Guggenheim fellowship. Since he let Scribner's handle all his finances for him, he probably assumed that his LHA earnings later wiped out this debt. However, when he finally signed his contract in May, 1933, he found that this $1000 was still on the books as an advance against the second novel.

2. All the references to the house and the people on Verandah Place were retained when "No Door" was reduced to a short story in FDTM.

3. YCGHA, Chapter 27.

4. HCL*46AM-15, unpublished portion of a letter, March 22, 1932.

5. FDTM, pp. 5-6.

6. SN, pp. 593-94.

7. *Letters,* p. 330.

8. *Letters,* p. 316.

9. *Short Novels,* p. 50.

10. *Ibid.,* p. 71.

11. *Ibid.,* p. 27.

12. *Ibid.,* p. 49.

13. *Letters,* p. 15.

14. PN 1, September to November, 1926.

15. HCL*46AM-7(30). Although the covers of the ledger and a few of its pages are still extant, most of the pages have been torn out.

16. HCL*46AM-7(36). This coverless, almost complete ledger contains only one date, "Amsterdam, Sat. Feb 14 1931 have been here since Wed. morning."

17. A good example of Wolfe's distaste for those who claimed Eliot as their own is his characterization of the Rhodes scholar, Sterling, "a devoted follower of Mr. T. S. Eliot," in OT&R, pp. 630-31. ("He was a most precious, a most subtle, elegantly sad, quietly bitter and disdainful fellow," etc.)

18. HCL*46AM-7(69), Notebook fragments. This particular entry, made in Paris, was dated 1928. The date was altered to 1924 later, when Wolfe chose it, along with other pages torn from pocket notebooks, for Eugene Gant's journal in OT&R, pp. 661-80.

19. Eliot's attitude in "The Hollow Men" is directly challenged in YCGHA, Chapter 29, "The Hollow Men."

20. The short paragraph in W&R, p. 449, about "a royalist from Kansas City, a classicist from Nebraska," is an unmistakable swing at Eliot.

21. PN 13, February to May, 1930.

22. *Short Novels,* p. 70.

23. HCL*46AM-7(70-k), two isolated diary passages.

24. *Letters,* p. 328.

25. Wolfe had underlined this phrase from Sir Thomas Browne's *Religio Medici* in his Everyman Library copy of *An Anthology of Prose from Bede to Stevenson,* HCL*46A-262.

26. See the conclusion to *Death the Proud Brother.*

27. Julia Wolfe's report of her telling Tom the main narrative of *The Web of Earth* may be found in William Fifield's "Tom Wolfe Slept Here," *Story,* XXII (March-April, 1943), 9-16. Although her account is almost incomprehensible, it appears that she sat with Tom waiting to catch a late-night bus home and reminisced for several hours. She first heard about the short novel when Wolfe wrote her May 29, saying "I have used many of the stories you have told me, together with others of my own" (LTM, p. 220).

28. Floyd Watkins has studied the relationship between Wolfe's story and the actual happenings in Asheville when the murderers escaped, in *Thomas Wolfe's Characters* (Norman, Okla., 1957), Chapter 4.

29. *Short Novels,* p. 146. For convenience all references are to this reprint, which is the same as the version which appeared in *Scribner's Magazine,* except that the characters' names are changed to those of the Gant family, as Wolfe had arranged them for publication in FDTM.

30. *Short Novels*, p. 145.
31. *Ibid.*, p. 151.
32. *Ibid.*, p. 152.
33. Maxwell Perkins, "Thomas Wolfe," *Harvard Library Bulletin*, I (Autumn, 1947), 275.
34. *Letters*, pp. 238-39.

16

THE WRECK OF THE "K 19"
AND OTHER TROUBLES

ALTHOUGH THESE MONTHS HAD PRODUCED TWO OF WOLFE'S
works that are notable for their structural integrity as well as for
their energy, the remainder of the year 1932 did not go smoothly.
This was regrettable, since Wolfe had at last reached a frame of
mind in which he accepted slow, painstaking piecework. "I will have
to content myself" he told George McCoy, with doing "one book at
a time." "I have outlined at the present time the material and plan
of eight books; enough work to keep me busy for years. . . ." [1] But his
first venture with one of these books went off the track. Early in the
year, as he transferred some completed episodes of his novel into
typed form, he began to concentrate on the express train sequence,
"K 19." Under urging from Scribner's to get something publishable
into shape ("They have begun to push me a little lately," he wrote
Mabel),[2] he had decided to develop this part of his larger novel,[3]
and they had announced the book for fall publication.

What was the whole narrative of "K 19"? The question is hard to
answer, but Wolfe's notes and the few chunks of manuscript that remain indicate this general plan: John Hawke is making a visit home
to Altamont. In a first-person narrative, he gives us the hurry of a
New York railroad station, a characterization of Abraham Jones
(who is seeing John off), and then a long train ride south. In this
section, "The Passengers," he sketches about a dozen Old Catawbans
on their way south. The longest of these characterizations, "The Man
on the Wheel," is concerned with the life and escapades of Robert
Bland,[4] a wild young man whom John has known all his life, both
in the South and in New York City. At the end of the novel, there is
a brief glance at the boom days in Altamont before John boards "K

19" once more for his return journey to New York.[5] Judging from the long train sequence adapted from "K 19" for the opening of *Of Time and the River,* the best portion of the manuscript was the train ride itself, which emphasized the young man's impressions of power and excitement as the panorama of the American scene sped past.

Wolfe worked hard on "K 19" all spring, for he felt he had to produce for his friends at Scribner's. When he brought an almost complete typescript to Perkins, however, the editor thought the work seemed hasty. As a matter of fact, the 250-page sequence about Robert Bland (or Robert Weaver, as he was later called in *Of Time and the River*) was a tedious first draft: it was the result of Wolfe's first attempt at dictation, a practice he had been forced into when he injured his right arm in late January.[6] Aside from several brilliant sections, "K 19" had neither the unity nor the sustained drive of Wolfe's three preceding publications. He and Perkins agreed that Wolfe should continue work on his large project, putting "K 19" aside.

However, Wolfe made raids upon the manuscript for other books, and at present a fragmentary version of "The Man on the Wheel" is the only portion that remains unpublished. Besides the train ride in Book I, *Of Time and the River* absorbed the train race for the opening of Book III, "Proteus: The City," and the material about Abraham Jones and about Robert Weaver (especially the quarrel with the dying man, Upshaw, at the Hotel Leopold). The short stories "Boom Town," "The Bums at Sunset," and "The Far and the Near," came from this manuscript, and many isolated passages in Wolfe's books, particularly prose rhapsodies and rhetorical catalogues, first went into typescript as part of "K 19."

In the middle of 1932, Wolfe was forced to move again when the building he lived in was sold. Fortunately, he found a vacant apartment a few houses up the street at 101 Columbia Heights, so that he lost only two or three days from his work. His life during this summer was not different from his routine of the previous fifteen months. In one apartment or another he spent hot days and nights trying to write, pacing the length of his room, smoking constantly, running his fingers through his hair, and drinking his thirty cups of coffee a day. Gradually his feeling of personal obligation to Perkins lost its power. He could not finish any book-length part of his work by fall. "... I am going ahead daily with my book," he wrote Henry Allen Moe in

July, "or one section of it, which no matter what my publisher's announcements and statements say, will be published when I am done writing it and when I think it is fit to be published." [7] In these months, heaps of manuscript pages piled up, for Wolfe no longer wrote in ledgers but used cheap typewriter paper or yellow second sheets, which bore anywhere from fifty to one hundred and fifty pencil-scrawled words, depending on the speed with which he wrote.

Since he had become totally occupied with his own writing, Wolfe had long given up his habit of heavy reading. Now whenever he picked up a book he chose an old favorite. "Upon the top shelf of my book case," he wrote Julian Meade, who had asked the information,

I have attempted to put some of the books which I use all the time and which I am able to read again and again. All I can do is to give you a few of the titles, at any rate it will tell you something of the books I like best. At the present time reading from right to left the books in my top shelf are as follows: my old college edition of "The Illiad" [sic] parts of which I sometimes read; the Bible which I read a great deal—I mean a few books, "Ecclesiastes," "The Book of Job," "The Song of Solomon," "Revelations;" Webster's Collegiate Dictionary which has in its own [way] the best reading in the world; the plays of Shakespeare; the poems of Coleridge; the poems of John Donne; "The Anatomy of Melancholy," "Ulysses," "War and Peace," "The Brothers Karamazov," "Leaves of Grass," "Moll Flanders;" the plays of Moliere, the poems of Heinrich Heine and a book of German lyrics. I delight in all manner of anthologies, I believe some people laugh at them but I have some great fat thick ones, all of them good ones, and I go back to them again and again. [8]

He might have added, as he did two years later in answering Lewis Gannett's query about "What a Writer Reads," *The Oxford Book of English Prose, The World Almanac,* and the poems of Wyatt, Herrick, Herbert, Milton, Blake, Wordsworth, Keats, and Browning. [9] Of the great, fat anthologies, he might have pointed out that George Beaumont's *A Book of English Poetry,* [10] with a corner turned down at Spenser's "Cantos of Mutability" and with pencil marks under all of the time passages in Shakespeare's *Sonnets* and *Rape of Lucrece,* was the one he opened most.

As the months of work on his second book elapsed, Wolfe did become more and more conscious of time. The year before, in an attempt to comprehend the concept of time, he had copied notes on philosophic theories of time from the *Encyclopedia Americana* and the *Encyclopaedia Britannica*,[11] which quoted James, Bergson, and Einstein. Then, time past and time flowing, "the specious present," were fascinating phenomena to him. By now, however, time was becoming a formidable enemy. After "K 19" was put aside, he began to lose confidence again, faced with the multiplicity of detail that arose whenever he touched any new subject. Now that he returned to his work on "The October Fair," the two pieces that he chose to deal with reflect a growing mood of somberness.

He had made occasional notes on the subject of death for the past two years. In the winter of 1930, he had seen a man die in the subway, and he began thinking about the ignominy of death in a metropolis: "Death in New York. Where do they go! Make a scene out of this—Eugene in New York 4 years—Never sees funeral—the daily obituary columns in newspapers (copy it)."[12] Turning back to these notes and remembering other deaths that he had witnessed in New York, he began to outline "The Book of the Dead." This idea gradually developed into the short novel, *Death the Proud Brother*, which was published in *Scribner's Magazine* the following year.

The other episode he worked over at this time was the quarrel sequence with Esther. This narrative, under the title "A Vision of Death in April,"[13] grew into a short novel that included an anatomy of jealousy, dreams and visions, memories of joy, shame, and jealousy —all fixed in one large pattern of paradoxes: springtime in the city and love's ending amidst the city's meager offering of spring.

While the short-novel form proved itself a good vehicle for Wolfe, at the same time he was filled with alarm whenever he considered how long it would take him to complete "The October Fair," for each episode he touched expanded in detail until it reached the proportions of a short novel. He seemed almost unable to control the situations that he took in hand. As he wrote to Dubose Heyward, "With me, it is now a question of eat or be eaten; of subduing the monster or being devoured by it, and above all of learning how to make an end. I think I've gone through most of the other stages. I am now an exalted master in sweating blood, beating my head against the wall, stamping across the Brooklyn Bridge in the middle of the night. I have learned almost everything, in fact, except how not to write a book in eighteen volumes. . . ."[14]

Although he had finished about four hundred pages of typescript for the new book, it was in scattered episodes, and more and more the breadth of the scheme seemed to overwhelm him. To get away from the tyranny of his teeming memory, he tried short vacations. He traveled to York Springs, Pennsylvania, and saw, for the first time, his father's people, whom he liked immensely.[15] He took an ocean voyage to Bermuda, which he loathed,[16] then returned to visit briefly in Boston and in Andover. Still the change did no good; he was confused, perplexed, and unhappy that the work was going so badly.

By the end of the year, Wolfe was getting very low on money and again had to concern himself with finances. Since he had run through the Guggenheim fellowship, the royalties from the first novel, and the $2500 prize money for *Bascom Hawke,* he now turned from his book to try to put together some more stories for *Scribner's Magazine.*

Early in 1933, he brought his "Book of the Dead" episodes into shape as *Death the Proud Brother.* He lifted the train race out of "K 19," and, fitting it to youth's first impressions of New York and the "ancestral voices"[17] from "The October Fair," he produced "The Train and the City." Just as he reached the bottom of his purse, *Scribner's Magazine* bought these two stories and asked him to prepare a third.[18]

II

Death the Proud Brother is a reminder that early in his career Wolfe had called Thomas De Quincey his master. The work invites comparison between Wolfe's fictionalized autobiography and De Quincey's *Confessions of an English Opium Eater.* Both are chronicles of feeling in a prose that adopts not only the diction of poetry, with its variety of associations, but even its verse rhythms. Both turn aside for direct address to the reader and for formal address to personified abstractions in the manner of the ancient orators. Wolfe's sketch, however, does include fictional elements; for example, an early draft of the section about the workman who fell from a high building indicates that this was a story Thomas Beer had told Wolfe about the construction of the Bergdorf-Goodman building.[19] Also, *Death the Proud Brother* is arranged for social criticism. Emphasizing violence and examples of heartless haste or curiosity, it carries a denunciation of man's pitiless attitudes toward his brother in the city. Although it is more than an impassioned record of personal experience (for details are adjusted or invented to build up theme and pattern), it stands as a revealing example of the borderline position that Wolfe's work occupies between fiction and confession.

Although *Death the Proud Brother* has the emotional power that comes from exact and sensitive detail, it remains, because of its turgid style, a work that discourages second reading. Even so, Wolfe's subject—that great commonplace, Man's mortality—provides opportunity for thematic variations of both humility and triumph as Wolfe climbs into his twentieth-century pulpit, echoing the seventeenth century preachers on our common doom: "Something of us all . . . lies dead here in the heart of the unceasing city, and the destiny of all men living, yes, of the kings of the earth, the princes of the mind, the mightiest lords of language, and the deathless imaginers of verse, all the hope, hunger, and earth-consuming thirst that can incredibly be held in the small prison of a skull, and that can rack and rend the little tenement in which it is confined, is written here upon this shabby image of corrupted clay." [20] As he relates his story of four deaths in New York, he unfolds the classic view that man, poor, weak, and fearful, attains a dignity in death that lifts him above all the living that surround him.

Wolfe's conviction that every man has an immortal destiny is reflected again in this work. Death is the "Proud Death" whose "awful chrysm" of grandeur is given to all "the nameless, faceless, voiceless atoms of the earth"; he is loved and welcomed. Die and become, the conclusion seems to say, for the narrator, after describing the grim death of the man in the subway, looks at the permanent forms in the midst of this change and finds comfort: ". . .I looked and saw the deathless sky, the huge starred visage of the night, and heard the boats then on the river. And instantly an enormous sanity and hope of strong exultant joy surged up in me again; and like a man who knows he is mad with thirst, yet sees real rivers at the desert's edge, I knew I should not die and strangle like a mad dog in the tunnel's dark. I knew I should see light once more and know new coasts and come into strange harbors, and see again, as I had once, new lands and morning." And the apostrophe to Death gives, for Wolfe, the final praise, "Have you not opened your dark door for us who never yet found doors to enter?" [21]

"The Train and the City" is a characteristic Wolfe fragment, containing an experience on a train journey, a declaration by a chorus of voices speaking out of ancestral consciousness, and, finally, an interpretation of the city. It includes a "moment," when the two racing trains pass, that represents the essence of fleeting life: ". . . we now had met upon the everlasting earth, hurled past each other for a moment between two points in time upon the shining rails, never to meet, to speak, to know each other any more, and the briefness of our days, the destiny of man, was in that instant greeting and farewell." [22]

Aside from the significance the story itself may have, "The Train and the City" is also a convenient illustration of Wolfe's use of his pocket notebooks. For his interpretation of the "Voice of the City," he thumbed through the notes he had made from overheard conversations and selected what he thought typical. In New York in March, 1930, he had recorded two Italian-American women talking in a speak-easy, so he now drew the "sweet accent of maternal tribulation" out of several pages of notes that run on in this fashion:

I did, I hit her very hard, my hand was burnin' fer a half hour. I smacked her on the behind.

Ah I do it t' make 'em mind, see. I don't want 'em to get too fresh, see. That's my on'y reason fer that—that's my on'y reason fer hittin' her—I'm afraid she'll hurt the baby—she bends her fingers back.

I said for God's sake please don't do that I gotta headache. [23]

In Atlantic City in April, he overheard one vacationer assuring another, "As far as my boss is concerned its bizness only an' as far as Mr. Ladd is concerned its my own bizness an' after 5 o'clock I'm my own boss," and so on. [24] Now he used this record for the "tones of lady-like refinement" in the City Voice. Selecting here and there from notes like these, Wolfe was able to compile an authentic impression of the ordinary New York city-dweller confiding his affairs to his friend.

The third contribution to *Scribner's* in this series, "No Door," should have borne the more accurate title "Work in Progress," for Wolfe had, with Perkins' advice, lifted sections out of his greater novel scheme to make up the bulk of the text. Using a simple framing device, Wolfe began with a first-person narrator provoked into reminiscence by the remarks of a rich patron who is entertaining him in his apartment by the East River. [25] The passage of prose-poetry, "Of wandering forever and the earth again...," prefaces (with very little relevance) four episodes that Wolfe labeled simply by dates.[26] The episodes, which were later broken up for publication in various books, follow in this sequence: "October: 1931," the framing material and remembrances of Brooklyn, the only parts that were retained under the title "No Door" in the collection *From Death to Morning;* "October: 1923," the furious reading at Harvard,[27] then thoughts of home, with the paean to Autumn, "October had come again...";[28] "October: 1926," impressions of England beginning, "Smoke-gold by day...";[29] "Late April: 1928," the visits of Esther to the garret,[30] and the incipient quarrel.[31] "No Door" has no artistic integrity of its own. It is chiefly notable as a collection of some of Wolfe's most memorable passages, and it concludes with a magnificent assertion of the triumph of life over material things as the narrator sees a vision of an old man who speaks as a kind of encouraging Ecclesiastes:

Some things will never change. Some things will always be the same. Lean down your ear upon the earth, and remember there are things that last forever. Behold: because we have been set here in the shift and glitter of so many fashions, because we have seen so many things that come and go, so many words forgotten, so many fames that flared and were destroyed; because our brains were bent and sick and driven by the rush, the jar, the million shocks of multitude and number, because we were a grain of dust, a cellulate, and dying atom, a dwarfed wanderer among the horror of immense architectures..., our hearts grew mad and desperate and we had no hope.

But we know that the vanished step is better than the stone it walked upon, that one lost word will live when all the towers have fallen down, we know that the vanished men, the dead that they motored to swift burials and at once forgot, the cry that was wasted, the gesture that was half remembered, the forgotten moments of a million obscure lives will live here when these pavements are forgotten, and the dust of buried lovers will outlast the cities' dust. Lift up your heart, then, as you look at those proud towers: for we tell you they are less than blade and leaf, for the blade and the leaf will last forever.[32]

These three selections, which appeared in *Scribner's Magazine* for May, June, and July of 1933, provided Wolfe with enough money to keep him going at the beginning of the year. As the months went by, he sold five more stories to *Scribner's Magazine,*[33] but what he really needed was another agent, for he had separated from Madeleine Boyd in unpleasant circumstances.[34] He needed now an agent for periodical publication who could turn more of his material into money for him. Realizing this, Perkins thought of Elizabeth Nowell, who had just left the Scribner's office to work for the Maxim Lieber agency, and he spoke to her about Wolfe in November. Wolfe gave her "Boom Town," and she sold it early the next year for two hundred dollars. Suspicious as usual, Wolfe had been dissatisfied with the payments that *Scribner's Magazine* had given him, and he was delighted when Maxim Lieber assured him that Scribner's were "exploiting" his talent. Nevertheless, the price for "Boom Town" was considerably less than he had been getting from *Scribner's Magazine,* and the agency made no other sales for him before June, when Perkins recalled the story manuscripts for publication in *Of Time and the River.* When Wolfe signed his contracts for *Of Time and the River,* he received another thousand dollars from Scribner's [35] and five hundred dollars from Heinemann. This money, with the payments for the five additional *Scribner's Magazine* stories, kept him from being dependent on Scribner's handouts for more than a year.

In one way, Wolfe benefited enormously from his contact with Maxim Lieber's agency, for he began here an unbroken association with Elizabeth Nowell. When Miss Nowell left Lieber's office and opened her own agency in 1935, Wolfe wanted her to handle all of his magazine publication. They talked over episodes from the huge manuscript that might be salable as separate stories, and during that year, Miss Nowell, who combed through all the sections of "The October Fair," sold "Old Catawba," "Gulliver," "Polyphemus," "In the Park," "Arnold Pentland," [36] "Only the Dead Know Brooklyn," "The Cottage by the Tracks," and "The Bums at Sunset." These were later collected, along with the *Scribner's* pieces, in *From Death to Morning* in the fall of 1935.

Miss Nowell, who had known Wolfe since her days as a reader on *Scribner's Magazine,* worked closely with him for the rest of his career. Since Wolfe was so suspicious in business dealings, it is a tribute to her personality that she was able to continue an association with him for such a long time. She was an attractive, generous-hearted girl with a ready wit and a tendency to good-natured raillery. Since she was competing in a man's world, she seldom allowed her essential warmth and sensitivity to emerge, and she played a role of a rough-talking, tough-minded Girl Friday. Very soon, a mutual affection and respect developed between Miss Nowell and Wolfe. She spent hours going over his work with him, the sort of thing no agent is expected to do. She gave her time partly because of gratitude to Wolfe for the chance to be his agent (this enhanced her reputation and brought her clients) and partly because she had a sincere interest in everything he wrote. The best illustration of her qualities and of her feeling for Wolfe is in a letter she wrote at the time his second novel was in the press.

All fooling aside, though, I want to try to say how much I think of your work. . . .Maybe I've got some kind of Yankee repression but goddamn it you must know about it whether I show it by sitting up all night working with you or by raving around like most of these other fool women. I can't help feeling self-conscious even now, and imagining your showing this to [Perkins]. . . .But you know I know you've got more talent and poetry and sincerity and greatness in your little finger than all the other writers I can think of put together. It's fallen on me to pick on you about all the nasty little details that magazine editors carp at and I'm afraid you'll always think of me as dragging you out of the Chatham bar or waving a blue pencil in your face. But underneath all of that I always get a tremendous inspiration out of your things and out of working with you. Well, you must realize too how grateful I am at the way you stuck with me and helped me these last two months. Maybe this sounds New-England-frost-bound or whatever you call it, but I've got tears in my eyes writing it, and I'll keep on showing you how much I do feel by working like hell on everything I can while you're away.[37]

As time passed, she became, in a sense, a minor Max Perkins to him. Principally, she spurred Wolfe into rewriting episodes as stories. In problems of revision, her influence was good, for she showed him how to cut his material, and she was often able, in her jocose manner, to persuade him to improve a story by some minor alteration. Whenever she gave advice, she did so cautiously, and Wolfe felt free to accept or reject it. In this relationship, Wolfe felt neither deference nor dependence; as a result, the friendship was a lasting one, and after Wolfe's break with Perkins, Miss Nowell grew to be his most trusted friend in the publishing world. Through continued hard work, Miss Nowell was able to sell a stream of magazine pieces that brought Wolfe an income large enough to support him, even if he had delayed the publication of his later books for years.

NOTES

1. HCL, unpublished portion of a letter, March 22, 1932.

2. *Ibid.*, April 28, 1932.

3. This idea, says John Hall Wheelock, probably came from Perkins, who had felt that Wolfe's main book would be the better balanced without the long train episode. Interview with me, December, 1950.

4. This character is based on Wolfe's friend, Henry Stevens, who later committed suicide.

5. Pieces of "K 19," chiefly about Robert Bland or Weaver, still remain in HCL*-46AM-7(34) and (35), and a few other pages are scattered here and there among the Wolfe papers.

6. See *Letters*, pp. 318-19. Wolfe finished "The Man on the Wheel" by April 21, 1932, and described it as "an 80,000 word MSS, the complete story of a man's life, part of my new book" (*Letters*, p. 340).

7. *Letters*, p. 344.

8. *Letters*, p. 324.

9. *Letters*, p. 480.

10. HCL*46A-105.

11. Wolfe used one of these entries for Eugene Gant's Paris notebook in OT&R, pp. 670-71.

12. PN 12, October, 1929, to January, 1930.

13. The bulk of this material became Book VI of W&R. Wolfe apparently wrote these episodes in 1931 and 1932, for his typist dated the pieces of manuscript as they went into typescript between June and August, 1932. HCL*46AM-7(55).

14. *Letters*, p. 351.

15. Wolfe's visits to his Pennsylvania relatives were the inspiration for the hearty welcomes of "His Father's Earth" (*Modern Monthly*, April, 1935), the dream of the good life associated with his father. This episode later made up one of George Webber's daydreams in W&R, pp. 88-90.

16. Wolfe made use of his Bermuda trip in a story (still unpublished) entitled "The Still-Vexed Bermoothes."

17. In "Whoever builds a bridge across this earth, whoever lays a rail across this mouth, whoever stirs the dust where these bones lie, let him go dig them up, and say his Hamlet to the engineers," the phrase "say his Hamlet" is obscure even in its context. It is a good example of Wolfe's tendency to sacrifice sense for sound when he hit upon a phrase that pleased him. He had meant to say that the builders should, when viewing these bones, comment on man's mortality and on the excellence of man now brought so low. Earlier notes for this passage read "speak of Yorick to the engineers."

18. LTM, p. 241.

19. HCL*46AM-7(49). In this version Stephen Hook, whom Wolfe modeled on Thomas Beer, was the sensitive witness of the terrible accident.

20. FDTM, p. 46.

21. FDTM, pp. 67-68.

22. *Scribner's Magazine*, XCIII (May, 1933), p. 290. This story became, with minor changes, the opening of Book IV in OT&R, pp. 407-19.

23. PN 13, February to May, 1930.

24. *Ibid.*

25. Wolfe seems to have based this episode on a visit to the apartment of David

Cohn, 2 Beekman Place, May 7, 1932, although it may have been at the earlier date indicated in n. 26, September, 1931.

26. Some of the episodes were cut out before publication. Wolfe's first plan for the chunks to be used in "No Door" is recorded in a list, HCL*46AM-7(51), Box 2:

1. Of wandering forever and the earth again
2. Brooklyn Scene (September: 1931)
3. October had come again   October ~~1923~~
4. The Hudson River Meets the Harbor   November 7, ~~1923~~
5. Time is a fable and a mystery   June ~~1927~~
6. The Station   May 3, ~~1928~~
7. The Man in the Window   ~~June: 1928~~ April late April.

In spite of Wolfe's cafeteria-style method of composition for this work, C. Hugh Holman feels that it has a "tight thematic structure." In a new edition of "No Door," reprinted in *Short Novels*, pp. 159-231, Holman has restored "The House of the Far and Lost" to the English scene in Part III.

27. Later published in OT&R, pp. 90-93.

28. *Ibid.*, pp. 327-44.

29. *Ibid.*, pp. 601-8, 611-13. Note that this chunk was not included in Wolfe's first list (quoted in n. 26). He had probably not yet written it when the first list was compiled, for it is the latest in composition (spring, 1933) of all the episodes in "No Door."

30. Later published in YCGHA, pp. 37-42.

31. Later published in W&R, pp. 554-55.

32. *Short Novels*, p. 230. This episode was later published in part in YCGHA, pp. 42-44.

33. "The Four Lost Men," "The Sun and the Rain," "The House of the Far and Lost," "Dark in the Forest, Strange as Time," and "One of the Girls in Our Party."

34. In 1931, Mrs. Boyd had delayed sending Wolfe his advance from the German publication of *Look Homeward, Angel* and had handled his money so irregularly as to cause suspicion of her honesty. After a violent scene in the Scribner's office, Wolfe discharged her.

35. Although Malcolm Cowley, in "Unshaken Friend," *New Yorker*, XX (April 1, 1944), 28-36 and (April 8, 1944), 30-43, stated that Wolfe received $5000 in advance royalties on OT&R, the Scribner's account books show only a total advance of $2050.

36. Later reprinted as "A Kinsman of His Blood" in HB.

37. HCL*53M-113F, March 1, 1935. Miss Nowell's continued devotion to Wolfe is further displayed in her publications after his death. She did research for six years (1950-56) to produce *The Letters of Thomas Wolfe*, the most important collection of documents and information that has yet come forth about Wolfe. Then she continued to work, even though stricken with cancer, to finish *Thomas Wolfe: A Biography*, the last chapter of which she finished just before her death in 1958. Her modesty caused her to play down her role in Wolfe's life when she wrote about him and to omit from the collection of letters Wolfe's strongest words of praise for her. Wolfe's statement, which appears in a letter to Vardis Fisher, July 17, 1935, should be recorded. He recommends Miss Nowell as an agent and then says, "... she's far and away the best agent I ever knew, absolutely honest and reliable, is not out to make money for herself—believe it or not, this is true—and is genuinely interested in your work" (HCL*49M-239).

17

TOWARD A "FINAL SET OF COMBINATIONS"

AT THE BEGINNING OF THE YEAR 1933, WOLFE BURST THROUGH the stoppage that had blocked the progress of "The October Fair." When he took a trip to Baltimore and Gettysburg with Max Perkins, they talked over his problems. As usual, Perkins gave Wolfe the necessary encouragement and probably made specific suggestions, for Wolfe wrote his friend, George Wallace, about his new outlook:

I was in a horrible, ugly and furious temper when you were down here, because after all my bloody sweating in the last two years I seemed to have gotten nowhere, and in fact, the whole game seemed to be lost. But just after you left in January I took a little trip to Baltimore and Washington, came back almost completely broke, in fact I was down to my last ten dollars and had no idea where any more was coming from, and in this mood I plunged into work and in the next month wrote over 100 000 words. I seemed suddenly to get what I have been trying to get for two years, the way to begin the book and make it flow, and now it is all coming with a rush.[1]

With the purpose of hurrying the book along, Perkins had very likely proposed that Wolfe use the "No Door" framing device—the narrator reminiscing about various experiences of his life. Since it would allow Wolfe to introduce scattered episodes that he had already written of his autobiographical narrative, it would rescue him from his most damaging obsession, that he must present a detailed, year-by-year account of his life. The suggestion was effective only in that it got Wolfe started again. He set to work on the early part of his book, and this outline jotted into his notebook indicates the area he was working in at this time:

Dinwiddie Scott [2]—Baltimore—my brother and
father—Dinwiddie's wife
Later Boston—the station
The Park Street Station
The Fury
The Books
The Food
Uncle Emerson and family
Professor Butcher and his classes
Home—arrest—disgrace—flight
The first year in the city
I was now twenty five years old [3]

After a brief but intense creative period, Wolfe turned over to Perkins in April a batch of six hundred typescript pages, bringing the total of his completed work to about one thousand pages.

Over the last three years, the only unifying plan that Wolfe had kept firmly in mind was the chronology of his own life; as a result, his narrative was gradually becoming a detailed life chronicle. As a "Note" to Perkins on his progress indicates, the book was still in four parts. The first, "Antaeus: Earth Again," included John Hawke's early life in Old Catawba, his stay in Boston, and his return home at the death of his father, which utilized some of the "K 19" train ride material. In the scenes at home which follow—the family squabbles, the drunken ride, the arrest—Wolfe intended to show the "frenzied dissonance and the tortured unrest in the lives of people from which the strong figure of the father has been removed." [4] Part II, now entitled "Proteus: The City," comprised Hawke's first year in New York. These two parts represented most of the work Wolfe had done: he had written "almost a first draft" of "Antaeus" and part of "Proteus." Of Part III, "Faust and Helen," he had only the last portion written ("A Vision of Death in April"), and of Part IV, "The October Fair," he had only notes.

Wolfe had not yet scrapped his Antaeus legend, for he told Perkins that the city was no longer the principal enemy of his hero. Another similarly Protean figure, "the million-visaged shape of time and memory" was now the Heracles who subdues Antaeus. With this change, Wolfe wished to raise the subtitle of his book to prominence. "It is now my desire," he wrote Perkins, "to call the whole book

Time and the River instead of *October Fair* as I think that *Time and the River* better describes the intention of the whole book." [5]

When Maxwell Perkins examined Wolfe's latest additions to his manuscript, the vigor and vividness of many scenes no doubt pleased him, but the lack of coherent narrative also made him fearful of further delay in publication.[6] After surveying the new material, Perkins wrote a brief criticism of it. He wished to put something of Wolfe's before the public in the autumn, and he therefore regarded the material in hand to be the bulk of the book and suggested an ending within the limits of what Wolfe had now given him to read. It is evident that the book employed the framework of reminiscence used for "No Door" because Perkins' first comment was "Make rich man in opening scene older and more middle-aged." Further, he suggested that for the ending the same passage be used that had concluded "No Door" ("Possibly ending for book with return to the city, the man in the window scene and the passages 'Some things will never change' ").[7] It was during this uncertain stage of the planning, when the novel and "No Door" were intricately connected, that Wolfe told his mother, "They have already planned to bring out a special edition of a short book early in the autumn and a long book later on. . . ." [8] It is a puzzle whether Perkins conceived an expanded version of "No Door" especially for the purpose of getting some of Wolfe's new work between hard covers or whether he thought only to reprint the short magazine version of the story when he saw there would be no novel ready for autumn. Although in September Wolfe was still talking about this publication ("Scribners are going to publish my story *No Door* in book form and if they agree. . .I want to dedicate the book to Ben"),[9] the project was never carried out.

To return to Max Perkins' criticism of Wolfe's incomplete manuscript, it is clear that, in view of Wolfe's large-scale methods, there was still too much work to be done in time for fall publication. Nor did Perkins yet understand Wolfe's struggle with "Amount and Number" or his methods of working out his material. Although some of Perkins' suggestions for using piecemeal material were excellent, as, for example, his suggestion, "Use material from Man on the Wheel and Abraham Jones for first year in the city and University scenes," [10] still others were of a kind to incite Wolfe to write for years—for example, the direction to supply more childhood reminiscences, or the suggestion to add more dialogue with Esther between the quarrel scenes, or, most particularly, the proposal to "write out fully and with all the dialogue the jail and arrest scenes." [11]

Nevertheless, since Perkins felt that the situation was under control and since Scribner's wished to relieve Wolfe of the necessity for writing magazine stories, in May, 1933, they offered him a contract granting advance royalties for the long-awaited novel. Wolfe must have had great misgivings as he affixed his signature, for the contract stated, "It is desirable that the said work should be published in the Fall of 1933, and said Author agrees to deliver to said Publishers a copy of the manuscript complete and ready for the press not later than August 1, 1933.[12]

Spring and early summer of 1933 were a period of hard work for Wolfe. He expanded the arrest and jail scene; he wrote out the impressions of England, the Coulson family scenes, and the Rhodes Scholar scenes; [13] he digressed into sketching out material that later developed in "Gulliver," "No Cure for It," and "God's Lonely Man." [14] But he did not meet the deadline for August. In fact, in early August he was sidetracked (perhaps by Perkins' suggestion) with boyhood reminiscences and with characterizations of his kin, especially his maternal aunts and uncles. He wrote to Perkins that he was completing this section of his book, which he called "The Hills Beyond Pentland," although he had written only a few unrelated episodes.[15] During this period, then, he never relaxed his efforts, but he often deceived himself, substituting the mere activity of writing for the conscious effort to complete a publishable volume.

In the past fifteen months, Wolfe had been unhappier and more unhinged than at any other time of his life. Entries in his pocket notebook during the previous year show the unhealthy state of mind that produced *Death the Proud Brother* and "A Vision of Death in April." Lists in May and June contain dark subjects for his writing: deaths, symptoms of madness, details of burning jealousy in love, situations of shame ("The Man Who Hit My Father in the Eye When He Was Drunk. For a Boy there is no more terrible thing than to see that his father is afraid before another man"), incidents of fear, examples of hatred and loathing, nightmares ("of the tender and corrupt children [16]—of their clinging lips—of incestuous horror—of having slept with one's teacher's wife [—] of returning to a place and being received quietly and without smiles and to find the houses closed the streets bare—nothing but shame and silence" [17]). In 1933 similar entries appear, a list of "Unhappy Scenes," a "Dirge" ("Why are we unhappy" [18]), and a meditation on loneliness and on the tone of loneliness in Job, Ecclesiastes, Everyman, Shakespeare, Wordsworth.

Besides these notes made for writing, Wolfe often recorded scenes of violence that he saw in his wandering. This is the end of a day in which he ran into two wife-beatings: "Went to the Lido, got pt. gin—went to Joe's, ate—walked to Atlantic Avenue—Rode to 4th Ave—on St car—came back to Clark St. on Subway—drunk woman crying and weeping and accusing man of beating her—negro elevator boy says to cop above "Dere's a fight downstairs—a man's beatin' on a woman." Cop runs into booth—gets gun and goes down. Horror! Horror! Horror!" [19]

He was more alone than ever. Perkins was his only real friend; other people he saw were mostly chance acquaintances. Because of his fretting over the book, he was drinking heavily again, as the handwriting in his pocket notebook often shows. In addition to the constant pressure of the book, he worried about money matters, not only for himself but for his sister Mabel in Washington and his sister Effie with her large family in Anderson, South Carolina. In this summer of 1933, his tension mounted. He worked long hours and then could not sleep. He began to lose weight. He felt exhausted and harried and was usually in a furious temper. Finally in September, he took a few days off for a trip to Vermont with his friend, Robert Raynolds. "...I was exhausted," he wrote his mother, "and could go no further—had an attack of ptomaine poisoning and sheer nervous fatigue—cramps in stomach and unable to hold food—so had to get away." [20]

During the reminder of the year, he continued to range from one episode to another in his manuscript, while his typist stacked the products of the summer's labor into neatly transcribed piles. As Wolfe filled in narrative gaps, he was crushed with horror at the profusion of details that rose up before him for each episode. Even the chronology of the book had lengthened when he investigated his father's ancestry for "The Hills Beyond Pentland" section. His turning aside to write of his father's world resulted in the story, "The Four Lost Men," a remembrance of his father, and an interpretation of Garfield, Arthur, Harrison, and Hayes, Presidents during his father's early manhood. In October, he was still feverishly scribbling, in hopes that somehow the whole work might miraculously assume final shape if he strove hard enough. He was so upset that he had lost his enormous appetite for food. He grew pale and dark-eyed, nervous and irascible. His inability to finish the book was like a disease that wasted his strength. After writing for hours, he would roam the streets, drunk and stultified. Sometimes when he was drunk he would call up Aline Bernstein and tell her he was dying. By the end of November, both his mental and physical health were so threatened that the Scribner's editors were afraid he would collapse.

No one could equal Wolfe's own account of his arrival at final despair. In *The Story of a Novel* he pictures both the impact of the dismal sights of the depression years on his sensibilities and the accumulated mental tension during his struggle to master his material. But he does not include all the details of his problem. He does not describe his additional anxiety about the need for more money. He does not tell his shame at his imposture in having accepted royalty advances from Scribner's and then having failed in his agreement to produce a completed manuscript. Nor does he confess his irrational sensitivity to the adverse criticism of his published work which came, amidst the praise, from various camps. "I was badly shaken," he wrote Perkins later, "time and again I was driven to the verge of utter self-doubt and despair by the sense of pressure all around me—the questions asked, the doubts expressed about my ability to write another book, the criticisms of my style, my adjectives, verbs, nouns, pronouns, etc. my length and fulness, my lack of Marxian politics and my failure to expound a set position in my writings. . . ." [21] In this atmosphere of national depression, personal obligation, financial need, and searching self-doubt, he sank at the end to that desperate condition he describes in *The Story of a Novel*:

"I still wrote and wrote, but blindly, hopelessly, like an old horse who trots around in the unending circle of a treadmill and knowns no other end nor purpose for his life than this. If I slept at night, it was to sleep an unceasing nightmare of blazing visions that swept across my fevered and unresting mind. And when I woke, it was to wake exhausted, not knowing anything but work, lashing myself on into a hopeless labor, and so furiously at it through the day; and then night again, a frenzied prowling of a thousand streets, and so to bed and sleepless sleep again, the nightmare pageantry to which my consciousness lay chained a spectator." [22]

In this distraught condition he sought Max Perkins for help and advice.

When Perkins suggested another survey of his progress, Wolfe put together all the manuscript of the story he had really been writing, the story of his life. The framing devices were discarded, the childhood of Hawke put aside and the sections about his mother's family. He drew up the most detailed outline that he had yet executed and, for the first time, saw his book as a whole, from the first Old Catawba scene, through the love affair with Esther, to the hospital scene in Munich. He took each separate episode, labeled simply "October 1920" or "The First Year in the City," and, under each, described what was written, what was yet to be written, and what purpose he had in mind in each scene. In this analysis, Wolfe gave the greatest amount of detail to his statement of purpose in each part. An example is the scene in which the boy visits his father dying of cancer in Baltimore. Wolfe's intent was:

1. To show in the meeting between the old dying man and his son the feeling that they are strangers to each other and the phantasmal dream-enchantment of time. The boy cannot believe this old dying spectre was ever his father or had anything to do with the life of his childhood and which now seems stranger than a dream. For this reason, he looks upon the old dying man as a ghost, an imposter of his real father, and in his heart he loathes him and wants to escape from him and the spell of black horror and unreality he casts on him.

2. To show in the description of the great hospital the conflict between the energies of life and death and its effect on youth: the young internes who have already been infected by a fatal, morbid, almost reckless, gayety of death. A brief description (already written but not typed) of the stimulation of the great drug of death upon the young internes (whom the boy has known previously) and his own revulsion and loathing of it. His desire to escape into life towards his vision of the shining city, the fortunate, good and always happy life that has no death in it.[23]

He divided up his crate of manuscript, tearing sections out of ledgers and placing them with the stacks of scrawled yellow typewriter paper. When it was all transcribed, Perkins said later, the typescript of the whole stood two feet high on the table.

It was on December 14, 1933, that Wolfe put himself entirely into Perkins' hands, and he felt relief for the first time in years. His hopes began to revive as he shifted the responsibility to his editor:

I don't envy you the job before you: I know what a tough thing it is going to be to tackle, but I do think that even in the form in which the material has been given to you, you ought to be able to make some kind of estimate of its value or lack of value and tell me about it. . . .Moreover, when all the scenes have been completed and the narrative changed to a third person point of view, I think there will be a much greater sense of unity than now seems possible, in spite of the mutilated, hacked-up form in which you have the manuscript; and I do feel decidedly hopeful, and hope your verdict will be for me to go ahead and complete the first draft as soon as I can; and in spite of all the rhythms, chants,—what you call my dithyrambs—which are all through the manuscript, I think you will find when I get through that there is plenty of narrative—or I should say when *you* get through—because I must shamefacedly confess that I need your help now more than I ever did.[24]

Perkins saw immediately that for publication the manuscript would have to be divided in two, so he persuaded Wolfe to drop the love story and to concentrate on the early portion of his narrative. Unfortunately, Wolfe as yet had only about half of this early matter completed. He set to work to finish the job as fast as possible, and many of the parts of the published book show his haste. Wolfe was conscious of this, as he told Martha Dodd (not quite accurately) after *Of Time and the River* came out: ". . . I wrote it in less than a year before it was published, at a time when I was horribly tired and when I had exhausted myself in writing the two books which are to follow."[25]

The manuscript that Perkins read was still a first-person narrative told by John Hawke. But by this time there could be no denial that the book was the "further adventures" of Eugene Gant. Wolfe agreed with Perkins that the family characters should resume their old labels and that the narrative point-of-view should be in the third person. In January, Wolfe sat down with renewed purpose and began to rewrite and fill in the gaps. He reviewed the general subject matter "from beginning to end," noting these scenes he had not yet written:

1. Robert Weaver
2. End of Dinwood Bland Scenes [26]

3. Introduction to Boston Scenes
4. Professor Butcher
5. Death of Gant
6. First Dinner at House [27]
7. Troy [28]
8. Hotel Leopold
9. Going abroad
10. England Ship
11. 1st Mo in Paris
12. End of Starwick Scenes
13. End of Europe Scenes
14. End of Ship Esther Scenes

As Wolfe's notes show, he was for the first time working from the very beginning with his rewriting and revision.

The First Episode

Prolog	500 words
Old Catawba	5000 words
The Platform	5000 words
The Train	15000 words
Baltimore	5000 words

Fill *the train* with "exultancy and joy" [29]

Despite Perkins' assumption of the burden, Wolfe did not relinquish to his editor the power to make final decisions. On the other hand, Perkins was eager to rush the manuscript toward publication much faster than Wolfe was willing to travel. Here began the year-long duel that Wolfe described in *The Story of a Novel*.[30] After a number of heated discussions about separate episodes, Wolfe finally agreed about March 1 that Perkins should go through the entire manscript with a blue pencil and that the decisions about scenes to be cut would be made all at once. Although this method sped up the progress toward a publication date, Wolfe was still revising and filling in gaps in the narrative. By April, he had an entire chapter outline for *Of Time and the River* that led finally to a place where he wrote "Finis."

Now that the book was on its way to completion, Wolfe's life was much happier. His great weariness had lifted, and he had regained his good humor. He was more devoted to Perkins than ever. In fact, his gratitude to Perkins was almost oppressive. He never ceased telling the Scribner's staff that Perkins had saved his life. After office hours the two would go out to Cherio's or to the Chatham Walk for drinks and dinner; later, they would return to the office to go over the manuscript from 8:30 to 10:30. Sometimes Wolfe would even sleep on the long table in the Scribner's library.

He had moved once again, to a new apartment in Brooklyn, 5 Montague Terrace, still keeping to a street by the harbor. With the change of address, his haunts changed slightly, and he spent hundreds of late-night hours in a little all-night coffee shop at the corner of Montague and Henry, regarding it as a sort of poor man's club. In his new quarters he did not work quite so steadily as before, but he accomplished much more toward his immediate end. By the middle of June, the manuscript of Books I and II was ready for proofreading, and after a great struggle most of the manuscript of the first three books went to the printers in July.

Besides revising and adapting the parts already in existence, during these months Wolfe turned out several completely new sections, the Hotel Leopold, Troy, and part of the Joel Pierce sequences, most of the episode of the three friends in Europe, the description of Eugene's frenzied writing and dreams in Southern France, and finally the introduction of Esther, producing in his haste some of the most swollen narrative passages in the book. Thus by September he had worked his way through to the end. Although he intended to review the whole, not only to rewrite rough portions but also to add a great many things, he never had the opportunity. To forestall these additions, Perkins sent the whole manuscript to the printers while Wolfe was on a two-week vacation at the Chicago Fair. When Wolfe returned in October, he was furious; he felt that his book could not possibly have its best effect, or even be comprehensible, unless he supplied the missing sequences. But Perkins persuaded him that, if he let him work another six months, there would only be a demand for another six months, and so on, for years.

Wolfe did make some additions and rearrangements while trying to correct proof in the fall: he toyed with section titles,[31] moved some of the prose rhapsodies from one place to another, and threatened to write whole new chapters. There was still so much to do, Wolfe felt, and he would not let go of the proofs. "He sat brooding over them for weeks in the Scribner library and not reading," Perkins said. "John Wheelock read them and we sent them to the printer and told Tom it had been done. I could believe that otherwise he might have clung to them to the end." [32] Although Wolfe pleaded for more time for revision, Perkins convinced him that immediate publication was the only course. As late as December, Wolfe made a few additions to the last two books. The principal change was in the conclusion. Formerly, the book had ended with the life and death symbolism of the people entering the ship; Wolfe now added the chance meeting of Eugene and Esther that implied their future.

Wolfe wished to acknowledge Perkins' help during the gestation and birth of the book in a preface to *Of Time and the River*, but the Scribner's staff persuaded him to withhold it.[33] He did include his dedication to Perkins (the most famous of the many acknowledgments by Scribner's authors) as a sincere statement of his appreciation and attachment. The last thing Wolfe did before *Of Time and the River* went to press was to prepare the statement about his planned six-book series that would appear as a "Publisher's Note" opposite the second half-title page. Besides making the announcement of his series, he wished to parry criticism of the inconclusive ending. It is interesting to see that in the first notes for this statement, *Look Homeward, Angel* was not included in the series, for Wolfe felt that his first book had made its own ending. Publication was set for March, 1935.

Of Time and the River was in print at last. Although he had growled and complained, Wolfe realized what Perkins had done for him in the past year. The editor had exercised a discipline that Wolfe himself did not possess. When Wolfe had his plan in outline, Perkins, acting as a conscience, prodded him to fill in that outline; when the outline grew, Perkins tried to hold Wolfe to the original plan. Wolfe had finished his first novel without any such guiding hand, and he brought to a close many a shorter piece by himself, but the new scheme was so vast that he could not even feel reassured when his common sense told him he could complete it part by part. If Wolfe had never surrendered his manuscript to Perkins, his drive to write would have kept him plodding along, despite mental anguish, until he found an end, but he might have spent years in this way and thus cut off opportunity for later work. But there were other pressures besides his own desire to triumph over his limitations. He had taken money from Scribner's, yet he had not fulfilled his contract. Then, after he had run through the Scribner's advance, he was reduced to spending his energies seeking money in magazine publication. At the end of 1933, then, he had no choice. He knew the book had to be finished in a hurry. And Perkins saw to it that Wolfe did finish it in a year.

II

But *Of Time and the River* was not the finished piece of work that *Look Homeward, Angel* had been. Nothing put together in this fashion could have been. There were so many false starts, so many plans, so many changes, that structurally the work had to suffer. Moreover, in the rush to complete *Of Time and the River* in 1934, Wolfe used in many episodes a narrative style that is particularly overblown. This hurried, tired writing is, paradoxically, the one that uses the most high-powered vocabulary. More than most writers, Wolfe had to stress control in order to keep from spending energy wastefully. Often the energy overflowed as he mechanically turned on the tap and let the highly charged words stream out. But not all this florid style is found in those sections written for the first time in 1934 (and at least one passage written that spring, the death of Gant, stands among the best in the book). Much more annoying and certainly irreparable in a six-month polishing, is the ranting and foaming of Eugene. His grotesque mutterings, his hysterical outbursts, and his battering his fists against the wall—all detract from the shy, hopeful, eager striving of the Eugene of the other scenes.

Like all of Wolfe's work, *Of Time and the River* contains a limited amount of action; besides this, isolated passages and characterizations tend often to distract the reader's attention from the central narrative. Although the same is true of *Look Homeward, Angel*, *Of Time and the River* differs greatly in narrative technique in two particular ways. First, encouraged to magnitude while reading *War and Peace*, Wolfe wrote many fully developed "scenes" for *Of Time and the River*, whereas *Look Homeward, Angel* has very few such scenes, and most of them are short. Although this use of scene rather than "summary" was a step forward for Wolfe, it unfortunately created new problems. Since he tended to ramble to extreme length, his editor often spent hours persuading him to whittle a scene down.

The second difference, the variety of literary forms that Wolfe assembled in *Of Time and the River*, is really a growth out of *Look Homeward, Angel*. The early version, "O Lost," had been cluttered with inept lyrical attempts and with crude "essays on various sub-jects" that Perkins cut out. Now, since Wolfe's skill in composing rhythmic incantations had improved and his leaning toward abstrac-tion had straightened up, the personal emotional statements and the editorializing find their place appropriately. But more than this, his linguistic gusto is displayed in an abundance of verbal experiments: between the covers of *Of Time and the River,* Wolfe has, in addition to his narrative, a great potpourri of dithyrambic chants, catalogues, exercises in word play, declamations, meditations, parodies, satiric sketches, short stories, essays, fantasies, and even journal notes.

The reason for the anthology-like nature of the book is partly the method of composition. Wolfe did not write it in straight running fashion as he did *Look Homeward, Angel,* but, as we have seen, he wrote episodes here and there, over the long period of time, for an ever-expanding narrative. When Scribner's pressed him to get the book into shape, Wolfe wanted to make use of materials he had la-bored over during all the years of his work on the novel series. Hence he gathered prose poems and narrative incidents from various places and lumped them into the first book to be published. On the whole, they are very well adapted to their places—"October is the time for all returning" to Eugene's thoughts of his dead father, the "Names of the Nation" to Eugene's hearing the bells of Dijon, the various "K 19" passages to the train rides. There are, of course, exceptions— the most hilarious being Eugene's sudden realization, as he steps out of his jail cell in Blackstone, that he prefers the poetry of Shakespeare to the poetry of Shelley.

In spite of the abundant variety, the book has some traditional structure: the simple unity of the travel novel is as old as story-telling, and the gradual awakening in the "discovery of life" novel is one of the commonest patterns in the twentieth century. Themes supplementing the narrative ought to aid in unifying the work, but Wolfe, absorbed in Eugene Gant's wanderings, seems to lose track of them. Yet *Of Time and the River* was only a part of a larger plan. Thus the book leaves some themes unfinished and others hardly be-gun. The theme of the search for a father, John Peale Bishop com-plains,[34] is not evident. Although one could point to several refer-ences that Bishop overlooked, Wolfe's notes show that the full de-velopment of the theme was to be in future volumes.[35] Then, too, the proem "of wandering forever and the earth again" reaches the resolution that love remains to succor man the wanderer, yet only on the last page of this fat volume is there an indication that love will offer certainty and strength. Wolfe also planned in the next volume, "The October Fair," an end to Eugene's fruitless questing and hungering. This answer was adumbrated in a Wolfe story published in 1934, "Dark in the Forest, Strange as Time." Here the dying German gives his advice to the young man: "Fields, hills, mountains, riffers, cities, peoples—you vish to know about zem all. Vun field, vun hill, vun riffer, zat iss enough." [36]

And within the simple narrative there are patterns of action that shore up the teetering structure. As part of Eugene's discovery of life, there are his rejections of one system or source of value after another [37]—the formulas of the Playshop, the culture-mill of teaching, the glittering life of the wealthy Hudson River people, the culture seeking of American expatriates, and, finally, Europe itself. The America-versus-Europe conflict, a continually recurring theme, is resolved in an affirmation of indigenous culture as against imported culture. Amidst these other strains runs Wolfe's usual theme of life value versus material value (as represented by the city). Finally, Frederick Ives Carpenter, in a letter replying to John Chamberlain's attacks on the book, points out the theme of the artist's development, which was to have been important in the whole novel series. "The 'controlling idea' of Wolfe's novels," he suggests, "may perhaps be described as the struggle of the human personality to develop the potential powers of creation, in spite of the forces that seem to frustrate it." [38] It is the "Starwicks," the defeatists, who represent the enemy that Eugene as an artist must overcome.

In spite of structural difficulties and in spite of embarrassing artistic offenses, *Of Time and the River* represents an advance beyond the first novel. However loose, its grasp embraces more; however unsteady, its aim is loftier. Most significant of all, the scope has widened from personal self-consciousness to include national consciousness as well. What the achievement might have been had Wolfe been able to carry out his early plan for a controlling myth is not worth a conjecture. At this point of his career, it was impossible for him not to become entangled in the toils of his own life sequence. Since the six-novel scheme that might have provided a suitable vehicle to comprehend this diversity was abandoned, *Of Time and the River* remains incomplete. The faults in proportion, style, and narrative, together with its unfinished state, stamp the book an artistic failure, yet it takes its place as one of those magnificent failures that is remembered for its outstanding parts while narrowly conceived successes are forgotten.

Whereas *Look Homeward, Angel* had a relatively quiet reception, *Of Time and the River* was the literary event of 1935. Within a month, Wolfe was swept into an important position in American literature. Not only did reviewers feel the breath of Melville and Whitman in the twentieth century, but they frequently used the term, Great American Novel, as they expressed hopes about the six-novel scheme. Most reviewers were stunned. The variety and the unequal quality of the writing caused bewilderment to Clifton Fadiman after his rush through a near half-million words: "If as a child, you ever clambered out of the thrill car of a death-defying scenic railway, you may recall the curiously divided state of your emotions. It was a toss-up as to whether you felt excited beyond the point of endurance or just enormously tired. Emerging at this instant from the nine-hundred-and-twelfth page of Thomas Wolfe's long-awaited 'Of Time and the River,' I have very much that scenic railway feeling, at once feverish and groggy. Just watching Mr. Wolfe release his magnificent, inexhaustible energy leaves me flushed and punch-drunk." [39] Other reviewers, like Howard Mumford Jones, snorted with irritation at the disproportion and the unrelieved intensity: "However powerful the book is in detail, the effect upon the reader who has to take it at a single stride is to exacerbate the nerves." [40] Indeed, the grievous faults in the book did not escape notice. The two principal strictures were on the over-emotional egoism of the autobiographical hero and the lack of structure. John Chamberlain's comment is representative of the first: "The weakness . . . lies in the character of the autobiographical Eugene Gant, who manages to riot through an adolescence and a young manhood without developing any selective power, any power of making distinctions, any power, in short, of thinking about America and its destiny. Eugene simply feels." [41] Robert Penn Warren's judgment sums up what many critics were saying about Wolfe's structure: "What, thus far, he has produced are fine fragments, several brilliant pieces of portraiture, and many sharp observations on men and nature; in other words, these books are really voluminous notes from which a fine novel, or several fine novels, might be written." [42]

But reviewers were tremendously excited over Wolfe's display of talent, his speaking with "a United States voice," [43] and his promise of greatness. Attacks on the book were modified by a genuine appreciation of Wolfe's gifts. Henry Seidel Canby, writing in the *Saturday Review of Literature,* labeled *Of Time and the River* an artistic failure; yet he went on to say: ". . . it is an important book, and Mr. Wolfe is an important writer. He has more material, more vitality, more originality, more gusto than any two contemporary British novelists put together, even though they may be real novelists and he is not. He stands to them as Whitman stood to the wearied 'Idylls of the King.' " [44]

NOTES

1. *Letters,* p. 365.

2. This character, later named Dinwood Bland, was planned as one of the passengers on the train. He later became Judge Rumford Bland in YCGHA.

3. PN 19, *ca.* September, 1932, to *ca.* February, 1933.

4. HCL*46AM-7(24-h).

5. *Ibid.*

6. Letter to Charles Scribner, April 18, 1933, quoted in part in Nowell, p. 217.

7. HCL*46AM-7(24-g).

8. LTM, p. 256.

9. LTM, p. 265.

10. HCL*46AM-7(24-g). This was a part of the abandoned work, "K 19."

11. *Ibid.*

12. From the contract in the files of CSS.

13. PN 20, *ca.* March to October, 1933. The impressions of England, beginning "Smoke-gold by day. . . ," he added to "No Door," which he prepared for publication during the spring.

14. An essay, originally part of John Hawke's story, which was published as "The Anatomy of Loneliness" in the *American Mercury,* October, 1941, and finally as "God's Lonely Man" in HB.

15. *Letters,* p. 381.

16. A discarded section from W&R entitled "What is Evil," HCL*46AM-7(56), explains this reference. The narrator sees a Broadway revue and watches the near-naked chorines run through their dance number. He is struck by one girl who has a tender innocent face but whose hips writhe in "the movement of sexual spasm." He remembers then a dream about children who had mature bodies.

17. PN 18, January to August, 1932.

18. PN 20, *ca.* March to October, 1933.

19. PN 18, January to August, 1932.

20. LTM, p. 264.

21. *Letters,* p. 439.

22. SN, p. 594.

23. HCL*46AM-7(24-l).

24. *Letters,* p. 398.

25. *Letters,* p. 478.

26. Cut before publication. This train passenger later found a place in YCGHA.

27. Never completed.

28. This episode concerns Eugene's impulsive train journeys up the Hudson River, OT&R, pp. 468-76.

29. PN 21, *ca.* January to April, 1934.

30. See also Malcolm Cowley's profile of Maxwell Perkins, "Unshaken Friend," *New Yorker,* XX (April 1, 1944), 28-36, and (April 8, 1944), 30-43, and Nowell, pp. 225-38.

31. The final discarding of his idea for the Antaeus legend may be seen in his last-minute use of the title for a random section of the European trip, OT&R, pp. 795-849.

32. "Thomas Wolfe," *Harvard Library Bulletin,* I (Autumn, 1947), 273.

33. For further details see Nowell, pp. 246-47.

34. "The Sorrows of Thomas Wolfe," *Collected Essays of John Peale Bishop,* ed. Edmund Wilson (New York, 1948), pp. 129-37.

35. "Suffice it to say that this last theme—the quest of a man for a father—does not become revealed until the very end of the book: under the present plan I have called the final chapter of the fourth and last part, ('The October Fair'), 'Telemachus'" (*Letters,* p. 244).

36. FDTM, p. 109.

37. Edwin Berry Burgum, in "Thomas Wolfe's Discovery of America," Walser, pp. 179-94, traces the rejections through all of Wolfe's novels.

38. Letter printed in the *Saturday Review of Literature,* XIII (January 25, 1936), 9.

39. *New Yorker,* X (March 9, 1935), 68.

40. "Social Notes on the South," *Virginia Quarterly Review,* XI (July, 1935), 456.

41. *Current History,* XLII (April, 1935), iii.

42. "A Note on the Hamlet of Thomas Wolfe," *American Review,* V (May, 1935), 207-8.

43. "U. S. Voice," *Time,* XXV (March 11, 1935), 77.

44. "River of Youth," Walser, p. 138.

Part V

THE VARIED ACTIVITIES OF A MAN OF LETTERS

18.

CAPTURED FUGITIVES:
FROM DEATH TO MORNING

PUBLICATION DAY FOR OF TIME AND THE RIVER BROUGHT THE end of a long period of work and set Wolfe off on another period of wandering, observing, and catching up loose ends. He has told in *The Story of a Novel* how he escaped to Europe in March, 1935, in order to avoid facing the reviews of his new book. He arrived in France on March 8, the publication date of the book. For almost a week he roamed the streets in a daze, fretting about its reception and feeling puzzled because he could not remember Paris landmarks as accurately as he thought he should. At last he worked up the courage to face the news and went to the American Express Office to get his mail. A cablegram from Perkins saying, "Magnificent reviews, somewhat critical in ways expected, full of greatest praise," did not dispell his worries. He paced and drank. At last he cabled Perkins: "You are the best friend I have. I can face blunt fact better than damnable incertitude. Give me the straight plain truth." [1] Perkins' reassurance came, followed on March 21 by a batch of excerpts from the reviews. Wolfe's elation was tempered by a suspicion that Perkins had excised passages that would trouble him. He was soon brooding over the comments on his autobiographical method and on the exaggerated behavior of his characters. Whipping himself into a froth, he jotted in his notebook:

It is one thing to profit by criticism, but no reasonabl[e] man can hope to profit by being torn limb from limb by 27 different people all pulling him apart in different directions. Before I left New York, for example, I saw an advance note of my book by one of the [——?] lady reviewers—the upshot of this was that all my people were monsters of the species—giants seven feet tall whose gentlest whisper was a bellow—It was all interesting enough she said but would it be so interesting...without the ranting violence of his language and his method [.] [H]is adjectives denote violence, altitude, size, immensity, etc.—Well, having got off to a good start taking away my adjectives, why not do a really good job and take away my nouns, pronouns, participles, verbs, adverbs, conjunctions, and parts of speech whatever—furnish me with a vocabulary of her own choosing... lock me up in a cell and thrusting the approved vocabulary and a sheaf of paper in my hands, hiss venomously: "Here, damn you—use this. And mind you write about something you know nothing at all about! We'll see if you can *really* write, you dog!" [2]

France was proving expensive, and Wolfe was lonely for a friend upon whom he could unload all his feeling about his work. He went to England at the end of the month, spending time at first with A. S. Frere-Reeves and his wife Pat, and then with Catherine Carswell and her Hampstead Heath literary group. Time and relaxation were soothing him, and after he saw his book on an American best-seller list he began to calm down. He did some reading and browsing, such varied fare as H. H. Richardson's *The Fortunes of Richard Mahoney,* Waugh's *Vile Bodies,* Thackeray's *Paris Sketch Book* and *The Book of Snobs.* He was entertained by Hugh Walpole. He went to the Old Vic for a performance of *Henry IV, Part II.* Through Henry Roberts of Heinemann, he met Robert Briffault and was awed by his learned discussion of the dominating cultures of past centuries. He stored away in his mind Briffault's prediction that America and Russia would dominate the twentieth century. He wandered about London and meditated on time and change as he gazed at the site of the Globe Theater and tried to conjure up a vision of Shakespeare's day.

He was beginning to get the perspective upon his own life and his own time that European trips so often thrust on him. Tom Wolfe had just published "A Legend of Man's Hunger in His Youth," and he now became aware for the first time that his youth was gone. A man of thirty-four years, he wrote in his notebook, "has reached a stage of life which is certainly not old, but which has lost the shine and fire of his first youth, and although he may not yet—or ever—be old enough 'to see life clearly and see it whole'—he is yet old enough to have seen and felt a kind of dimension." [3] He then listed the ages of some of his literary contemporaries—Hemingway, Faulkner, Fitzgerald, Caldwell—and wondered about his accomplishment.

He soon headed for Germany, where he planned to spend some of the reichmarks that he had earned since the publication of *Schau Heimwartz, Engel* in 1931 but that the Nazi government would not allow to go out of the country. He sailed to Holland the last of April, passing through Amsterdam, where he responded joyously to its spring freshness, its flowers, and its gin ("It makes you Bee," he put in his notebook).[4] He went on to Berlin, where he found the most gracious welcome he had ever received. He divided his time between his friends at the publishing house, Rowalt Verlag, and his friends at the American Embassy, where Martha Dodd, the captivating daughter of Ambassador William E. Dodd, became his social secretary. He was in Berlin two weeks before he had time to make an entry in his notebook: "a wild, fantastic, incredible whirl of parties, teas, dinners, all night drinking bouts, newspaper interviews, radio proposals, photographs. . . . May never do it again but it was interesting and worth seeing and people told me startling things."[5] The great beauty of Northern Europe in the spring and the cordiality of his hosts in Berlin refreshed Wolfe's spirits and cleaned away the corrosions of the past four years.[6] He was now ready to go home.

As the newly recognized American spokesman, Wolfe felt a special significance in the fact that his ship docked in New York on the Fourth of July. Newspaper reporters greeted him for interviews. He felt like a dignitary. Max Perkins was waiting for him at the pier, and together they roamed the city. They lunched on the East River in a restaurant that had been converted from an old coal barge. From the roof of the Prince George Hotel in Brooklyn, they gazed at New York harbor and the towered density of Manhattan in the sunset. Back across the river, they went from bar to bar celebrating until almost dawn. In the Village, Wolfe pointed out the 8th Street garret where he had written *Look Homeward, Angel*. Perkins led the way up the fire escape to climb in the window, and Wolfe wrote on the wall "Thomas Wolfe lived here."[7] He never felt happier in his life. The joy of that day so lived in his memory that he recalled it for Perkins in the last words he ever wrote: "I shall always think of you and feel about you the way it was that Fourth of July day three years ago when you met me at the boat, and we went out on the cafe on the river and had a drink and later went on top of the tall building, and all the strangeness and the glory and the power of life and of the city was below."[8]

II

For the fall publishing season, Scribner's planned to follow up the success of the new book with a volume of short pieces—all the scattered magazine stories that had not appeared in *Of Time and the River*. Perkins wanted *The Web of Earth* to survive the impermanence of magazine publication, and he especially hoped that this collection would clear all these bits out of the way so that Wolfe would not try to work them into his subsequent novels.

Wolfe was determined this time to see the book through the press himself. Despite all the praise that had come to him with *Of Time and the River*, Wolfe felt a resentment-in-retrospect over Perkins' handing his manuscript to the printer without his consent. A foreboding note appeared in a letter Wolfe wrote from Colorado while he was traveling in the summer. "...you must not put the manuscript of a book of stories in final form until after my return to New York. If that means the book of stories will have to be deferred till next spring, then they will have to be deferred, but I will not consent this time to allow the book to be taken away from me and printed and published. . . . I really mean this, Max. I have money enough to live on for awhile now." [9]

On his return from the West, Wolfe approved the versions of his scattered pieces that had been selected by the Scribner's staff for publication in the new book. In fact, with the exception of "No Door," all the stories were to appear in the book without significant change from the way they had appeared in magazines.[10] Wolfe chose the title, *From Death to Morning*, to describe the change of mood implied by the arrangement of the stories, which ran from the dejection of "No Door" to the affirmation of *The Web of Earth*. But his title especially reflected the movement from darkness to light in *Death the Proud Brother*, which Wolfe had told a lecture audience in Colorado he regarded as the best piece of writing he had done up to 1933. He was soon correcting galley proof, and the book was published on November 14, 1935. The pieces included in it, various in intention though they seem, had all been part of Wolfe's huge autobiographical manuscript. Two of them, "The Bums at Sunset" and "One of the Girls in Our Party," had come from the panorama of America he had written in Europe in 1930; they were part of the diversity of material worked finally into *Of Time and the River*, Book VII, which depicted Eugene Gant's yearning to return home. Some parts of "The Face of the War" had been cut from *Look Homeward, Angel*. "Only the Dead Know Brooklyn," originally part of a survey of Brooklyn during the depression entitled "The Locusts Have No King," was to have been part of "The Death of the Enemy." "In the Park" was lifted from Esther's monologue, "The Good Child's River." "The Far and the Near," which Wolfe referred to in his notes as "the engineer fantasy," was a vision that came to Eugene Gant as he stared out of his window during one of the quarrels with Esther.[11] "The Four Lost Men" and "Circus at Dawn" were drawn from the book of reminiscences, "The Hills Beyond Pentland."

The book illustrates, beyond what *Of Time and the River* had demonstrated, Wolfe's variety in tone and method. It offers the brutal realism of "The Face of the War" (which had been admirably suited to the *Modern Monthly's* special war issue)[12] as well as the nostalgic glance at the American past in "The Four Lost Men." It contains "Gulliver," an essay on the tall man as an outsider; "The Men of Old Catawba," an excursion into historical legend; and "Only the Dead Know Brooklyn," a dramatic monologue ironically revealing the gulfs that separate human beings from one another.

But a brief summary of the origins of these stories and sketches distorts the picture of Thomas Wolfe at work. They did not all come into being merely through the agency of the scissors. *The Web of Earth*, as we have seen, was expressly written as a short novel for publication in *Scribner's Magazine*. Other items in the collection went through a series of steps before they achieved their present form. Enough evidence exists for commentary on three of them that can indicate something of Wolfe's methods of putting a short selection into publishable shape and can show what kind of advice and help he received.

Details are available that reveal the gradual emergence of "Dark in the Forest, Strange as Time." Wolfe made this entry in his notebook on December 18, 1926, while he was getting ready to return home from Europe: "Saturday—On the Train Again—In Alsace Lorraine [—] I came yesterday from Munich to Zürich—Got there last night—Began to snow in Munich in the morning—Down through Bavaria—in the hill country—flurrying snow—Ground white—the consumptive who rode with me in the carriage—His rather young and handsome wife at Munich."[13] This remained in his notebook and in his memory for several years. When he was at work on his second novel, filling in scattered episodes of his hero's European wanderings, he wrote a description of the crowd in the railroad station and their joking farewells. Sometime in 1933, he returned to this scene, revised and enlarged it, adding imaginative hints about the wife's furtive betrayal of her husband and developing the dialogue between the young traveler and the consumptive. He turned this version over to Alfred Dashiell to consider for publication in *Scribner's Magazine*. After Dashiell had accepted it and made a few suggestions, Wolfe revised it again, returning it to Dashiell with the remark, "I've got to have another crack at this in proof, and know I can improve it." [14]

From a brief note this material grew into another one of Wolfe's symbolic studies in contrast: life and death, spring and winter, vitality and decay. The voluptuous wife is surrounded by the jocose banter of the crowd with its healthy sexual suggestiveness. The consumptive, whose eyes are "burning steadily with the fires of death," turns his back to the lively crowd as he departs for his winter seclusion. All the contrasts—the young traveler's vigorous seeking, the dying man's wisdom and resignation; the food and luxury of the diner, the atmosphere of death in the compartment; the young man's meditation on the mixture of brute desire and creative spirit within himself —are resolved in the conclusion. As the young traveler leaves the compartment and joins the parade of the living, he senses that he, the dying man, and all the passengers are going in the same direction toward a common silence.

In its earliest version, "One of the Girls in Our Party" had been one of the vignettes woven among the wanderings of David Hawke.[15] It stood merely as Miss Blake's letter beginning, "England was the first place we went to. . . ." When Wolfe needed money in 1934, he dug it out of his crate of scraps, added the introductory dialogue, supplied Mr. Singvogel's spiel in dialect, and sold it to *Scribner's Magazine*. He worked it over again after it had been accepted and improved the conclusion to suggest the native's thoughts turning to home.[16] It began as a light satire on Cook's tours in which Wolfe hitched together details from guidebooks with remarks he had overheard from American travelers. By the time he was finished with it, the color of American life had burst through to give the whole story another dimension.

"In the Park," one of the series of anecdotes about Esther Jack's father, was probably written in 1931. Perhaps Perkins suggested that this episode about the two priests and the automobile ride could stand by itself for magazine publication. At any rate, in 1932 Wolfe went over it, expanding the details of the ride in the new horseless carriage and providing a conclusion about dawn and the songs of waking birds in the park.[17] He shifted a paragraph from the middle to serve as the beginning: "That year we were living with Aunt Bella. . . ." When he could not sell the story to *Scribner's,* he gave it to Miss Nowell at the time she first began to act as his agent, in 1933. She tried to get him to make a better explanation of how the stalled car was started again (rather than have the weeping driver just lean on the hood) but Wolfe never got around to it.[18] In 1935, she made a few revisions herself, shifted the order of some statements, got Wolfe's approval, and sold the story to *Harper's Bazaar* while he was in Europe. In June, 1935, the first part of Esther's story went before the public. But not until *The Web and the Rock* did readers know what rich personalities they had been introduced to— Joe Linder and Esther Jack.

From Death to Morning perplexed the reviewers. Although they were used to Wolfe's mammoth productions, they felt uneasy seeing his sprawling manner and abundance of detail used within short forms. "Only in the broadest sense of the word are most of them short stories," declared Hamilton Basso.[19] "Mr. Wolfe takes the form of the short story and twists it and shapes it to his own ends," wrote Edith Weigle.[20] Even so, Wolfe's unique stamp came through and received its tribute. "With the exception of a slight but heavy-handed satire," said Peter Munro Jack, "these stories are Mr. Wolfe's peculiar property; they belong to him with the certainty of style and introspection —no other writer can match them and they show the most striking literary personality of our day." [21] Nevertheless, this collection has not held its place beside Wolfe's novels.[22] He is a writer whose effect is cumulative, and short selections divorced from the larger context of his autobiographical narrative lack the force they might otherwise have. Over the years, readers have responded to these stories and sketches in proportion to their familiarity with his other work. Only the two short novels, *Death the Proud Brother* and *The Web of Earth,* are developed fully enough to stand up well by themselves.

NOTES

1. *Letters,* p. 434.

2. PN 26, March 21 to April 26, 1935. He refers to Isobel Paterson's remarks in the *New York Herald-Tribune Books,* February 24, 1935.

3. *Ibid.*

4. PN 27, April 27 to June, 1935. He was jotting notes for a character like Mr. Bendien of YCGHA, Chapter 33.

5. *Ibid.*

6. For the details of this visit to Berlin, see Chapter 22.

7. UNCL, unpublished letter, Maxwell Perkins to John Terry, November 1, 1945.

8. *Letters,* pp. 777-78.

9. *Letters,* p. 485.

10. In the published volume, only Part I of "No Door" appeared under that title. The Hawke family was changed back to the Gant family in *The Web of Earth.* "Polyphemus" and "Old Catawba," although they formed two sketches in magazines, were joined together as "The Men of Old Catawba."

11. In an even earlier version, it, too, had been a part of the montage of America written in 1930. See *Letters,* p. 243.

12. This issue also featured a symposium on "What Will I Do When America Goes To War?" with articles by John Dewey, Archibald MacLeish, Elmer Rice, Sherwood Anderson, Van Wyck Brooks, and Reinhold Niebuhr.

13. PN 2, November, 1926, to September, 1927.

14. *Letters,* p. 400.

15. *Letters,* p. 243.

16. A note to Dashiell accompanied the manuscript: "Here is the story: my intention was to have those parts which I have underscored in pencil separated from the rest of the text by short spaces and italicized. . . .I rewrote the last page to get a better order—Please note that the last sentence is *not* italicized." HCL, unpublished, undated letter.

17. A note in a ledger, HCL*46AM-7(36), dates the revision.

Published	Unpublished
Look Homeward Angel	In the Park
Bascom Hawke	

18. Miss Nowell's footnote, *Letters,* p. 457, indicates that she did not remember dealing with "In the Park" as early as 1933. In HCL*46AM-12(4), there is a letter in which she discusses her suggestions about the story, and another (53M-113F) dated January 31, 1934, states: ". . . I'm still hoping you'll do something with the automobile story sometime."

19. *New Republic,* LXXVI (January 1, 1936), 232.

20. *Chicago Tribune,* December 14, 1935, p. 16.

21. *New York Times Book Review,* November 24, 1935, p. 6.

22. This volume is the only one of Wolfe's books which did not sell out in its first edition. Of 7500 copies, about 1000 were remaindered in 1940—although in recent years the book has gone into reprints both in hard and soft covers.

19

THE STORY OF A LECTURE

THOMAS WOLFE HAD BEEN GIVING SPEECHES ALL HIS LIFE—
usually to patient friends. But in the summer of 1935, when he was
invited to lecture at the University of Colorado Writers' Conference,
he was a little worried about a formal appearance as an "American
novelist." As soon as he returned from Europe, he set to work to
compose the lecture. He drew up some notes under such headings as
"Some Problems of a Writer" and "The Artist in America." It is clear
he had in mind criticisms about his form that had goaded him, because notes for his introduction list "a few general misconceptions"
that ordinary readers have about novels and go on to misconceptions
that critics have about form.[1] At length, however, he turned to the
subject which interested him most, the story of his own struggle to
write *Of Time and the River.* He had on hand the discarded introduction to *Of Time and the River* in which he acknowledged his debt
to Perkins, and he had material about the reception of *Look Homeward, Angel* in the unused preface to the Modern Library edition.
Drawing from these remnants, he worked out a lecture which ran
seventy-four typewritten pages before it was finished.

The offer of $250 plus an expense-paid trip to the West was a sign
to Wolfe of what his newly won fame could bring him. He found,
too, that the Colorado State Teacher's College at Greeley would offer
him another $75 for a stopover and talk there. "It sounds pretty soft,"
he wrote Robert Raynolds, "but what I'm looking forward to with
panting thirst is the chance of seeing some of the West." [2]

Leaving New York by train July 27, Wolfe accumulated a sense of
the immensity of his country during the next two days, especially as
he watched the Great Plains unroll beside him. When he arrived in
Greeley, July 29, he felt "instantly at home" under the bright blue

clarity of the Colorado sky.[3] Even though Greeley is east of the Rockies, still this was country for Gulliver. From his talk at the State Teacher's College, he went on to Boulder on July 31. He arrived after the conference had been underway a week but in time to join a round-table discussion on "Poetry and Intelligibility" with Robert Frost, Robert Penn Warren, Thomas Hornsby Ferril, the Western poet, Whit Burnett and Martha Foley, short story editors, Dixon Wecter, the brilliant young historian of American culture, and George Reynolds, the grand old man of Colorado University and a distinguished scholar of the Elizabethan Theater. Wolfe was in good company. The following week he was scheduled to participate in another round-table conference on "Social Responsibility and the Modern Author." As the week went on, he was "astonished" at the serious professionalism of the conference and the high quality of the talks. In fact, when he saw the program of evening lectures on "What is a Short Story," "The Recent Southern Novel," and "What Poetry Thinks," he felt his own title, "The Making of a Book," looked narrow and dull.[4]

On the evening of August 6, he seemed almost to have adopted the role of the hairy-eared natural genius among the intellectuals as he stood up to give his lecture. In a halting, stammering voice, the man whose book had been the outstanding novel of the year addressed his audience, "I do not feel that I can talk to you about trends in the modern novel or attempt to tell you what the modern novelist is doing or attempt an analysis of what he has done the last five or ten years or what he will do in the five or ten which are to come. I cannot tell you how to write books; I cannot attempt to give you rules and suggestions whereby you will be enabled to get your books published by publishers or your stories accepted by popular and high paying magazines. . . ."[5] His diffidence dissolved as he described his own literary experience. His story was long and slow-paced, but he held his audience. His dedication to his work was infectious, and the sounds, the scents, the sights of American life were laced through his speech. Halfway through, he apologized for his verbosity and offered to stop, but the audience shouted him on. Continuing, he rehearsed all the agonies of putting *Of Time and the River* together with Perkins' help. After an hour and forty minutes, he ended as humbly as he had begun: "I came here resolved that whatever else I said to you, I was going to try to tell you the truth without pretense or evasion about the way I wrote a book. . . . I have tried to tell you the true story of the artist as a worker rather than of the artist as a fine fellow with fine critical, aesthetical notions. . . ." [6] He had won his hearers as much by his unpretentious presence as by what he had to say. Wolfe's talk that evening was the most memorable event of the conference.[7]

For the aspiring young writers attending the conference, contact with Wolfe in his formal appearances or in the informal workshop sessions was very valuable. He preached the gospel of hard work, and he showed them his own experience as an example. While he was there, he arranged for three of the students to send manuscripts to be read at Scribner's, and he wrote to Perkins about them.[8] He earned the lifelong gratitude of Dixon Wecter by putting him in touch with Perkins, who helped him get *The Saga of American Society* into publishable form.

Not all the time was spent in the classroom or lecture hall. Wolfe met generous Western hospitality. It was ten days of good food, good talk, and late-night parties. The night of his lecture, he sat on the floor of Edward Davison's kitchen, equipped with a bottle of whiskey, a saucer of ice, and a large glass, and discoursed on space and time with Joseph Cohen of the philosophy department until 5:00 A.M. Since he was seething with ideas for writing, he talked continually of his proposed "Book of the Night." His new friends at the university were amazed at his enthusiasms for the American scene when they took him one night to the nearby mountain town of Longmont. As he watched the Model A's come into town and the people saunter along the sidewalks, he raised his arms in the air and cried, "Oh, this is Saturday night in America!"

After the conference, Thomas Hornsby Ferril took Wolfe for a trip into the mountains. They went up into Gilpin County to the reconstructed gold-mining town of Central City, where the Teller House no longer had its entrance paved with bricks of solid silver but still displayed to tourists its "Face on the Barroom Floor." They drove through Rocky Mountain National Park, spent a day at the Ferril cabin in Grousemont, and then went on to Colorado Springs.[9] Here Wolfe caught up with his old friend and New York University colleague, Desmond Powell. Powell took Wolfe over to the faculty club at Colorado College, where he spoke briefly to a room packed with professors and whatever wives and students could squeeze in.

The next two weeks were all a headlong rush. Wolfe took in Denver, Santa Fe, the Painted Desert, and the fantastic geological phenomena of Arizona and Nevada, landing finally at the Roosevelt Hotel in Hollywood, a block from Grauman's Chinese Theater.

For the visiting celebrity, a tour of Hollywood usually means moving picture stars and studios. Wolfe was fascinated by the glitter and the mechanical ingenuity as he surveyed the MGM studio, saw the "Mutiny on the Bounty" set and Tarzan's jungle, met Clark Gable, Warner Baxter, Frank Morgan, and (most impressive of all) Jean Harlow, who was then at the peak of her platinum career. He found the same neon, fairy-tale atmosphere at the RKO studio. He blinked in the glow of fame when he discovered how well screen writers and directors knew his work. "I have met several," he boasted to Perkins, "who have a copy of every story I ever wrote, including the college stuff of Chapel Hill days. . . ." [10] The outcome of the Hollywood visit, according to the story Wolfe told back in New York, was the offer of $1000 a week as a screen writer.[11] He did not consider it because it was not the kind of work he wanted to do and because he knew movie scripts were co-operative enterprises in writing that made demands he could never endure.

He headed north for a stopover in San Francisco and Palo Alto, where he met Kathleen and Charles Norris. Then he returned to the East by way of another kind of glitter in Reno, where he sensed a frontier gaiety in the wide-open gambling palaces and sporting houses. A stay in Salt Lake City was not too short to prevent his getting a permit to buy liquor in the State of Utah. Wolfe's journey sobered off to become a solemn pilgrimage when he stopped in St. Louis. From the outset of his trip, he had planned to look up the place where Julia Wolfe had operated the "North Carolina" boarding house during the St. Louis Fair in 1903. Now, in mid-September, he was there to bring back the moments of a past self three years old in the house where his brother Grover died. The visit to the site, like all returns to places long left behind, overwhelmed him with the strangeness of familiarity in the midst of change. The emotional impact of this experience began a seething which boiled over two years later when Wolfe wrote "The Lost Boy," his most intense treatment of the search for lost time.[12] The success of this story vindicated once more Wolfe's method of seeking out experience.

II

The writers' conference lecture was a loosely structured piece in Wolfe's conversational style, a good example of his early use of dictation. As an informal talk on the practical problems of a writer, it had been ideal in the semi-professional atmosphere of the Writers' Conference. Perkins knew that publication would make Wolfe vulnerable to critical attack, so he did not offer any encouragement to get it into print. But Elizabeth Nowell saw it as a fascinating autobiographical essay, for it summarized Wolfe's career as a novelist, it presented an honest, humble account of how *Of Time and the River* came into existence, and it generalized about the problem of the artist in America. She cut it down to half its size [13] and sold it to the *Saturday Review of Literature* to be published in three installments from December 14 to December 28, 1935. Wolfe jotted down seventeen possible titles, such as "An Apprentice Speaks," "Penance More," and "A Young Man's Life and Letters," before he called it simply *The Story of a Novel*.

He had not paid much attention to what Miss Nowell was doing with his lecture. But when Scribner's decided to bring out *The Story of a Novel* as a small book, Wolfe, dreading the permanence of a hard-cover version, spent late January and early February working over the manuscript. He put back many paragraphs that Miss Nowell had cut and added a whole new section, the series of nightmares that forms the climax of the essay. When he finished, it was almost as long as the original lecture. This time Max Perkins had no part in his book.[14] It came from the press in an edition of 3000 copies on April 21, 1936.

This little book made many new friends for Wolfe. It showed the reading public an entirely new personality. Here was no ranting, exulting, self-pitying Eugene Gant. Thomas Wolfe stood before them in all humility saying, "I am not a professional writer; I am not even a skilled writer; I am just a writer who is on the way to learning his profession and to discovering the line, the structure, and the articulation of the language which I must discover if I do the work I want to do." [15] He told a story of stumbling and groping with an earnestness which revealed a man wedded to his task.

In many places the style, too, seemed new—a conversational tone, suggested by parenthetical remarks and by the frequent use of "and" to join parts of sentences; simple declarative statements, occasionally made rhythmic by a series of parallel clauses; commonplace words, sometimes clustered for emotional effect. This homely ease enabled readers to identify themselves with him as he unrolled his account of how a rather ordinary young man of humble origins achieved fame and wondered how it happened:

I would go home at night and look around my room and see that morning's coffeecup still unwashed and books on the floor and a shirt where I had thrown it the night before and great stacks of manuscript and everything so common and familiar-looking and so disorderly, and then I would think that I was now "a young American writer"; that somehow I was practising an imposture on my readers and my critics because my shirt looked the way it did and my books and my bed—not, you understand, because they were disorderly, common, familiar, but just because they looked the way they did.[16]

The book had this unpretentious manner partly because in the beginning it had been dictated and then it had been delivered as a talk to a live audience. For once, Wolfe was a man speaking to other men rather than a writer pouring himself out to a void. But the stylistic strength was also due to the presence of Miss Nowell, for the lecture had been too verbose. When she cut it, she cut mostly by paragraph, but sometimes she removed a repetitious sentence, and often she whittled four adjectives down to two, or three phrases down to one. She slashed at the manuscript in a way that Perkins had never done and that Wolfe would never have permitted him to do. She could tinker with his work because she had no jurisdiction over publication. Wolfe did not get his back up because he did not feel he had to accept her changes or to argue with her about them. He had learned, too, that magazine space was limited. He knew that Miss Nowell could please magazine editors and that later he could restore what he liked for publication in permanent form.

What happened in his own reworking of *The Story of a Novel* is that Wolfe did not bother to replace words, phrases, or sentences. When he prepared it for book form, he rescued paragraphs that had been cut, for these had frequently added important facts or illuminated the detail of his plunges into the deeps of memory. Then, wishing to increase the emotional intensity as he approached the end, he added new, imaginatively colored material, the dreams of guilt and time, which he would not have used on the lecture platform.

This accumulation of circumstances together with some hard work on Wolfe's part made *The Story of a Novel* more than an exposition of a writer's problems. It became a memorable contribution to confession literature. It was a patterned product with a series of emotional peaks mounting toward a final anguish that brought out Wolfe's moment of recognition: "I knew at last I had become a writer." Once again, Thomas De Quincey is standing in the background, for *The Story of a Novel* has an over-all resemblance to *The Confessions of an English Opium Eater*. In subject matter, Wolfe's urgent need to write corresponds to De Quincey's craving for the mighty drug. In structure, Wolfe follows De Quincey's sequence: the book begins with an autobiographical sketch and an account of the first acquaintance with writing; it moves on to describe the delights of creative intensity, "that bright flame with which a young man writes who has never been published"; it descends to the horrifying dreams, "the nightmare pageantry to which my consciousness lay chained a spectator." In style, Wolfe's rolling periods, when he soars above his conversational stride, reach the bizarre rhetorical heights which are the special mark of De Quincey's romantic prose.

The work is reminiscent of De Quincey for another reason beyond the fact that Wolfe's favorite subject was self-revelation. In 1932, when Wolfe worked on the story of David Hawke's stormy parting from Esther, he used the title "A Vision of Death in April," echoing De Quincey's title "A Vision of Sudden Death." [17] Consciously imitating De Quincey's arrangement in *The Confessions of an English Opium Eater*, he planned two sections called "The Pleasures of Love" and "The Pains of Love." [18] From this old manuscript he imported some of the dream agonies into *The Story of a Novel*, using them as the "dreams of Guilt and Time." [19] To them he added further dream work about the university and the stacks of uncorrected papers. *The Story of a Novel* is, then, a curious mixture of autobiography and fiction, for the dream sequence is an elaborate fiction based on anxiety dreams that had troubled Wolfe throughout his career. He had developed these nightmare passages in order to darken the picture of his hero unhinged by jealousy. They were easily transferred to illustrate another kind of mental torment as Wolfe described his despair over "the making of a book."

But Wolfe's debt to De Quincey is not what makes this book a "confession." Wolfe in his honesty was making a public acknowledgment of Perkins' help in bringing *Of Time and the River* into being. Critics who were already repelled by Wolfe's plethoric style or the eccentricities of his hero now had a new club to beat him with: his method of composition. *The Story of a Novel* brought Wolfe's early career to an end. Its publication set in motion the trouble that Perkins feared, and Wolfe eventually had to declare his independence of Scribner's. But the book also marks the beginning of new growth and further control of the powers Wolfe had released in the last five years.

NOTES

1. PN 28, June to September, 1935.

2. HCL, unpublished letter, July 8, 1935.

3. Wolfe said this twice, first in a letter to Mrs. J. M. Roberts, May 20, 1936 (*Letters*, p. 518), and later in an interview with Edward Miller in June, 1938 ("Gulping the Great West," [*Portland*] *Oregonian*, July 31, 1938).

4. Program of The Sixth Annual Writers' Conference, July 22 to August 9, 1935.

5. HCL*46AM-7(50), typescript of the lecture.

6. *Ibid.*

7. This was the general impression among students enrolled at the conference, according to Kate Pearson, a high school teacher from St. Paul, Minnesota. Francis Wolle, a professor in the Colorado English Department, records this impression of the evening: "The lecture was at one and the same time a thrilling and an irritating experience. He swayed like a captive elephant behind the lectern, stuttered and stammered and for some time could not get beyond 'Ladies and gentlemen.' But he said that he had never before attempted to talk about his writing or the way he did it. Then he went on more or less revealing his soul as he does in his novels, but all in a hesitant, awkward, lumbering way. It distinctly was not just an ordinary lecture but a startling and exhausting experience." Letter to me, August 21, 1959.

8. See *Letters*, pp. 483-84, although the details of his comments have been cut out of the published letter.

9. Pack Memorial Library, letter from Thomas Hornsby Ferril to Myra Champion, September 5, 1951.

10. *Letters*, p. 487.

11. Frank A. Dickson, "Look Homeward, Angel," *Anderson* [*South Carolina*] *Independent*, August 21, 1948; HCL 53M-113F, The Purdue Speech; and *Letters*, p. 488, n. 2.

12. For an admirable critical discussion of this story, see Louis Rubin, *Thomas Wolfe, The Weather of His Youth* (Baton Rouge, 1955), pp. 47-51.

13. It had run 74 pages of elite type; when she finished, it was 44 pages of pica type. For further details on the marketing of the manuscript, see Nowell, pp. 301-2.

14. Perkins did, however, persuade Wolfe to cut out three paragraphs which he deemed "too political." UNCL, unpublished letter, Perkins to John Terry, October 29, 1945.

15. SN, p. 562.

16. *Ibid.*, p. 569.

17. This part of De Quincey's *The English Mail Coach* also contains a "dream fugue."

18. HCL*46AM-7(24-v). These titles were never used.

19. HCL*46AM-7(55). Some of this dream material had been already used in OT&R, pp. 892-93.

Part VI

NEW DIRECTIONS AND OLD LANDMARKS

20

HOW EUGENE GANT BECAME
PAUL SPANGLER

WE HAVE SEEN THAT DURING THE YEARS THOMAS WOLFE worked on his second novel he had floundered through frequent changes in plan and had hindered his progress by digression. Some of the retrenching had come about because he adopted new attitudes toward his material. Some of the digressions had been forced on him because he needed to do something in a hurry to get money, but most of them had developed out of another kind of necessity, the compulsion to continue writing even after his creative energies were exhausted. His way of working was something like that expressed by Joyce Cary's Gulley Jimson, the artist who said, "When you can't paint, paint. But something else." The root of his difficulties, however, was this: he lacked a plan which could attract and hold his creative powers until it was completed. As a result, he fell back upon the narrative line of his own life, on which he knew he could always string his beads without committing himself until a final arrangement.

Although he was never again to tangle himself so hopelessly as he had in the early thirties, his experience with *Of Time and the River* did not teach him to master his problems of composition. In fact, in *The Story of a Novel* he spoke of his preparing countless notes, lists, and descriptions, calling this activity his "research," his "method." Plainly, he was ready to follow out the same course for his future work, although, of course, a great deal of the "exploration" of his resources was already done. Thus he became involved in a variety of undertakings as he moved toward his next major publication.

During the months between his return from the West in the fall of 1935 and his next vacation trip to Germany the following August, Wolfe's work fell into three overlapping areas of concentration: the continuation of his six-volume series; the development of "The

Hound of Darkness," a book about nighttime in America; and an entirely new venture, "The Vision of Spangler's Paul," a novel about one man's discovery that life does not turn out as he expected.

He was living in Manhattan now, overlooking the East River from the fourteenth floor at 865 1st Avenue, where today he might have gazed with satisfaction at the neighboring United Nations building. His days of Brooklyn obscurity were over. He had some time for friends now. He often spent the evening at the Perkins' house, which was close by at 246 East 49th Street. He began sitting for a portrait by Perkins' son-in-law, Douglas Gorsline. He accepted invitations to cocktail parties and dinners. But gradually his socializing tapered off, and he settled back into his routine of working from noon till sleep time, well after midnight.

He first tried to settle down to complete "The October Fair," the story of Eugene Gant's passionate interlude with a fair lady in the October of her life. But he had purged himself of the most pressing need to write that book back in 1932. More attractive was the next volume, "The Hills Beyond Pentland." Since it dealt with recollections from childhood, it seemed easier to handle because it allowed his memory to roam freely for detail.

Obviously, Proust's *Remembrance of Things Past* had been uppermost in Wolfe's mind when he conceived the book. It centered on Eugene Gant's attempt to write about an episode in his childhood, when Uncle Bacchus came to visit the Gant family in Altamont. Wolfe toyed with schemes to provide a framework for these memories. One placed Eugene Gant in a Munich hospital, thinking of home and childhood as scattered memories of that time descended upon him. Another, probably the earliest, had Eugene sitting in his apartment, his "little cell" in Brooklyn, trying to write about the arrival of his Uncle Bacchus but never getting to that episode. For as he set the scene (the child lying on the grass in front of his house at three o'clock in the afternoon), his recollections proliferated. He reconstructed the details of the street, of the Negro market boys riding by on their bicycles, of the baker's delivery truck, of the history of that truck, its owners, and its accidents, and so on. Eugene Gant, speaking in the first person, was to guide the reader through a maze of reminiscences in the way that Delia Hawke had done in *The Web of Earth*.

The climax was to be a recapture of the past and an imprisonment of it in a permanent form, a triumph over time. One impassioned statement by the narrator (later prefixed to *The Web and the Rock*) indicates the intention of the book: "Could I make tongue say more than tongue could utter? Could I make brain grasp more than brain could think? Could I weave into immortal denseness some small brede of words, pluck out of sunken depths the roots of living, some hundred thousand magic words that were as great as my hunger, and hurl the sum of all my living out upon three hundred pages—then death could take my life, for I had lived it ere he took it: I had slain hunger, beaten death." [1]

Although the "Publisher's Note" in *Of Time and the River* had stated that "The Hills Beyond Pentland" was already written, it was by no means ready for publication. Wolfe had in typescript the sequence about the boy and the street on which he lived; a description of "The Return of the Prophet Bacchus" for a reunion of Civil War veterans; Eliza Gant's tales of Bacchus and other Pentland kin; an account of Uncle Bascom's visit from Boston, which included Bascom's bitter denunciation of his father, Major Thomas Pentland; and sketches of Eliza's boarders and their talk, from which "The Four Lost Men" had already been taken for publication. Followers of Wolfe's work who have wondered what the announced volume, "The Hills Beyond Pentland," contained can now see that, with varying degrees of alteration, this material finally made its way into print in the first nine chapters of *The Web and the Rock*.[2]

Wolfe had not turned back to this material since 1933, but he had planned by now to place at the beginning of the work an impressionistic mélange similar to the prologue he had once worked on for his second novel. This was "The Book of the Night," a sketch of America after dark that had interested Wolfe since 1930. Since Wolfe himself was a night wanderer, he had observed a great variety of human activity during the night hours. In fact, he had already turned his attention to night backgrounds in *Death the Proud Brother*, "Only the Dead Know Brooklyn," and the famous train ride to the North in *Of Time and the River*. Perhaps he was again inspired by his master, James Joyce, whose "Work in Progress" on the Night Mind Wolfe knew well.[3] Whatever the reasons for his interest, Wolfe included the "Book of the Night" on his informal list of projected publications in 1935,[4] and in April, when he had set down notes for "The Frame of Hills Beyond Pentland," he planned to call the first chapter "The Beast of the Night." He described it as a "great medley of thoughts, scraps, chants, a child's impressions." The second chapter was then to be "Three O' Clock." [5]

But the trip to the West Coast in the summer produced a marked effect on Wolfe's plan for this preliminary "medley." Although specially labeled as an American writer, Wolfe had known nothing of the vast area of the nation across the Mississippi. Now, awed by the spaciousness of the prairie, stirred by the mountain scenery, dazzled by the strange earth formations of desert and canyon, refreshed (as all transcontinental travelers have been) by the opulence of California, he felt driven to incorporate his new sense of American space and configuration into his work. Moreover, he wished to place himself squarely in a tradition which he felt had been dominant in American writing. "It seems to me," he scribbled on an odd sheet, "that all American writing of the first mark has had in it a quality of darkness and of night—I mention Poe, Hawthorne, Melville, Whitman (most decidedly), Mark Twain and Sherwood Anderson." [6]

For the prologue to "The Hills Beyond Pentland," accordingly, what he had first conceived as a mixture of childhood reminiscences became "The Hound of Darkness," a series of scenes being enacted simultaneously all over America on a single night. It would be, in effect, the "Buried Life" of the nation. Into this simple framework Wolfe could bring any night incident that he had witnessed during his wandering and that he sensed was characteristic of a particular locale. He chose the night of June 13, 1918, and transported a number of his recent experiences back in time to that point.

As his plan developed, the influence of motion picture technique upon him is apparent for the first time. Looking down on the nation, he begins panning in from distance, he drifts into montage with emphasis on sound: the train whistle hoots, "Ho-Idaho-ho-ho-ho-ho"; the corn rustles, "coarse and sweet"; the leaves whisper, "Promise, promise, promise, promise." [7] Then he opens a series of scenes in dialogue. He set down his notes, too, in scenario fashion. "Scene: A night of dazzling light above America. As the action begins, the body and bones of the American continent are revealed from East to West." [8] Among the various outlines he drew up, the following is representative:

1. A blazing moonlight above America
2. A nearer view—the Sea

3. Nearer—the Corn in Illinois—a negro on a country road down South—screen doors slamming—streetcars —the leaves—a seaside resort in New England.
4. The Pelt of America
   a) Two Mexicans near Santa Fe
   b) Before a Drugstore in the South
   c) Mr. Saltonstall reading the Transcript
   d) The Sailors in the Tunnel under the River
   e) A Train going across Indiana
   f) Nigger bootblacks in a Tobacco Town
   g) The Whores in New Orleans
   h) The little fairy back room boy in Troy, N. Y.
   i) The House at Malbourne in Virginia
   j) A Boy and a Girl
   k) Grandma Gant and Augusta
   l) The Coal Crew—Altoona, Pa.
   m) (perhaps this should be last—Bacchus in a day coach)
   n) A Boy in a Bar in Hoboken

Clearly, the purpose of "The Hills Beyond Pentland" had changed. Formerly, Wolfe had set out to recreate the "golden weather" of his childhood and to use anecdotes of relatives and neighbors as particles of this atmosphere. Now, he would enlarge the scope of the work and would place a national stamp upon the work. A draft for a new title page reads:

> The Hills Beyond Pentland
> Man's Vision of His Lost,
> His Found, His Ever Real America [10]

Wolfe would take up the great problem of the American Dream, its fading and the ever-present possibility of its being realized. Notes in the big ledger he was using show some of the means by which he thought to handle it: "Alone by afternoon there in your father's house and so desiring perfect glory in America. Two Sections: I The Unknown North (to supplement His Father's Earth). II The West Unvisited." Further, scraps from a political speech are followed by the note, "How then did the 'hope and promise of America' of which the Honorable Pickens Gaffney had so eloquently spoken touch the lives of these people?" [11] Wolfe would scale down from his panorama of the whole body of America to the scrutiny of a typical American town. He prepared a general heading, "The Body and Soul of Altamont," then set down notes that would serve for the "Body": population figures and a careful catalogue of the buildings around the Town Square.[12]

II

Besides getting *From Death to Morning* and *The Story of a Novel* ready for publication, Wolfe spent the fall and winter planning and writing scenes for "The Hound of Darkness." [13] But all this activity came to an end sometime in early 1936. For about a year, a crisis had been developing. It arose out of accumulated resentments— about the reviews of *Of Time and the River* and *From Death to Morning,* about criticisms heard during the Colorado Writers' Conference, about reverberations from the magazine publication of *The Story of a Novel.* Further, Wolfe had been upset by his two lawsuits. The first had been brought against Wolfe by his discharged agent, Madeleine Boyd, who demanded a percentage of the royalties on his recent books. The second had been brought by Wolfe himself against Murdoch Dooher in order to recover valuable manuscripts he had foolishly allowed this young man to offer for sale. During the year Wolfe had enjoyed the warmth and brilliance of fame's limelight, but he had become a good target, too.

When his inward seething had become intolerable, Wolfe went to Max Perkins to talk over a creative remedy that would give him peace. The outcome was a decision that affected his work for the remainder of his career. He made up his mind to set aside work on the hexology in order to demonstrate that he could write a more objective, "non-autobiographical" novel—a short one that would not take much time. "He was going to put on the title page," Perkins reported, "what was said by Prince Andrei, in *War and Peace,* after his first battle when praise fell upon those who had done nothing and blame almost fell upon one who had done everything. . . .'Prince Andrei looked up at the stars and sighed; everything was so different from what he thought it was going to be.' " [14]

Wolfe called his new book, "The Vision of Spangler's Paul." He got the name "Spangler" for his hero from Spangler's Spring, a site on the battlefield of Gettysburg near the place of his father's birth (Spangler's Run he had called it in old Gant's dream in *Of Time and the River*). Wolfe had tried once before to demonstrate that he was more than an autobiographical novelist. Now, for his second attempt, he went back to the sketches about "Monkey" Hawke that he had done in 1930 and 1931 and transferred the ape-like features to both Paul Spangler and his father.

In order to show that he could handle other material besides his own experiences, he determined to try a narrative point of view that he had not used before—the detached observer—and to set his scene in an earlier time. He decided that the book should have "An Introduction by a Friend." The friend, Robert Mason, a lawyer about thirty years senior to Paul Spangler, speaking in the first person, would not only tell about Paul but he would also recount stories of old times in Libya Hill. Wolfe's notes show a great many false starts, but he finally got underway, alive with the excitement of a new venture. He began to spin out the story of Paul Spangler's father, his appearance in Libya Hill, how he pulled the circus wagons out of the mud, his stage coach journey with Zack Joyner, his faith in brick as building material, and what changes he wrought upon the town.[15] Most important of all was a sequence about Robert Mason and the courthouse bell that Wolfe completed as a unit sometime in May, 1936, and sold to the *American Mercury* as "The Bell Remembered."

Wolfe was proud to display this first evidence that he could follow the "totally objective" method. "The Bell Remembered" develops two of Wolfe's most characteristic themes: the father-and-son relationship and the recapture of lost time. But a combination of new and yet somehow familiar details carries the narrative: the recreation of a village square in the 1880's, the excitement of the bell's announcing court in session, the child's awe of the war veterans with their wounds and boasts, the Judge's brusque but sensible treatment of his son's hero worship, the boy's discovery in a history book of his father's heroism under fire, the impact of the discovery in stamping that day in the boy's memory.

Since "The Vision of Spangler's Paul" was to have as its principal idea that life does not always turn out as we expect, several ramifications grew out of this initial conception. First of all, Wolfe thought to make Paul Spangler face some of the problems of the artist in America. Paul was to be such a dedicated writer, so devoted to the muse, that he was in bondage to his task. Wolfe's book was entitled, for a time, "The Return of the Bondsman Paul," with a quotation from The Acts of the Apostles on the title page: "And Paul said, I would to God that not only thou, but also all that hear me this day, were both almost, and altogether such as I am—except these bonds." Then too, this book about discovery through disillusionment began to take over one of the themes of "The Hills Beyond Pentland," the vanishing of the American dream, as another title page reveals:

> The Vision of Spangler's Paul
> The Story of His Birth, His Life
> His Going To and Fro in the Earth
> His Walking Up and Down in It:
> His Vision also of the Lost,
> The Never-Found, the Ever-Here America
>
> With an Introduction
>
> by
>
> A Friend [16]

Although this playing with titles and mottos was nothing new for Wolfe, it tells a good deal about the turns his writing would take. As the novel about Spangler expanded to cover that character's whole life, one might expect that sooner or later Wolfe would return to the autobiographical track. And sure enough, by June, 1936, one of the tentative outlines labeled "Mr. Spangler Year by Year" logs the experiences of Thomas Wolfe.[17] Later outlines show that Wolfe was ready to take over material that he had already written in order to fill out Spangler's early life. Soon he had transferred Eugene Gant's afternoon meditations in front of his father's house and all the other "Hills Beyond Pentland" sketches to his new scheme. And though over the next two years the hero's name changed from Paul Spangler to George Spangler to George Josiah Doaks (known as Joe Doaks), Wolfe was always writing the same story, and this is how the character George Josiah "Monk" Webber of *The Web and the Rock* came into existence.[18]

But even though Wolfe absorbed old material into his book, that material underwent a great deal of revision, and new blending of his experiences began to take place. Hitherto all of Wolfe's characters had their counterparts in real life. Now Wolfe began to allow his imagination a little more freedom. For example, the character Nebraska Crawford (later surnamed Crane) seems possibly to have been shaped from two of Wolfe's closest boyhood friends: Max Israel, who was a good baseball player, and Henry Harris, a dark-eyed, bronze-skinned lad whose mother looked like an Indian.[19] Further, the emotional depth of the young hero's attachment to Nebraska had its beginnings in "The Hills Beyond Pentland" sketches, because there the admired boyhood companion was brother Ben.[20] Later in Wolfe's writing, the aging Nebraska may have been drawn from a professional baseball player whom Wolfe met on the train when he returned from the West in 1935 or from other major league players whom he became acquainted with. At any rate, Wolfe's imagination fused these images together to form both an individual and a type— of strength, courage, athletic ability, all that a boy might want to be. Wolfe even supplied an appropriate siring for Nebraska. Since he had long planned to introduce the defeat of the Masked Marvel into one of his reminiscent chapters, he now made Nebraska Crawford's father the hero of the occasion, scrawling out this addition to be inserted in the midst of the episode in which Nebraska rescues Spangler from the West Side boys. The result of this care was the creation of the one successful character who moved from childhood to maturity with George Webber in Wolfe's final manuscript.

III

With the ever-lengthening "Introduction by a Friend" and the expansion of material high-jacked from "The Hills Beyond Pentland," Wolfe had not done much with his new book to develop the idea of lessons learned through disillusionment. He had been skirting around the edges of the problem, taking a long time getting started. But by May of 1936, he began work on a later section of the novel. He began preparing the background for Spangler's entrance into the literary world. He began writing about a publishing house like Charles Scribner's Sons.

What this meant was that he had become engrossed in his new venture and had decided to abandon the pretense of not writing about his own life. He had decided to return to the notion that his own experience, heightened, could take on the quality of legend. All this seems clear from the description he sent to Heinz Ledig in June:

...it is by far the most objective book I have ever written, although, of course, like anything that is any good, it comes right out of my own experience, from everything I may have learned or found out during the course of my life. If I succeed in it, I want it to be a kind of tremendous fable, a kind of legend composed of all the materials of experience. The general idea is...the story of a good man abroad in the world—shall we say the naturally innocent man, the man who sets out in life with his own vision of what life is going to be like, what he is going to find, and then the story of what he really finds. It seems to me that this is the story behind "Don Quixote," behind "The Pickwick Papers," behind "Candide," behind "Gulliver," and even it seems to me behind such works as "Faust" and "Wilhelm Meister." [21]

The very models he cites were indications that Wolfe's book would move into the realm of comedy and satire. Indeed, this change from transcript of life to criticism of life was to result in indecision about the organization of the book for the next two years. As he shifted back and forth, writing now on one section of the manuscript and now on another, Wolfe's satiric attitude toward the experience of his recent years seemed to clash with the nostalgic view of his earlier years.

But at the time he wrote to Ledig, he was in a satiric period. He had long planned to make use of his intimate acquaintance with the staff and operations of his publishing house. Scribner's was now his New York family and community. Since he knew the editors, the readers, the secretaries, the business staff, the magazine staff, the bookstore staff only a little less well than the citizens of Asheville, and since Perkins had passed on a good deal of gossip and anecdote about happenings in the office over the years, Wolfe had assimilated the atmosphere of the publishing house well enough to handle it with confidence. He planned to convey the corporate personality of Scribner's by covering a full day at James Rodney and Company, as he called the house, beginning with characterizations of the three dominating figures, each symbolized by an animal: The Lion (Charles Scribner), The Fox (Maxwell Perkins), and The Goat (Whitney Darrow, the business manager, whose occasional stupidities about literary values had irked Wolfe).[22] To precede his survey of "A Day at Rodney's," Wolfe described each animal in his bestiary rising from sleep, following his early morning routine, and then arriving at his office. Hurriedly scrawling on yellow second sheets, Wolfe worked for about two months until he had exhausted both himself and his interest in the Rodney material.[23]

Meanwhile, additional tensions had built up, in spite of his attempt to dominate them. First of all, his lawsuits baffled and enraged him. When he finally settled the Boyd case in May, it cost him $650 plus lawyers' fees, although Wolfe had voluntarily added $150 to the settlement. The grounds for contention in the Dooher case were multiplying: Murdock Dooher continued to sell the Wolfe manuscripts he had, pocketing the money for himself. Further, Wolfe had quarreled with Scribner's and with Perkins over the royalties on *The Story of a Novel*.[24] But he endured the greatest pain of all when Bernard De Voto's article "Genius Is Not Enough" appeared in late April. In his brilliantly satiric manner, De Voto flayed the author and slashed at his work, declaring his books to be the products of a Scribner's assembly line. A hint of Wolfe's unstable condition as a result of all these pressures comes in a postscript to a letter. He had dictated a letter to Kent Greenfield in which he discussed De Voto's article; then at the end he scribbled hysterically: "The letter, of course, is written to *you*—and is confidential. It does not matter about De Voto, Canby, or the rest—but I am just through with legal trouble and not through with it yet—they have got all my money, all my manuscripts—so don't give this to them." [25] By summer, Wolfe was brooding over a decision whether or not to leave Scribner's.

In mid-July he sat, tired out, shaken in confidence, and emotionally bruised, composing a letter "To All Publishers" (which in the end he never sent), stating that his relations with Scribner's were still good but he wanted to seek a new publishing arrangement. And with all his honesty and his readiness for self-revelation, he declared, "In all fairness, I should here state that I think my physical resources which have been generous are at the present moment depleted, that the kind of vital concentration which has at times in the past attended the art of creation is diffused. But I think these things may come back, and that there is a possibility I will do better work that I have yet done." [26]

Still, he had been through periods of despair before, and he knew himself better now. He had even predicted his present state in a letter to Mrs. Roberts in May, saying "I am probably in for several thousand hours of hell and anguish, of almost losing hope, utterly, and swearing I'll never write another word and so on, but it seems to have to be done in this way and I have never found any way of avoiding it." [27]

He needed another respite to give his reservoir a chance to fill. He decided to go to Germany to see the Olympic Games. Since he was having trouble getting his accumulated royalties out of Germany, he felt he might as well spend them there. He knew that Ernst Rowalt would entertain him magnificently, and he knew, too, that the German edition of *Of Time and the River,* published in April, had been well received. He put his problems behind him, looking forward to another journey.

NOTES

1. HCL*46AM-7(56), in a typescript labeled "The Street."
2. However, Chapter 8, "The Child by Tiger," was written later; and Chapter 5, "Aunt Mag and Uncle Mark," in a more extended version, had been cut from the pages of "O Lost."
3. Wolfe's library contained not only *Anna Livia Plurabelle* (HCL*46M-350) and the March, 1928, issue of *transition,* which contained the beginning of Book III of "Work in Progress" (HCL*46A-498), but also the symposium, *Our Exagmination round his Factification for Incamination of Work in Progress* (Paris, 1929).
4. PN 27, April to June, 1935.
5. PN 26, March 21 to April 26, 1935.
6. HCL*46AM-7(70-aa).
7. HCL*46AM-7(52), "The Hound of Darkness" ledger.
8. *Ibid.,* p. 7.
9. *Ibid.,* p. 66.
10. HCL*46AM-7(50), on the back of p. 26 of the Colorado lecture.
11. HCL*46AM-7(52). For "The Unknown North," see W&R, Chapter 5. "The West Unvisited" seems never to have been written.
12. *Ibid.,* p. 44 and HCL*46AM-7(53), p. 400.
13. "Gentlemen of the Press," published in HB, is one of these scenes.
14. "Thomas Wolfe," *Harvard Library Bulletin,* I (Autumn, 1947), 274.
15. This material, altered and rearranged, appears in HB, Chapter 7, "The Stranger Whose Sermon Was Brick."
16. HCL*46AM-7(53).
17. PN 30, June 7 to *ca.* August 1, 1936.
18. The curious cry of the market boys "Paul, Paul," W&R, Chapter 2, is a leftover from "The Vision of Spangler's Paul."
19. Max Israel was Tom's best friend in his early boyhood; Henry Harris was his best friend at the North State Fitting School. Wolfe's remark in a letter to Arthur Mann probably refers to Max Israel: "I've got the man, I knew him as a child—he never made the Big League, but he could have. I mean he would have looked real in a Big League uniform because, as I saw at the dinner, it was from just such fellows that the Big League players come" (*Letters,* pp. 722-23).
20. HCL*46AM-7(53). "And at the same moment he sees the image of the brave companionship of Ben. What is there to fear?" Cf. W&R, pp. 63-64.
21. *Letters,* p. 526.
22. Another character, "The Great Baboon," was never developed.
23. By chance, the manuscript pages of this material were dated by the typist, running from May 23, when Wolfe was writing "The Lion at Morning" (HB, pp.

162-85), up through June 12, when he was finishing the work on Foxhall Edwards (YCGHA, pp. 438-98). After Wolfe's death, Perkins as literary executor insisted on several changes in the sketch of "The Lion."

24. See the exchange between Perkins and Wolfe in April (*Letters*, pp. 503-9).

25. *Letters*, p. 530.

26. *Letters*, p. 538.

27. *Letters*, p. 518.

21

PAUL SPANGLER'S VISION OF EVIL: "THE CHILD BY TIGER"

WOLFE'S RESERVOIR MAY HAVE RUN DRY IN THE EARLY SUMMER, but it was overflowing when he returned to New York at the end of September, 1936. He had rested, observed, meditated; and all the misgivings and shifts of attention that had accompanied the approach to the new book were brought under control. He explained to Thea Voelcker: "...although my conscious mind was busy with all the things and places I was seeing and the people I was meeting, I think my unconscious mind must have been busy at my book, because now that I am back the whole plan, from first to last, has become clear to me, and I think I know exactly what I want to do." [1] Although the clarity and confidence were temporary, this period was the most productive of his later career. In the next three months, he was to contribute more to the bulk of his final manuscript than in any other period of comparable length. He hired a secretary and began to dictate, following what he now established as his habitual method of composition, a method that pointed to greater strength in his writing.

Wolfe had been developing this method since 1935. He was following his most natural impulse in the use of language, and he was making it necessary for himself to revise his work carefully. Although he actually pursued a variety of methods over the next two years, his commonest procedure was something like this. First, he would dictate to a secretary—sometimes one who took shorthand but more often one who sat at the typewriter taking down his words directly. Pacing about the room, he would let the words flow, diving into his memory, at times glancing at a few notes scribbled on a scrap of paper, occasionally using for guidance a typescript of material he had written years before.

Taking this dictated version, which was either triple-spaced or single-spaced with extremely wide margins, he would revise it, working between the lines or in the margins and sometimes filling the backs of the sheets or scribbling a four- or five-page insertion. When this revised version was retyped, it became a part of his treasure of usable manuscript, and from this point one of several courses might develop. Perhaps an episode had enough integrity to become a magazine story or sketch. If so, Elizabeth Nowell would spot it as she looked over Wolfe's recent work and make suggestions about what might be done with it. After Wolfe made necessary changes for periodical publication, a suitable version would go off to an editor. But Wolfe's problem in getting editors to accept his work was excessive length. Luckily he had Miss Nowell's assistance here. Otherwise he would never have bothered to please an editor by excising, say, a thousand words, for by the time a story was returned with a request for reduction in length, he was likely to be working furiously on another project and to be unwilling to leave it. But Miss Nowell would take over and cut out the thousand words, very carefully marking her suggested excisions with parentheses and placing numbers in the margin indicating the number of words cut. After triumphantly adding up the numbers, page by page, to the required total, she would return the manuscript to Wolfe for his approval. Spared the terrible task of initial decision on what was to go, he would look over the manuscript, accepting some cuts, rejecting others, making a few changes of his own; and at length, the shortened version would appear in the *American Mercury,* the *New Yorker,* or one of the other magazines commonly found on the newsstand.

Or perhaps the sketch would have a less eventful history after its first revision. It would lie in his packing box until it was pulled out to be integrated into a larger section of his book. Usually very little alteration was considered or needed at this point: Wolfe would polish it a little more; add a little more; supply an occasional transition; at times, lift out a portion to be placed elsewhere in his sequence. Sometimes, however, during one of his periodic wappenshawings, Wolfe would interweave two, three, or even several sketches, rewriting enough to create a new whole.[2]

Clearly, Wolfe had developed more craftsmanship since his

troubles with *Of Time and the River*. He had learned a great deal about himself and about the way he must work: he should write out everything at length and whittle away at it later. And he had especially learned about the simple mechanics of revision from having to meet the restrictions of magazine editors on wordage.

With these improvements in technique came a decision about the subject matter for the new book he was working on. He ceased fretting over the question that troubled his progress in the spring: whether he could write a "non-autobiographical" novel. He had found that he could only do his best work when he felt free to draw upon his own experience whenever he wished. Now he was ready to assemble the entire body of his book, and it would be made up of layers of memory from his own life.

He began making notes on the characters who would appear in his books. This procedure led to his dictating plans for the revision of chapters he had already overhauled more than once since the time they had formed part of "The Hills Beyond Pentland": "The narrator —'I.' (The narrator 'I' of the book is a child known as Spangler's Paul: at the beginning of the book he is twelve years old. When the action starts he is lying on the grass before his uncle's house in North Carolina. This is the chapter which has already been written in first draft with the title 'The Names of the Caliban Paul.') The revisions that must now be made are as follows: The boy instead of being before his father's house is before his uncle's...," and so on.[3] As he proceeded with the notes for revision, Wolfe planned the thematic development of the conflict his hero feels within himself, the clash of heritages from father and from mother. He described the boy's situation: his mother is dead, his father (who lives in "open defiance of convention and public disapproval with an attractive but notorious woman in the community") has broken from his wife's family. The boy, living with his mother's people, is filled with horror at the slovenly mountaineer atmosphere. He longs to associate himself with his father's world of "warmth and radiance," and he creates in his mind an idealized vision of the unknown North from which his father migrated. The main lines of what became the first nine chapters of *The Web and the Rock* were now being established.

Continuing, Wolfe dictated a series of sketches of the people who would populate the community surrounding Spangler's Paul, the people who live on his street, the people whom he knows on the

East side of town, those whom he encounters from the West Side, the people whose activities in the town are carried on chiefly at night. The notes about characters run through Spangler's career to the time he begins teaching in the North at The School for Utility Cultures.[4]

Still dictating daily, boasting in a letter to Jonathan Daniels that he was spouting five thousand words a day, Wolfe began another sequence. Again he traced the ever-widening circle of Spangler's experience, but this time he was setting down the first draft of the core of his book, a series of episodes involving Spangler with the other characters. He filled out gaps in his hero's childhood under the heading "The Town," including there "Nigger Dick," a brief version of "The Child by Tiger." He went on to his account of Spangler's college days, entitled "The State," which consisted principally of an early characterization of Jerry Alsop (here named Big Ben Jolley). He continued on to "The City," which covered the adventures of young Southerners in New York. He jumped over Spangler's love affair with Esther Jack to material entitled "Oktoberfeste," in which Spangler's fight at the October Fair is prefaced by a sketch of Munich. He finally wound up with "The Earth," Spangler's encounters with Daisy Purvis and Lloyd McHarg.[5]

While the creative torrent was flowing, Wolfe drove himself without stint, pouring out the words by the hundreds of thousands—and even declining to attend an election-night party despite his zealous support of the Roosevelt cause. By the time he broke off exhausted in late December, he had a working base for his book. This new material and the hoard of odd manuscript he had accumulated over the past six years was in its raw, crude state a richer ore than that from which he had extracted *Of Time and the River,* and it formed eventually the bulk of his two posthumous novels.

II

Reviewing his rough drafts, Wolfe began to work some into shape for magazine publication. Still caught up in a kind of dream of past time, he took the episode "Nigger Dick" and began work on what became "The Child by Tiger," the outstanding short story of his career. Elaboration increased its length considerably and brought it to a second version. It underwent further revision after Miss

Nowell suggested cuts in order to make magazine publication possible. Wolfe gave the story another full overhauling this time, strengthening his style by lopping off adjectives and adding vigorous active verbs.[6] This story, which he had passed over as he followed his outline for *Look Homeward, Angel* and which he had first developed in 1930 as an illustration of the variety of American life, had now evolved into an inquiry into the springs of evil in human nature.

"The Child by Tiger" offers a real demonstration of Wolfe's creative ability. The bloody justice wrought upon Will Harris, alias James Harvey, who had shot and killed five Asheville citizens, provided the bare bones of the story. Harris, a strange Negro, had wandered into town in early November, 1906, when Tom Wolfe was six years old. Nothing was known about Harris except that he bought some overalls and high-top boots at a store and a second-hand rifle with some cartridges at a pawnbroker's. He was next heard from the night of the shooting, November 13.[7]

In his earliest retelling of the story, Wolfe had used Vachel Lindsay's title "The Congo."[8] He had probably intended to emphasize the "basic savagery" of the Negro desperado. But in the six years that had passed since this initial draft, his attitude toward the Negro people had undergone change along with the general enlargement of his sympathies. Possibly, too, a reaction to the Nazi scorn for Jesse Owens (for whom Wolfe had cheered victoriously at the Olympic Games)[9] had contributed to his more enlightened view.[10] Now, rethinking and embellishing the Will Harris story, he used his material to uncover the hidden violence of all humankind.

Wolfe molded the situation to his new book by having the story focus on Dick Prosser, "the child by tiger," through the eyes of the boy, Paul Spangler. (For comment on the story, it is convenient to refer to the expanded version that appears in *The Web and the Rock;* there, of course, Spangler's name has been changed to George Webber.) Wolfe invented the series of incidents that opens the story and developed a character very different from the original, Will Harris. Dick Prosser is introduced as the boys are playing football. As he coaches them on handling the ball, other features of his character are woven in by the narrator's reminiscence. He is a model for the boys, since he is knowing and practised in manly, athletic skills. Prosser, who was at one time a soldier, has shown them how to box, how to shoot (a detail that establishes the murderous accuracy of his marksman's eye), how to build a fire, how to "tote a burden." As the story continues, Wolfe prepares his enigma by giving Prosser a complicated series of characteristics. As the Shepperton house servant and chauffeur, he is seen to be orderly, precise, even somewhat austere. He has a deeply religious strain: he reads the Bible, he sings hymns as he works, he intones like a preacher when he warns the boys about the Judgment Day.[11] He demonstrates his stoicism when drunken Lon Pilcher crashes into the Shepperton car and then smashes Prosser in the face with his fist.

Although the boy's-eye view sees only these external displays, George Webber senses the buried turbulence that is just below the surface when he sees the sudden flash of fury in Dick Prosser's eyes. Wolfe uses rather obvious animal imagery to suggest the latent savagery: Prosser treads about noiselessly as a cat, he bares his teeth, his eyes go small and "red as rodents'."

Midway through the narrative, Wolfe steps aside in Melvillian fashion to play paradoxically with the symbols of good and evil, reason and unreason, the known and the unknown. Snow falls on the night that Dick Prosser runs wild. The white snow comes down from the North, George Webber's father's country, which has symbolized an ideal world associated with light and reason. The snow comes into the South, the land of the murky, irrational Joyners, his mother's people. But so mixed are the qualities of light and dark that the snow is a "demonic visitant" from the unknown North which blows down to accompany the wild outbreak of Dick Prosser's darkness. "Thus, at the head of those two poles of life will lie the real, the truthful image of its immortal opposite. Thus, buried in the dark heart of the cold and secret North, abides forever the essential image of the South; thus, at the dark heart of the moveless South, there burns forever the immortal splendor of the North." [12]

Wolfe's story is a study of the undeniable presence of that darkness. Underlying Dick Prosser's model behavior, the beast waits to snarl forth; underneath the civilized veneer of Libya Hill's inhabitants lurks a barbarism thirsting for blood. After Prosser has broken out on his shooting spree, Wolfe employs the animal imagery to uncover the brute nature of the white citizens as he describes the menacing growl of the crowd. The baying of the bloodhounds reflects the relentless fury of the human pack in pursuit of Prosser.

Wolfe holds firmly to the boy's point of view as the details of

Prosser's evening of frenzy are revealed to George and Nebraska by snatches of rumor from the crowd. Wolfe follows out the narrative of the chase by means of a summarizing device: "From time to time news would drift back to them." Here Wolfe made use of the true story of Will Harris as he had heard it. In Asheville in 1906, Harris had killed a Negro who came home to discover Harris with his wife. He shot the policeman who was called to the scene. He charged up Asheville's Eagle Street, shooting at every moving object. He killed one man in the street and another in the door of a shop. When a hotel resident opened his window, Harris's shot struck just below the sill. In Pack Square, one of his bullets pierced straight through a telephone pole, killing Policeman Bill Bailey. Harris was captured two days later when he had run out of ammunition, and his riddled body was brought back and hung in the window of the undertaking rooms of Hard, Bard, and Company.[13]

Wolfe handled the facts as he knew them in order to maintain narrative interest and added what was necessary to develop his theme. He either ignored or forgot the details of the two men killed on the street but made his Dick Prosser shoot accurately at the man in the window, taking the top of his head off. He used the death at the telephone pole to contrast ironically with a grotesque scene in the midst of the slaughter: a drunken police magistrate dressed in evening clothes attempts to declare Prosser under arrest and escapes a bullet by fool's luck. He continued to employ animal imagery in following Dick Prosser's flight—like a noble and canny beast alone in the snow-covered woods and fields or plunging through the icy waters of Cane Creek for a mile in order to throw off his pursuers. He described Prosser's last-ditch stand before the mob as typical of the heroic figure young George Webber had admired: Prosser fell back "as slowly and deliberately as a trained soldier retreating in good order, still firing as he went" until his last bullet was gone. And with that puzzling stoicism and that passion for ritual and order he had displayed as the Shepperton house servant, he sat down quietly at the edge of the creek, "unlaced his shoes, took them off, placed them together neatly at his side" and then stood up to face the fire of the oncoming mob.

Wolfe was able to make an effective scene out of the account of Harris's body at the undertaking parlor because he was able to bring George Webber and the other boys there to look at the "ghastly relic of man's savagery" and to see their fellow citizens as "the mongrel conquerors of the earth." As they listen to the boastful tales of the killing, they sense the "something hateful and unspeakable in the souls of men."

One final scene takes the story into another realm. George and his friends go back to Dick Prosser's room in the Shepperton house, where his Bible lies open at the Twenty-third Psalm. As Mr. Shepperton reads it aloud, the scene underscores ironically the bitter details of Dick Prosser's end. The Lord had led him beside the icy waters of Cane Creek and had made him lie down in snowy pastures. When he walked through the valley of the shadow of death, he had been ripped to a tattered hulk by the bullets of violent men.

But along with these ironies, the peaceful pastoral rhythms of the psalm allay the emotions aroused by the blood-drenched narrative, and we move to a contemplative distance as the story closes. Wolfe makes George Webber think of it all in later years, and as the images melt together in his mind, they recapitulate the stages of his knowledge of Dick Prosser up to the reading of the psalm in the clean-swept little room. Webber thrusts aside Psalm Twenty-three as an inappropriate text, and he meditates upon a more suitable psalm, Blake's "The Tiger," with its insistent question about the existence of evil and savagery in the universe. Dick Prosser and his inexplicable nature become the symbol of the paradoxical blend of evil and innocence in man, "a projection of his own unfathomed quality, a friend, a brother, and a mortal enemy, an unknown demon —our loving friend, our mortal enemy, two worlds together—a tiger and a child." [14]

From the memory of childhood play, from the memory of a lurid tale heard from fellow townsmen, from the memory of W. O. Wolfe in Pack Square pointing out the bullet hole drilled cleanly through the telephone pole, from the thronging memories of Asheville's faces, Wolfe brought the details to fuse imaginatively into an exciting story, full of darkness and hurrying feet, which rose to become a vision of the oldest question about the human condition. Wolfe was able to achieve this success probably because he knew just enough about Asheville's bloodiest hour to grasp its reality but not enough so that his imagination was overwhelmed by his memory.

NOTES

1. *Letters,* p. 545.

2. For example, Chapter 2 of W&R, "Three O'Clock," was one of Wolfe's type-scripts running seventy-five pages. It was made up of the following pieces, most of which were written at different times: a dissertation on North and South Carolina, a meditation on names, a boy's aunt calling him to do an errand, a characterization of Nebraska Crane (Crawford, Drake), the defeat of the Masked Marvel, a digression on poor whites, the attack of a gang of boys on George Webber.

3. HCL*46AM-7(24-r).

4. *Ibid.* The typescript, entitled merely "Characters," breaks off after 131 pages.

5. The composition of this material can be dated because of a list of tabulations Wolfe jotted down. He added up the estimated number of words he had written for "I Have a Thing to Tell You," "Oktoberfeste," "A Child By Tiger," "Characters," "Town," "City," "Earth." They amounted to "180,250 total words as of Dec. 4" (HCL*-46AM-7[61]). The section "The State" is not included in this list. Perhaps he dictated it at some other time, but the form, the spacing, and the paper are exactly the same as for the sections labeled "Town," "City," and "Earth."

6. HCL*46AM-7(55) and (56). Versions in manuscript and typescript show the stages through which the story passed.

7. I am grateful to Myra Champion for information about Will Harris and his violent end, my account of which comes mostly from an article in the *Asheville Citizen,* November 16, 1906, a reprint of which appeared in the memorial issue of the *Citizen,* September 10, 1937. Some additional details were supplied by Mrs. Mabel Wolfe Wheaton.

8. *Letters,* p. 243.

9. Martha Dodd, *Through Embassy Eyes* (New York, 1939), p. 212.

10. Wolfe's behavior toward the Negro in his life and his attitude toward the Negro in his writings show a man struggling against a cultural prejudice that surrounded his early life. In his later years he was outwardly ready to treat Negroes in the same way he treated anyone else. Colored bellboys at the Hotel Albert and the Hotel Chelsea say they got on well with him. Parnell Kennedy, bellboy captain at the Chelsea, occasionally joined Wolfe in his room for a drink. In fact, Kennedy asserted that, when Wolfe got surly from over-drinking, he was the only one in the hotel who could handle him. Elmer Davis, doorman at the Harvard Club, found Wolfe always friendly and ready to chat and to ask about all his family. William Braswell, in "Thomas Wolfe Lectures and Takes a Holiday" (Walser, p. 73), records Wolfe's gracious behavior to Kendall Taft's cook. As for L. Ruth Middlebrook's anecdote in "Reminiscences of Thomas Wolfe," *American Mercury,* XLIII (November, 1946), 545, that at N. Y. U. Wolfe refused to ride with a Negro elevator operator, it is an example of a complicated fit of temper. Wolfe became enraged at one of the elevator operators, but it perhaps had less to do with the fact that he was a Negro than the fact that he was a New York City dweller. Wolfe was angry at the undue sense of authority the man assumed. In his notebook, he commented: "The American city temper is cowardly, vicious and cruel—servile and cringing when it is powerless; arrogant and overbearing when it holds the reins. Never put a uniform on an American not even for running an elevator. He can't stand it." PN 3, Fall, 1927, to September, 1928.

In his writing, however, he reveals that he looked on the Negro as an inferior being. He would not capitalize the word "Negro," and he always referred to a Negro girl as a wench. His imagery usually shows revulsion, and generally he treats the Negro characters in animalistic terms. Niggertown in Altamont is a jungle, Ella Corpening's skin is her pelt, Aunt Maw's disgruntled servant is a poor brute, and so on. But the jolt that Wolfe's social conscience got in Germany seems to have helped him toward overcoming his color prejudice. Dick Prosser in "The Child by Tiger" is treated with admiration and sympathy, even though he is a murderer, and he stands brother to the white citizens, even if it is to symbolize the tendency to violence in all human beings.

11. Floyd Watkins has pointed out that Wolfe drew Prosser's phrases from a famous sermon, "De Dry Bones in De Valley," *Southern Folklore Quarterly*, XX (June, 1956), 136-49.

12. W&R, p. 140.

13. Floyd Watkins has an excellent discussion of "The Child by Tiger" in *Thomas Wolfe's Characters* (Norman, Okla., 1957), pp. 102-9. He compares the correspondences between Will Harris' desperate career and Wolfe's story. Oddly enough, he seems to assume that Wolfe had the old newspaper accounts before him, for he points out the details that Wolfe "unfortunately omitted." Wolfe had only heard the story; he did no research.

14. W&R, p. 156.

Part VII

THE SOCIAL CONSCIENCE

22

A POLITICAL AWAKENING:
I HAVE A THING TO TELL YOU

THE MATURITY OF WOLFE'S WRITING SINCE THE PUBLICATION OF his second novel is displayed in other ways than improved technique. His deeper understanding of human relationships had grown gradually as his slumbering social conscience was aroused. Finally, he had been jolted fully awake during his stay in Germany in 1936. Over the next two years, his life and his writing were to show not only further extension of his social sympathies but also his realization that politics is just a more complex form of ethics.

"For the first time in my life," Wolfe wrote his old friend Billy Polk after returning from Germany, "I have become passionately interested in politics, not only here at home but also in the vexed and tragic states of Europe." [1] Wolfe's two trips to Germany in 1935 and 1936 had taught him a lesson. These two observations of Germany, one year apart, are twin chapters of his life which show how his own experience was central to any social views he held. They also represent the context out of which the short novel *I Have a Thing to Tell You* arose, and they brought about the first steps toward the social awareness of Wolfe's later writing.

Most of his life Wolfe had not paid much attention to politics and international affairs. When he read the newspapers, he usually turned first to the sports section. He was ill-informed, then, about the ominous developments in Europe in the 1930's. What he had observed about European nations was only a tourist's view, for during his trips abroad he spent his time sight-seeing, when, that is, he was not working all alone struggling with his problem of self-expression. He knew more about European restaurants than about European social problems.

325

As a result, his attitude toward Germany was based on his casual contacts with the people as he passed in and out of the country during European tours. And that attitude shifted according to his moods. For example, he had resented the Prussian arrogance of German students whom he had brushed against, and he had loathed the neckless German tourists whom he had watched stuffing themselves with sausages on a trip up the Rhine. Probably some post-World-War animosities still lurked within him. Later, however, he had come to love Munich and the southern Germanic people of Austria. In his writing he began to identify his father's country in southern Pennsylvania with a Germanic cleanliness, generosity, and vitality.

When Wolfe went to Europe in 1935, he was unprepared to criticize the upheaval that had changed the Germany he had last seen during his brief stay in the Black Forest in 1930. During the rise of Nazism in the early thirties, he was too buried in his work to be aware of its evil. His only contact with an anti-Fascist force in America was with V. F. Calverton and his *Modern Monthly* staff. He thought Calverton was an insincere opportunist, and he distrusted his whole Trotskyite group. Although stories of the Nazi persecution of the Jews could not have failed to reach his ears, he seems to have discounted them with the skepticism that the postwar generation had come to have about atrocity stories. As for the anti-Semitic propaganda, it accorded with his own notions about the Jews. News of such events as the bloody June purge of 1934 he must have missed completely, because his first impressions of the "New Germany" were eminently favorable.

Spring was bursting out when he arrived in May, 1935, and the "well-kept cleanliness" [2] of Berlin and an air of prosperity struck him as a bright contrast to the gloom of France and England sunk in the depths of the Great Depression. Then, too, the German people impressed this American nationalist as possessing the kind of cultural solidarity and vitality that he felt America so sadly lacked in depression days. His coming was colored by the success the German edition of *Look Homeward, Angel* had achieved and by the news of the recent reception of the long-awaited second novel in America. The pleasant delirium of fame was further intensified by the whirl of entertainment his publisher, Ernst Rowolt, provided and by the personal attention he received from Martha Dodd, the attractive daughter of the American Ambassador. [3]

Fame had never tasted so sweet in America. For six weeks he was the center of literary interest in Berlin. Literary figures who had not appeared in public since Hitler's rise to power came forward to meet the visiting foreigner. It seemed as if the arrival of a well-loved American writer had awakened the withering roots of culture wherever they lay in the capital. Wolfe left in mid-June with happy memories and a feeling that he had become a part of Germany's cultural heritage along with Goethe and Schiller, whose shrines he had visited in Weimar with great reverence. Of politics there had not been much talk, except at the Embassy where he had engaged in argument and discussion with Martha and Bill Dodd, Jr. In spite of Wolfe's deep respect for Ambassador Dodd as a scholar and historian, yet an earthy Tar Heel, Wolfe would not accept all his criticisms of Germany under the Nazis. He left Germany "with many of his illusions intact, though some were wavering."[4]

In order to understand how it was possible for Wolfe to be attracted to German Fascism, it is worthwhile to compare his first impressions of Nazi Germany with those of Martha Dodd. Young Miss Dodd was a graduate of the University of Chicago, where her father was a professor of American History. She was an eager, uncritical liberal (excited, for example, by Ella Winter's *Red Virtue*) who worked on the literary staff of the *Chicago Tribune*. When she first arrived in Germany in 1933, she was impressed with the German people as kindly, polite, happy, and orderly. She found the merchant class in particular much more pleasant and honest to deal with than the French shopkeepers. She was so moved by the spirit of the people, and so intoxicated by the shouting, the singing, the colorful military displays, that she felt she was witnessing a national rebirth. In spite of the fact that her father was daily offering official protests against the outrages and brutalities of the Storm Troopers, she so sought to excuse the excesses that at the family dinner table she was called "The Young Nazi." So much was she bedazzled by her position at the center of social life at the Embassy, then, that a couple of months passed before she became fully aware of the large-scale offenses against human decency that the Nazi regime was carrying out.[5]

Miss Dodd's introduction to the glamor and prestige of diplomatic life and Wolfe's response to adulation temporarily blinded each of them to sights that less emotional, less self-centered people easily perceived. Wolfe was further troubled by an inadequate understanding of what freedom meant. He quibbled that he was free to criticize the Jews in Germany, whereas in New York he was not. He compared the freedom he himself enjoyed in Berlin with the injustice of his being sued for breach of contract in New York by an agent whom he had discharged for mishandling his affairs.

But by the time Wolfe made his next visit to Germany in 1936, grave events had taken place that should have alerted anyone to the threat of Fascism. Italy had invaded Ethiopia and conquered the country soon after Addis Abba had fallen. Anti-Semitic outrages increased in Germany. German troops had marched into the Rhineland. General Franco had landed at Cadiz with the Spanish Foreign Legion and Moorish troops.

Wolfe's voyage across the Atlantic in late July, 1936, had begun with a series of political arguments aboard ship, and he arrived in Berlin full of questions. This time he found out truths to which his eyes and ears had been closed the previous year. He listened to Martha Dodd's new chronicle of Nazi abominations, and now he believed them. More than anything, he sensed the atmosphere of distrust everywhere he went. His personal experiences built up irritation and finally revulsion at what he saw was happening. He became suspicious of his financial dealings with his publisher, and at length even quarreled with his friend, Ledig. Obstacles to his taking a German girl across the Austrian border for an Alpine holiday annoyed him. Problems of taking currency in and out of the country enraged him. But when in Aachen he witnessed the apprehension of a German Jew who was fleeing by train across the German-Belgian border, he was horrified. All the notes that he had made in his pocket notebook, arguing with himself about Fascism, lists of arguments "For" and "Against," were meaningless now.[6] He returned to America extremely sobered.

II

Wolfe's change of mind about Nazism shows itself first in his short novel, *I Have a Thing to Tell You,* published in three installments in the *New Republic* in March, 1937, and later in a more extended form in *You Can't Go Home Again.* Its very title indicates something of the urgency with which Wolfe felt that he must write out of his new knowledge.[7] But this work was brought into being in ironic fashion.

In order to cut his expenses for his European vacation, Wolfe had made arrangements with North German Lloyd to write three articles for their trade magazine, *Seven Seas,* in return for a half-price passage on one of their liners. He tried to write the travel articles, making beginnings in his notebook to describe travel in Germany or the Olympic Games. But he found that he could not, with any honesty, reflect happiness about what he had found in Germany. He might have set down some facile pieces on the beauties of Berlin or on the Tyrolean Alps, but his inner oracle forbade him.

After his return to America, he wrote to the *Seven Seas,* trying as delicately as possible (he certainly wanted no more trouble about breach of contract) to be relieved of his obligations. "...everything I do," he told the editor, "everything I create, comes from the whole texture of my experience—from everything I have seen, thought, felt or known. As I think of these proposed articles, I find it very difficult to isolate them from this whole fabric, to separate them from lives and events and feelings which would be proper and essential in a work of the imagination but which I feel would not only be improper but decidedly unwise in a series of travel articles for a travel magazine." [8] It seems clear as the letter continues that Wolfe still loved Germany and the German people. He implies that if he praised or showed his approval of the present state of affairs, he would only be disloyal to a people who perhaps would one day throw off the Nazi yoke. He enclosed $150 to make complete payment for his passage, tourist class.

He then set to work, no doubt muttering "Ich kann nicht anders," which was his own special incantation whenever he had won a struggle to follow an inner necessity. In his notebook he had already set down his title and a few scattered statements and phrases, such as "I am going to tell you a little story and it's a little story that may hurt me too" and "whereon the pillars of this earth are founded" and "brothers, we must brothers be." He had even included a fragment of a statement that would make clear that he carried an anti-Semitic prejudice: "I don't like Jews, and if most of the people I know would tell the truth about their feelings I wonder how many of them would be able to say that they liked Jews." He had drawn up a list of the "Personae (from First to Last)" who could appear in a narrative that

covered his entire summer tour, and it contained one group of people
who were to become the principal figures in his story:

On the Train
to Paris
{
Tommy Mayaski
The German Woman
The Young Sculptor
The Little Man [9]

As plans shaped themselves in his head, he decided to focus on his
final journey by train out of Germany, and he drew together from his
memory all the political revelations made to him by his friend, Heinz
Ledig, and placed them in one scene just before the central character's departure from Germany. In the next weeks, he dictated 30,000
words, his first version of *I Have a Thing to Tell You*.[10] It was part
of his new book, one of Paul Spangler's later encounters in the process
of maturing. After drastic cutting it was ready for magazine publication.[11]

When the work appeared, Wolfe surprised his readers with a piece
that was obviously based on his own experience yet displayed a new
Wolfe manner. Told by Paul Spangler in the first person,[12] the opening passages about waking and having breakfast in the German hotel
have the studied detail and the short sentences of the Hemingway
style, which Wolfe admired very much.[13] Throughout the work, the
style remains a constant index to the feeling the story evokes. After
the quiet beginning, it mounts in intensity until the capture of the
little man trying to escape on the train. Occasional muted lyric passages describe the beauty of the land Spangler must leave forever,
and, finally, in the emotional peak of the farewell itself, the rhythmic
repetition of Wolfe's oratorical style appears: "To that old master,
now, to wizard Faust, old Father of the ancient and swarm-haunted
mind of man, to that old German land with all the measure of its
truth, its glory, beauty, magic and its ruin—to that dark land, to that
old ancient earth that I had loved so long—I said farewell." [14]

The rather spare version in the *New Republic* is not nearly so
effective as the longer narrative that Wolfe intended for his big
manuscript. The final published version in *You Can't Go Home
Again*, with additional material about the Olympic Games and about
the encroachments of Nazism, follows a pattern of gradual revelation into which Wolfe packed the essence of his experience in Berlin.[15] Avoiding sensationalism, the story is unique. It is an attack on

Nazism, not through a tale of violent conflict, torture, or espionage, but through a record of the way its evil, like most great evils, pervades the consciousness of a human being who merely passes near it.

In this section of *You Can't Go Home Again,* Wolfe first shows how fame and love temporarily ease the tortured mind of George Webber (as Paul Spangler is finally named).[16] Then the series of episodes in George Webber's departure that follows provides all the evidences that Nazism is a "plague of the spirit." George's friend, Franz Heilig, describes how an ordinary man's personal life suffers from Nazi interference. Regulations thwart his relations with his girl, racial investigation complicates his plight as an illegitimate son and further threatens that he will lose his job as a librarian.[17] The scene at the railroad station shows the widespread suspicion that Nazism breeds, for the three people who come to bid George goodbye all eye one another uneasily. This scene, with its frequent references to homosexuality, also suggests a climate of decadence in Berlin. Else von Kohler accuses Franz Heilig of jealousy over George. They argue about Herr Grauschmidt's drawing of George, which has made him look like a "sugar-tenor." Another argument ensues about Grauschmidt's effeminate manners and tastes. Karl Lewald refers to his wife in purposely mistaken English as "mein hosband" and, joking with George, hopes that he, too, will someday have a "good hosband." The tension among the passengers who are George's companions on the train builds up through trivial chit-chat about the difficulties of travel and the problem of taking currency out of the country. It increases as George hides $30 in a vest pocket and others exchange small amounts in German marks to hoodwink the inspectors. It reaches its climax in the detention of the escaping Jew who had hoped to take his little savings with him. The last event, the crossing of the border, brings relief to all the passengers—even the German woman who had nervously rationalized about the government's action in holding the poor Jew behind. They have got "out," and for George Webber "out" takes on another meaning than exit or escape. It signifies a self-willed exclusion, for he knows that he will have to write honestly about what he has seen and felt and that he can never return to Germany, "the other half of his heart's home."

Punctuating the narrative of the train journey are frequent reminders about freedom and brotherhood. Adamowski is seen reading *The Saga of Democracy.* He can hardly wait to return to the United

States, his adopted country, and breathe the air of freedom again. The mixture of nationalities in the train compartment—German, American, and Polish—intensifies the theme of brotherhood. All are strangers, politely distant from one another at first. Then they join in the simple ritual of breaking bread together and unite over Adamowski's box lunch—only to have one of their "family of earth" snatched from their midst. The most telling indictment of the Nazi system is in the sense of betrayal the situation forces on George Webber. He feels a murderous fury at the German officials who hustle the Jew away, yet he is afraid to implicate himself. He holds in his hand the few coins the little man had given him, feeling they are "blood-money." He, as well as the others, can scarcely bear to return the look the prisoner gives them: "And in that gaze there was all the unmeasured weight of man's mortal anguish. George and the others felt somehow naked and ashamed, and somehow guilty. They all felt they were saying farewell, not to a man, but to humanity; not to some pathetic stranger, some chance acquaintance of the voyage, but to mankind; not to some nameless cipher out of life, but to the fading image of a brother's face." [18]

I Have a Thing to Tell You is a well-defined mark in Wolfe's career in both thought and composition. In order to purge himself of guilt for having been deceived by the veneer of Nazism, Wolfe acknowledges the claims of human brotherhood with a strength that his self-centered individualism had not allowed to emerge before. As a composition, it is a product of independent work and care that tells how much Wolfe had learned from working with Miss Nowell on *The Story of a Novel.*

But Wolfe continued to carry a sense of guilt about his pro-Nazi period. In his plans for his book, he used the phrase "Fair Medusa" to symbolize fame, for in Germany fame had temporarily turned his heart to stone.

NOTES

1. HCL, unpublished letter dated October 12, 1936. He wrote in the same vein to Jonathan Daniels on October 23.

2. Wolfe used the phrase in a letter to Thea Voelcker (*Letters*, p. 545), who stood for the portrait of Else Von Kohler in YCGHA.

3. Much of the information about Wolfe's stay-over in Berlin in 1935 and 1936 has been taken from Martha Dodd, *Through Embassy Eyes* (New York, 1939), pp. 86-95, and H. M. Ledig-Rowolt, "Thomas Wolfe in Berlin," *American Scholar*, XXII (Spring, 1953), 185-201.

4. Dodd, p. 94.

5. Dodd, pp. 18-45.

6. PN 31, August 20 to *ca.* September 30, 1936. For details, see Nowell, p. 332.

7. Wolfe's title is an ingenious use of the phrase he often heard on the lips of H. M. Ledig, who prefaced his explanations of the political situation with "Nun will ich Ihnen 'was sagen." He planned the story in Paris, just after crossing the German frontier (*Letters,* p. 541).

8. *Letters,* p. 544.

9. PN 31, August 20 to *ca.* September 30, 1936.

10. For Wolfe's consideration of another title, "I Have Them Yet," see Nowell, p. 337.

11. The first version, labeled "The World: The Bright Angel (March, 1935-October, 1936)" ran fifty pages of single-spaced typescript with very wide margins. Wolfe revised it, making cuts, additions, and a great many changes in phrasing to produce a second version of ninety-three pages, double-spaced. This was the version used for *You Can't Go Home Again.* With Miss Nowell's help, Wolfe cut this down to sixty-four pages, with magazine standards of length in mind. When Miss Nowell sold the reduced version to the *New Republic,* it was accepted subject to further reduction in length. She followed her usual practice of going over the piece and marking suggested cuts. Wolfe approved them. Thus, for magazine publication the work went through four versions, the last one being Miss Nowell's cutting. This short version has been reprinted in *Short Novels,* pp. 236-78.

12. This is the only published piece in which Wolfe's central character is called "Paul" Spangler.

13. HCL*46AM-7(70-h). In notes, probably for his talk on the "American Novel" at N. Y. U. in 1929, Wolfe offers extended praise of the style in *A Farewell to Arms.* "Hemingway says one thing and suggests ten more," etc.

14. *New Republic,* XC (March 24, 1937), 207.

15. Most of Chapter 38, "The Dark Messiah," YCGHA, pp. 625-33, was added in February, 1938. Wolfe wrote it while trying to answer a letter from Donald Ogden Stewart, head of the League of American Writers, who was polling American writers about their views on the Spanish Civil War.

16. Revising the material Wolfe left in his final manuscript stack, Edward Aswell fashioned the "Dark Messiah" chapter in the following way: taking Wolfe's "A Spanish Letter" (described in n. 15), he placed pages 6-7, 15-20, and 9-14 in that order, drew some additional material from Wolfe's writings on fame and the poet, then supplied an introduction and some transitional paragraphs.

17. Heinz M. Ledig (upon whom Wolfe based the character, Franz Heilig) thought that Wolfe had gone to his hotel room each evening and recorded their conversations verbatim (H. M. Ledig-Rowolt, "Thomas Wolfe in Berlin"). This is not true. Wolfe would occasionally set down in his notebook Ledig's habits of phrasing, but that is all. For example, "Zis little man with his pipe," and so on—PN 31, August 20 to *ca.* September 30, 1936. After Wolfe's return to America, he asked someone, perhaps Miss Nowell, to go over the letters from Ernst Rowolt and to make a list of unidiomatic phrases he could use as a model for the dialogue.

18. YCGHA, p. 699.

23

THE EMERGENCE OF JOE DOAKS

So impelling was Wolfe's creative momentum at the end of 1936 that he did not cease work even when a libel suit exploded in his face in early December. Because of Wolfe's fictional portrait of her as Mad Maude in "No Door," Marjorie Dorman sued both Wolfe and Scribner's, sending Wolfe into an Olympian rage and into a long, half-humorous denunciation of Perkins, which ended ". . . and now you have got me into a $125,000 libel suit." [1] Although he took time off to consult with lawyers and to indulge in lengthy confabulations with the Scribner's staff, he contined his writing until Christmas Day, when he broke off, exhausted, in order to take a six-week tour through the South.

Wolfe had learned that these vacations were necessary in order to keep himself from going stale from fatigue. And he also knew that new sights and fresh observation were a splendid means for stocking his memory and for jogging him into comparison, judgment, and knowledge. He stopped off first in Richmond, bumping into a Modern Language Association Convention by chance. He ignored or insulted any former colleagues from New York University he met there. But the chance did lead him into a pleasant evening with the Vanderbilt group, John Crowe Ransom, Robert Penn Warren, Allen Tate, Cleanth Brooks, and Caroline Gordon. He went on to New Orleans, where he sampled all the delicacies the city could offer, from dinner at Antoine's to a poor-boy sandwich.[2] With a group of newspaper men, friends of Hamilton Basso, he spent some late evenings, after one of which, shuddering with hangover, he declined to address a Sunday School class for his cousin, Ollie Wolfe. In New Orleans, Wolfe first met William B. Wisdom, who began his unsurpassed Thomas Wolfe Collection by asking Wolfe to autograph copies of his books. After a stopover in Biloxi, Wolfe headed east to Atlanta.

The trip to the South had flanked Asheville, but now Wolfe decided to end his "exile," as he called it, and to stop there on his way north. But a misunderstanding in a telephone conversation with family members made him think he still would not be welcome. So he passed on by, stopping first in Raleigh to see Jonathan Daniels and then going on to Chapel Hill, where he renewed acquaintance with Albert Coates, Phillips Russell, and Paul Green and paid a call on the aged Horace Williams.[3] After seeing other old friends on his way, including James Boyd, with whom he could talk about his projected work, he arrived in New York in time to work hard with Elizabeth Nowell toward the final version of *I Have a Thing to Tell You*.

But something else had happened during these weeks that would have its ultimate effect on Wolfe's work. He had had time away from his task to think about his association with Scribner's and his relationship with Max Perkins.

The Perkins-Wolfe friendship had satisfied deep-seated emotional and intellectual needs for each man. Perkins, who had five daughters, came to look on Wolfe as a son; Wolfe, who had sought the stability of authority, looked to Perkins as a father. In fact, Wolfe had told his brother, Fred, back in 1929, "This man has been more than a friend, he has been a father to me, and, strictly between ourselves, I think of him as a father and care for him as such." [4] Certainly, over the years Wolfe sorely needed Perkins' editorial assistance, but beyond this, he turned to Perkins for advice on his financial dealings, his relations with his family, his love affairs, his choice of living quarters, and a multitude of other problems that called for decision.

But Wolfe's career meant something special to Perkins, too. Maxwell Perkins had wanted to be a writer. His talents found an outlet not only in the creative criticism he gave to the manuscripts of young authors but also in the suggestions of subjects, themes, or organizational patterns he made to established authors on the Scribner's list.[5] When he happened upon Wolfe's extraordinary but uncontrolled genius and when Wolfe appealed to him for aid on *Of Time and the River*, his opportunity to work closer to the forge, to feel its glow and see its sparks, gave him the greatest pleasure of his editorial career.[6] In addition to professional satisfactions, Perkins' rather suppressed nature seemed to get vicarious release through his friendships with Scribner's authors. If he enjoyed the robustness of Will James, John Thomason, Jr., and Ernest Hemingway and if he drew a secret thrill from the youthful escapades of Scott Fitzgerald, then he must have experienced a powerful substitutional fulfillment in the unrestrained vigor of Wolfe's whole life and manner.[7]

But mutually beneficial though their association may have been, it was still a teacher-pupil relationship. An apprentice must become a master, and Wolfe felt ashamed at the length of his apprenticeship. He felt especially guilty about Perkins' assistance on *Of Time and the River*. When the book made its spectacular entrance on the American literary scene, Wolfe began to nurse a sore artistic conscience. From Europe he wrote to Perkins:

More than ever before, I have come to realize how much the making of a book becomes an affair of honor to its maker. The honor of the artist— his whole life, all his character and personal integrity, all that he hopes and wants and dreams of, everything that gives his life any value to him —is at stake each time he produces any work....I hope to God that you and I have come through this ordeal honorably....You, I think, have done so in your great labors with me as an editor and a man. As for myself, the victory, if I have really won it...is not entire and whole as I would make it." [8]

He had used *The Story of A Novel* as a detergent for that guilt. But when public acknowledgment of Perkins' help drew critical sharpshooting upon his work, Wolfe's disturbance was aggravated further, and his connection with Perkins became strained.

An artist's works are his brain children, and any slur cast upon the legitimacy of their birth can awaken a destructive jealousy powerful enough to blight a friendship. These critical attacks were to Wolfe aspersions upon his artistic virility. He felt De Voto had put into print a slanderous myth "that I am unable to perform the function of an artist for myself." [9] This analogy between the sexual powers and the creative powers of the imagination helps to explain Wolfe's sensitivity to criticism. When he accused Perkins of assuming powers of censorship over his writing, he complained that the result would be the "enervation and castration of my work." [10] Thus, his frequent cries of pain over having sections cut from his work were not mere overstatements, and his outburst to Madeleine Boyd, reporting the

cuts on *Look Homeward, Angel* ("They are taking the balls off me"),
was not just jocose obscenity.

Wolfe stated his grievances about Perkins and Scribner's at greatest length in a letter dated December 15, 1936, and mailed a month
later from New Orleans. The principal trouble was Perkins' tutorial
supervision of his work. Perkins had insisted on excisions in *Look
Homeward, Angel*. He had persuaded Wolfe that publication of
"K 19" was inadvisable. He had argued for cuts and changes in *Of
Time and the River*. He had agreed too readily (Wolfe thought) to
the postponement of "The October Fair" [11] and "The Hills Beyond
Pentland." Now he frowned on Wolfe's writing about the publishing house of James Rodney and Son. In his letter, Wolfe became
impassioned, almost hysterical, as he declared his determination to
say what he pleased in "The Vision of Spangler's Paul": "And I
shall wreak out my vision of this life, this way, this world and this
America, to the top of my bent, to the height of my ability, but with
an unswerving devotion, integrity and purity of purpose that shall
not be menaced, altered or weakened by anyone. I will go to jail
because of this book, if I have to. I will lose all my friends because
of it, if I have to. . . . I will be exiled from my country because of it,
if I have to. . . . But no matter what happens I am going to write
this book." [12]

Perkins denied that he exercised control over Wolfe's work. What
he wrote once to Scott Fitzgerald he might have said to any
Scribner's author: "Don't ever *defer* to my judgment. . . . I should be
ashamed if it were possible to have made you; for a writer of any
account must speak solely for himself." [13] But Wolfe's case was different. He had needed help and had asked for it. After the ordeal of
the second novel was over, Wolfe was somewhat like the subject of
hypnosis—not ready to "go under" in Perkins' presence, but too uncertain to maintain his integrity if Perkins made suggestions, had
doubts, or showed indifference. Thus it did not matter whether
Perkins consciously imposed his influence upon him or not. What
did matter was that Wolfe felt a restriction of his freedom. For
Wolfe to develop as a novelist, it was absolutely necessary that he
declare his independence.

He had thought about severing relations with Scribner's since the
summer of 1936. But Perkins was always so reasonable and reassuring whenever Wolfe discussed his position that Wolfe felt a break

with Scribner's would be a kind of betrayal. As a result, Wolfe began to look for a pretext to quarrel with Perkins—over money, over politics, over the right to write about the House of Scribner.

At length, the libel suit provided the occasion, for Wolfe wanted to fight the case, while Scribner's wanted to avoid the expenses of extended litigation. When, in February, 1937, Scribner's persuaded Wolfe to settle out of court and to pay what Wolfe considered a "blackmail fee to the Dorman family," Wolfe felt he had good reason for leaving. He did not consider the excessive cost of taking the case to court, although the amount he paid to lawyers even at this point, $1350, was almost as much as his share of the settlement paid to the Dormans. All he could see was that his little backlog of earnings was wiped out and that his royalty report for the second quarter, dated June 30, showed he owed Scribner's $1115.[14] He was back in the same slough in which he had been mired in 1933 and 1934, when financial pressures had influenced his submission to Perkins about *Of Time and the River*.

Yet not quite. He had a major reputation now and a sizable stack of manuscript, and both advantages would help Elizabeth Nowell's sales to magazines. Still, if he were to spend time revising episodes into a form suitable for magazine publication, he would not get on with his book.

Hurt, angry, and discouraged, Wolfe decided to get out of New York, and he made his long-postponed trip to Asheville at the end of April. After finding he was welcome there, he decided to rent a cabin and return in the summer to live in the mountains as his friends Hamilton Basso and James Boyd were doing.

II

These new turns of events shook his confidence and smothered the creative fire that had blazed during the fall. After the settlement of the libel suit, he began to worry about money and turned his attention to magazine publication. He poked around in his packing case and came up with a considerable haul. He revised a section of the Daisy Purvis material to become "'E': A Recollection," which was sold to the *New Yorker*. He wrote a beginning and ending for a sketch about a Japanese sculptor, gave it the title "Mr. Katamoto," and sold it to *Harper's Bazaar*. He pulled together one of the Esther

Jack scenes, "April, Late April," for publication in the *American Mercury*. He wrote "Chicamaugua" out of the Civil War experiences told him by his Uncle John Westall, whom he had seen in Burnsville in April. He reworked a story, "No More Rivers," about a member of the James Rodney publishing house. These, together with last-minute polishing on "The Lost Boy," which had been sold to *Redbook* in February, and on "The Child By Tiger," which brought the staggering sum of $1200 from the *Saturday Evening Post*, occupied more time than Wolfe wanted to give, but they kept him financially independent of Scribner's.

This scramble to get dollars made Wolfe's practice of working on a number of projects during a short period more complex than usual. Still, work on the big manuscript had continued intermittently since February. But the imaginative spell that had produced and governed his torrential dictation during the last months of 1936 had been broken by litigation and worry, and uncertainties about his aims and progress set in again. In the first place, he knew that he had disparate bodies of material that he was trying to weld into a single unit; the childhood memories and experiences, the successive disillusionments of maturity, and the love story of "The October Fair" were the largest groups. His plans would shift and he would draw up some outlines designed to channel off certain episodes into a separate volume and other outlines reorganizing the main scheme of "The Vision of Spangler's Paul," bringing in material he had written years ago. But since all the material was related to his own life, it was difficult to keep from thinking of it as one book. Although he had set aside one hexology, it looked as if another were going to develop.

A second problem had arisen because the libel suit had put him in debt: he wanted to publish another book as soon as possible. Of all the fragments in his hoard, the Esther Jack material was nearest completion, and he began to sift through that.[15] His impulse was to write, and whether he would be filling in gaps in the development of "Spangler's Paul" or rounding out a separate volume, he would at least be moving toward some end which could evolve as he wrote. With pencil in hand again (for he could not afford a secretary to take dictation), he started work with Spangler's introduction to the literary life through Esther Jack. He fashioned his satire on the publishing house of Rawng and Wright, releasing some of his pent-up spleen about publishers in general and uncovering a long-buried animosity toward Horace Liveright in particular. He went on to the literary party at which Spangler meets Seamus Malone, a brilliant satiric portrait of Ernest Boyd that makes him seem, in parlor conversation, the same outrageous iconoclast who penned *Literary Blasphemies.*[16]

The satiric indulgence of this spring cooled resentments that had boiled up at the settlement of the Dorman case. These writings are evidence that Wolfe could control and direct his emotional disturbances toward a healthier product than he had been able to achieve a few years before. But for Wolfe's literary purposes, they vary in their success. The scenes about the publishers or the party do not carry the narrative very far forward. They are scarcely more than a series of satiric characterizations, although they show that Wolfe had not lost his touch for comic exaggeration. On the other hand, the scenes between Esther and the young author develop the story through dialogue and event. More than this, the scenes have just the right kind of imaginative shaping to make them fit well with the material he had already written about the love affair. Both Esther and her young lover are treated with satiric detachment, yet they still display the same qualities and motivations that mark the characters Wolfe had created in the early 1930's. Particularly effective is the counterpoint of their thoughts after their violent love-making. She is blindly overcome by the wonder of their unique love; he is selfishly absorbed in hopeful expectations that his book will be published.[17]

The winter's agitation wrought still a third change upon the manuscript in progress. It grew out of one of the alternate plans Wolfe had jotted down while on his first trip South. Perhaps he felt more acutely his position as an innocent dupe; and perhaps his distorted picture of himself in the clutches of Marjorie Dorman and her scheming lawyer or under the tyrannical control of the Scribner's commercial interests made him decide to emphasize the ridiculousness of his situation. Or perhaps he judged that the new book had not been reflecting the spirit of *Pickwick, Don Quixote,* or *Candide.* He decided to reshuffle what he had and to make his hero seem a bewildered, comic average man by calling him Joe Doaks. He set down his first outline sometime in January. He made the first public announcement in the *New Republic,* March 10, 1937, that the tentative title of his book was "The Life and Times of Joseph Doaks." [18] He altered the hero's name to Doaks in the recently written satires [19] and allowed him his first public appearance under that name in "Mr. Malone" in the *New Yorker*, May 29, 1937.[20]

Wolfe seems at first to have conceived of this reorganization of material as a single book that would begin with Joe's arrival in New York.[21] But later, as one might expect, it grew to embrace all the material he had been working on for his central manuscript.

At any rate, the name Doaks came to govern all the new work Wolfe began from July, 1937, to February, 1938. And the very name itself is the sign of the long road Wolfe had come in recent years: his alter ego had changed from a superman to the very type of the common man. The new material had its special stamp, too. Social criticism or satire, and usually both, characterized everything begun in these next months. The title pages, varying from "The Ordeal of the Bondsman Doaks" to "The Lives of the Bondsman Doaks," displayed a new motto that conveys the change in spirit that took over now:

> It was all very well to dissemble your love,
> But why did you kick me downstairs? [22]

Wolfe's ability to satirize himself had been increasing in these recent years of trouble. It is an important element of the detachment with which he came to view his autobiographical hero. It was a fortunate resource at this time, when he was torn in half by the breach of one of the strongest personal attachments of his life and when he was about to turn his back on the life he had made for himself in New York. It was in this unsettled frame of mind that he nailed the lid on his packing case and headed for Asheville to spend the summer.

NOTES

1. Perkins gives an amusing account of this in a letter to Ernest Hemingway, December 9, 1936, *Editor to Author*, ed. John Hall Wheelock (New York, 1950), pp. 118-19.

2. For details, see Nowell, pp. 365-69.

3. George Stoney, "Eugene Returns to Pulpit Hill," *Carolina Magazine*, VI (October, 1938), 11-14.

4. HCL*53M-113, unpublished letter dated November 25, 1929.

5. See, for example, Perkins' remarks in *Editor to Author* about Fitzgerald's *This Side of Paradise*, pp. 19-20; Van Wyck Brooks' biography of Emerson, p. 48; Roy Baker's *Native American*, pp. 170-74; Marcia Davenport's *East Side, West Side*, pp. 286-94; and his suggestions to Marjorie Kinnan Rawlings about a boy's book, pp.

83-84; to Dixon Wecter about a book to be called "The Troublemakers," p. 182; to John Thomason, Jr. about a modern *Don Quixote*, pp. 114-15. Other examples are scattered throughout the volume.

6. *Editor to Author*, pp. 101 and 116.

7. Wolfe indicated to Perkins that he recognized this: "There is also a tendency among people of active and imaginative minds and temperaments, who live themselves conventional and conservative lives, to indulge vicariously their interest in the adventures and experiences of other people whose lives are not so sheltered as their own" (*Letters*, p. 590).

8. *Letters*, pp. 438-39.

9. *Letters*, p. 556.

10. Wolfe uses this phrase in two different letters to Perkins (*Letters*, pp. 591, 601).

11. In 1931 Mrs. Bernstein had protested to Perkins against the publication of a book in which she would be a character. After this Perkins continued to feel uneasy about "The October Fair."

12. *Letters*, p. 587.

13. *Editor to Author*, p. 30.

14. The payments had been deducted from his account in three installments, February 23, April 1, and May 3. Wolfe took this blow hard, because his royalty report on February 1 had shown a balance of $1114.63, and he had earned another $498.11 by June 30.

15. To avoid confusion, I have referred to the character based on Aline Bernstein as Esther Jack, although up to now Wolfe had named her Esther Jacobs, except in the earliest episodes, where her name is Alice or Irene. Now, in spring, 1937, and this is another indication of his shifting plans, he changed the name to Rebecca Feitlebaum. He settled on the name Esther Jack in the summer of 1937.

16. HCL*46AM-7(55). Wolfe's autograph manuscript, running 1052 pages, becomes W&R, pp. 487-586, plus the sketch "On Leprechauns" (published in HB), which had been Wolfe's introduction to Mr. Malone.

17. W&R, pp. 510-11.

18. Another idea, fortunately abandoned, which Wolfe conceived of sometime during these years was to write "The Education of Boob McNutt." An outline, HCL*-46AM-7(24-e), promised a fascinating character named Oswald Omniballs, who was a friend of the hero.

19. In Wolfe's published work, Joe still remains in one passage as a hypothetical figure. See W&R, pp. 492-95.

20. The chronology of all these changes is based on the following evidence. In the autograph manuscript for the satiric material, Wolfe does not use the first person point of view, as he had done in all the work written the previous fall. He uses the third person and calls his central character "our hero," "our young man," "our young author," although his name is George Spangler. Wolfe must have begun this work in March and completed it in a few weeks. By May 12, the part of it entitled 'Mr. Malone" was in page proof for the *New Yorker*, and the hero's name was now Doaks.

21. W&R, pp. 219-22, was the opening chapter. The description of the railroad station, however, had once been a part of "K 19."

22. From Isaac Bickerstaff's poem " 'Tis Well 'Tis No Worse." With comic bitterness, Wolfe calls it "my favorite poem" in a letter to Hamilton Basso, July 29, 1937 (*Letters*, p. 646).

24

THE BURDEN OF NEW YORK: "THE PARTY AT JACK'S"

THOMAS WOLFE'S RETURN TO ASHEVILLE IN JUNE, 1937, WAS intimately connected with his cutting off relations with Scribner's and Maxwell Perkins. He turned homeward to fill the emotional void created by his loss of Perkins' friendship—of which he had written, "it is like death to me." [1] But this flight to a protective stronghold was the last token of personal instability that Wolfe was ever to display. By the time he decided to re-establish himself in New York in September, he had finally conquered his over-dependence on emotional supports and had arrived at the position in which he had placed Eugene Gant at the end of *Look Homeward, Angel*. His struggle to attain his independence was to him a terrible ordeal, and many times during the next year he summed it up as reaching a final knowledge that "you can't go home again." By "home" he meant not only Asheville but "back to your childhood, back to . . . your people, back to the father you have lost, and back to the solacements of time and memory." [2] This statement represents a real about-face for Wolfe, a turning away from his concern for the way things used to be to an acceptance of "the way things are" and from a yearning for security to a realistic recognition that change is necessary and good.

His "exile" from Asheville, which he had complained about since 1929 and which some of his friends thought was a self-dramatizing pose, had been real. When he returned from Europe in 1931 and visited his sister Mabel in Washington, he heard for the first time all the details of how family and friends had reacted to *Look Homeward, Angel*. He was so overcome that after their late-night talk he did not go to bed but left Mabel's house and went to Gettysburg. Her frankness had made him feel that he was not wanted there. Al-

343

though this misunderstanding was soon cleared up, he did not venture home to Asheville as he ordinarily would have done. Henceforth, he rejoined the family circle only at occasional reunions in Washington, when his mother came up from Asheville and brother Fred came down from Pennsylvania.

As time passed, he made his reapproach to Asheville as warily as if it were a military campaign. First, there was the gathering of intelligence and consideration of possible quick thrusts into Southern territory to literary or historical society meetings. This was followed by scouting expeditions into the South. In the winter of 1936-37, Wolfe faced preliminary skirmishes when he stopped in Raleigh to see Jonathan Daniels, who six years before had found that the South had been "spat upon" in *Look Homeward, Angel.* He went on to Chapel Hill, the locale hardly less prominent than Asheville in his first book. Here he conquered with his friendly manner and found a warm greeting from his old college friends. Finally, in April, 1937, he mustered his force for the full-dress operation. He made his attack from the rear, stopping over in Burnsville in the Smokies, where he witnessed the shooting of James Higgins in a frontier-style settling of a grudge. "I thought the advance line of fire from Asheville had just moved up on me," he later told Mabel.

That first return was a triumph. The reunion of the loquacious Wolfes at the Old Kentucky Home was constantly interrupted by friends telephoning and dropping in. The fame Tom had gained through *Of Time and the River* provided him with a prestige that smoothed most of the Asheville feathers he had ruffled. Even the Westall relatives, who had been outraged by his first novel, now came to see him. The always hearty cousin, Henry Westall, offered the disarming greeting: "I thought I was the only reprobate in the family till I read your book. Now I know we're all sons-of-bitches." Tom visited old haunts and saw with some wistfulness the changes brought by the intervening years. But generally he was in the best spirits, booming out jokes wherever he went. He toured the Smokies and finally selected a cabin for the summer at Oteen. He returned to New York for eight weeks of work in order to arrange as much material as possible for Elizabeth Nowell to sell to magazines.

He came back to Asheville the second time at the end of June, determined to "set a spell and think things over." It would be his season of withdrawing. He was not only emotionally jittery but physically worn out from the long stints of work broken only by frenetic travel. Doctors in New York had warned him, he told Mabel when he arrived, that he needed a ninety-day rest or he would collapse. But he could not stop work. His last novel had been published over two years ago, and he still had not vindicated himself by bringing out a mammoth work to stun or silence his critics. Accordingly, he had shipped his packing case full of manuscript down to Asheville, and for his summer's work he had two aims: to put his big manuscript in order and to "do a big piece of work." Perhaps, he thought, the complete change of scene would generate his creative powers as his European trips had done. At any rate, he hoped so and reassured himself by recording his vows fervently but humbly in a letter to Hamilton Basso: "to rebuild here in my brain again these past fifteen years or more of youth, of conflict, and of wandering. And from this substance, this accumulation of a life worn down—I pray, a little brighter, and freer, I hope, from the degrading egotisms all men know in youth—here to strike out, I hope to God, a living word: to do out of the substance of my one life, my single spirit, a better and truer work than I have ever done." [3]

The big piece of work he had in mind was "The Party at Jack's," the second draft of which he had completed just before he left New York. He had long planned to write about a party at which Alexander Calder had entertained the Bernstein family and guests with a circus of mechanical animals and dolls.[4] He had also been intrigued by the fictional possibilities in an evening at the Bernstein apartment, seven years before, which had been interrupted by a fire. The Marguery at 270 Park Avenue, where the Bernsteins lived, was a luxurious hotel and apartment building eleven stories high that covered an entire city block, from Park to Madison between 47th and 48th Streets. It housed in its expensive suites prominent industrialists, financiers, society leaders, and stars of the entertainment world. The building was built on stilts over the railroad tracks running to Grand Central Station. The fire started about 8 P.M. in the sub-basement, which contained some furniture showrooms. The smell of smoke soon broke up the Bernstein family dinner, and the cook in a panic locked herself in her room. After Wolfe broke down the door and rescued the cook, the whole group escaped by means of the private elevator opening into the apartment.[5]

Two engine companies fought the fire for two hours while a

throng of two thousand people watched outside the fire lines. Apartment dwellers, who had been preparing to go to dinner or to the theater, streamed out of the building, some in dishabille. Two people lost their lives in the fire: one, an aged lady who was ill in her room and who collapsed as she was being helped down the stairs from the eleventh floor; the other, William Cass, aged fifty, an elevator operator, who was smothered by smoke in his stalled elevator after Fire Chief John Kenlon ordered the electric power in the building shut off.[6]

Since in these recent months of 1937 Wolfe had been writing about parties—his hero's meeting with the critic Seamus Malone and with the poetess, Rosalind Bailey—he had come to see the opportunities for characterization and criticism that social gatherings afforded. He turned now to use his remembrance of the circus performance and the fire at 270 Park Avenue, and his memories of several gatherings of Mrs. Bernstein's literary and theatrical friends, and to present a diverse social picture. He had the literary model of Proust's *Sodom and Gomorrah* in mind,[7] and very likely, too, the opening chapters of Huxley's *Point Counterpoint,* which he had read and admired in 1929.

Wolfe exercised more than usual care in keeping his material under control. A few notes remain as evidence of his concern for narrative focus—Mrs. Jack was to be the center of activity, the young lover was to observe the behavior of the guests and react to the atmosphere of luxury, aimlessness, and moral corruption all around him. Other notes show his planning of movement among character groups and shifts in topics of conversation during the party.[8]

His intention to do a long story which Miss Nowell could turn into expense money was soon left behind. By the time he was working his way through a second draft, scrupulously revising his dictated copy and adding long stretches of narrative, his vision had run away with him. He proposed to epitomize New York society and to criticize the social structure which supported it, and he had established October, 1929, as the time. In June, just before moving down to his cabin, he showed this version, now over 50,000 words, to Miss Nowell, who not only pleaded with him to whittle it down but also offered her usual helpful criticism.

In Asheville he started his third version of "The Party at Jack's." He had sent out word that he needed a secretary, stipulating only that he wanted one who would not be shocked by anything he said and who would not fall in love with him. Young Martha Wrenshall, a champion swimmer but a very poor typist, took the job. She swam at the Country Club pool every morning, then drove out to Oteen to get Wolfe out of bed about noon. They worked together until dark, with Wolfe dictating slowly, gauging himself to her speed, as he paced up and down in front of the cabin porch. When not interrupted by visitors, he would work at night revising his pages.

At the end of the summer, he was able to report what had happened to the story as he had reworked it: "I have completely rewritten it and rewoven it. It was a very difficult piece of work, but I think it is now a single thing, as much a single thing as anything I've ever written. I am not through with it yet. There is a great deal more revision to be done...." [9] Since it had reached its present length, over 80,000 words, Wolfe now considered integrating it with other materials from "The October Fair" and moving toward book publication.

This was the state in which "The Party at Jack's," the most complex episode Wolfe had ever attempted, was to remain. Subsequent events banished the need for immediate book publication. Other problems pressed upon him in the next months, forcing him to set the final revision aside.

II

"The Party at Jack's: A Study in Depths," as Wolfe called it, is one of the major works of Wolfe's later career. He had brought it through three versions now, and it was near enough to completion so that critical assessment is possible without much difficulty. But it should be clearly understood at the outset that in bringing this work into print Edward Aswell of Harper, who prepared the manuscript to be included in *You Can't Go Home Again,* must be credited with the final shaping. Aswell used Wolfe's sequence faithfully, but he made a great number of cuts, reducing the bulk by about one-fifth. Other problems posed by the unfinished condition of the manuscript demanded more exact editing. Aswell wove together and rearranged some of the passages in the midst of the party that Wolfe had left in variant versions; he altered the style of three sections that Wolfe had written years before in his more florid manner and had not yet rewritten; and he rewrote and expanded the concluding three pages of the story.[10] Thus, all but the pages at the end are Wolfe's, almost all of the organization is his, but the final proportioning and polishing are Aswell's.

The main narrative line is deceptively simple. The Jacks are seen rising from sleep and going about the activities of their day, Mr. Jack to his office, Mrs. Jack to her arrangements for an evening party. The maids, doormen, and elevator men of the apartment building are introduced and take their places in the preparations. In the evening, the party reaches its height when a circus of mechanical dolls entertains the guests. The performance is interrupted by a fire that drives all the tenants from the apartment building and causes the deaths of two elevator men. The fire out, the Jacks return to the security of their apartment and retire to bed complacently.

But the vitals of the story are in its social criticism—criticism of capitalism and its class structure, of urbanization, and of materialistic pride. Mr. Jack is made a prince of capitalistic society. His wealth has accumulated through neither creativity nor service. As a stock market speculator he has gathered a fortune by means of other men's energies—by gambling on the successes or failures of other men's business endeavors. His world knows no other value than money. Every man has his price, and any trickery or dishonesty is condoned as the accepted means to the important end. The treasure-center for the strivers of all classes is the city, but only the wealthy can buy the privileges of space and air, privacy and protection, in its oppressive confinements. Mr. Jack's palatial apartment is his chateau, from which he looks every morning exulting in his dominance of the city and from which he ventures daily to maintain his rule.

His life is surrounded by the conspicuous display and consumption of the leisure class—simple, tasteful, fabulously expensive furnishings, sumptuous feasts, elegant women, a retinue of servants, limousines. The social and intellectual interests of Mr. Jack's circle follow the latest modes. At the party they discuss the Sacco-Vanzetti case with humanitarian zeal because it is in vogue. Mr. Hirsch, the financier, is, in drawing-room conversation, an opponent of child labor, a foe of the sharecropping system, a friend of the mill hand; yet much of his income derives indirectly from the sweated labor of child, sharecropper, and mill worker. The whole group reveal mildly radical social and economic opinions in their party small-talk, out of need to swim with the current fashion: Mrs. Jack declares herself a socialist at heart and indulges in the appropriate kind of name-dropping ("Oh, I knew Jack Reed. He used to come to Mable Dodge's place"). The Medicis of this world support the arts, but they have become so decadent that they cannot patronize any work that has true vigor and integrity. Piggy Logan's circus, with its performing dolls, is the sign of a sterile and infantile enthusiasm.[11]

Penetrating deeper, Wolfe shows that the materialism of these people has affected their vitality as humans: they are as lifeless as Piggy Logan's dolls. Their failure to believe in or care about anything beyond the vanity and power of wealth has withered their passion and intensity. "They tilled the wasteland and erosion had become fashionable. They were bored with love, and they were bored with hate. They were bored with men who worked, and with men who loafed. . . . They were bored with marriage and with single blessedness. They were bored with chastity, and they were bored with adultery." [12] Mr. Hirsch does not pursue Lily Mandell with passion and murmur, "Thy navel is like a round goblet, which wanteth not liquor." Stephen Hook is too weary to express the true responses he has to life. "Love's bitter mystery had broken no bones for Mr. Jack, and so far as he was concerned, it could not murder sleep the way an injudicious wiener schnitzel could. . . ." Amy Carleton's jaded appetites have gone beyond drink, sex, and drugs; her restless seeking can find an awakening moment only when the blaze of the apartment house fire threatens the life of a trapped tenant.

Looking about him, George Webber draws the conclusion Wolfe wishes to set before us. If all this ennui has an economic basis, if all these idle lives derive their leisure from the toil of the millions who support this system, then a double devastation prevails when the economic rights of men are violated.

This idea is complicated further when even those members of the working class closest to the world that Jack built are corrupted by it. The Jacks' servants adopt the code of their masters and live a demeaning, parasitic existence. The maids steal clothes and household goods, the chauffeur pads the bills for gasoline and tires, all regale themselves at parties below stairs to which invited guests of the police force contribute barrels of bootleg beer.

On the other hand, the contrasts between the characters of both classes make "The Party at Jack's" the single work of Wolfe's which shows the strong influence of Marxian thought. Although in a letter to Miss Nowell Wolfe tried to avoid the Marxian label, his very words seem to confirm what he denies: "As to the rest of it, the social implication that, I fear, would make the piece anathema to any of the older publishers, I simply cannot help it. It is simply the way I feel and think: I hope and believe there is not a word of conscious propaganda in it. It is certainly not at all Marxian, but it is representative of the way my life has come—after deep feeling, deep thinking, and deep living and all this experience—to take its way." [13]

The class struggle is pointed up in a number of ways. All who serve the Jacks are caught in a dilemma between their class feelings of hatred for the system they help to uphold and their human feelings of gratitude toward the individuals of the upper class who patronize them. Nora, Mrs. Jack's maid, appreciates her place but she reveals an envious hostility to Mrs. Jack for her extensive and costly wardrobe and for her sexual freedom—products of class privilege not available to servants. The elevator man, John Enborg, conscientiously carries out his duties and protects the people he works for from intruders, but he resents their lack of appreciation for his efforts.

The problem of class loyalty in the class struggle is dealt with explicitly in the clash between old John Enborg, who respects and defends "the kind of people we got here," and Henry, the doorman, who actively furthers the position of his own class through the labor union. Henry maliciously warns John:

You know what's going to happen to you if you don't watch out? You're gettin' old, Pop, and you'd better watch your step. You're goin' to be caught in the street some day worryin' about what's goin' to happen to the people in this place if they have to ride up in the same elevator with a delivery boy....

You're goin' to get hit, Pop. And it ain't going to be by nothin' small or cheap. It ain't goin' to be by no Ford truck or by no taxicab. You're goin' to be hit by somethin' big and shiny that cost a lot of dough. You'll get hit by at least a Rolls Royce—by one of the people in this house.[14]

In the end, John meets his death while evacuating the apartment dwellers during the fire. One of the frightened tenants flips the wrong switch, shutting off the power to the elevator. John, caught between floors, is smothered by the smoke.[15]

But the class war and the ideal of the classless society gets its most powerful statement through symbolism. The fire starts underneath the magnificent fourteen-story structure and smokes out all the tenants. Nor can the firemen smother this fire that disrupts the order of the tenants' world. When all of the inhabitants have emerged from the great structure (and they represent, like America, a conglomeration of the nations of the world) [16] and when they stand together on the level of the courtyard, the class barriers no longer exist, and a spirit of brotherhood reigns over the scene. Dwellers who have never spoken to each other chat in neighborly fashion; wealthy tycoons and social registerites mingle with cooks, butlers, chauffeurs, courtesans, and entertainers.

But despite the symbolic suggestions of revolution and the millennium, "The Party at Jack's" is very different from the usual proletarian novel. There is no division of characters into evil-willed owners and stout-hearted workers. Wolfe provides sufficient complexity to his characterizations and mixes virtues and faults so that he brings his people to life. Mr. Jack is anything but tyrannical. He smiles at the chicanery of his underlings (although his attitude is also a manifestation of conspicuous waste); he conducts his financial affairs only in the accepted ways, with the attitude, "business is business"; he has a great affection for his family. He is even a little amusing as he takes his exercises in the morning and as he refuses to be disturbed from a good night's sleep worrying about his wife's lover. He is pitiable when his eyes fill with tears in acknowledgment that he cannot share his wife's life in the theater. Nor does Wolfe denounce the Jacks' circle as heartless. They would never say, "Let them eat cake"; and, at times, they support right action militantly, even though for the wrong reasons. As for Mrs. Jack and her daughter, they are much more attractive and sensible than their servants. Indeed, Mrs. Jack herself is a worker, "a formidable little dynamo"; while Nora, her maid, is a shiftless hypocrite. Moreover, the outstanding spokesman for the working class, Henry, is an over-righteous, unsympathetic figure. The reader feels, therefore, that, above the pattern of class struggle, Wolfe looks down god-like with mingled pity and censure upon his modern Babylon.

Because he fails to restrict his attitude, Wolfe's symbols are rather free. In a symbolic range that extends beyond but still embraces the suggestions of a social uprising, his symbolism presents an apocalyptic vision of the downfall of a civilization. Possibly, the words of the Biblical prophets had been running in Wolfe's head when he

reworked the first section of "The Party at Jack's." He refers to proud
and stiff-necked people; he describes the bejeweled, long-necked
women whom Jack liked in a manner suggestive of Isaiah's denunciation of Israel's fashionable women; he sees the city (over which
Jack murmurs "My City. Mine.") thrusting its towers upward with
"Assyrian" insolence.

The apartment building, as a symbol of materialistic pride, is an
"arrogant boast of steel and stone." But it has no solidity. Beneath it
rumble the trains that cause the building to tremble each time they
pass. More than just the suggestion of the shakiness preceding the
stock market crash, more than just an image of revolutionary rumblings, these earth-shaking tremors represent warnings of the collapse of the whole society. We are first made aware of the trembling
shortly after Mr. Jack arises from sleep; he has just been looking
out over the city in the dawn, and he has had a sudden vision: ". . . it
seemed to Mr. Jack as if all life had been driven or extinguished
from the city and as if those soaring obelisks were all that remained
of a civilization that had been fabulous and legendary." [17] Wolfe intended to give emphasis to these earth tremors by ending the story
with Mr. Jack, who is startled for a moment by the vibrations and
then shakes off his fears with a shrug. "Trains again," he mutters.[18]
In the middle of the story, Wolfe makes an allusion to the sinking
of the *Titanic*, which he then builds into another gigantic image of
a doomed society as the people pour out of their apartments: "It was
really like the scene of an appalling shipwreck—like a great liner, her
life gored out upon an iceberg, keeling slowly with her whole great
company of people—the crew, the passengers, the rich, the poor, the
mighty, and the lowly—assembled now, at this last hour of peril, in
a living fellowship—the whole family of earth, and all its classes, at
length united on these slanting decks." [19]

With this variety of aims, Wolfe had to struggle hard to make his
elements coalesce. He presented his social criticism through direct
statement, through action, through comparisons among characters,
and through symbol. More than this, he had to integrate the whole
mixture with the progress of his autobiographical pilgrim. He fitted
George Webber into his whole scheme very neatly. As an observer
at the party, he looks around him at pampered effeminacy, adultery,
profligacy, false humanitarianism, all placed in a luxurious seat of
honor. He realizes that he too is caught up in the moral corruption

of this world, for he, as the lover of Mrs. Jack, is a part of it. He realizes, too, that, like the servants, he risks being tainted if he keeps his place in these surroundings. As a man and as an artist, he must break off his affair and escape from this false world.

The interweaving of George Webber's decision with the main story line brings about the enrichment of the characterization of Esther Jack so that she becomes the most interesting figure in the story. She is part of the world that Jack built, she has invited these friends, she has arranged for Piggy Logan's circus. But she is not like the others because she has an exquisite enjoyment of living. She is zestful, passionate, generous, and as a worker and creator, she contributes to society. Giving her these qualities, Wolfe draws her in the dimensions of the child and the maiden—gleeful over her party, her dress, her appearance, her friends' compliments; yet at the same time, her face marked by signs showing age and maturity, she plays the role of the mother and the overseer of the household.[20] Then, Wolfe builds her into a symbol of the eternal feminine. Compared with her portrait painted in 1901, she shows scarcely any alteration. Stephen Hook, glancing from the portrait to the original, meditates upon her agelessness:

Had he not been beside her at the launching of the ship? Had they not been captives together among the Thracian faces? Had he not lighted tapers to the tent when she had come to charm remission from the lord of Macedon?—All these were ghosts—save she! And she—devouring child of time—had of this whole huge company of ghosts alone remained immortal and herself, had shed off the chrysalis of all these her former selves as if each life that she had lived was nothing but an outworn garment, and now stood here—*here!* Good God!—upon the burnt-out candle-end of time—with her jolly face of noon, as if she had just heard of this brave new world on Saturday—and would see if *all* of it was really true tomorrow.[21]

This picture of captive prizes and classic temptresses reinforces Wolfe's chanting of the burden of New York by reminding us of the passing of ancient civilizations. At the same time, the symbolic power of Mrs. Jack—she has now become the image of woman in all her stages, child, mate, mother—increases the dramatic tension of George Webber's decision to leave her.

Wolfe's attempt in "The Party at Jack's" to combine a diversity of elements for a complex statement is an indication of the way he was moving near the end of his career. But although we can applaud what he left in an unfinished state, we need not assume he would have perfected it. Indeed, one of the faults that would not have been eliminated in further revision is, oddly enough, that the central scene, the party itself, does not sparkle as a party. Wolfe had neither the feeling for social amenities nor the gift of wit to enliven a social mingling. The result is that character sketches dominate this part of the story.

Then, too, since Mr. Jack and several of his guests are grouped and labeled as Jews, the social criticism has an unpleasant anti-Semitic tone that mars the story in its present state, and Wolfe probably would not have changed it in a last revision.

But far outweighing these faults are the clearly evident virtues. "The Party at Jack's" is a rich mixture, and with apparent struggle, Wolfe has managed to control its multiplicity. It is given form and significance by ideas that emerge through symbol and image, character and action. It stands as the last large-scale unit Wolfe added to his long manuscript, and it indicates the final direction of his social concerns and his maturing craftsmanship.

III

Wolfe was only able to work intermittently during those two summer months in Asheville, for he was constantly interrupted by visitors and invitations. He was glad to be welcomed back to home ground, but he discovered that he was more vulnerable here to intrusions upon his time and privacy. For one thing, he saw the delicacy of his position: the newly returned and recently forgiven prodigal did not wish to offend friends and acquaintances who sought him out as a celebrity to speak at a fund-raising dinner or to join an evening party. For another, he felt a stronger obligation to spend time with his mother, his sister, and his brothers than he had felt toward friends in New York. Finally, he really enjoyed re-splicing the old connections in Asheville and submerging himself in the flood of talk that had always been characteristic of the friendly Asheville folk and the Wolfe family in particular. He thus faced, in more distressing extreme, his old dilemma of the emotional need for the society of fellow beings and the professional need for privacy. Just because he went off to a mountain cabin without a telephone did not mean he could protect his working time. And his own good nature did not allow him to turn away callers without inviting them to help reduce the five gallons of white corn whiskey he had in store. He complained to Hamilton Basso of "the hordes of thirsty tourists who just happen in casually," and he summed up his problem to Miss Nowell. ". . . my stay here this summer has really resembled a three-ring circus. I think people have wanted to be and have tried to be most kind, but they wore me to a frazzle." [22]

By the end of the summer, he reached the conclusion that he could no longer stay in the Asheville community and survive. In the last week of August, he moved from Oteen to the Battery Park Hotel for some of the rest and privacy he had not found in his secluded mountain retreat. He complained of headaches; he worried fretfully about the lack of progress on his big book; he spoke to his brother Fred about his fear of death before he could set down all that he must say. He disappointed the members of the Wolfe family, particularly his mother, by announcing that he would return to New York on September 2.

For Wolfe, going North again meant facing the reality of his severed relations with Scribner's. As yet there had been no formal move. Now, with desperate impulsiveness, he put in telephone calls to several New York publishers and bluntly stated, "This is Thomas Wolfe. Would you be interested in publishing me?" Most publishing house representatives did not know what to make of these strange long-distance calls and thought the procedure some sort of hoax.[23] But odd though it may be, the calls led ultimately to his establishing a new publishing relation with Harper and Brothers in December.

This period of withdrawal to Asheville was short, but it provided Wolfe with opportunity for learning and decision. He discovered that a return to Asheville was impossible. Fame brought the same excitements and distractions he had found seven years earlier in New York, except that in Asheville the personal impact of his work created greater tensions. The Asheville people, he told Miss Nowell, "are still, in a friendly way, living over the whole vexed experience of *Look Homeward, Angel* and of having the culprit back in their midst." [24] He found, too, that the old problem—that no one understood him or what he was trying to do in his writing—was ever present. He was now even more of an outsider. Time and change had not only altered the Asheville he knew but it had altered him.

He completed the last part of the lesson that you can't go home again. His step into the future began with the search for a new publisher. As for his writing, the time had not been entirely wasted. He had worked out his story of the decline and fall of modern American society, and he had gathered, too, information about the failure of Asheville's principal bank and the political corruption surrounding it that would supply him with the story of the rise and fall of Libya Hill's false prosperity.

NOTES

1. *Letters*, p. 603.
2. *Letters*, p. 707.
3. *Letters*, p. 628.
4. Calder's circus had been all the rage in Paris between 1927 and 1930, and its fame had spread to New York. His dolls performed as acrobats, sword-swallowers, bareback riders, and trapeze artists to appropriate circus music that blared from a phonograph while Calder as ringmaster announced the acts and distributed peanuts among the drawing-room audience. *Current Biography*, 1946, pp. 89-91; and Geoffrey T. Hellman, "Everything is Mobile," *New Yorker*, XVII (October 4, 1941), 25-33.
5. Letter from Edla Bernstein Cusick to me, March 7, 1961.
6. "Two Die as Blast Rocks the Marguery and Routs Guests," *New York Times*, January 4, 1930, pp. 1-2; January 5, 1930, p. 22.
7. Wolfe twice refers to the work as "Proustian" (*Letters*, pp. 631, 648).
8. HCL*46AM-7(24-v).
9. *Letters*, p. 651. The development and expansion of "The Party at Jack's" may be seen in examining its various versions, HCL*46AM-7(59). Wolfe had apparently done a brief sketch of the party and the fire sometime in the early 1930's. A few typewritten pages of this remain. The first draft of the story as a whole had been dictated in the spring of 1937. The typescript runs 126 pages, triple spaced. The story begins with Mrs. Jack's preparations to receive her guests. Rather few guests appear in the party scenes. One of the characters is Mrs. Jack's son, Freddie. The story ends with Mr. Jack's going to bed.

The second version has 194 numbered pages of double-spaced typescript, beginning with Mrs. Jack's preparations for the party. To these have been added about twenty unnumbered pages to make a new opening, which consists of a description of the apartment building and a conversation between two elevator men about a panhandler (cf. YCGHA, Chapter 13). This version differs a great deal from the first version in style and in the addition of characters and events. Roberta Heilprin, Jake Abramson, Stephen Hook, Lawrence Hirsch, Amy Van Leer (later named Carlton), and others now come into the story. The second version was used by Miss Nowell, with a great many cuts, for the magazine publication of "The Party At Jack's" in *Scribner's Magazine*, May, 1939. At Miss Nowell's request, Wolfe had altered the conclusion so that the story ended with Mrs. Jack. This version has been reprinted in *Short Novels*, pp. 282-323.

For the third version, Wolfe drew upon material he had written in 1933 about Mr. and Mrs. Jack going through their morning routines. The story begins with Mr. Jack asleep, dreaming of his childhood in Germany, goes on to Mrs. Jack's rising from bed and starting her day. This all adds about 100 pages to the second version. Wolfe also revised and expanded some other scenes. The story ends with Mr. Jack's going to bed, since it had begun with him. But it is an unfinished version. Some parts of the earlier material have been reworked and others have not. Some of the scenes about the guests at the party have variant forms. Mrs. Jack's son, who in the second version is called Ernie, is cut out and his lines given to Mr. Jack without the necessary changes in characterization being made. This is the version Edward Aswell used, with cuts and changes, for Book II, "The World That Jack Built," in YCGHA.

A few notes remain that show some of Wolfe's plans for revision between versions two and three, HCL*46AM-7(24-v):

> Make Mrs. Jack into something else—a dress designer.
> Turn Ernie into Mr. Jack.
> Work train into Mrs. Jack's room.
> Make youthful lover think the things about the people and the
>   party.
> Make Old John tap against the elevator walls.

Except for the fourth, all these items are scratched out, indicating that Wolfe made the changes.

10. Wolfe had ended as he began, with Mr. Jack, who feels the trembling of the building as the train passes beneath it. For YCGHA, Aswell chopped off these pages to place greater emphasis on George Webber. In the penultimate episode (in which George bids good-night to Esther), Aswell expanded Wolfe's brief statements about Webber's thoughts in order to spell out more clearly the reasons why Webber is going to break from Esther.

11. Wolfe's merciless satire of Calder in this caricature seems to have had some legitimate basis. The performance at the Bernsteins was a most childish affair. Mrs. Bernstein's daughter, Edla, recalls: "Mr. Calder invited most of the guests, but we were permitted to have a few friends in, I don't remember who now, but Tom was among them. It was a real mess. Calder put nails in the walls and bookshelves to string up various apparatus and scattered peanuts around to give it a proper circus atmosphere. The last straw was when he sprayed ammonia about to lend a truly animal flavor....it was all highly unpleasant—so much so that there was some sort of comment about it in Walter Winchell's column." Letter to me, March 7, 1961.

12. YCGHA, p. 224. For all quotations from "The Party at Jack's," references will be to the page numbers in YCGHA. Further, the young man will be referred to as George Webber rather than Spangler, since this is the name Wolfe gave him as he prepared his last work for publication.

13. *Letters*, p. 652. William F. Kennedy, in "Economic Ideas in Contemporary Literature—The Novels of Thomas Wolfe," *Southern Economic Journal*, XX (July, 1953), pp. 42-43, has offered the first critical interpretation of this story which goes beyond the literal narrative. Building on a suggestion from Aswell, he reads the story as economic allegory: the fire is the depression, the guests are the business leaders, the employees in the building are the workers. When the fire is put out, the old economic order is restored.

14. YCGHA, pp. 209-10.

15. To sharpen his social criticism, Wolfe changed details about the fire at 270 Park Avenue. Among other things, he made both of the people who lost their lives employees, and he made a careless tenant, rather than the fire chief, responsible for shutting off the power.

16. "There were German cooks and French maids, English butlers and Irish serving girls. There were Swedes and Danes and Italians and Norwegians, with a sprinkling of White Russians. There were Poles and Czechs and Austrians, Negroes and Hungarians" (YCGHA, p. 293).

17. YCGHA, p. 150.

18. Edward Aswell later changed the conclusion. See n. 10.

19. *Scribner's Magazine*, CV (May, 1939), 58. This passage, retained by Miss Nowell for magazine publication, was cut out of YCGHA by Aswell.

20. When Aswell cut many of the references to her age, he dulled the sharpness of this contrast.

21. YCGHA, p. 253.

22. *Letters*, pp. 645, 653.

23. Edward Aswell, "Thomas Wolfe Did Not Kill Maxwell Perkins," *Saturday Review of Literature*, XXIV (October 6, 1951), 44.

24. *Letters*, p. 653.

25

PUBLISHERS AND POLITICS

When Wolfe returned from North Carolina, he wanted a place where he could work undisturbed. He sought seclusion in the heart of the city. Some time earlier Perkins had recommended the old Chelsea Hotel on West 23rd Street, which had been the center of New York social life in the late nineteenth century, with the opera house, the theaters, and Delmonico's clustered around it. Perkins knew that Edgar Lee Masters enjoyed the quiet, old-fashioned homeliness of his apartment at the Chelsea, and he concluded it was just the place for Wolfe, especially since the high-ceilinged, spacious rooms would keep him from feeling cramped. By November Wolfe had moved into these new quarters. He told no one his address, received all his mail through Elizabeth Nowell's office, and set to work, desperately anxious to get his manuscript in shape. He wrote to Scribner's lawyer, Cornelius Mitchell, "My funds are almost exhausted, and after two years of constant, nerve-wracking interruptions of all sorts, I am faced now with the necessity of getting on with my work without further delay, if I am going to support myself at all." [1]

The Thomas Wolfe who had greeted old friends in Asheville and who now set up shop in New York again was a middle-aged man. He was bulkier than he had been in his early thirties, maintaining his weight at about 230 pounds, never dropping below two hundred as he used to. Thirty-seven years had brought him a paunch and a bald spot on the back of his head. He had just begun to wear glasses, for the headaches he had suffered in Asheville were caused by eye strain. He liked to characterize himself, in Falstaffian terms, as having grown fat and old. If he had, he carried the age with dignity, for he now took care of his clothes and his appearance, as if he were aware that he was a public figure. Still, there was an ease and comfortableness in his manner which suggested shirt sleeves rather than a coat, and there was a colloquial homeliness to his talk, along with an earnestness which no longer seemed tortured. Nor was he self-conscious about his height. The loneliness of his early years continued, but rather than a defensive irritability, that loneliness now carried a resigned acceptance of the common human condition of isolation. Wolfe had spoken in recent years of wanting to marry, but his dedication to his work would probably never have allowed the intimate intrusion of another person into his life.

The wild eagerness of his youth had become a sober, reflective curiosity about the swiftly changing patterns of life around him. His friendliness with casual strangers, his honest concern about their affairs, their homes, their families, had broadened until he seemed to carry an air of kindly interest into any gathering. But he still had the powder for explosions. He had a good store of indignation to direct at social or personal injustice. Or he could occasionally be surly when some difficulty blocked progress in his work, and he took to drinking while he fought it out with himself.

His routine was lonely and rigorous. He got at his work about noon, dictating to his secretary until six or preparing sheets for her to type as he drank innumerable cups of coffee. After she left, he worked into the evening until he had dinner sent up from the hotel restaurant or stepped next door to Cavanaugh's for a couple of mint juleps and a steak. After dinner he would pass the time of day with the cashier or coat check man at Cavanaugh's or would chat with hotel residents or the bartender at the Chelsea. Then he would return to write until two or three in the morning. Some days he went uptown to Elizabeth Nowell's office or met his lawyers to discuss his one remaining lawsuit, the attempt to recover his manuscripts from Murdoch Dooher. Later, when his friendship developed with Harper editor Edward Aswell, he spent some week ends at the Aswell home in Chappaqua. Once in a while, a friend like James Stokeley or Norman Pearson would drop in to the Chelsea, and Wolfe would talk with him about his writing. Sometimes he would compare notes on the literary game with Edgar Lee Masters or with Fred McIsaacs, a pulp fiction writer who lived at the Chelsea.

Wolfe was torn between concentrating on one section of his manuscript in order to get a volume published soon and filling out the general shape of his autobiographical narrative. Anticipating that a new publisher would want to see some of his work before committing himself to publication, he had selected "The October Fair" section, for it seemed the most nearly finished part. He began piecing chunks together, rewriting, expanding, and filling in transitions for narrative coherence. Over the next few months, though filled with indecision about whether it would become the volume announced in 1935 or a part of his new narrative, Wolfe produced the entire account of his hero's meeting with Mrs. Jack and the beginning of the love affair.

But work on other sections was being planned or started, too, and fruits of his Asheville trip began to mature. Wolfe's vision generally seemed to intensify when he was away from the area he was writing about. Most of his dithyrambic chants about American earth had been done in Europe, "The Party at Jack's" had been written in Asheville, and now in New York Wolfe began to write about what he had discovered in North Carolina. He wrote the scarcely fictional "Return," which included accounts of his journey through the Southern Appalachians, the murder he had witnessed in Burnsville, and his reception in Asheville.[2] The phrase "you can't go home again" began to appear in notebooks and outlines as the title of a book or a section of a book.

The pain of his separation from Maxwell Perkins needed to be soothed by writing. He sketched out a couple of outlines about their relationship that he entitled "The Farewell to the Fox," and he jotted in his notebook the opening sentence of his final justification: "I have of late, dear Fox, been thinking of you very much, and of your simple yet your strange and fascinating name."[3]

Not all his moods were somber. The adventures of Joe Doaks were to have a comic prologue. Wolfe indulged himself in happily spent time and effort on a series of sketches called "The Doaksology," done in the manner of Dickens' comic history of the family name in Chapter I of *Martin Chuzzlewit*.[4] This genealogical parody, which turns up gulls, dupes, cuckolds, and generally trouble-prone fellows, begins, "This Doaks (or Doakes—for the name has almost as many varieties as a dog has fleas) came from a celebrated family that has branches in every quarter of the globe." In Roman times, Caesar commented on their skill in battle: ". . . facile doctissimi eorum

Doxiensi sunt." Evidence of the Doaks family in medieval France is preserved in a fourteenth-century song:

> Le droict des amants est jouer
> Le poulette et le coq;
> Les droict du seigneur es d'aimer
> La femme du Monsieur Doque
> Plan—plan—rat—ta—ta—plan
> La femme du Monsieur Doque

Sir Guy Le Doaks is knighted by Richard the Lion-Hearted, who plucks a lemon from a bough and gives it to Sir Guy as a symbol of his house and line. A later knight, Sir Doaks Le Greal, is unable to relieve a damsel in distress, for he is too stupid to understand her problem. In the sixteenth century, Hugh Doaks of Kent boards ship for the colonies, a sequence in Wolfe's mock-Elizabethan style as supposedly set down in a chronicle of "Old Robert Somervil." Down through the years, the Doakses emigrate to America, the Doacks branch to Pennsylvania with the German colonists, the Doakes branch to old Catawba—although some still remain in Europe to carry on the family tradition: for instance, the Doaks investors in the South Sea Bubble and the famous Ebenezer Doaks, a devotee of Pantisocracy.[5] "The Doaksology" reflects Wolfe's basically healthy attitude toward his troubles. He was able to satirize his hero by giving him a simpleton's heritage.

Meanwhile, he was making some progress toward getting a new publisher. He had been despondent at first about the results of his long-distance calls from Asheville. But Houghton Mifflin had followed up the news that he had left Scribner's and had begun preliminary talks with him. Wolfe was feeling some uneasiness about the way these talks were going when Miss Nowell called to ask if he wanted to see Edward Aswell of Harper. Through a mistake in telephone connections, Harper had missed an early opportunity to take up Wolfe's invitation when he called from Asheville. When Aswell accidentally discovered that Wolfe was available, he contacted Miss Nowell immediately and, as she arranged, went down to the Chelsea to talk business. Aswell and Wolfe liked each other right away, and their business talk soon became the conversation of two friends. Until five o'clock in the morning, Aswell listened to Wolfe's long tale of his interrupted work and his reasons for leaving Scribner's. On the spot, Aswell made an offer of $10,000 for advance royalties on Wolfe's next book, sight unseen.[6] In the next weeks, Wolfe came to know and trust Aswell, and he felt confidence in Cass Canfield, the president of Harper and in Eugene Saxton, the senior editor. He decided to accept the offer on December 19, and he signed a contract for a book to be called "The Life and Adventures of the Bondsman Doaks" on December 31, 1937. It is clear that his commitment to Harper came about because of Aswell's instantaneous offer, which restored his sagging confidence, and because of Aswell's admiration for his work. "I think it is going to turn out to be a wonderful experience," he told Anne Armstrong, "I feel that the man is quiet, but very deep and true: and he thinks that I am the best writer there is." [7]

Wolfe ended the year with great expectations. He felt he was valued; he no longer would feel uncertain about the acceptance or rejection of his work. No more would he be tempted to put responsibility for decision on Perkins. He was free and happy. It was a new beginning.

II

The day Wolfe signed his new contract with Harper, he dictated a letter to Mrs. Edward Aswell, thanking her for a Christmas gift, a copy of Huxley's *Eyeless in Gaza*. In commenting on the book he revealed that he had been pondering the question of the social responsibility of the artist:

...apparently Huxley's ideal is a kind of non-partisan man—or rather, a man who is partisan only in his belief in life. And yet, I wonder if in this world of ours today we can be non-partisan. Of one thing I am sure: the artist can't live in his ivory tower any more [;] if he is, he is cutting himself off from all the sources of life. Tremendous pressure is brought to bear from all sides upon people like myself: we are told that we must be partisan even in the work we do. Here I think the partisans are wrong: and yet a man does feel today a tremendous pressure from within—a kind of pressure of the conscience. . . .I wish it were possible for me to feel like Candide that the best thing in the end is to tend one's garden. A tremendous lot can be said for that, a tremendous lot of good, but somehow garden tending doesn't seem to be the answer either, the way things are today.[8]

In the last two years, Wolfe had been moving toward a solidification of his social and economic views. The development of his social involvement had been long and slow. In his early career, his all-absorbing drive to become an artist, his desire to guide his life toward experience that would provide him with strong impressions, and his struggle for self-expression largely blinded him to the problems of social man. When the 1929 crash came, he had just established himself as a novelist, and he was too buried in his own problems of getting his work done to notice the onset of the Great Depression. It was forced to his attention by the losses that members of his own family suffered and by the poverty and suffering that he began to observe during his stay in Brooklyn. The effect of these events and scenes soaked in over the years, bringing him to the point at which it was almost impossible to finish "The October Fair," which dealt with the enthusiasms and despairs of his youth. At last in 1938, he had just about decided to throw it aside. Writing to Donald Ogden Stewart, he revealed why his feelings had changed: "... one day I got a letter from a person who was speaking about art and love and beauty. It was a good letter but after I had read it I looked out of the window and across the street I saw a man. He was digging with his hand into a garbage can for food: I have a good memory for places and for time and this was half-way through December 1932. And I know that since then I have never felt the same way about love or art or beauty or thought they were enough." [9]

Observations of social injustice in the great land of plenty whose praises he wanted to sing brought him, first, to a citizen's awareness of and awakened interest in social reform through political action and carried him, finally, to a resolution to attack social wrong with the only lance he had, a pencil. Wolfe was always politically somewhat naive, but ever since he had shaken off the Menckenian anti-democratic attitudes that he had acquired at Harvard, he had been politically a man of good will. He unfailingly supported the Democratic party. After Al Smith's defeat in 1928, he was angry. He felt that all the reactionary forces in America had triumphed and the little people had been trampled on.[10] In the thirties he was an eager Roosevelt partisan—which set off countless political arguments with Maxwell Perkins, who was an anti-New-Deal Democrat. Perkins' favorite comparison in discussions about the movement toward reform was between Erasmus, the man of compromise, and Luther, the man of revolution. He felt that the world needed more men like Erasmus to prevent violence and disaster. Wolfe, who in moments of decision was fond of quoting Luther's words, "Ich kann nicht anders," favored taking strong action.

Memories of these discussions rose up in 1936, when Wolfe first began to sketch out the characterization of Foxhall Edwards, and they led to his first treatment of America's forgotten men in the moving meditation on the suicide of "C. Green," who jumped from the Admiral Drake hotel. Wolfe had stepped temporarily out of his garden. At this time he wrote to Mrs. Roberts, revealing that he was choosing sides in the social struggle, yet guarding himself from becoming a mere propagandist:

...by instinct, by inheritance, by every natural sympathy and affection of my life, my whole spirit and feeling is irresistibly on the side of the working class, against the cruelty, the injustice, the corrupt and infamous privilege of great wealth, against the shocking excess and wrong of the present system, the evidences of which are horribly apparent [,] I think, to anybody who lives here in New York and keeps his eyes open. I think the whole thing has got to be changed, and I'll do everything within the province of my energy or talent to change it for the better, if I can, but I am not a Communist, and I believe that the artist who makes his art the vehicle for political dogma and intolerant propaganda is a lost man. I think almost every great poet and every great writer who ever wrote and whose works we all love and treasure has been on the side of the oppressed, the suffering, the confused and lost and stricken of the earth.... But really isn't this just another way of saying that every great man or any good man is on the side of life, and although I am myself the son of a working man, I go so far as to say that an artist's interest, first and always, has got to be in life itself, and not in a special kind of life.[11]

But by late 1937, the prologue to World War II was being enacted. The Spanish Civil War had been raging for more than a year. The United States and the other democratic powers, shunning responsibility, stood by to watch German and Italian military might slowly grind the Spanish Loyalists under the wheels. Japan had invaded China in the middle of the year, and the United States, bound in instinctive isolationism, seemed to ignore the destruction of American missions and the sinking of the gunboat, *Panay*, and went on shipping war materials to Japan. Hitler, eager to expand the territory of the Reich, daily preached his blood-and-soil doctrine, and he was getting ready to take over Austria. To all appearances, the Communists seemed the only force opposed to the advance of Fascism.

By this time, Wolfe's mounting interest in social issues brought him into contact with a number of Marxist intellectuals. Through his friendship with Sherwood Anderson, he came to meet, among others, Ella Winter, who eagerly awaited a novel of social protest from his hands ("our" book, as she called it); [12] Clifford Odets, who wanted him to plug his play, *Clash By Night;* [13] George Seldes, who wanted him to go to Washington to picket against U.S. neutrality in the Spanish War; [14] and Michael Gold, who wanted him to contribute to the *New Masses*.[15] Apparently, word had traveled far about Wolfe's radical inclinations, for he even got an invitation to address an American Student Union group at the University of Pennsylvania.[16]

Besides these personal requests, he received, in early 1938, other encouragements to stand up and be counted. Donald Ogden Stewart of the League of American Writers, polling American authors, wrote him, "Are you for or are you against Franco and Fascism? Are you for or are you against the legal government of the people of Republican Spain?" [17] Freda Kirchway, editor of the *Nation,* asked him to contribute to her survey on the question, "How to Keep Out of War." Clifton Fadiman invited him to contribute his credo to the *Living Philosophies* series, which were to be published individually in the *Nation* and later to be collected in a volume.

Bombarded from all sides, yet wanting above all to get his work done, Wolfe held his head in his hands. "What to do?" he wrote Mrs. Roberts.

Like you, I have become in the last few years tremendously involved with the state of the world—as my consciousness of life has enlarged, my consciousness of self has dwindled: there are things now that so afflict me in the state of man that I think I would take up arms against them, or give my life to stop them—but what to do? There is hardly a day goes by now but what people—for the most part, I think, sincere and genuine people—call me up or write me, and ask me to sign my name to a petition or proclamation of some sort, to go to Washington with a group to protest to the President about the state of things in Spain; to appear with a group at the French Consulate and protest to the French Consul about the state of things in Spain; to serve on committees of protest about the condition of the sharecroppers in the South—about the imprisonment of Tom Mooney

—about the violation of civil liberties in various places—about the Scotts-boro boys—about the Moscow trials—for or against the Stalinists or Trotskyites—but what to do, what to do? [18]

Wolfe could not help but respond both as a citizen and a writer. He published a letter in the *Nation,* April 2, a thumping attack on isolationism and a plea for "collective action" by the democratic states. But since he was a creative writer, most of his action took literary form. If he gave his views on Spain, he would not write an essay: to the *Nation* he sent a piece of irony, a parody of a letter to the editor commenting on Franco's invitations to the tourist trade.[19] His reply to Donald Ogden Stewart's letter became a long, introspec-tive account of his impressions of Nazi Germany—so searching, in fact, that he did not send the letter but saved it to revise for his autobiographical novel.[20] It now makes up the bulk of "The Dark Messiah" in *You Can't Go Home Again.*

For his Doaks book, he planned, soon after his return from North Carolina, to make Asheville (under the name Libya Hill) the principal example of what happened to the smaller cities of America in the 1929 crash. He had now heard at first hand about the failure of the Central Trust Bank, the loss of the city funds it held, and the political scandal that surrounded it. From New York, he wrote back to Mrs. Roberts and to his cousin, Jack Westall, for further informa-tion, newspaper accounts of the court trial of the bank officials in 1931. He began to draw together old and new material that would take Doaks through the depression days in both Libya Hill and metropolitan New York.

The hardest-hitting piece that came out of this period was "The Company," which Wolfe gave to Mike Gold for publication in *New Masses,* January 11, 1938.[21] It represents Wolfe's highly personal re-action to the ethics of big business and in particular to the way the National Cash Register Company treated his brother-in-law, Ralph Wheaton. Ralph, Mabel's husband, had devoted years of loyal serv-ice to his company; then, when he was well along in years, he was fired because business had fallen off in his area.

Wolfe had already satirized the "One Hundred Club" in an un-published portion of *Look Homeward, Angel.* He accumulated more material when he stayed with the Wheatons in a room over their garage on the last trip to Asheville just before *Look Homeward, Angel* was published, at which time he also met the district manager of the company. For his Doaks book, he conceived a character (drawn, to some extent, from both his brother, Fred, and his brother-in-law, Ralph Wheaton), Jim Doaks, who was to represent the little man, complacent and conservative, who defended ruthless, unhampered business procedures as "the American way of doing things." Now, taking the old material from his first novel and his new impressions of the National Cash Register Company and firing them with an aroused sense of justice, Wolfe wrote "The Company," the story of Jim Doaks and the Federal Weight and Scales Company. Since this story in Wolfe's longer version finally found its permanent place in *You Can't Go Home Again* as one of George Webber's series of discoveries, it will be convenient to use the names George Webber and Randy Shepperton in discussing its qualities.[22]

Wolfe's satirical method in "The Company," with its mixture of anger and laughter, makes its social criticism wholly different from that in "The Party at Jack's" and more biting. In making George Webber, the observer, remain unperceptive until the end of the story, Wolfe allows the reader to penetrate the rather heavy irony himself. The narrative focuses first on "the pink-cheeked Santa Claus," the back-slapping Mr. Merritt, and begins to build up the cheapness of his hypocrisy: "... he winked at George in such a comical way that all of them had to grin. Then he gave George a big cigar." The straight-faced narrator, emphasizing the "aura of good fellowship" Mr. Merritt exudes, moves to shop-talk and then makes an innocently simple transition to the mysterious workings of the company ("before long George began to pick up a pretty good idea of what it was all about").

In the explanation, Wolfe turns military and religious terms to good mock-heroic effect. The hierarchy of overseers and underlings have their rank and responsibility like an army chain of command. The company president's words, "There's your market, boys! Go out and sell them," accompanied with a finger flourished at the map of the country, are surrounded with grandeur and placed beside the famous sayings of Napoleon, Perry, Dewey and Grant. The inhumanity of American business enterprise comes under scrutiny in the economic Heaven and Hell with which the company rewards and threatens its employees. The Hundred Club, for all company men who make one hundred per cent of their yearly quota, provides a one-week, expense-paid junket to Bermuda or Cuba. "Twelve or fifteen hundred men, Americans, most of them in their middle years, exhausted, overwrought, their nerves frayed down and stretched to the breaking point" get an annual respite with intoxicating sherbets and winsome houris in the company's economic paradise. And woe to those whose names are not on the register of the Hundred Club. Economic damnation yawns beneath their feet, for President Paul S. Appleton III is "a theologian who, like Calvin, knew how to combine free will and predestination." Those who do not strive to reach the Company Heaven, even though their quota is raised after each fulfillment, cannot be saved.

After this mock-religious analysis, Wolfe returns to the narrative for George Webber's discovery of how this uniquitous system has shaped Mr. Merritt. After George has overheard Merritt's snarling accusation against Randy Shepperton for "not getting the business," he sees him come out of the office, change face in an instant, and burst forth, "Well, what d'ya say, folks? What about one of Margaret's famous meals out at the old homestead?" And the fable ends with George's vision of the toiling Egyptian slaves, whipped on by a hierarchy of overseers, each, from the Pharaoh on down, lashing his subordinate, at work to build the great pyramid.

Although the whole story hangs on one incident, Wolfe has so festooned it with clichés, booster talk, slogans (although he finally omitted the most Rabelaisian of the lot: "Let Federal Service You"), hypocritical veneers, and mock-prophetic executive visions that he avoids the over-simplified didacticism common to the fiction of social protest. By means of satiric distortion, Wolfe lays bare the brutalities of white-collar existence, and he denounces by implication the whole idea of "creative salesmanship"; that is, the forcing of sales upon customers who have no need for the product, a vicious mechanism of advertising and marketing that exhausts the economic vigor of a nation.

Despite its appearance in *New Masses*, "The Company" has no distinctive Communist flavor. Wolfe was ready to combat inhumanity, but he would march under no special banner. For one thing, he was such an individualist that he could not have tolerated the discipline imposed on writers by the Communist Party. For another, he was too irritated by the patronizing intellectual snobbery he encountered in discussions with literary Communists. They treated him, he growled, like "a poor benighted son of a bitch who doesn't know his ass from the House of Morgan." [23] More than anything else, he had lived long enough to realize that the Communist vision of a millennium did not square with the realities of human behavior. Arguing about economic equality with S. L. Solon, Wolfe replied, "Don't you think that's the old Christian spirit all over again? It'll probably work out about the same way too." [24]

His notes during this period show that he was searching himself to decide just what his political position was. What emerges is the picture of a person who upholds the rights of man that are traditionally associated with democracy (though he does not understand them all) but who feels that the economic framework of American capitalism must be changed. With hindsight one can see that these views make him a supporter of the bloodless revolution of the Roosevelt regime. Probably the fullest summation of his views is contained in the following fragment, jotted down in the spring of 1938:

If I had to state my politics I'd call myself a social democrat. And by a social democrat I would understand a man who believes in socialism and communized socialism [i.e., not the National Socialism of Nazi Germany], and in democracy but not individualized democracy [apparently he means in representative government and not pure democracy].

I do not believe in the abolition of private property, in the class warfare, or in the so-called dictatorship of the proletariat. I do not believe also in the abolition of free inquiry, or that the ideas represented by "freedom of thought," "freedom of speech," "freedom of press" and "free assembly" are just rhetorical myths. I believe rather that they are among the most valuable realities that men have gained, and that if they are destroyed men will again fight to have them.

I do not think there is any great "Communist danger" in America at the present time.

But I do think there is a grave Fascist danger, and it is with Fascism that I am concerned.

And again, in another fragment Wolfe elaborates one important distinction: "So far from believing that the idea and practice of democracy is dependent for its existence on the survival of the modern capitalist system, and that its destiny is indispensably joined with that of capitalism, I should say that if democracy is to survive at all, it can do so only through the radical modification of capitalist society, as it now exists. . . ." [25]

These remarks are certainly not profound, nor do they, in their simple way, penetrate the social problems of the world in the late 1930's. But as a crude ideological statement, they show the basic position from which Wolfe launched the social criticism that dominated this final period of his writing. They also show that Wolfe's fear of Fascism had grown not only because of the rumblings in Europe but also because he distrusted the American economic framework and saw potential evil in the American people themselves. In his letter to the *Nation* denouncing isolationism, he stated: "Just as the foundations of Fascism are rooted in the hopelessness and despair of a bankrupt and defeated people who, having nothing more to lose, submit to any promises of gain—this would be apparent to anyone who visited Germany as I did in 1928 and 1930—so does the success and growth of Fascism depend upon submission, and flourish upon compromise and vacillation." [26] All of Wolfe's usual scorn for defeatist attitudes, all of his revulsion at lack of vitality, had taken on a political construction.

However Wolfe might define his position and whatever labels he might paste on the objects of his hostility, there was still something wrong in America that he could not name. It displayed itself in greed, in cowardice, and in flabbiness of belief among the citizenry and in visual squalor on the landscape. In the privacy of his notebook, he probes the "nameless wound":

Is it not true that having known faith and freedom in this land, and an image of free institutions, the very words that once gave life and hope to us have been so befouled and slobbered over by the politician getting votes, that they have now gone dead and stale and foul for us—and that Croesus with his filthy money-bags at stake invokes the Constitution and the Ten Commandments in a single breath, howls out that liberty—his own liberty to get—is in dire peril?

. . .is it not true that. . .even the *promise* of that high and glorious fulfillment has been so aborted, corrupted, made dropsical with disease, that its ancient and primeval lineaments are no more to be seen? Is it not true that we were given here for the enrichment and improvement of man's life a golden wilderness, and that we have almost made of it a wilderness of horror, ugliness, and confusion. Is it not true that we began here with an ideal of a free man's life, enlarging and fulfilling its whole purpose in an atmosphere of free and spacious enlightenment—and is it not true that what we have is for the most part just a mongrel and disordered mob—a jargon of a thousand tongues, the mouthpiece of a million vicious and sensational rumors—but with no faith, no freedom, no belief—a slave-like swarm without the dignities of slavery—a duped, doped horde who seek or want no remedy for the diseases that prey upon them—and themselves so vicious, infamous, and base, that one does not know which is more hateful or more odious—the fools who take it or the knaves who dupe?

He goes on to condemn the American scene: "the thousand dreary architectures," "the rusty rackets of its elevated," "the wasteland horror of its little shops, hot dog stands, grease and food emporiums, shooting galleries." [27]

It is because Wolfe identifies himself with his nation that he can make this bitter outburst, for he cries out, "We've got to *loathe* America, as we loathe ourselves. With loathing, horror, shame and anguish of the soul unspeakable—as well as with love—we've got to face the total horror of our self-betrayal, the way America has betrayed herself." [28] This passage has all the intensity of the writhing of the sinner. But as Dante taught, evil must be comprehended before it can be purged, and Wolfe is acknowledging national guilt. Or one might extend Socrates' words about the necessity for self-criticism to apply to national criticism: The "unexamined nation is not worth living in"; [29] and Wolfe is scrutinizing the national condition. From this willingness to face whatever he found abhorrent comes Wolfe's importance as an American bard. He would not be a mere chauvinist; he would revile as well as praise.

This ambiguous attitude was certainly not a new one with Wolfe. He revealed it in *Of Time and the River* and *From Death to Morning*, which, in spite of paeans to the American land, presented scenes of violence and horror and expressed revulsion at rural and metropolitan corrosion. But the mingling of love and loathing was a more potent mixture now. His critical awareness of American shortcomings only produced a stronger yearning for the American dream to come true.

In this state of mind he turned out "A Prologue to America," the last piece of writing he published in his lifetime. It appeared in the February, 1938, issue of *Vogue* ("the ladies' corset and hosiery encyclopedia," he apologized to friends).[30] Drawn from his "Hound of Darkness" scenario, revised to become the fleeting impressions of a wanderer rather than a series of scenes in dialogue, and whittled down to five thousand words to suit the editors, the work is somewhat disorderly because of uncertain shifts in point of view between the narrator and the characters. But the double attitude is unmistakable. Wolfe's American scene is both splendid and tainted:

"Across the width of Indiana the merits of Carter's Liver Pills are blazoned in the moon"; Lakeshore Drive is "the best shirt-front on earth" with the "million miles of brutal jungle that is called Chicago" behind it. In his eagle-eye view, Wolfe swoops from the "hackled moonlight on the Rocky Mountains," down to the gaudy façade (like a "splendiferous chop-suey joint") of Grauman's Chinese Theater in Hollywood. Alongside the happy enthusiasm of teen-agers dancing the Big Apple, he sees the brown-shirted thugs on the Pleasanton police force. Some passages completely merge beauty and ugliness—the image of Pittsburgh with its "hell's beauty in the blasted land," and of Times Square, a blink of advertising, with its "jeweled pollen of the lights that climb in linkless chains." [31] But the nighttime sweep across the continent ends with optimism and with a sense of impending development in the nation: "For there is something marching in the night; so soon the morning, soon the morning—oh America." A descent into the dark night of the soul is necessary before illumination.

NOTES

1. *Letters*, pp. 662-63. Mr. Mitchell's firm, Mitchell and Van Winkle, is said to have inspired Paget & Page in Wolfe's unfinished sketch, "Justice is Blind," published in Walser, pp. 91-100.

2. Considerably cut, this appears as Part II of "The Return of the Prodigal," published in HB. Wolfe never finished it.

3. PN 32, September 14, 1937, to early 1938.

4. Miss Nowell's comment (*Letters,* p. 718, n. 2) that "The Doaksology" was originally Joyner material, written in 1936-37, and that it later became Chapters 2-6 of HB is in error and has caused some confusion already (e.g., C. Hugh Holman, *Thomas Wolfe* [Minneapolis, 1960], p. 24).

5. HCL°46AM-7(54).

6. Edward Aswell, "Thomas Wolfe Did Not Kill Maxwell Perkins," *Saturday Review of Literature,* XXXIV (October 6, 1951), 45.

7. *Letters,* p. 695.

8. *Letters,* pp. 698-99. Wolfe had been quizzing himself in his notebook:

> Is a writer "political" or not?
> Is Shakespeare "political?" Yes
> Is John Keats? No
> Is P. B. Shelley? Yes
> Is Byron? Decidedly
> Is Dickens? Yes
> Is Thackeray? No

and so on. PN 33, early 1938 to April 25, 1938.

9. HCL°46AM-7(59), unpublished letter, written about February, 1938, most of which was later used for YCGHA, Chapter 38.

10. *Letters,* p. 150.

11. *Letters,* pp. 519-20.

12. HCL*46AM-12(4), January 11, 1938.

13. *Ibid.,* telegrams dated December 3, 19, and 31, 1937.

14. *Ibid.,* April 25, 1938. Wolfe's reply to Seldes' letter refuses but displays interest.

15. *Ibid.,* undated letter.

16. Wolfe refused. HCL*46AM-15, unpublished letter, April 18, 1938.

17. Stewart's letter has been lost. But Wolfe quoted the questions in his letter, cited in n. 9.

18. *Letters,* p. 738.

19. Published May 21, 1938. Reprinted in *Letters,* pp. 752-54. Wolfe, taking no chances of being misunderstood, wrote an accompanying note to Freda Kirchway, assuring her it was "wrote sarcastical."

20. The next form it took was entitled "A Spanish Letter," thirty pages of typescript which Wolfe intended to publish separately. HCL*46AM-7(59).

21. This was a real testimonial to Wolfe's liking for Gold and his respect for the anti-Fascist power that *New Masses* represented. He could have sold it to another magazine for $400.

22. YCGHA, pp. 129-40.

23. HCL*46AM-7(70-aa).

24. S. L. Solon, "The Ordeal of Thomas Wolfe," *Modern Quarterly,* XI (Winter, 1939), 44-53.

25. HCL*46AM-7(70-aa). These statements are found among other similar fragments written on yellow second sheets.

26. *Letters,* p. 735.

27. HCL*46AM-7(70-aa).

28. *Ibid.*

29. The words in Jowett's translation of Plato's "Apology" are "the unexamined life is not worth living."

30. *Letters,* p. 702.

31. *Vogue,* XCI (February, 1938), 63-66, 150-53, 161.

Part VIII

THE HAND OF THE LIVING AND THE HAND OF THE DEAD

26

"LET HIS NAME BE WEBBER"

Wolfe had not seen Maxwell Perkins since his retreat to Asheville in the summer of 1937. After his return to New York in September, he suffered intensely from the self-enforced separation. "I can only tell you straight from the heart," he wrote Perkins, "that I have not had anything affect me as deeply as this in ten years, and I have not been so bereaved and grief-stricken by anything since my brother's [Ben's] death." [1] But Wolfe did not want to see him. He was so "sore inside" that he needed more time to heal. When the incredible lawsuit with Murdoch Dooher came up for a hearing in February, 1938, it provided an occasion to end the estrangement, for Wolfe had asked Perkins to appear as a witness. Wolfe was deeply moved by the very anticipation of the reunion and a little apprehensive, too. He was afraid that a renewal of the friendship would tempt him to begin going to Perkins with his problems once more. Or at least that the very presence of the man to whom he had clung for support would unsettle the feeling of independence he had struggled so hard to achieve. Wolfe saw Perkins on the evening of February 1 and on the day the case was scheduled, February 8. He came through his ordeal well; Perkins was no longer the awe-inspiring father figure. The lawsuit dominated the talk, and even after the victory in court there was not much chance for intimate conversation because Barnet Ruder, a rare book dealer and one of the witnesses for Wolfe, remained with them. "I'll always regret that the rare book man was along," Perkins said later, for this was the last time he saw Tom Wolfe.[2]

With his docket cleared of lawsuits and with the test of facing Perkins safely passed, Wolfe could now turn with a freer mind to getting something ready for Harper. The $10,000 vote of confidence

Aswell had given him brought with it a grave obligation. As he surveyed his work, he recognized what had frequently crept forth in his trial outlines of the Doaks book: that he had disparate bodies of material to deal with.[3] He could not make all his autobiographical reminiscence suit his conception of a book about a modern Don Quixote's "adventures of the road." He therefore drew up a long "Statement of Purpose" addressed to Edward Aswell that was intended to get him beyond this impasse.[4]

This new plan, which would be governed by the theme of change and maturity ("You can't go home again"), showed that Wolfe wished to cover only the span of his life from 1929 to 1937. The agonies of his hero's early love affair, he felt, need not be included. For his method of organization, Wolfe returned to "K 19"—even using the opening chapter of that abortive work, the hero's entry into Pennsylvania Station, for the first chapter after the prologue.[5] The hero was to meet a mixture of home folks on the train, Nebraska Crane, Jerry Alsop, Judge Bland, Jarvis Riggs, and others. Each meeting would bring to mind early memories—"Time Sweeps," Wolfe calls them—in this way making use of material written about boyhood days. The hero, who is unnamed because Wolfe now thought the name, Doaks, suggested cartoons and slapstick, has the same gorilla-like disguise that George Spangler had worn in 1936.

After running about twenty pages, the "Statement of Purpose" stops. Wolfe never sent the letter. He could not send it because he could not sacrifice the full treatment of his autobiographical self that he had been creating for years. One can imagine Wolfe stamping around his rooms at the Chelsea full of a hundred indecisions and at last the "gray-lipped thing" arising within him to say, No. He formed a new plan, giving his hero a new name that was symbolic of what he resolved at last to do. Jottings on a scrap of paper show him playing with an idea, "Weaver, Weber, Webber." His decision is recorded on another scrap, "Let his name be Webber." [6] He now set out to weave together all the material he had and to supply transitions as needed for splicing. He set up his title page:

THE WEB AND THE ROCK

A Story of the Voyage of Everyman:
His Going To and Fro Upon the Earth;
His Walking Up and Down In It;

And His Desire For Home: His
Vision of the Lost, The Found, the
Ever-Real, The Never-Here America [7]

The new title offered wholesale possibilities for symbolism. Generally, the web is the fabric being woven on the loom of time, but the particular fabric is the life of Wolfe's Everyman, George Webber. Further, his hero is an artist, a weaver of words, and he weaves not only his mimetic tapestries but also a web of trouble in his life. His name, Webber, and that of his maternal ancestors, Joyner, suggest the earnest artisan as well as the person of humble origins. The City, as the rock, is barren but at the same time has a substantiality that provides a footing for the life that swarms upon it. Foxhall Edwards, too, is a rock. His solidity offers support for the hero, but since a rock is unchanging, his presence is uncongenial to artistic growth.

Into this enormous book was to go almost everything he had written, the nighttime impressions from "The Hound of Darkness," the boyhood scenes from "The Hills Beyond Pentland," the Esther Jack material from "The October Fair," the fragments of "K 19," pieces cut from *Of Time and the River*, the "Introduction by a Friend" from "Spangler's Paul," together with everything he had created about the Joyners, the narratives about George Spangler and Joe Doaks, everything about James Rodney and Company, about the Libya Hill land boom, about bankers, lawyers, sports writers, book reviewers, college professors, and so on. He even planned to squeeze in chunks already published in *From Death to Morning*, such as "The Four Lost Men." It would be easy. He was compiling a complete autobiographical sequence again.

Wolfe spent all spring as a weaver and joiner putting his material in order—with, as always, painful hesitations and changes. But he needed to get a book in shape and, as he had said in November, "I am less and less inclined to monkey with it now." [8] His revisions were extensive, for this was the principal job. But he had great gaps to fill in, too. Starting at the beginning, he had to complete the chronicle of the Joyners. He dismembered his "Introduction by a Friend," taking the parts that applied to early days, and then went on to develop the characters of "Bear" and Zack Joyner as nimble-witted frontiersmen who performed fabulous deeds. He had a stock character in mind: "Zack Joyner. He is David Crockett, he is Lincoln, he is

Paul Bunyan all rolled up in one." [9] He planned to include the Civil War period by bringing in a reunion of Confederate veterans in 1878. "Chicamauga" was to be "Rance Joyner's Tale."

As Wolfe went on with his reshuffling, his procedure chiefly was to group together all the "material masses" that applied to distinctive periods of his life and to fit them into a rough order, throwing out some old variants but leaving in his manuscript stack any sketch that might possibly be integrated when he returned for a final revision. For example, this was his assembly and tentative arrangement for the section that covered the childhood of George Webber:

Book III
The Web and the Hound
(1906-1916)

Chapters:

>Caliban (Three o'clock)
>The Child Caliban
>The Street

Book [IV]
Caliban

Chapters:

>Characters: People Of The Street
>Himself (1908)
>Two Worlds Discrete (The Joyner And The
>   Webber World)

>The Child By Tiger
>Aunt Maw And The Orphan Girl
>The Old Red Irish
>The Great House
>The Image Of The Circus And His Father's Earth
>The Second Thing On Sunday
>The Baker's Truck

Book [V]
The Winter's Tale (1913)

Chapters:

>Home From The Mountains
>The Street Of The Day [10]

One item calls for comment as an example of Wolfe's amalgamation of old and new material. Back in 1930, he had written about "Monkey" Hawke's travels with the circus. In 1936 he reworked this episode to become one of young Spangler's daydreams and set down this reminder: "Note: the circus scenes must be made more of a vision (must I not depend much more on the visionary than I have in these hauntings of old lost time?)." [11] Other material he had written about the Pennsylvania farm country then became converted into the boy's intuitive vision of his father's native place. Now combined as "The Image of the Circus and His Father's Earth," these pieces, originally intended to serve other purposes, were now ready to be made part of George Webber's private legendizing about his father.

Wolfe went on to spend several days harmonizing scattered writings about his hero's college years, even blending in some old pages cut from *Look Homeward, Angel* about Professor Randolph Ware. Moving George Webber's career to New York City, Wolfe assembled a varied body of material: impressions of metropolitan noise and crowding; Webber's further association with the college friends, Alsop and Randolph; [12] sketches of Nebraska Crane as a professional baseball player; a partially developed characterization of Webber's cousin, Dexter Joyner, a cornfed aesthete; a characterization of Monty Bellamy,[13] whose yearnings to be a Broadway actor Wolfe planned to transfer to Dexter Joyner; meditations on loneliness and unhappiness in the city; an erotic fantasy about a chance meeting with a rich and beautiful lady that had been cut from Eugene Gant's reveries at Harvard.

Next Wolfe wrestled with an enormous and confusing mass of writings about Esther Jack, and at length he established a tentative order that contained intrusions about Webber's trips to Libya Hill and to Europe. As he worked, he would pencil in a simple transition in order to arrange a sequence—such as his putting "and arm in arm they went back to his room again" at the end of a chapter called "The Quarrel: Pursuit and Capture" so that a scene set in Webber's room could follow.[14] At other times he would shape a chapter from several elements—an example is a chapter called "The First Party (Mrs. Jack and the Celebrities)," which was fashioned from a narrative about a party, an impassioned appreciation of New York City, a mixture of passages from "Prologue to America," and a characterization of Stephen Hook (a figure based on Thomas Beer).[15] But this complicated story of the love affair with Esther Jack, together with her memories of her childhood, Webber's attempt to publish his book, and Wolfe's musings on love, jealousy, madness, remorse, the arrogance of the rich, and so on, was going to require a lot more work in revision. Accordingly, in his manuscript sequence Wolfe left duplicates and variant versions to await a later bout.

Wolfe could not stand all this revision as a daily duty. He jumped ahead to fill in some later gaps, writing principally about Jarvis Riggs, political corruption, and the fall of the bank in Libya Hill. It was at this time that the character Judge Bland, who had been only a passing figure cut from *Of Time and the River*,[16] took on proportion as an evil presence grimly surveying the activities of Libya Hill.

But Wolfe's book still had no end. Late outlines show that Wolfe planned the last portions to be "You Can't Go Home Again" (based on his return to Asheville) and "The Farewell to the Fox" (Webber's statement of belief addressed to Foxhall Edwards). But, as Wolfe's annotation for his working outlines indicates, "The Farewell to the Fox" was only "partly done." [17] Two interruptions occurred that suggested to Wolfe a conclusion. One came on April 13, when Clifton Fadiman wrote asking him to contribute to the collection of "Living Philosophies." Wolfe pondered this request and even began to write out some trial passages. He finally declined on the grounds he had too much to do.[18] But he had been pushed into asking himself questions. What did he believe in? Could he articulate his philosophy of life in general terms? Could he describe the changes in his thinking since he published his first two books?

The second was an invitation from Purdue University to give a lecture at the annual Literary Banquet, May 19, 1938. Here was an opportunity like the one that gave rise to *The Story of a Novel*. Wolfe could talk about the experiences of recent years that had produced changes in his views and about the huge book he had built on those experiences. Besides, he would get paid for it. He knew he was not a top-flight speaker, but as he told a friend, he could "do a hell of a lot of stammering for three hundred dollars." Gathering thoughts engendered by Clifton Fadiman's proposal and relating them to George Webber's career, he went ahead enthusiastically to dictate a speech for the Purdue students that declared, as he told Miss Nowell, "what convictions and beliefs I now have, not only about writing, but about the life around me from which I draw the sources of my material. . . ." This credo, then, could be used for the conclusion of the book. When it was reworked, it would stand as an epilogue in the form of a personal address, "The Farewell to the Fox," which "would be a kind of impassioned summing up of the whole book, of everything that has gone before, and a final statement of what is now." [19]

When Wolfe accepted the engagement at Purdue, he gave himself a deadline. He would finish boxing in *The Web and the Rock* before he left for Indiana. He could then take a vacation trip to the West, for he was bone-weary and needed a rest before he tackled the "tremendous labor of writing and revision" that the book still needed.[20]

He wondered if he should let Edward Aswell look through the manuscript while he was gone. Not only did he have parts that showed diversity of purpose but he also had many incomplete sections—about Libya Hill politics, about lawyers, about James Rodney and Company, about Nazi Germany, about European wanderings—and a number of sections that existed only in title or note—about the Hampstead Heath literary group, about Hollywood, about the Rocky Mountain region, about Oberammergau ("The Bartered Jesus"), about the birth of a baby in a Manhattan hospital ("The Nativity"), and so on.[21] "I don't know whether it would be a good idea to let him read it now or not," he wrote Miss Nowell. "I know where I stand, but it is like presenting someone with the bones of some great prehistoric animal he has never seen before—he might get bewildered." [22]

Wolfe spent his last week in New York working with a secretary to make a final assembly of his "enormous skeleton." He labeled each section, indicating its place in the book, and he drew up a fourteen-page rough table of contents.[23] He felt the manuscript could stand editorial inspection after he let Miss Nowell go through it looking for excerpts to try on magazine editors. She broke through her usual veneer of toughness to tell him she was now convinced he was the Great American Novelist.[24] Then Edward Aswell came down to the Hotel Chelsea on May 17 to pick up the manuscript and see Wolfe off. He found him in his shirtsleeves, excited and happy, letting the bartender pack his clothes while he made last-minute additions to the manuscript stack and threw other chunks aside to remain in his treasure crate. Finally, with apologies, explanations, and qualifications about its unfinished state, Wolfe bound the manuscript up in two enormous packages and gave it to Aswell to read. Not too fagged out to feel happy and relieved, he boarded his train.[25]

II

From this journey, Thomas Wolfe never returned to work again. Yet as he traveled everything seemed to go well. At Purdue he met a responsive audience of three hundred people, who were fascinated by the huge man twisting uncomfortably in his dinner clothes and stammering out his opening words in a deep voice.[26] Soon his earnestness took over to give energy and flow to his words. At ease, he did not follow his prepared speech too closely, and he tossed in side remarks when he wished. He was speaking "out of the workshop" he said, and he took half of his time with a good-humored account of his own struggles as a writer. Midway through, his tone changed as he began to talk about the awakening of his social conscience. He used to think that the artist should only concern himself with the true and the beautiful, that he should not let social problems intrude upon his work. He went ahead now to tell "how and why, and by what degrees and stages I have come to feel differently." He described how he became aware of the gathering darkness of the early thirties through public disasters, private tragedies, political turmoil, and subdued faces. The years "of letting the weather of life and of humanity soak in upon my consciousness had taken me out of the more narrow provinces of myself and my work." He went on in mounting periods to recount the personal disillusionments that came to him with fame and then reached a climax with a revelation of his faith in the common people.

From this grim loss, and from the desolation of these new discoveries, I had derived, by a strange paradox, a new sense of life, a newer and it seems to me, a better hope. For at the bottom of the well, at the rock bottom of the soil, in the whole corrupt and shoddy structure of the upper honeycomb, I had begun to see and understand and feel the common heart of man, and finally, I had come to see that this, no matter how much it gets betrayed, is the thing that can never be betrayed; no matter how much it gets corrupted, is the thing that finally can never be corrupted; no matter how much it gets defeated, is the thing that can never be defeated. . . .[27]

After the program, he relaxed with members of the English department at an informal party. His coat off and a drink in his hand, he discussed the Spanish war and his Loyalist sympathies. Gradually, as the talk turned to modern writers, he gave his opinions of Hemingway, Dreiser, Lewis, Dos Passos, and Lardner and, encouraged to a story-telling mood, he relayed New York literary gossip. He was having such a good time with his new friends that he persuaded them to continue the party for two more days in Chicago with him.

The joy of wandering was ahead of him. Vaguely he thought to take a couple of weeks and head for the Northwest, but following whim was an old course for Wolfe. He just wanted to move across the continent again, and he wanted to try the speed of a new streamliner. The gusts of Western air had been blowing the glooms of West 23rd Street out of his mind ever since he had left. Good fellowship, variety of scene, and freedom from work were restoring his old feeling of appreciative possessiveness about the American land. He found the Midwest "fat as a hog and so fertile that you felt that if you stuck a fork in the earth the juice would spurt—one thousand miles of fat, flat, green, hog-fat fertility—barns, houses, silos, towns— the whole repeating in the recessions of a gigantic scroll—very restful, somehow, after the torment of New York and four million words of manuscript." [28] In Oregon, new sights inspired new enthusiasms: "The streams and creeks and rivers swarm with fish—not 6 inch, 12 ounce ones—but great salmon, steelheads, etc. that weigh from 10 to 30 pounds. The forests are dense with enormous fir trees four and six feet through. . . ." [29]

Then in Portland he got a unique chance to extend his view of the West. Edward Miller, Sunday editor of the *Oregonian*, and Ray Conway of the Oregon State Motor Association were planning to find the answer to this question: "Is it feasible and sensible to tour the Western national parks within the time limits of the average man's vacation? If so, what does it cost?" [30] They were going to try a two-week tour at full gallop and invited Wolfe to come along. He could not turn the offer down. Besides getting a sense of the variety and scope of his country, he would be able to say after the trip that he had been in every state of the Union but Texas.

Starting from Portland on June 20, Wolfe and his friends swept south to Arizona and back up to Washington by July 2. Their sightseeing took them through all the major parks, Crater Lake, Yosemite,

General Grant, Sequoia, Grand Canyon, Bryce Canyon, Zion, Grand Teton, Yellowstone, Glacier, and Mount Rainier. Wolfe took notes furiously—the usual sort of trivia that pinned down memory for him.[31] He was not just gazing at the scenery; he was getting the feel of his country. "The national parks are, of course, stupendous," he wrote Miss Nowell, "but what was to me far more valuable were the towns, the things, the people I saw—the whole West and all its history unrolling at kaleidoscopic speed." [32]

Back in Seattle again, he found good news, a telegram from Edward Aswell. "Your new book is magnificent in scope and design, with some of the best writing you have ever done. I am still absorbing it...." [33] This reassurance was all he needed. His note-taking shows the itch to write was coming again. His letters to Miss Nowell reveal that an effervescence built up by his travels was about to overflow: "This is a country fit for Gods—you've never seen anything like it for scale and magnificence and abundance: the trees are as tall as the Flatiron Building.... The East seems small and starved and meagre by comparison...." [34] He was getting ready to add 200,000 words to George Webber's adventures. Since in Seattle he had looked up the Westall kin, descendants of his great-uncle Bacchus, he had something more to say about the Joyners too.

But he never had the chance to say it. Exhausted by the rush of the preceding two weeks, he caught pneumonia, which reopened an old tubercular lesion in his right lung and released the germs into his blood stream. After two months of wasting away in Seattle hospitals and after unsuccessful surgery in Baltimore, Thomas Wolfe was dead of tuberculosis of the brain. His manuscript, containing what was most precious to him in life, was once more in the hands of an editor.

NOTES

1. *Letters,* p. 675.

2. UNCL, unpublished letter from Maxwell Perkins to John Terry, November 9, 1945.

3. There are eleven fairly full outlines scattered among material in HCL*46AM-7(24-s) and (24-u), with such captions as "Portions of MSS (To Be Gotten Together)," "Material Masses for Joe Doaks," and "Synopsis For the Ordeal of the Bondsman Doaks."

4. The first part of this is reprinted in *Letters,* pp. 710-19.

5. This material was finally published in YCGHA, pp. 48-56.

6. HCL*46AM-7(61).

7. HCL*46AM-7(24-u).

8. *Letters*, p. 683.

9. HCL*46AM-7(61). Floyd Watkins, in *Thomas Wolfe's Characters* (Norman, Okla., 1957), pp. 147-51, shows that Wolfe also drew on the stories about North Carolina Governor Zebulon Vance.

10. HCL*49M-209(19). Most of this material was published in W&R, Chapters 1 to 9. "Himself (1908)" appeared in HB as "No Cure for It." Some of "The Old Red Irish" had already been published in OT&R, pp. 160-66, and "The Great House" (Eugene's glimpse of the Vanderbilt mansion) had been cut from OT&R. Editor Aswell did not print these pieces. "The Baker's Truck" became W&R, Chapter 7, "The Butcher."

11. HCL*46AM-7(24-v).

12. Wolfe calls him Ravenel. Aswell changed the name to Randolph.

13. Based on Lacey Meredith, Wolfe's college friend who was night cashier at the Hotel McAlpin in New York.

14. HCL*46AM-7(56). For the published version, see W&R, Chapters 40 and 41. Aswell added another day.

15. *Ibid.* For the published version see W&R, Chapter 30.

16. HCL*46AM-7(65). The passages were about Eugene Gant meeting the blind man, Dinwiddie Martin, on the train and going home with him in Baltimore to encounter his shrewish wife.

17. HCL*46AM-7(24-s).

18. HCL, unpublished letter to Clifton Fadiman, May 3, 1930.

19. *Letters*, p. 751.

20. *Letters*, p. 765.

21. HCL*46AM-7(24-s).

22. *Letters*, p. 764.

23. See Appendix, where this table of contents is printed in full.

24. HCL-46AM-12(4), unpublished letter, May 11, 1938.

25. HCL*49M-209(30), Aswell's account of Wolfe's last night in New York, published in Nowell, pp. 416-17.

26. William Braswell, "Thomas Wolfe Lectures and Takes a Holiday," Walser, pp. 64-76.

27. HCL*49M-209, The Purdue Speech.

28. *Letters*, p. 766.

29. *Letters*, p. 771.

30. Edward Miller, "Gulping the Great West," [*Portland*] *Oregonian*, July 31 and August 7, 1938.

31. A selection of these notes has been published: Thomas Wolfe, *Western Journal* (Pittsburgh, 1951).

32. *Letters*, p. 774.

33. *Ibid.*

34. *Letters*, pp. 774-75.

27 ~~~~~~~~~~~~~~~~~~~~~~~~~

THE WEB OF ILLUSION AND
THE ROCK OF REALITY

IN THE FALL OF 1938, OCTOBER RAINS FELL ON THE GRAVE OF
Thomas Wolfe, but his ghost walked in the office of Edward Aswell
at Harper and Brothers. Aswell had, on his own authority, offered
Wolfe the generous advance on his next book without seeing it. His
publishing house had backed him up, but now the book was incomplete and its author dead. A heavy responsibility weighed on him to
create something publishable out of the mass of material that Wolfe
himself had found almost ungovernable.

In the summer, he had telegraphed encouragement to Wolfe, calling his book "magnificent in scope and design," but he soon came to
think of it as chaotic.[1] Sifting through the pages, he could not even
keep the names of the characters straight, for he found direct and
oblique references to Wolfe's autobiographical hero under all his
names, Eugene Gant, David Crockett Hawke, John Hawke (in the
first person), Paul Spangler, George Spangler (nicknamed Monk),
Joe Doaks, George Webber. A woman appeared, variously named
Alice, Irene, Esther, or Rebecca, who was a Mrs. Jacobs, Jack, or
Feitlebaum. George Webber was an only child, but John Hawke had
a stuttering brother named Lee and Joe Doaks had a brother who
did not stutter named Jim. Although George Webber's mother died
when he was a boy, Mama turned up under different names in the
later part of the manuscript.

Aswell had been associated with Wolfe for only six months before
the fatal vacation trip, but he could turn for aid to two people who
had worked with Wolfe for years. Maxwell Perkins had been named
literary executor in Wolfe's will, and he was ready to help anyway,
for he had a large emotional stake in Wolfe's writing. He not only

gave Aswell a free hand to select from the book manuscript what was publishable but he answered questions and gave advice whenever he was consulted. The second person, Elizabeth Nowell, knew more about Wolfe's recent work and intentions than anyone else. She continued to be the agent for magazine publication, and she was ready to serve Aswell with the same vigor she had given so generously to Wolfe. She took Wolfe's rough table of contents and annotated it for Aswell, identifying the sections and their origins and indicating, when possible, what Wolfe had planned to do with this part or that.

With the help of Perkins and Miss Nowell, Aswell soon had the manuscript under control. Of the four major parts into which Wolfe had divided it, he put aside the first about the Joyner ancestry; he reserved the last part, which covered George Webber's later education and was entitled "You Can't Go Home Again," for a later volume; and he set to work to fashion parts two and three into a single book, using Wolfe's title, *The Web and the Rock*.[2] The material about Webber's childhood and youth was fairly easy to deal with. For the most part, Aswell had only to remove most of the carefully hoarded scraps from "K 19" and *Of Time and the River* that Wolfe had not wanted to give up without one more attempt to salvage. Then, too, as Aswell lived with the manuscript, he became familiar with Wolfe's method of knitting material together and began to practice it himself. He was, for example, able to take three different pieces Wolfe had written about the people in George Webber's neighborhood and from them to construct Chapter 6, "The Street of the Day," and Chapter 8, "The People of the Night."[3]

A few other alterations were necessary, mostly to establish transitions. Also, Aswell did not want to invite any more libel suits, so he wrote to members of the Wolfe family asking about the sources of the characters. A few names and identifying characteristics had to be changed; for instance, Wolfe's chapter "The Baker's Truck" became "The Butcher" by judicious substitution of a few words here and there.[4]

With the third part of the manuscript, which Wolfe had entitled "Love's Bitter Mystery," Aswell had more of a tussle. Wolfe had tried to write about his love affair for eight years. He had worked on it in different moods in 1930, 1931, 1932, 1935, 1937, and 1938, but he was never really satisfied with what he was making of it. After a spell of writing or revision, he would set it aside and go on to something else. Thus Aswell had before him a mass of undigested gobbets, some of which came from the period of Wolfe's passionate outpourings, some from his period of satire about Joe Doaks, and some from his period of social criticism. Some episodes had gone through cycles of revision, others had lain untouched for six or seven years. Then, too, some of the material appeared in different combinations—for example, Wolfe had taken early scenes with Mr. and Mrs. Jack, with Lily Mandell, and with other members of the theatrical circle and had worked them into "The Party at Jack's."

Wolfe had always planned a simple sequence for his lovers: meeting, falling in love, happiness, jealousy, quarrels, and parting. But since he had returned to fairly exact autobiographical chronology in his narrative, his love story extended over several years and was interrupted by travels and reunions. All Aswell knew was what Miss Nowell told him: that Wolfe intended to rewrite the whole in his less plethoric style.[5]

Taking this disparate collection of chapters, Aswell did a piece of creative editing. He concentrated Wolfe's attenuated love story, rearranged sections, placed together all of Webber's European wanderings and memories of Esther, toned down the violence of Webber's horrible denunciations, and made a coherent, effective narrative out of what Wolfe had left him. The one insurmountable problem was how to work in "The Party at Jack's," with its symbolic prophecy of the crumbling of class structure. Finally, because of its tone and its theme, which suited the mature years of George Webber, he had to follow Wolfe's arrangement and hold it for the next volume.

The conclusion of *The Web and the Rock* proved to be both easy and difficult. Long ago Wolfe had planned to end "The October Fair" with the reflections of his hero in a Munich hospital. He had worked over this section several times, but since he always had trouble with endings, he was not ready to let go of it yet. In his manuscript he left two versions,[6] one of which he revised hastily in order to bring "Love's Bitter Mystery" to a conclusion. He had, at least, attempted a transition to the final part of the book by bringing in the phrase, "You can't go home again." But it was no real finish. Since Aswell did not feel he had the right to add anything himself, he took what he had. He pieced the two versions together and left the material in its unsatisfactory state.[7]

From the time of his first bewilderment over the manuscript,

Aswell had labored about eight months to construct a book in eight narrative units. Using Wolfe's words where he could, he wrote a few paragraphs, which he placed in italics, linking the large narrative chunks together. *The Web and the Rock* was published, very late in the spring schedule, on June 22, 1939. No acknowledgment was made of Edward Aswell's guiding hand, even though he did more to bring Wolfe's book into order than Maxwell Perkins had done with *Of Time and the River*.

II

When Wolfe turned away from the Gant hexology to write a book about "the innocent man discovering life," he had in mind, as he told his friends, works like *Don Quixote, Candide, Pickwick Papers, Wilhelm Meister's Apprenticeship* and *The Idiot*. Of these books, *The Web and the Rock* is most like *Don Quixote* in its philosophical core, because, more than just telling a story about an education in living, it deals with the problem of illusion and reality. As Cervantes had shown both the folly and the wisdom of imaginative self-deception and both the limitation and strength of holding fast to fact, so Wolfe presents this double view. In a way Wolfe is tackling the same problem he had treated in *Look Homeward, Angel*—the conflict between idealism and realism. But the character George Webber is a more effective symbolic creation than Eugene Gant.

Cervantes employed two characters who represented the polarity of the human psyche, with its tendencies to both idealism and realism. Wolfe uses one character who swings back and forth—gloriously transcending harsh fact by imagination but becoming entrapped by illusion; happily recognizing "things as they are"[8] but shrinking before stark realities. By presenting Webber's ever-widening world of experience, Wolfe follows his hero's stumbling search for equilibrium.

For the psychological origin of these two ways of looking at life, Wolfe sets up a simple dualism of reason and irrationality in his character. George Webber has a divided heritage: his father is a Northerner, his mother a Southerner. The North represents reason, order, and control. The South represents the realm of the unconscious, with all its inherent powers and dangers: intuition, impulsiveness, violence, superstition. But a pull too far in either direction is harmful. As young Webber sees it, "If you get too North, it gets no good. Everything gets frozen and dried up. But if you get too South, it is no good either, and it also gets rotten. If you get too North, it gets rotten, but in a cold dry way. If you get too South, it gets rotten not in a dry way . . . but in a horrible, stagnant, swampy, stenchlike humid sort of way. . . ." [9]

The boy fears his maternal endowment. He hears "lost voices of his kinsmen long ago" as he listens to ruminative tales from his great-aunt Maw (a symbolic mother-name and suggestive, too, of devouring) or his Uncle Mark. He sees a picture of mountaineer ignorance, superstition, poverty, and laziness. As George looks at the town of Libya Hill, he recognizes that the present-day poor whites of the West Side come from the mountains. Since they seem to him brutish and malevolent, he recoils in horror at the thought of his connection with them and their ways.

This poor-white world is one kind of reality he cannot face. He cannot endure the spectacle that "destroyed every proud illusion of the priceless value, dignity and sanctity of his individual life." The spawning of human life in this poverty-ridden section of town does not seem possible. Could man in his dignity be begotten this way? "Why, they had got him between brutish snores at some random waking of their lust in the midwatches of the night! They had got him in a dirty corner back behind a door in the hideous unprivacy of these rickety wooden houses, begotten him standing in a fearful secrecy between apprehensive whisperings to make haste, lest some of the children hear!" [10]

With relief George turns to the figure of his father, a symbol of solidity who builds houses with brick. He is a rational, orderly man, a skilled worker surrounded by the sights and odors of masculinity. George creates an elaborate illusion about his father's world. It seems to him full of light, warmth, and bright colors; it has a romantic quaintness "like a Currier and Ives print." His father's place of origin in Pennsylvania is brought to him in a vision of opulence and generosity. The cities of the North are to George like Dick Whittington's dream of a London paved with gold. A golden light bathes the vision of the city, from the morning sun "that shines through ancient glass into a room of old dark brown" to the evening splendor of the theaters "shining with full-golden warmth and body on full-golden figures of the women, on fat red plush, . . . and on the gilt sheaves and cupids and cornucopias." This brave new world combines all young George's dreams of triumph and fame.

The city flashed before him like a glorious jewel, blazing with countless rich and brilliant facets of a life so good, so bountiful, so strangely and constantly beautiful and interesting, that it seemed intolerable that he should miss a moment of it. He saw the streets swarming with the figures of great men and glorious women, and he walked among them like a conqueror, winning fiercely and exultantly by his talent, courage, and merit the greatest tributes that the city had to offer, the highest prize of power, wealth, and fame, and the great emolument of love. There would be villainy and knavery as black and sinister as hell, but he would smash it with a blow, and drive it cringing to its hole. There would be heroic men and lovely women, and he would win and take a place among the highest and most fortunate people on earth.[11]

Later, when George travels North to New York, he is too excited by the approach to the golden city to allow the reality of the garbage dumps and grimy factories to trouble him. He maintains his illusion as long as he can against "the life of subways, of rebreathed air, of the smell of burned steel, weariness, and the exhausted fetidity of a cheap rented room." [12] But finally, the illusion blasted, he finds himself, lonely, unhappy, unloved, and unrecognized among the crowd of "ciphers" who inhabit the city.

George Webber's boyhood in Libya Hill provides plenty of evidence of what life is really like. Chance mutilations and deaths occur on the street where he lives. The violence and cruelty of which men are capable are displayed all around him—especially in the "inhuman vitality" of the butcher and his wife and in the lynching of Dick Prosser. Wide-eyed, he absorbs it and accepts it: "Great God! this being just the way things are, how strange, and plain, and savage, sweet and cruel, lovely, terrible, and mysterious, and how unmistakable and familiar all things are!" [13] But this does not prevent him from indulging in the intoxication of illusion, which is occasionally interrupted by stories of the Joyner past, such as the account of the unfathomable behavior of Major Joyner, whose dreams of learning and culture led to the neglect of his wretched, starving children.

When George Webber goes to college, illusion surrounds two of his mentors, Jim Randolph, the athlete, and Jerry Alsop, the would-be intellectual. George looks on them as gods or fathers, but as his experience grows, he levels them down. He comes to recognize that each of these figures is himself overcome by a failure to face reality. Jim Randolph romanticizes himself as a leader and general paragon without seeing that he can only assume this role among adolescents. Jerry Alsop, who plays Doctor Pangloss to Webber's Candide, is betrayed by his whole view of life.[14] His bright-colored reading of literature cannot perceive the lower depths of Dickens's pessimism and his understanding of good and evil is as elementary as a checkerboard.

Webber's English teacher, Professor Ware, the man of fact, is equally limited. He has "trapped himself among petty things." [15] Nevertheless, he is able to speak prophetically about the further education of George Webber and even to offer a key to imaginative control: "You will never make a philosopher, Brother Webber. You will spend several years quite pleasantly in Hell, Getting the Facts. After that, you may make a poet." [16]

The promise of the shining city associated with his father's world lures Webber to New York. Here he spends his years in hell, getting the facts, and he becomes a writer. Even in his reading he has begun to penetrate beyond words, "to stare straight through language like a man who, from the very fury of his looking, gains a superhuman intensity of vision, so that he no longer sees merely the surfaces of things but seems to look straight through a wall." [17]

But his loneliness in New York gives rise to another fantasy. With all the elaborate detail of wish-fulfillment, he conjures up a vision of a beautiful, rich, devoted woman who welcomes him to her house, her library, and her bed. And the second half of *The Web and the Rock* presents the realistic re-enactment of this fantasy.

George Webber falls in love with Mrs. Jack, a beautiful Jewish woman who is a fashionable member of the New York theatrical set. As a scene designer for the theater, she takes her place easily in Webber's world of illusion. It seems at first that his boyhood dream of triumph in the glittering city and his youthful erotic fantasy have both come true. After a time, he recognizes that the great love of his life is only an adulterous affair, and he tires of the pretensions that swirl around her life in the theater. When her friends in a publishing house reject his book, his imagination churns up new fantasies, this time in jealous hatred of the woman who truly loves him and believes in his genius. As he broods, overcome by mad delusions, visions of her betrayal visit him, and scenes of dishonored, emasculated men entrapped by a Jewish *belle dame sans merci* play through his mind. The happiness disappears, and Webber and the woman descend to mean-spirited altercations. The affair breaks up as Webber embarks for Europe.

He wanders fitfully through several countries until a crack on the head in a Munich beer hall subdues him. In the concluding chapter, Webber carries on an imaginary dialogue between himself and his body, and he learns to accept the limitations of flesh. The conclusion is a poor one for this book, for it is unrelated to the love story and it has little to do with the problem of imagination. With further work on his manuscript, Wolfe would have cleared up this difficulty, for a more satisfactory conclusion to "Love's Bitter Mystery" is fore-shadowed in a chapter that Wolfe had added to this part of his book in 1937.[18] In a scene just after the publishers have returned his book, Webber says soberly to Esther Jack:

The shining city of my youth and dream is a warren of grimed brick and stone. Nothing shines the way I thought it would—there is no Perfection. And instead of the proud Gibson girl of childhood fancy, I met—you.
. . .The world is a better place than I thought it was. . .a far, far better and more shining place! And life is fuller, richer, deeper—with all its dark and tenemented slums—than the empty image of a schoolboy's dream. And Mrs. Jack, and other women, too. . .are greater, stronger, richer people than a Gibson girl. . . .I have soiled my soul and scarred my spirit by inexpiable crimes against you. I have reviled you, Mrs. Jack, been cruel and unkind to you, repaid your devotion with a curse, and put you out of doors. Nothing is the way I thought it was going to be, but, Mrs. Jack, Mrs. Jack—with all your human faults, errors, weaknesses, and imperfections, your racial hysteria, and your possessiveness—you are the best and truest friend I ever had, the only one who has ever stuck to me through thick and thin, stood by me and believed in me to the finish. You are no Gibson Girl, dear Mrs. Jack, but you are so much the best, the truest, noblest, greatest, and most beautiful woman that I ever saw or knew, that the rest are nothing when compared to you.[19]

The critical response to *The Web and the Rock* was divided—praise for the new display of controlled power, blame for old sins of excess. For instance, Howard Mumford Jones wrote in the *Boston Transcript,* "There are episodes. . .more brilliantly written, more powerfully seen than can be found in the work of any other recent novelist. There are also passages which contain as much genuinely bad writing as can anywhere be found." [20] Many reviewers recognized that the second part of the book picked up the autobiographical narrative from *Of Time and the River*, and they did not care for the old Wolfe manner in contrast to the new. George Stevens, writing in the *Saturday Review of Literature*, summed it up: "If *The Web and the Rock* had been published as two novels, it would be possible to say that the first half was Wolfe's best novel, the second half his most disappointing." [21] Others, as might be expected, were critical of the structure. As Clifton Fadiman expressed it, "The book ends, rather oddly, with a European-travel section, sufficiently interesting in itself but somehow tacked on, superfluous." [22]

Aswell had printed an excerpt from the "Statement of Purpose" (which Wolfe had written in February, 1928, but never sent to him) as a prefatory note by the author. Among other things, it said, "This novel. . .marks not only a turning away from the books I have written in the past, but a genuine spiritual and artistic change. It is the most objective novel I have written." This note did Wolfe's reputation no good at all, because the statement referred to a book more like *You Can't Go Home Again*. Most critics took issue with it to say that Wolfe was critically blind to think he was taking a new direction. With the general reader, however, Aswell's painstaking labor was rewarded. Harper had a publisher's success, with even the first edition running to 31,126 copies.

It is unlikely that Wolfe would ever have rewritten the old material that went into the love story in *The Web and the Rock*, for over the years he had revised and rearranged the episodes again and again. Nor would he ever have cast the material aside, for it drew upon the most important relationship of his adult life. Even though in planning his next publication he had considered abandoning it several times, he always ended up by working it into his new scheme. A close look at the second half of the book as it now stands suggests that he was right to hold on to it. If the point is granted that this portion of the unfinished work is structurally defective (and especially that the travelogue at the end is digressively out of place), yet it still may be argued that the last half of *The Web and the Rock* has been abused.

If it seems stylistically intemperate, Wolfe's writing in that portion of the book is still appropriate to a story about a passionate and sensitive young man responding to the excitements of the golden or the brazen metropolis and appropriate to a story of love and terrible jealousy. In fact, critics who have quailed at the sections about George Webber's troubled love affair have usually done so on the wrong grounds. They find the anti-Semitism, the violent quarrels, and Webber's motiveless malignity too painful—the products of a mentally unhealthy state. But they seem to ignore the fact that Wolfe wished to set forth his "Vision of Death in April" on a Wagnerian scale and that the style builds the scenes and meditations they find too strong. Wolfe scarcely excuses his hero. "An evil splinter passed through his brain like a poisoned arrow," he writes as he is about to describe one of Webber's jealous states. A genuine criticism of Wolfe's unsatisfactory motivation for Webber's unjust treatment of Esther is that in writing autobiographical fiction he was unable to see or to admit that Esther is rejected because she is a mother-substitute. Thus Wolfe did the best he could with the rejection and attributed it to madness: "That spring—in the green sorcery of that final, fatal, and ruinous April—a madness which was compounded of many elements took possession of him and began to exert completely its mastery of death, damnation, and horror over the whole domain of his body, mind, and spirit." [23]

Further, this "October Fair" material contains one of Wolfe's finest characterizations, his picture of Esther Jack. Nor is the handling of Esther a set piece. She is developed over a series of chapters and eventually plays an important part in what Wolfe has to say about art, about intellectual gluttony, and about a way of looking at life itself.

She is introduced casually. A few identifying tags are pinned on her: she slips her wedding ring on and off her finger nervously, she cups her hand to her ear and inquires, "Hah?" She is merry and not at all self-conscious. When Webber sees her in the context of the theater, he associates her with "busy hands," and he respects her competence. When their love affair begins, she has an admirable directness and frankness: "'Listen,' she said, 'there is nothing to tell between you and me. There is nothing to explain. When I saw you on the boat I knew that I had always known you, and it has been the same way ever since.'" [24]

The enrichment of the characterization begins when Wolfe presents her as the embodiment of Webber's recapture of lost time. As she weaves her web of language, she brings alive not only her past but the whole atmosphere of the nineties and the early twentieth century. The web of reminiscence goes back to her childhood: back to a letter to her "Dere Uncle Honeys" about her dog, Roy; back to her memories of her father, Joe Linder, who speaks with an actor's rhetoric, full of word-play on famous lines from the stage and the exaggerated joking typical of a man who loves children; back to her excursions with her father to see the designer of the Brooklyn Bridge or to talk backstage with the great actor, Richard Brandell.[25] Esther's treasury of images has been built up by the variety that is characteristic of city life. The impressions are vivid because even as a little girl she could fasten onto little details and feel a sensuous response to them. She tells Brandell:

Sometimes it's a leaf, and sometimes it's a pocket of a coat and sometimes it's a button or a coin, and sometimes it's an old hat, or an old shoe on the floor. Sometimes it's a tobacco store, the cigars tied up in bundles on the counter, and all of the jars where they keep the pipe tobacco.... Sometimes it's the design of the elevated structure across the street where a station is, and sometimes it's the smell of bolts of new, clean cloth, and sometimes it's the way you feel when you make a dress—you can feel the design go out of the tips of your fingers into the cloth as you shape it, and you feel yourself in it....[26]

Webber recognizes this as her "vital quality of joy" in living.

Using Esther, Wolfe gives a unique twist to the Golden Age myth. Her pictures of her early years have the golden glow, and New York is her Garden of Eden. Wolfe had Milton's garden in mind as he developed the story of the love affair. What is now the third paragraph in the chapter, "April, Late April," had begun (before Aswell cut it): "'Sweet is the breath of morn, her rising sweet, with charm of earliest birds'—and that is the way the springtime came that year. Not the whole glory of the great plantation of the earth could have outdone the glory of the city streets that Spring." [27] Esther is the Eve of that city garden, and even after Webber leaves her, the words "With thee conversing I forget all time" go through her head as she thinks of her Adam.[28] There is no serpent and there is no apple to bite in this story. If there is any fall of Man, however, it is through George's knowledge of good and evil about city existence.

In fact, it is through Webber's shifts in feeling toward Esther that Wolfe conveys his own double attitude toward urban life. In his life with her at first, Webber sees all the vigor and enterprise of the city as a social and cultural center, besides all the charm of the old and the ordinary. He sees her life in the theater, her place in café society, her sense of the intricate detail of the city's face—the old furniture shops, the brownstone houses, the bazaar of the Lower East Side. Later, he associates her with the abuses of privilege, with the corruption and heartlessness of city life, from Park Avenue, "a world of lives that had no earth in them, a world of burnished myrmidons," to the common pavements trod by men whose juiceless existence is betrayed by the withered vocabulary of "Sure, I know! I know! You're telling me! . . .I know! You know how it is, don't you? . . .Nah-h!" [29]

Since Wolfe wanted his own love of life to prevail in all his work, he uses the character of Esther to express his abiding optimism during the time that George Webber is overcome by a sense of defeat in his life and his work. Even after Webber quarrels with Esther and abuses her and she sees momentarily the brutalities of city life as he saw them, Esther brings forth affirmation in the same way David Hawke stood up to challenge in Boston. As she gazes around her, she questions what she finds:

Had the city suckled at its iron breast a race of brute automatons, a stony, asphalt compost of inhuman manswarm ciphers, snarling their way to ungrieved deaths with the harsh expletives of sterile words, repeated endlessly, and as rootless of the earth, and all the blood and passion of a living man, as the great beetles of machinery they hurled at insane speed through the furious chaos of the streets?

No. She could not think it was true. Upon this rock of life, and in these stupendous streets, there was as good earth as any that the foot could find to walk upon, as much passion, beauty, warmth, and living richness as any place on earth could show." [30]

And her eye picks out, in the city scene, symbols of life struggling against weakness and time: hospital patients soaking up air and sunshine, the river flowing ceaselessly, and a tree growing between brick walls putting out its April leaves.

Wolfe even gives to Esther the answers to Webber's problem of artistic expression. She herself is an artist who knows that persistence and hard work are the means to success. [31] She also has the perception to see the universal in the particular, "a forest in a leaf, the whole earth in a single face." She is therefore able to discern the root of

Webber's problem, that he feels fear and defeat because of his creative megalomania. Her solution, which she thinks over while Webber is making another kind of self-assessment in a Munich hospital, is a simple one:

What horror did you want to flee? Must you forever be a fool without a faith and eat your flesh?
"The horror of eight million faces!"
Remember eight—know one.
"The horror of two million books!"
Write one that has two thousand words of wisdom in it.
"Each window is a light, each light a room, each room a cell, each cell a person!"
All rooms, all windows, and all persons for your hunger? No. Return to one: fill all that room with light and glory, make it shine as no other room ever shone before, and all life living on this earth will share it with you.[32]

All that has been said about the function of Esther in *The Web and the Rock* reveals something, too, of the genuine abundance with which the book overflows. Not only in the second half of the book but throughout the whole, there are scattered catalogues, panoramas, montages, poetic sermons, and editorials which, when added to the variety of characters and vignettes, bulk out an impression of teeming American life. And not merely of contemporary life. Wolfe shows quite frequently an ability to examine his scene and, like an archaeologist contemplating an artifact, to imagine the history of human travail behind every object. Here, for example, is a passage about the identity, the sense of "Place," in the Lower East Side of Manhattan:

Call it an old saddle, worn by an old rider and sweat-cured by an old horse; call it an old shoe, a battered hat, a worn chair, the hollowed roundness of an old stone step that has been worn by seven centuries of feet—in these things you will find some of the qualities that made the East. Each drop of sweat, each drop of blood, each song, each boy's shout, each child's cry, had worked its way into the lintels of the East, had got into each dark and narrow hallway, was seasoned there into the creaking of each worn step, the sagging of each spare rail...."[33]

The Web and the Rock has that same anthology-like quality found in *Of Time and the River,* but it has a thematic development absent from the earlier book.

NOTES

1. HCL*49M-209(19). Aswell labeled his notes (and included was his annotation of Wolfe's table of contents), "Notes I made to help bring order out of chaos." Further, in an interview with me in 1949, Aswell said that when he first went to work on the manuscript it was "a mess."

2. See Appendix for Wolfe's division of the book into parts and chapters.

3. When the book was in galley proof, "People of the Night" was cut out. Probably Aswell was afraid this assembly of vicious characters might provoke more lawsuits. The character Judge Bland made his first appearance in this chapter.

4. The alterations were of this sort: W&R, p. 130, "sausages and sandwiches" had been "pies and cakes"; W&R, p. 118, Lampley's cut had been a burn.

5. HCL*49M-209(19). Elizabeth Nowell's notes to Aswell, written on the table of contents, read: "He told me he was going to rewrite Oct. Fair—that he'd been too close to it when he did it, that it would now be rewritten as 'emotion recollected in tranquility' and typical of all young men in first love affair." Further: "When we did April Late April for Mercury I exclaimed at difference between old, lush, too-adjectival style of early Oct. Fair as compared to his new style (Summer '37). He agreed and tried to tone it down, make it less personal, less over-written, etc. Later when we were discussing all the stories we sold that year, I said I liked April Late April least and he agreed. He would sure have rewritten Oct. Fair in new style."

6. A third version was placed at the end of the whole manuscript as part of "A Farewell to the Fox."

7. C. Hugh Holman, in an excellent survey of Wolfe scholarship and criticism, "Thomas Wolfe, a Bibliographical Study," *Texas Studies in Language and Literature,* I (Autumn, 1959), 427-45, has raised the question of a need for critical editions of W&R and YCGHA.

8. Wolfe perhaps used this phrase because it was the one Shaw's Don Juan used to describe the kind of reality found in Heaven, as opposed to the kind of illusion in which the inhabitants of Hell indulged (*Man and Superman,* Act III).

9. W&R, p. 15.

10. W&R, p. 60. Walter F. Taylor, in "Thomas Wolfe and the Middle-Class Tradition," *South Atlantic Quarterly,* LII (October, 1953), 546, sees George Webber's abhorrence of slum dwellers as a reflection of Wolfe's middle-class attitudes. On the contrary, it betrays a rejection of recent origins in a lower class.

11. W&R, pp. 91-93.

12. W&R, p. 229.

13. W&R, p. 21.

14. In one earlier draft Wolfe had given him the name Pangleek.

15. Wolfe's portrait of Edwin Greenlaw here is astute. He describes him as a great teacher, but as a scholar who, in spite of his dedication to research, "wasted himself compiling anthologies."

16. W&R, p. 217.

17. W&R, p. 273.

18. Chapters 32 to 35 of W&R, written in the spring of 1937, were among the last additions Wolfe made to the Esther Jack story.

19. W&R, pp. 522-23.

20. July 1, 1939.

21. June 24, 1939, pp. 5-6.

22. *New Yorker*, XV (June 24, 1939), 69-70, reprinted in Walser, pp. 149-53.

23. W&R, p. 539.

24. W&R, p. 361.

25. All this material is based on stories that Mrs. Bernstein had told Wolfe. Brandell is Richard Mansfield.

26. W&R, p. 421.

27. Cf. W&R, p. 441. Note, too, how the rest of the passage echoes Eve's speech, *Paradise Lost*, IV, 650-57.

28. W&R, p. 688. This is *Paradise Lost*, IV, 639.

29. Louis Rubin, in *Thomas Wolfe, The Weather of His Youth* (Baton Rouge, 1955), pp. 101-12, sees five stages in George Webber's "romance with the city" in the two posthumous novels.

30. W&R, p. 574.

31. The "arc" from inception to completion of an artistic work (W&R, p. 462) was Mrs. Bernstein's metaphor as she discussed her own work.

32. W&R, p. 686.

33. W&R, p. 324.

28

A LONG WAY FROM HOME

WHEN HE FACED THE WORK ON THE NEXT VOLUME, ASWELL HAD an easier time assembling it, for he did not have a souvenir collection to deal with.[1] Wolfe had not been writing about the later years of his autobiographical hero long enough to have a hodge-podge of extraneous pieces to cram here and there into his narrative. But at the same time, Aswell had in his hands a crude product. Since this was mostly work that Wolfe had turned out in the last two years, it had been laid aside to season, but it had not yet been brought back into the workshop to be revised or reassembled. Much of it was hastily done first draft. All of the hero's adventures with Lloyd McHarg had been dictated hurriedly in late 1936 and had sat untouched since. Almost all the sketches about the House of Rodney had been scribbled out in early 1936 and still awaited revision. Some sections were incomplete. No scenes with Foxhall Edwards and George Webber together had been written at all. Indeed, Wolfe's emotional response to his return to Asheville in 1937, which inspired the title "You Can't Go Home Again," had not been given its full fictional treatment and had to be cut out of the book. Editorial doctoring was badly needed.

Aswell's critical service here was a sensible reordering. Whereas Wolfe had placed his episodes to follow the chronology of his life (even though it meant breaking up groups of chapters he had written in thematic blocks), Aswell rearranged them into units. He grouped together all the pictures of boom days in Libya Hill. He gathered up the scattered reactions to George Webber's book. He made the European trips into one. He placed the material about fame in the best possible sequence.

Besides cutting and rearranging, Aswell tampered with Wolfe's style as he had not done before. With dictated first drafts, that tampering was absolutely necessary. But beyond this, Aswell was aware of the criticism that had been directed at stylistic instability in *The Web and the Rock,* and he altered sections of the manuscript Wolfe had written in the early 1930's in order to make them conform to the later style which dominated the book. Some passages were tidied up by Aswell in a way that would have improved several of the rhetorical pronouncements in Wolfe's earlier novels. Thus the famous passage "What Is Man?" (which had originally been a part of Wolfe's chapter, "The Ship," in *The Web and the Rock*) was made more precise and less repetitious by the editorial pencil. Here, for example, are changes Aswell made in one section of it:

WOLFE'S MANUSCRIPT

Behold his works:

He needed speech to ask for bread—and he had Christ! He needed songs to sing in battle— and he had Homer! He needed words to curse his enemies—and he had Dante, he had Voltaire, he had Swift! He needed cloth to cover up his hairless, puny flesh against the seasons—and he wove the robes of Solomon, he made the garments of the great kings, he made the samite for the young knights. He needed walls and a roof to *shield him from his enemies, to cover him from cruel seasons, and to propitiate him with his God, and he made Blois and Chartres and Fountains Abbey!* He was born to creep upon the earth, and he made great wheels; he sent great engines thundering down the rails, he launched great *engines in* the air, he put great ships *like this one* upon the *strong* sea.

Plagues wasted him, and cruel wars destroyed his strongest sons, but fire, flood, and famine could

ASWELL'S REVISION

Behold his works:

He needed speech to ask for bread—and he had Christ! He needed songs to sing in battle— and he had Homer! He needed words to curse his enemies—and he had Dante, he had Voltaire, he had Swift! He needed cloth to cover up his hairless, puny flesh against the seasons—and he wove the robes of Solomon, he made the garments of the great kings, he made the samite for the young knights. He needed walls and a roof to shelter him—and he made Blois! He needed a temple to propitiate his God—and he made Chartres and Fountains Abbey! He was born to creep upon the earth— and he made great wheels, he sent great engines thundering down the rails, he launched great wings into the air, he put great ships upon the angry sea.

Plagues wasted him, and cruel wars destroyed his strongest sons, but fire, flood, and famine could not quench him, no, nor the inexorable grave: his sons leaped shouting from his dying loins. The shaggy bison with his thews of thunder died upon the plains; the fabled mammoths of the unrecorded ages are vast scaffoldings of dry, insensate loam; the panthers have learned caution and move carefully among tall grasses to the water hole—*yet there is not one of these that could not stamp man's life to powder with a movement of his fast strong foot.* Man *lived among* the senseless Nihilism of the universe *because he loved life. He believed in life and hated death.* There is *only* one belief, *there is only* one faith, *and in* that *belief* is man's glory, *in that belief is* his immortality, *in that belief is his triumph over eternity.* That *belief* is a belief in life *instead of death.* Man *has loved* life, and because of this he is great, he is glorious, he is beautiful. *He loves life* and his beauty is everlasting. He *has lived* below the senseless stars and *he has written* meanings in them. He *has lived* in fear, in toil, in agony, and in unending tumult, but if the blood foamed bubbling from his wounded lungs, at every breath he drew, he would still love life more dearly than an end of breathing.[2]

not quench him. No, nor the inexorable grave—his sons leaped shouting from his dying loins. The shaggy bison with his thews of thunder died upon the plains; the fabled mammoths of the unrecorded ages are vast scaffoldings of dry, insensate loam; the panthers have learned caution and move carefully among the tall grasses to the water hole; and man lives on amid the senseless nihilism of the universe.

For there is one belief, one faith, that is man's glory, his triumph, his immortality—and that is his belief in life. Man loves life, and loving life, hates death, and because of this he is great, he is glorious, he is beautiful, and his beauty is everlasting. He lives below the senseless stars and writes his meanings in them. He lives in fear, in toil, in agony, and in unending tumult, but if the blood foamed bubbling from his wounded lungs at every breath he drew, he would still love life more dearly than an end of breathing.

The hand of the editor intrudes more often in *You Can't Go Home Again* than readers have suspected. By this time, Aswell identified himself with Wolfe to the extent that he felt free to play author with the manuscript. Whereas Aswell's part in *The Web and the Rock* may be likened to that played by Ezra Pound, "the greater craftsman," in bringing Eliot's *Waste Land* into final form, his contribution to *You Can't Go Home Again* is like George Kaufman's doctoring of a faulty script for the stage.

Once again, Aswell linked the narrative blocks together by writing summaries to be set in italics.[3] The book was ready for the fall publishing season in 1940 and was issued without any notice of Aswell's editorial presence.

Since it came from the same manuscript as *The Web and the Rock,* the new book continued to play contrapuntally with illusion and reality—this time in the hero's pursuit of fame, "the bright medusa." Webber finds that fame in his home town only stirs up hostility. When his novel, *Home to Our Mountains,* hits Libya Hill, good friends suffer from malicious gossip as a result of Webber's portraits, and injured fellow townsmen send letters threatening his life. In New York, fame only invites people to use him, and Webber once again plays his role as the innocent dupe. A wealthy man is eager to be George's patron, until *Home to Our Mountains* fails to win the Pulitzer Prize. One woman seizes upon him for social opportunity ("'I want you to use your influence to get me into the Cosmopolis Club,' she whispered passionately"). Other women seek him because they want rescue from sexual or spiritual bankruptcy. Later George observes that fame has turned Lloyd McHarg, America's most honored man of letters, into a restless automaton. It is too bad that Aswell did not make some use of Wolfe's resolution of the search, an allegorical dialogue reminiscent of *Everyman.* Webber awakes one morning in Brooklyn to find that fickle Fame has walked out on him and only Dame Care remains. He addresses her: "Dame Care—why must you stay when all the rest of them have gone? They were a goodly company at first—Youth, Hope, and Vanity—and those four graces, Fame, Beauty, Fortune, Love—Dame Care, there was a time when I was not alone and you were with me. Now all of them are gone, save you, whom I had so forgotten—now won't you leave me too?.... Then, Care," he says, "if not the fairest of your daughters, the most faithful —follow me. In you, at any rate, chaste comrade of my sleepless night, and grave companion of our mortal sorrow, I have met a faithful woman." [4]

Closely associated with the search for fame is Wolfe's treatment of the predicament of the American artist who tries to express the quality and variety of his experience. Much of what Wolfe says is only a reflection of his own personal problems as a writer. *You Can't*

Go Home Again contains in George Webber's conversations with Randy Shepperton a defense of the autobiographical method. Webber attempts to make a distinction between the artist drawing upon his experience ("Man Creating") and the artist living as a social being ("Man-Alive"). The trouble is that the two become confused for Webber. And he admits it: "If only I could tell myself that every word and phrase and incident in the book had been created at the top of my bent and with the impartial judgment of unrancorous detachment! But I know it is not true. So many words come back to me, so many whip-lash phrases, that must have been written in a spirit that had nothing to do with art or my integrity." [5] To be truly impersonal and objective, he feels, he must strive harder after truth, to be what he calls "more autobiographical." The remedy is "to withhold nothing, to try to see and paint myself as I am—the bad along with the good, the shoddy alongside of the true." He is groping for a form, a vehicle to carry this truth. He is trying to write "something— a story—composed of all the knowledge I have, of all the living I've seen. Not the facts, you understand—not just the record of my life— but something truer than the facts—something distilled out of my experience and transmitted into a form of universal application." [6]

The paradox of George Webber's life as a novelist is that although he must immerse himself in the swirl of life and although he has unusual perception of the problems of humankind, he still has a sense of alienation from the people around him. In his Brooklyn apartment, neighbors like Mr. Marple are pleasantly friendly, but they have no more understanding of what he is doing than if he were an international spy. If Webber feels like a freak when he talks to ordinary people (for instance, the waiter who has "a great idea for a story"), he is equally worried by his distance from the intellectuals of his time. Since there is nothing fashionable about dealing with the great commonplaces, he feels isolated as he watches many of his contemporaries go down one cultish by-path after another.

As Wolfe follows George Webber's career, his moods and postures vary. There are times when he is the Whitmanesque superman overlooking the expanse of America ("Don't be frightened, it's not so big now, when your footstool is the Rocky Mountains"). There are times when he looks with a Spenglerian eye upon the human vermin scampering through their mazes of urban life. But, for the most part, he directs a sensitive critical scrutiny upon the social scene.

The distinguishing mark of *You Can't Go Home Again* is Wolfe's social criticism, and it takes a variety of forms. It is presented directly through scene and action in "I Have A Thing to Tell You" and "The Company." It is a whispered symbolic warning in Book II, "The World That Jack Built" (Aswell's title for "The Party at Jack's").[7] It emerges constantly in contrasts of suffering and luxury or of oppression and privilege—as in Webber's sight of the human derelicts seeking shelter from the winter night in public toilets near the towered wealth of Manhattan skyscrapers. Sometimes other characters besides Webber focus on it. Nebraska Crane, whom Wolfe wished to picture as the "man of nature," plans to settle down to farming when he retires from baseball. He refuses to be a part of the misuse of land for real estate speculation in Libya Hill, for he "conceived of the land as a place on which to live and of living on the land as a way of life."[8] Judge Rumford Bland, the blind man whom Wolfe made into an evil Tiresias, sees into the corruption of Libya Hill politics and chuckles with malicious satisfaction as he penetrates the pious veneer of Parson Flack, the political strong man of Libya Hill. Several characters become comic targets for social protest, but the hilarious snobbery of Daisy Purvis, the British charwoman who discourses on the Prince of Wales or the dwindling estates of the aristocracy, is given a sober turn when George Webber sees her heartless scorn of the English poor. Sometimes Wolfe himself as narrator voices his criticism directly, as in the long consideration of C. Green, the average American city-dweller, the product of the melting pot, the psychologically stunted victim of metropolitan life who has to commit suicide to assert his identity.

The narrative takes George Webber through the period of speculation, crash, and depression. What he sees makes him question the direction America is taking and ponder the apparent loss of spirit in its people. One of the many meanings of the statement "You can't go home again" is that you can't go back to an older America. Wolfe's emotional tension in facing up to change was so great that a motif of decline and fall recurs throughout the book. Webber sees the ruin of his home town, the decay of his beloved Germany, the crumbling of the capitalistic system represented by Mr. Jack, and a spirit of weariness and defeat everywhere he goes.

Yet, in the same way that Wolfe revealed to the audience at Purdue his faith in the common people despite all his disillusionments, so here he shows his faith is alive. It comes through in the shifting scenes of suffering humanity, in the contemplation of the suicide of "C. Green," in "The Promise of America," and in the final optimism of Webber's statement to Foxhall Edwards: "I believe that we are lost here in America, but I believe we shall be found." This is the faith that underlies his whole farewell letter to Fox. And it is a consciously self-deceptive faith. He agrees with Fox, the preacher of pessimism, that evils will continue to plague man. "Man was born to live, to suffer, and to die, and what befalls him is a tragic lot. There is no denying this in the final end. *But we must, dear Fox, deny it all along the way.*" [9] It is characteristic of Wolfe to put it in these terms —declaring the vital importance of the dream. For Wolfe had found the way of life for the "innocent man" who discovered that nothing was the way he thought it was going to be. He must be able to recognize evils and weaknesses and identify them clearly for what they are. But his life is worth living only if he struggles against them with a faith that they shall not prevail.

Because Wolfe's work frequently reveals a patronizing attitude toward the Negro, the Jew, the Irishman, or any person who does not come from old American stock, this statement about faith in the American people needs to be proved. A good example for argument is the chapter "The Promise of America," in which Wolfe pictures as strivers for fame a Negro boxer with his "black panther's paw," a Southern poor-white baseball player with "lean face steady as a hound's," and a Jewish student with "his greasy hair roached back in oily scrolls above the slanting cage of his painful and constricted brow." The adjectives and figures of speech are pejorative—even suggesting a lower level of creature. But what is important is that Wolfe as narrator identifies himself with each of them. For they are invoked as examples when he invites all seekers for fame to take a look at America: "O brothers, like our fathers in their time, we are burning, burning, burning in the night." We cannot question Wolfe's sincerity as he concludes: "So, then, to every man his chance—to every man, regardless of his birth, his shining, golden opportunity— to every man the right to live, to work, to be himself, and to become whatever thing his manhood and his vision can combine to make him —this, seeker, is the promise of America." [10]

Home may be a place of security, but it is also a place of ignorance and prejudice. Tom Wolfe had come a long way from home.

Since *You Can't Go Home Again* shows new facets of Wolfe's talent, it is regrettable that it is not a more satisfactory book as a whole. Although all Wolfe's books since *Look Homeward, Angel* lack cohesiveness, *You Can't Go Home Again* seems more choppy than any of the others. More than this, what Wolfe has to offer is spread more thinly over his pages. Had he lived, he would have spent a much longer time than he expected on this part of the manuscript before he was willing to let it go. It would have been a longer book, a denser book—perhaps his greatest book.

But despite its piecemeal quality and its lack of the Wolfean abundance, it was surprisingly well received. Coming as it did at the end of the 1930's, the social criticism had a powerful appeal. Further, the subdued manner of the autobiographical hero, who is mostly an observer of the action, led most reviewers to sense a maturity and resolution they had not found in Wolfe before. These comments are typical: "George Webber does grow up, not merely by fiat," "a Thomas Wolfe matured in understanding," "the new novel is far and away the finest, the most mature book he ever wrote," "he had become adult enough to draw some age-old truths about life," "this is the book of a man who had come to terms with himself." [11] For the first time, there was complaint that the publisher was not dealing fairly with the public or with Wolfe. Hamilton Basso in the *New Republic* denounced Harper and Brothers for their jacket blurbs that Wolfe had undertaken a new work in 1936 and "after several years" of labor had delivered to them the finished product before he died.[12] Basso knew that some of this writing had been done before 1936 and that Wolfe's later plans were still incomplete.

Having published the story of George Webber, Aswell picked through the remains to see what more might be gleaned. He took the incomplete history of the Joyners and a few other salvageable bits, added to them some of Wolfe's fugitive pieces scattered in various magazines, and published what he had gathered under the title, *The Hills Beyond,* in October, 1941. To this volume he appended "A Note on Thomas Wolfe" in which he revealed at last his part in the production of *The Web and the Rock* and *You Can't Go Home Again.* Although Aswell did a good deed in rescuing "The Lost Boy" from the oblivion of periodical publication, the rest of this volume has little value except as it shows the variety of things Wolfe turned his hand to.

The title piece about John Webber and the Joyners was written intermittently between 1933 and 1938, although old Looky Thar had walked the stage in *Welcome to Our City* [13] and the pompous Theodore had made his first appearance in *Mannerhouse*. It does not represent, as Aswell's note implies, the final phase of Wolfe as a writer.[14] The only part in which the Wolfean fire smolders is the story of young Edward Joyner that had been published as "The Bell Remembered" in 1936. The collection of anecdotal improvisation and the creation of legendary figures like Bear and Zack Joyner have attracted the interest of folklorists and regionalists but scarcely anyone else. With his excursion into tall tale and folk humor Wolfe tried hard. Unfortunately, it is all as consciously imitative as his attempts to write "folk drama" in his student days. He was working in a dead tradition like an antique-maker. The kind of legendizing that came naturally was the conversion of his own experience into living legend. He worked best recording the tales of home or the folkways and folk speech of city dwellers as they added color to the life of his autobiographical hero.

II

With the publication of *The Hills Beyond* we come to the end of a unique story of how a man wrote the kind of books he did and of how those books took on their published form. Although the story has been long and complicated, we should not lose sight of the fact that Thomas Wolfe's literary career was unhappily short. He passed from the literary scene only nine years after he entered upon it with *Look Homeward, Angel.*

He left behind a sizeable shelf—four huge novels and three volumes of shorter pieces. It is an uneven product, and more hands than his own fashioned it. Yet whatever is valuable or censurable is his own, for he was responsible for the themes, the characters, the episodic action, and the style.

It adds up to a remarkable achievement, wrought through struggle and persistence. All his work arose from "the material and experience of his own life"; [15] thus he was always on the job. When not writing, he sought experience, observed human activity critically, and pondered his responses to what he found. What he was after was the apprehension of that "condensed and heightened form of reality" [16] he called legend. Since the legend was to be distilled from multiplicity, he was sometimes staggered by his attempts to cope with "the billion forms of America." [17] He thought it was an American problem. But it was a twentieth-century problem and an urban problem—besides that, it was a problem for a man with an unusually vivid memory. He overcame it to extract a full measure of the life of his own time. In his cyclorama of the American scene and in his capture of the American temper, Wolfe left a living memorial of a segment of twentieth-century American life. He was able to characterize both the American of the 1920's, restless, individualistic, striving, and the American of the 1930's, sick with the economic ruin around him, yet believing in the latent resources of the nation and its people.

But Wolfe's work is not important merely because it can be read as social history. He raised his autobiographical hero above the level of realism to become an archetypal figure engaged in the quest for self-discovery and forced constantly to readjust his focus on life as he went along. And as he spun out the adventures, Wolfe asked essential questions about the great unsolved problems of mankind. Where do we come from? Where do we go? What is reality? What endures in the midst of change? What is the nature of man? What accumulation does he bring with him? What forces affect his life? How can he find happiness? With questions like these woven into the fabric of his books, Wolfe reveals a kinship with the great writers of world literature.

He called his pieces of autobiographical fiction novels. Because literary criticism of prose narrative was (and still is) in a rudimentary stage, Wolfe encountered the charge that he was not writing novels at all, and he was profoundly disturbed by it. If now we turned to Northrop Frye's distinctions among novel, confession, romance, and anatomy, we could perhaps employ a cumbersome, hyphenated term that would apply more accurately than the word novel.[18] But since editorial advice or arrangement pushed Wolfe's work toward the novel and since a set of usable critical terms has not been firmly established, we should let the label "novel" stick. One way or another, the quality Wolfe shares with the great novelists is his ability to create a little world and to people it with vital, memorable characters. A novelist, in Phyllis Bentley's apt metaphor, is a man perched on a high wall who describes to a group of listeners, unable to see over the wall, the activities of life on the opposite side.[19] In this situation, the author's task is that set down by Conrad, "to make you hear, to make you feel—it is, before all, to make you see." A writer of sufficient scope erects, or assumes, an acceptable metaphysic for this fictional world, and he repeats general truths of human nature that will find agreement in the hearts of his listeners. His characters, blocked from the scrutiny of the audience by the wall, must be sketched out vigorously and, for sympathy, their conduct must accord with general ethical notions. Since the events selected must seem significant to this audience, the subject matter should have a basic appeal for the "common reader."

Wolfe meets these requirements. He created a satisfactory fictional world, alive with characters of blood, bone, marrow, passion, feeling, because he tried to see in his individual experience what was universal. Though he sometimes could not step beyond his own personality and though he often failed to be orderly, we accept his world. As he sits, dangling his long legs over the wall, looking into the world of memory, he colors his scene for us excitedly with vivid, highly sensuous speech, which occasionally drops into quieter tones or explodes into mocking laughter. Since he is expansive, his world is bursting with variety; and since his people, in their relationships with each other and the world, are confronted with man's common problems, they are kin to us all. In order to hold us within the spell of his recreated world, he takes time to sing in dithyrambic strains, to survey the landscape as far as he can see, or to envision the promise of a nation. When we tire, he draws us back again as he reminds us soberly of the nature of man, his nobility, his savagery, and the puzzle of his destiny. Whatever Wolfe's lapses in taste and judgment, he has four basic essentials of a great novelist: scope, variety, emotional intensity, and a concern with common experience.

This is what he accomplished even though his time was up at the age of thirty-seven. As he lay on his hospital bed in Seattle, he thought with anguish of the work he had still to do. Yet, coming close to death had brought a mood of acceptance. "I know now I'm just a grain of dust," he said to Perkins in his last letter, "and I feel as if a great window has been opened on life I did not know about before." [20] Tom Wolfe would have liked to write about what he saw through that window.

NOTES

1. Of the thirty-four groups of chapters Wolfe had arranged in his final manuscript, twenty-four formed the basis for W&R and only eight for YCGHA.

2. HCL*46AM-7(59). Cf. YCGHA, pp. 435-36.

3. To see how Aswell tried to use Wolfe's words for these italicized transitions, cf. YCGHA, p. 398, paragraphs three and four; and the two final paragraphs of "God's Lonely Man" in HB, pp. 196-97.

4. HCL*46AM-7(65). Part of this appeared as "Fame and the Poet" in *American Mercury*, October, 1936. Aswell was apparently uneasy about allegory and did not even reprint this among the collected pieces in HB. Wolfe's figure of Dame Care is drawn from Goethe's *Faust*, Part II, Act V.

5. YCGHA, p. 355.

6. YCGHA, pp. 385-87. One suspects that the word "transmitted" was a typist's error for "transmuted."

7. Aswell took the title from one of Wolfe's chapter headings. William F. Kennedy, "Economic Ideas in Contemporary Literature—The Novels of Thomas Wolfe," *Southern Economic Journal*, XX (July, 1953), 42-43, notes that the title also means "the world that money built."

8. YCGHA, p. 80.

9. YCGHA, p. 737.

10. YCGHA, pp. 505-8.

11. These excerpts are from the following reviews: Stephen Vincent Benét, *Saturday Review of Literature*, XXII (September 21, 1940), 5; Henry Hart, *New Masses*, XXXVII (October 22, 1940), 25-26; *Newsweek*, XVI (September 23, 1940), 46; Burton Rascoe, *American Mercury*, LI (December, 1940), 493-94; J. Donald Adams, *New York Times Book Review*, September 22, 1940, p. 1.

12. CII (September 23, 1940), 422.

13. Edward Goodnow, who played the part in 1923, could still recite the lines when he was interviewed in 1949.

14. Aswell's statement has led critics astray in talking about Wolfe's possible future if he had lived. Muller suspected it might mean a decline of powers, and Rubin felt it showed a return to strength because Wolfe was once more writing about "the country and people he knew best."

15. SN, p. 572.

16. HCL*46AM-7(56), The World, the Oktoberfest, p. 1.

17. SN, p. 611.

18. Frye's discussion of "the four forms of fiction," in *Anatomy of Criticism* (Princeton, 1957), is the most penetrating theory of fiction in our time. But to follow his suggestions for the labeling of hybrid forms of fiction and call Wolfe's work novel-romance-confession-anatomy would be to adopt an unwieldy term.

19. *Some Observations on the Art of Narrative* (New York, 1948).

20. *Letters*, p. 777.

APPENDIX

THOMAS WOLFE'S ROUGH OUTLINE
OF HIS LAST BOOK

This typescript was left with Wolfe's final manuscript in the hands of Harper editor Edward Aswell. Each piece in the manuscript bundle was labeled according to its place (e.g., "Part I, Book I, The Joyner Genealogy"). The fact that only three "Books" are numbered and that none of the "chapters" is numbered indicates that Wolfe intended to revise extensively and to do a great deal of reweaving. A couple of items are crossed out, presumably by Aswell, who then moved the episode in question to another section of the manuscript. A few pieces here and there had no label, possibly because they were put into the manuscript after Wolfe's secretary, Miss Gwenn Jassinoff, had finished typing the rough outline. These were probably some of the "chapters" added in Aswell's handwriting.

The whole typescript is scribbled up with chatty explanatory notes by Elizabeth Nowell, who tried to indicate to Aswell what she knew of Wolfe's intentions for this piece or that. In the early part of the typescript, Aswell has marked an "X" by most of the items he chose for The Web and the Rock and for the title piece in The Hills Beyond. Some of the items chosen for You Can't Go Home Again in the last part of the typescript he marked with Roman numerals. In the first half of the typescript, most of the unused items are marked "Out" or "Dup[licate]."

Most of the items are identifiable—from their place in the posthumous novels, from their presence among the stack of eighty-one "Rejected Passages," HCL*46AM-7(65), or from copies found elsewhere among the Wolfe papers. The notes on the following pages indicate only briefly the nature of the material; nor do they indicate much of the duplication in varying versions that Wolfe included in his stack of typescript.

THE WEB AND THE ROCK

Part I

The Hound of Darkness
(1793-1916)

Book I

The Web and the Root
(1793-1881)

Chapters:

The Prologue [1]
Old Catawba [2]
Old Catawba—The Sons of Martha, etc. (a variant) [3]
The Joyner Genealogy [4]
A Digression On Myths
There's Always Hercules (How Libya Hill Got Its Name)
The Division Of The Tribe (The Great Joyner Schism and How It Came About)
Cosmopolis: How Certain Joyners Went To Town
The Plumed Knight: Theodore (In Which Town Joyners Achieve, For The First Time, A Gentleman)
The Battle of Hogwart Heights
Theodore's Children

Part I

The Hound of Darkness
(1793-1916)

Book

The Last Reunion (March 18, 1878)

Chapters:

Chickamauga: Rance Joyner's Tale [5]
Rance Joyner's History (Two versions) [6]

1. "Prologue to America," published in *Vogue*, XCI (February, 1938), 63-66, 150-53, 161.
2. Published in FDTM. This had been cut from the opening of OT&R.
3. HB, Chapter 1.
4. This and the following eight items make up a longer version of HB, Chapters 2-6. However, "There's Always Hercules" was cut out. This section was about Bear Joyner's exploits as a wrestler. He was fond of the legend of Antaeus, the Libyan giant; and the challenge, "whoever comes through Libya must throw me," is how Libya Hill got its name.
5. Published in HB.
6. Some of this material went into W&R, pp. 73-82.

Part I

The Hound of Darkness
(1793-1916)

Book II

The Web and The Wheel
(1881-1906)

Chapters:

A Stranger Whose Sermon Was Brick [7]
The World Lost But Not Forgotten
The Bell Remembered
The World Comes In [8]

Part I

The Hound of Darkness
(1793-1916)

Book III

The Web and The Hound
(1906-1916)

Chapters:

Caliban (Three o'clock) [9]
The Child Caliban [10]
The Street [11]

7. This and the following three items make up a longer version of HB, Chapters 7-10. The material had originally been part of the "Introduction by a Friend" in "Spangler's Paul."

8. A longer version of HB, pp. 342-44, which had included material about the visits of Confederate generals to the house during the 1880's.

9. W&R, Chapter 2.

10. This was probably material from the "Introduction by a Friend," some of which went into W&R, pp. 3-7. There may have been some duplication of material in the previous item.

11. A series of brief characterizations of many of the figures in W&R, Chapter 6. HCL*46AM-7(24-r).

Part I

The Hound of Darkness
(1793-1916)

Book

Caliban

Chapters:

Characters: People Of The Street [12]
Himself (1908) [13]
Two Worlds Discrete (The Joyner And The Webber World) [14]
The Child By Tiger
Aunt Maw And The Orphan Girl [15]
The Old Red Irish [16]
The Great House [17]
The Image Of The Circus And His Father's Earth [18]
The Second Thing On Sunday
The Baker's Truck

Part I

The Hound of Darkness
(1793-1916)

Book

The Winter's Tale (1913)

12. A series of extended characterizations (drawn up for "Spangler's Paul"), much of the material in which went into W&R, Chapter 6. With this material Wolfe had included other characterizations he grouped as "People of the Night," HCL*46AM-7(24-r). Aswell's chapter with that title was cut from W&R when the book was in proof.

13. Published as "No Cure for It" in HB.

14. Probably this material became W&R, pp. 8-12, 68-73, and 91-94.

15. This material, which had been cut from LHA, became, in a shortened version, W&R, Chapter 5.

16. Three unused chunks of material, all cut from OT&R, characterized the Irish of Altamont in contrast with the Boston Irish. Included is material that had already appeared in OT&R, pp. 160-66.

17. An unused passage about the Willetts family (based on the Vanderbilts). Cut from the train sequence in OT&R.

18. This and the next two items appear in W&R, pp. 86-90, 83-86, and 118-31.

Chapters:

Home From The Mountain
The Street Of The Day [19]

Part I

The Hound of Darkness
(1793-1916)

Book

America Unvisited

Chapters:

The Four Lost Men

Part I

The Hound of Darkness
(1793-1916)

Book

The Night of the Hound (June 7, 1916) [20]

Chapters:

The Fantasies: Clara Kimball Young
The Pencil Merchant

19. Another version of the material which went into W&R, Chapter 6. Written originally for "The Hills Beyond Pentland," this material follows the first-person narrator's memories of the street, the saloon, his paper route, the houses he delivered papers to, and the people who lived in them.

20. The following series of dramatic scenes had been written for "The Hound of Darkness." "The Newspaper," included in HB as "Gentlemen of the Press," is the only one which has been published. Wolfe apparently did not intend to use them in this form, because already he had reworked part of "The Wind from the West" into the Chicago section of "Prologue to America." And he had taken the phrases from "The Mexicans" and from "The Lovers" (the demand of "Promise" and the whispering of the leaves) and worked them into a piece entitled "So Soon the Morning" and then made that a part of his book entitled "The First Party" (see W&R, pp. 474-75). Other material here which is of interest: "The House in Boston" pictures Mr. Saltonstall reading a review while an Irish voice speaks outside his window; "The House at Malbourne" shows Foxhall Edwards and some friends discussing President Wilson. "The Seaman" has been crossed out and moved to Part IV, Book [VIII], "The Quest of the Fair Medusa."

The House at Malbourne
The Lovers
The Mexicans
The Newspaper
The House In Boston
The Whores
The Drug Store
~~The Seaman~~
The Wind From The West
The Rock In Maine
Walpurgisnacht

Part II

The Web And The World
(1916-1924)

Book

Chapters:

The Rise Of The Bank (1916-1924) [21]

Part II

The Web And The World
(1916-1924)

Book

Pine Rock (1918)

Chapters:

Jim Ravenel [22]
Alsop At 20
Characters: Gerald Alsop
The Priest At Pine Rock
Counting From The Left: Preacher Reed
The Torch

21. Aswell used only a part of this, YCGHA, pp. 360-62.
22. This and the following five items form W&R, Chapters 10-12.

Part II

The Web And The World
(1916-1924)

Book

The Rock (1923)

Chapters:

Approach To The City (1923) [23]
Alsop and Ravenel
Monty Bellamy (The Rock: 1923) [24]
Nebraska Crane [25]
Nebraska Crane: The Game [26]
The Sporting Writer (1925)—(for Nebraska Crane) [27]
The City Patriots (1923)—(The Southerners in New York)
Hero's Twilight (Jim Ravenel)
Why Are We So Unhappy? [28]

Part II

The Web And The World
(1916-1924)

Book

The Village Immortals (1923)

Chapters:

A Note On Experts: Dexter Joyner [29]

23. The bulk of W&R, Chapters 13-15, is made up of the sections "Approach to the City," "Alsop and Ravenel," "The City Patriots," and "Hero's Twilight."

24. An unused passage, originally written for "The October Fair": a long characterization of Bellamy, a young Catawban who, living in New York, yearns to be an actor.

25. An unused passage (much like YCGHA, pp. 338-40) in which Spangler telephones Nebraska Crane after a return from Europe.

26. An unused passage, about baseball as the American national game, which had been cut from OT&R. A small part of it appears in OT&R, pp. 206-7. Wolfe had intended to rework it and tie it in with Crane as a big-league ball player.

27. Published as the first part of *A Note on Experts: Dexter Vespasian Joyner* (New York, 1939).

28. W&R, pp. 274-78.

29. Published in part in *A Note on Experts*.

The Rock (The City: 1923—The Aesthetic Days) [30]
The City Enigma [31]
The Desire For The Whole: The Effort Of Memory [32]
Love And Glory: A Fantasy [33]
~~On Loneliness: At 23 (a note to follow Fantasy~~) [34]
Beryl Drunk And Beryl Sober [35]
~~Night Eye~~ [36]
~~Mrs. Morton~~
The Medical Students [37]
Dinwood Bland: The Hospital (1923)
Dinwood Bland: The Woman
The Story of ~~Robert Bland~~ (One Of The Catawbans Who Came To
The City) [38]

Part II

The Web And The World
(1916-1924)

30. W&R, pp. 260-61, is at least a part of this section.

31. W&R, pp. 228-32.

32. W&R, pp. 261-64.

33. W&R, pp. 279-93. This had been cut from OT&R, where it had been one of Eugene's fantasies during his lonely life in Boston.

34. Published as "God's Lonely Man" in HB, but one paragraph from it probably appears in W&R, p. 275. Aswell crossed out the item here and inserted it in two other places below, but then used it with neither of those groups of chapters. See nn. 59 and 106.

35. An unused passage, part of Wolfe's satire on the Greenwich Village aesthetes. It concerns Beryl Endicott in Lloyd McHarg's book (Carol Kennicott of Sinclair Lewis' *Main Street*) and the kind of people who return from the big city to bring "beauty" to the home town.

36. This and the following item were apparently out of place, for each is set in a European scene. The items appear again in this rough outline, written in by Aswell, at the end of the list of chapters in Part III, Book [IX], "The Sundering Flood." The first item appears in W&R, pp. 641-48. The second is an unused passage, written originally for OT&R, about Eugene and a widow he met in Paris.

37. This and the following two items are unused passages, cut from OT&R, about Eugene's adventures in Baltimore on his journey north to Harvard. The first item concerns a group of hard-drinking, cynical hospital internes. The next two concern Dinwood Bland (the first characterization of Judge Rumford Bland), the blind man who is receiving eye-treatment at the hospital and who takes Eugene home to meet his sharp-tongued wife.

38. An unused section, a collection of fragments left over from "K 19," which Wolfe hoped to combine with his characterization of Dexter Joyner, whose name is written under the crossed-out "Robert Bland."

Book

Utility Cultures, Inc. (1924-1927) [39]

Chapters:

Spurgeon [40]
Mahoney [41]
The Two Friends [42]
The Diabetic [43]

Part III

Love's Bitter Mystery
(1925-1930)

Book

The Meeting With Esther [44]
(1925)

Chapters:

The Voyage Home: The Ship (1925)
The Ship: Meeting With Esther (1925)

39. None of the materials grouped here were used by Aswell for Wolfe's post-humous books because there was no narrative; they were only a series of character sketches, written or dictated at different times and for varying purposes.

40. A long character sketch of Chester Spurgeon, one of the faculty members at the School for Utility Cultures, who moves from the New Humanism to Marxist literary criticism (cf. the paragraph about Spurgeon, YCGHA, p. 410). Wolfe based the character on his colleague, Edwin Berry Burgum.

41. A long character sketch of John J. O'Mahoney, another faculty member, a second-generation Irishman who became an aesthetic snob. Wolfe probably developed this character out of stories which Perkins had told him about Scott Fitzgerald's friend, Julian Van Cortland.

42. A sketch of two faculty members who work together as a team. Wolfe probably based these characters on his friends, Henry Carlton and William Manley, who left N. Y. U. to write radio scripts together.

43. A series of fragments, pages written at different times about Hugh Desmond, a faculty member who is troubled with diabetes and is later afflicted with tuberculosis and dies. Wolfe based the character on his friend and colleague, Desmond Powell, who had to leave New York and go to Colorado for his health.

44. The materials grouped here became W&R, Chapters 17-25, with very little cutting or change. The piece entitled "The Two Playwrights," however, was not included. This piece was probably another sketch of Carlton and Manley that had been written for "The River People" and that Wolfe hoped to integrate with these materials on Webber's early life with Esther.

The Two Playwrights
The Letter
The Theatre
The Birthday (October, 1925)
Together
Esther's House
Esther's House: Her Quality Defined (The City and The Country
    America)
The Old House
The New World (First Weeks With Esther)
The New World: Discovery

Part III

Love's Bitter Mystery
(1925-1930)

Book

The Good Child's River [45]
(1926)

Chapters:

Penelope's Web
~~Esther Away (September-December 1926)~~
In The Park
Stein And Rosens
~~Stein And Rosens~~ Stephen Hook

Part III

Love's Bitter Mystery
(1925-1930)

45. Most of the material grouped here went into W&R, Chapters 26-27. "In the Park," which had once been a part of "Penelope's Web" but which had already been published in FDTM, was set aside. "Esther Away" was a duplicate of "Her Face Remembered," Part III, Book [V], and was crossed out at this place in the rough outline, perhaps by Wolfe himself, because it has a European setting and does not fit this group. "Stephen Hook" may have been an early and extensive characterization of Hook (who is based on Thomas Beer), parts of which very likely are found reworked in W&R, pp. 476-78, and YCGHA, pp. 233-36.

Book

The Magic Years [46]

(1925-1927)

Chapters:

The Coming of Spring (1926)
April Late April (1926)
Esther At Work (1926)
The First Party (Mrs. Jack and The Celebrities)

Part III

Love's Bitter Mystery
(1925-1930)

Book

Boom Town [47]

Chapters:

K 19 (1926) [48]
The Homecoming (1926)—(Boom Town: The Company) [49]
The Company
Two Trains: The North And The South [50]

46. With some rearrangement, this group of materials became W&R, Chapters 28-30.

47. This group of materials stands as a good example of the sections of the big manuscript that Wolfe left in rough form. The first three items plus "Boom Town" are ready to form a narrative sequence (they make up the bulk of YCGHA, Chapters 5-9), but they were each written at different times with diverse intentions in mind. The other items are tossed into this group, probably because Wolfe thought he could use some paragraphs or passages from them when he made his revision (or they were pieces that came from this chronological period of his autobiographical narrative and he could not yet bring himself to put them aside).

48. Some of this chunk, which had been written for the "Joe Doaks" pattern, was used in YCGHA, pp. 51-55. Wolfe scrawled at the end of it, "Note (This is incomplete: the purpose of K 19 when completed is to introduce several characters—Alsop, Joyner, Dinwood Bland (the blind man), the President of the Bank and other people who will play a considerable part later in the book)."

49. This and the following item make up YCGHA, Chapter 8, "The Company." The two items consist of typescript materials for the first and last parts of the chapter; a copy of the short version of "The Company" in *New Masses;* and a typescript of the material about the One Hundred Club that had been reworked from an LHA passage cut out of that book.

50. An unused passage, cut from OT&R, about waiting at the station as some passengers are getting ready to go South, while "I" am waiting to head North.

Boom Town (1926) [51]
Deeper South (note—to follow Boom Town) [52]
Mr. Gilmer And The Women Talking [53]
The Quality of Gus [54]

Part III

Love's Bitter Mystery
(1925-1930)

Book

Chapters:

Her Face Remembered (October, 1926) [55]
Dark In The Forest, Strange As Time (December 1926)

Part III

Love's Bitter Mystery
(1925-1930)

Book

Life and Letters (1928) [56]

51. Several versions of the story "Boom Town," including a copy of the one printed in *American Mercury*. Pieces of the story are scattered through YCGHA, Chapters 5, 6, 7, and 9.

52. An unused, grotesque sketch reflecting the crudity of life in South Carolina towns.

53. An unused passage, cut from OT&R. Members of the Hawke family talk with one of the boarders.

54. Two unused sequences. The first includes about a hundred pages of memories and anecdotes about the stuttering brother, cut from OT&R (although some had appeared in OT&R, pp. 392-98). Some pages indicate that the "Names of the Nation" (OT&R, pp. 866-69) had originally been a part of this long automobile ride through the South, which accounts for the word "brother" that is sprinkled throughout that passage. The second item, cut from LHA, describes Luke Gant, the sailor, taking the starved Eugene to a cafeteria in Norfolk. Aswell has written in, "Gus: The Cafeteria," at the end of this chapter list.

55. A longer version of W&R, pp. 623-27.

56. Somewhat cut, this material appears as W&R, Chapters 32-35, except that the last item was set aside and later published under the title "On Leprechauns" in HB.

Chapters:

Rawng and Wright (March-April: 1928)
Waiting For Glory (March-April 1928)
Hope Springs Eternal
Mr. Malone
A Digression on Leprachauns

Part III

Love's Bitter Mystery
(1925-1930)

Book

A Vision Of Death In April (1928) [57]

Chapters:

A Vision Of Death In April
The Time Magic And The Color Green
The Goat Cry
The Dreams Of Time: The Medusa
The Quarrel: The Street
The Quarrel: Remorse
The Quarrel: Pursuit And Capture
The Quarrel: Together Again: The Weaver At Work Again
The Quarrel: (Probably a duplicate)
The Quarrel: (Probably a variant)
The Nature of Jealousy Defined
The Memories Of Death

57. Cut and rearranged, this group of materials appears in W&R, Chapters 36-42. Three items were not used. The first, "The Dreams of Time: the Medusa," is a nightmare sequence, part of which had appeared in OT&R, pp. 892-93. Eugene dreams of ancient Greece; he sees a beautiful Helen-like woman who welcomes him to her arms, but when he embraces her, she turns out to be the snake-haired Medusa. The second item, "The Nature of Jealousy Defined," is an essay on jealousy and its causes. The third item, "Memories of Death," cannot be identified. Two other pieces were added to this section, and their titles were written in by Aswell at the end of the list of chapters. The first, "An Image of Peace," may have gone into YCGHA, Chapter 1. The second, "The Parting," became W&R, Chapter 42.

Part III

Love's Bitter Mystery
(1925-1930)

Book

Death The Proud Brother

Chapters:

~~The Locusts Have No King~~[58]
Death The Proud Brother (1928)
The Station Revisited (April 1928) [59]

Part III

Love's Bitter Mystery
(1925-1930)

Book

The Sundering Flood (1928)

58. This item is crossed out here, and the title was added, in Aswell's hand, to Part IV, Book [VII], "The Quest of the Fair Medusa." It is difficult to identify the material that this title represents, for Wolfe used the title for several pieces that he kept in his packing box—although generally the material was about Brooklyn. One batch was a series of scenes all over America, with the recurrent phrase, "What shall I do now? Where shall I go?" that later was worked into "Prologue to America." Another piece with the same recurrent phrase pursued a series of scenes in Brooklyn, including the conversation with Mr. Marple (YCGHA, pp. 401-5). Other items included under this title seem to have been a piece about the environment of the city-dweller (YCGHA, pp. 427-29) and the monologue, "Now is duh mont' of March," (YCGHA, pp. 429-31). Another item bearing this title was a short story about a telephone conversation, which was sometimes called "Hello, Adelaide." "Only the Dead Know Brooklyn" had once borne this title and was included in this batch of material. Another item carrying the subtitle "Rats' Alley" depicted four tough-talking characters who ridicule a religious tract they have found on the street.

59. An unused passage from "K 19", in which the narrator, going to Pennsylvania Station with Abe Jones, feels a revulsion against the crowding, snarling city Jews, but then looks at his friend and feels his prejudice ebb away.

In the list of chapters after this item, Aswell has written "Loneliness" and "Only the Dead Know Brooklyn."

Chapters:

Some Things Will Never Change (Late April, 1928) [60]
A Woman's Letter (May, 1928) [61]
Dark October
The People In The House [62]
Katamoto (1928) [63]
Comfortless Memory (Paris: June, 1928) [64]

Part III

Love's Bitter Mystery
(1925-1930)

Book

The Spell of Time (~~1928~~) [65]

Chapters:

Im Dunkeln Wald (Freiberg Im Breisgau, June 18, 1928) [66]

60. Originally published as a part of "No Door," this was used later as a part of YCGHA, Chapter 4.

61. This and the following item contain some duplication and exist in more than one version. "A Woman's Letter," however, was altered by Wolfe so that, instead of Esther's going on a voyage, Webber is the journeyer. It became W&R, Chapter 43. "Dark October" is a longer version of W&R, Chapter 49, which also contains the material about "forever," YCGHA, p. 14.

62. A series of character sketches, written in 1932, about the people who live in the building where David Hawke has his apartment. It includes a brief sketch of Mr. Takiyaka, who later became Katamoto, and the conversation with Mr. Wakefield, YCGHA, pp. 405-8.

63. This item probably contained the magazine version, which was published in *Harper's Bazaar*, and a longer version, which formed the basis of YCGHA, Chapter 3.

64. This became W&R, pp. 634-41. To this chapter list, Aswell has added by hand "Night Eye," and "Mrs. Morton," for which see n. 36.

65. At the beginning of this chapter list, Aswell has written in "Ambleside," "Time Is a Fable," and "Esther Away." Wolfe apparently moved the first two items to this place, for they were added, in Miss Jassinoff's hand, after "Dark In The Forest, Strange As Time" and then crossed out. They appear in W&R, pp. 627-28 (the subtitle for "Ambleside" was "The Toothless Tailor") and pp. 626-27, 629-33, and 648-49. For "Esther Away," see nn. 45 and 55.

66. An expressionistic piece, never used, about the search for a father.

Part III

Love's Bitter Mystery
(1925-1930)

Book

Oktoberfest (October, 1928) [67]

Chapters:

The City of Munich
The Pension
The First Visit To The Fair (with two variant versions)
The Hospital (with a variant version)

Part IV

You Can't Go Home Again
(1930-1938)

Book

The Ring and The Book
(1930)

Chapters:

The Station [68]
Webber: Aet. 29 [69]
K 19: The Passengers [70]
Alsop: 32 [71]
K 19: Nebraska Crane [72]
The Hidden Terror: Dinwood Bland [73]
The Blind And The Dead [74]

67. This material became W&R, Chapters 46-48 and 50.
68. A 1938 revision of a Doaks manuscript, which became YCGHA, pp. 48-51.
69. Aswell used this passage for W&R, pp. 258-61.
70. A revision from "A Statement of Purpose," which went into YCGHA, pp. 53-57.
71. An unused passage, one of the "Time Sweeps" from "A Statement of Purpose."
72. A part of "A Statement of Purpose," which went into YCGHA, pp. 56 and 63-69.
73. A part of "A Statement of Purpose," which was used for YCGHA, pp. 81-85.
74. A part of "A Statement of Purpose," which was used for YCGHA, pp. 85-88
and 71-78, although some material from the canceled chapter, "People of the Night"
(prepared in proof sheets to be Chapter 8 of W&R), was worked in with these pages.

The Book And The Town [75]
The Book And The Man [76]
Writing And Living [77]

Part IV

You Can't Go Home Again
(1930-1938)

Book

The Fall of The Town [78]
(1930)

Chapters:

The Ruin Of The Town: The Cause (November, 1930)
The Fall Of The Bank (1930)

Part IV

You Can't Go Home Again
(1930-1938)

Book

The Lion And The Fox [79]
(May 7, 1932)

75. A combination of materials, some about Gant, some about Doaks, which, cut and altered, became YCGHA, pp. 325-30 and 341-51.

76. A piece of "An Introduction by a Friend," which was altered to become YCGHA, Chapter 24. Edward Joyner was changed to Randy Shepperton by Aswell.

77. Part of "An Introduction by a Friend," which, cut and altered, became YCGHA, pp. 333-37 and 371-88. Again, the change from Joyner to Shepperton was Aswell's.

78. This material, considerably altered and perhaps rewritten by Aswell, became YCGHA, pp. 363-72. Wolfe had Parson Flack gazing grimly over the town (pp. 371-72), not Judge Bland.

79. This is the title of one chunk of Wolfe's manuscript, but the date is 1929. Presumably 1932 is a typist's error here. Somewhere in this part of the manuscript, perhaps here, Wolfe had apparently placed about forty pages of typescript—at present included in HCL*46AM-7(59)—which describe the House of Rodney and the acceptance of the author's book for publication (some of which went into YCGHA, Chapter 2) and perhaps the account of Fox asleep, pp. 438-43.

Chapters:

The Ring And The Book (1930) [80]
And Now He Had The Letters [81]
The Faculty Meeting (1930)–(Utility Cultures, Inc.) [82]
Names (conversation between George Webber and Robert Joyner:
New York–1930) [83]

Part IV

You Can't Go Home Again
(1930-1938)

Book

The Party At Jack's (1930) [84]

80. This item is difficult to identify, but it probably did not contain any material that went into W&R, Chapter 29, to which Aswell gave the title "The Ring and the Book." It probably contained the material which became YCGHA, Chapter 23, "The Lion Hunters," and it is Webber as a literary lion who is referred to in the title of this whole section, "The Lion and the Fox."

81. This became YCGHA, pp. 333-38.

82. An unused fragment, in which Gant or Spangler, just returned from Europe, prepares to go to the first department meeting of the college year at the School for Utility Cultures. Most of the piece is devoted to a sketch of James Hocker, a poet who is interested in Proust. The sketch is probably based on Wolfe's colleague, John Varney.

83. An unused passage about the associations which Doaks (changed to Webber) attaches to names—Smith, Jones, Percy, and so on.

84. Cut and slightly revised, the material grouped here became YCGHA, Book II, "The World That Jack Built." Wolfe had not finished it: there is some duplication among the different parts; there are some pages from "First Party" which Wolfe had placed with the party scene but had not yet integrated with the main story; there are some passages which Wolfe had written earlier and had not yet decided whether to include or set aside; there are some pages which are intended for magazine publication, but which probably would not have been used for the book; there are some characters who bear one name in one part, another name later.

"Morning" and "Morning: Jack Asleep" were not used. They depict Mr. Jacobs (Jack) dreaming of his childhood in Germany and his Latin recitations in the classroom. Aswell also cut the bath scene out of "Jack Afloat," and he cut out a part called "The Madman," about Jack's partner, Rosenthal, from one of the early sections. He cut out the conclusions (Wolfe had one for the book and one for a magazine) which take Mr. or Mrs. Jack back to bed again. He moved one part to "The Locusts Have No King" chapter, pp. 423-27 (beginning, "The party was in full swing now"). Aswell also wrote the last paragraph on p. 186 and perhaps wrote the paragraph on p. 261 beginning "Yes, that was it! That was the answer!" and the conclusion to the whole story, pp. 320-22, expanding a couple of Wolfe's paragraphs.

Chapters:

Morning
Morning: Jack Asleep
Morning: Jack Erect
Morning: Jack Afloat
Morning: Mrs. Jack Awake
Morning: Mrs. Jack And The Maid
Morning: Jack And His Wife
Morning: The World That Jack Built
The Great Building (April, 1930)
The Elevator Men
Before The Party (Mrs. Jack And the Maids)
Piggy Logan
The Family (Mr. Jack, Alma, etc.)
The Party Beginning
The Guests Arriving
The Lover
Mr. Hirsch Was Wounded Sorrowfully
Piggy Logan's Circus
The Guests Departing: The Fire
The Fire: The Outpouring Of The Honeycomb
The Fire: The Tunneled Rock
After the Fire: These Two Together
One Of The Girls In Our Party [85]
Daisy Purvis

Part IV

You Can't Go Home Again
(1930-1938)

Book

McHarg (January, 1931) [86]

85. This item and the next are out of place and belong in the next section. "One of the Girls in Our Party" appeared in FDTM, and Wolfe hoped to work it in somewhere. "Daisy Purvis" became YCGHA, Chapter 32.

86. Greatly cut and somewhat toned down, this material became YCGHA, Chapters 33-37.

Chapters:

The Meeting
Bendien And Stoat
The Journey
The House In The Country
The Return

Part IV

You Can't Go Home Again
(1930-1938)

Book

Exile And Discovery

Chapters:

'E(Mrs. Purvis: London—1930-31) [87]
The Lion At Morning [88]
The Fox Awake [89]
Old Man Rivers [90]
No More Rivers [91]
Nebraska Crane: 1931 [92]
Ike Brown [93]
A Question Of Guilt (George Webber To Robert Joyner—1932) [94]

87. A revision of part of "Daisy Purvis" that had appeared in the *New Yorker*, July 17, 1937.

88. Cut and revised, this was published in HB.

89. Cut and slightly rearranged, this became YCGHA, pp. 443-98, although it may also have included the material about Fox asleep, pp. 438-43.

90. An unused section, a satirical sketch about Mr. Rivers of the House of Rodney and the clubs he belonged to, based on Robert Bridges, the editor of *Scribner's Magazine*, 1914-30.

91. A short story about Otto Hauser, an editor at the House of Rodney, some bits of which were worked into YCGHA, Chapter 2. For information about Wolfe's troubles with this piece, which was largely a character sketch of his friend, Wallace Meyer, the reader who had first seen merit in "O Lost," see Nowell, pp. 321-23.

92. Used for YCGHA, pp. 57-63.

93. Unused material about Abe Jones and his wife.

94. This and the next four items are materials originally written for "An Introduction by a Friend" for "Spangler's Paul." Aswell wove some parts of it together and rewrote it to become YCGHA, Chapter 26. However, pp. 330-33, the material in which bears the title "A Question of Guilt" in one Wolfe manuscript, may also have been a part of this.

The Question Of Guilt (Brooklyn, 1932)
Permanence And Change: A Question Of Brick (Brooklyn, 1932)
Father And Son (Brooklyn, 1932)
A Letter On Homelessness (To Robert Joyner: 1932)
Guilt And Time: A Dream (1933) [95]
The Time Dreams: Memory [96]
Fox And Foxman (November, 1933) [97]
The Past: Seen Like A Flash [98]

Part IV

You Can't Go Home Again
(1930-1938)

Book

The Quest Of The Fair Medusa [99]
(1935-1936)

Chapters:

Nightfall In Brooklyn: 1934 [100]
"He Struck The Board—" [101]
Steve's Place (1934) [102]
Last Poem (Brooklyn, 1934) [103]

95. A version of the dream of the return home, similar to Part I of "Return of the Prodigal" published in HB.

96. An unused passage, cut from OT&R, in which Eugene remembers his twelfth birthday, his paper route, his going to school, and Ben's gift of a watch.

97. An unused fragment, a hastily dictated account of how the narrator jumped from a moving train and broke his arm. For this episode in Wolfe's life, see *Letters*, pp. 318-19.

98. A duplicate of most of the materials in "The Quality of Gus." See n. 54. After this item, Aswell added in handwriting "What Is Man," a piece cut from the chapter "The Ship," which he revised and placed in YCGHA, pp. 432-36.

99. Aswell had written in at the beginning of this group of chapters, "The Locusts Have No King," for which see n. 58.

100. An unused passage, part of which is similar to YCGHA, pp. 399-401.

101. An unused passage, originally a part of "K 19" or "The October Fair," about the anguish of a writer who is pacing his room.

102. This probably was another title for the piece which Wolfe had called "A Great Idea for a Story," although Aswell listed (in handwriting) "A Great Idea for a Story" at the end of this group of chapters. It appears in YCGHA, pp. 414-23.

103. This probably was some material which had to do with the quest for fame—possibly the passage beginning, "Go, seeker, if you will, throughout the land...," YCGHA, pp. 505-8.

The Great Games (1936) [104]
Morning In Brooklyn: The Faithful Woman [105]
Dr. Turner [106]

Part IV

You Can't Go Home Again
(1930-1938)

Book

I Have A Thing To Tell You [107]
(1938)

Chapters:

Last Farewell
Fame And The Poet (Part I)
Fame And The Poet (Part II)
Van Paget And Page

Part IV

You Can't Go Home Again
(1930-1938)

Book

104. This was pp. 6-20 of the piece Wolfe called "A Spanish Letter," his revision of his long-unsent letter to Donald Ogden Stewart, which recounted his change of feeling about Germany. Somewhat rearranged, this material appears in YCGHA, pp. 622-33.

105. An unused section of Wolfe's "Fame and the Poet" material, an allegory in which Dame Care remains faithful to the writer although Fame has deserted him.

106. This became "A Portrait of a Literary Critic" in HB. At the end of this list of chapters, Aswell has added, by hand, three items: "The Seaman," "On Loneliness," and "A Great Idea for a Story." An arrow indicates the last item was to go between "Steve's Place" and "Last Poem." "The Seaman" was one of "The Hound of Darkness" scenes, in which a sailor declares that the air in Brooklyn stinks. "On Loneliness" became "God's Lonely Man" in HB.

107. This group of materials included the long version of "I Have a Thing to Tell You," YCGHA, Chapter 39-44, and the materials on fame, pp. 501-8 and 622-25, together with the allegory, "Fame and the Poet," which appeared in *American Mercury*, October, 1936. "Van Paget & Page" was an unfinished sketch about lawyers, which, with some cutting and revision, Aswell published under the title "Justice is Blind" in Walser, pp. 92-100.

Chapters:

Return (1937) [108]

Part IV

You Can't Go Home Again
(1930-1938)

Book

A Farewell To The Fox [109]
(1937)

Chapters:

Invocation To The Fox: The Hospital
Old Pine Rock And The Village Immortals: A Survey
Ecclesiasticus: The Fox
Even Two Angels Not Enough (Berlin: 1935)
Credo

108. An unfinished account of the return to Asheville. Aswell cut down the length, changed the central character's name to Eugene Gant, paired it to the piece about the dream of the return, and published it as Part 2 of "The Return of the Prodigal" in HB.

109. Aswell cut, revised, and rearranged these materials and made them into YCGHA, Chapters 45-48. He also added some passages from "A Spanish Letter" about Germany. Since just before Wolfe left on his fatal journey the last part of his manuscript and the "Purdue Speech" were inextricably connected, it is impossible to say just how much of his valedictory material Wolfe would have included or what the final words of his book would have been. Aswell took the prophetic conclusion to "I Have a Thing to Tell You" and placed it at the end of YCGHA.

A LIST OF SOURCES AND
OF WORKS CITED

I. UNPUBLISHED MATERIAL

(Accession numbers are given for Thomas Wolfe material in the Harvard College Library.)

HCL*46AM-7(15) to (18). Manuscript drafts, manuscripts, and typescripts of one-act plays, 1918-20.

HCL*46AM-7(1) to (4). Manuscript drafts and typescripts of "The Mountains," a one-act play, 1920-21.

HCL*46AM-7(5). Typescript of "The Mountains," a play in three acts and a prologue, 1922.

HCL*46AM-7(6) to (8). Manuscript drafts and typescripts of *Mannerhouse* in its early stages, 1921-23.

HCL*46AM-7(9) and (10). Typescripts of *Mannerhouse*, 1924-25.

HCL*46AM-7(11) and (12). Manuscript drafts, typescripts, casting notes, and set drawings for *Welcome to Our City*, 1922-23.

HCL*46AM-7(13) and (14). Typescripts of *Welcome to Our City*, 1925.

HCL*46AM-7(19). Manuscript fragments of "The House of Bateson," 1922(?).

HCL*46AM-7(20) to (22). Manuscript notes and drafts for plays, sketches, and essays, 1920-24.

HCL*46AM-7(23). Manuscripts and typescripts of "Passage to England" and "The 1925 Sketches," plus manuscript journal notes, 1924-25.

HCL*46AM-7(24). Outlines, synopses, and working notes for literary projects, 1926-38, including outlines and memoranda for "O Lost," "The October Fair," "The Good Child's River," *Of Time and the River*, etc.

HCL*46AM-7(25). Two notebooks containing the Autobiographical Outline prepared for "O Lost," 1926.

HCL MS 326F. Seventeen volumes containing the manuscript of "O Lost," 1926-28.

HCL*45M-156F. Typescript of "O Lost," 1926-28.

HCL*46AM-7(26). Typescript pages and passages deleted from "O Lost" in the preparation of *Look Homeward, Angel*, 1926-28.

HCL*46AM-7(28) and (29). Manuscript drafts of "The River People," plus memoranda and journal notes, 1928.

HCL*46AM-7(30). Fifteen volumes containing manuscript notes, outlines, sketches, drafts, and episodes for "The October Fair," 1928-31. Included are three volumes of manuscript drafts which were originally written for "O Lost," 1926.

HCL*46AM-7(31). Three volumes containing manuscript drafts for "The Good Child's River," 1930-31.

HCL*46AM-7(32). Manuscript outlines, notes, and fragments of literary work, 1928-31.

HCL*46AM-7(33) to (35). Manuscript notes, drafts, fragments, and episodes of "K 19," 1930-32.

HCL*46AM-7(36). Manuscript drafts and a fragmentary typescript of *A Portrait of Bascom Hawke,* 1926-31.

HCL*46AM-7(37). Manuscript drafts and typescripts of *The Web of Earth,* 1932.

HCL*46AM-7(38) to (44). Manuscript drafts and fragments of episodes for *Of Time and the River,* 1930-34.

HCL*46AM-7(45) and (46). Typescript drafts and fragments of episodes for *Of Time and the River,* 1930-34.

HCL*46AM-7(47). Typescript of *Of Time and the River,* including some pasted-up pages of galley proof from Wolfe's magazine publications.

HCL*48A-848. Galley proofs for *Of Time and the River.*

HCL*46AM-7(49) and (51). Manuscript drafts, fragments, and typescripts for Wolfe's magazine publications, 1933-35.

HCL*46AM-7(50). Manuscripts and typescripts of Wolfe's lecture at the Colorado Writers' Conference and of *The Story of a Novel.*

HCL*46AM-7(48) and (52). Manuscript and typescript drafts, fragments, and notes for "The Hills Beyond Pentland" and "The Hound of Darkness."

HCL*46AM-7(53). Manuscript drafts and typescripts for "The Vision of Spangler's Paul."

HCL*46AM-7(54). Manuscript drafts and typescripts for the episodes about Joe Doaks.

HCL*46AM-7(55) and (56). Manuscript and typescript drafts, fragments, and notes for *The Web and the Rock.*

HCL*46AM-7(57). Final typescript of *The Web and the Rock.*

HCL*46AM-7(58) and (59). Manuscript and typescript drafts, fragments, and notes for *You Can't Go Home Again.*

HCL*46AM-7(60). Final typescript of *You Can't Go Home Again.*

HCL*46AM-7(61). Outlines, notes, and sketches for Wolfe's late writings, 1935-38.

HCL*46AM-7(62) and (63). Notes, manuscripts, typescripts, and final typescript for *The Hills Beyond.*

HCL*46AM-7(65) and (66). Rejected passages from Wolfe's posthumous novels.

HCL*46AM-7(67) and (68). Miscellaneous and unidentified sheets, manuscripts, and typescripts.

HCL*46AM-7(69). Thirty-three pocket notebooks, 1926-38, plus fragments of other pocket notebooks.

HCL*46AM-7(70). Miscellaneous autobiographical and literary notes, work charts, pedagogical material from New York University, reviews, etc.

HCL*46AM-8. Wolfe's academic notebooks, term papers, examinations, exercises, 1908-24.

HCL*49M-209. Letters, notes, and papers of Edward Aswell pertaining to Thomas Wolfe.

HCL*53M-113F. Additional Wolfe materials found in the possession of John Terry at his death. Letters, essays, academic materials, fragments of plays, notes, outlines, etc.

HCL*48M-211. Letters from Thomas Wolfe to Mrs. J. M. Roberts.

HCL*46AM-11. Typescript of the published portions of the letters to Mrs. Roberts in *Atlantic Monthly,* December, 1946, to February, 1947. Included are fragments of a commentary by Mrs. Roberts.

HCL*46AM-12. Correspondence received and business papers.
  (1) Legal papers.
  (2) Letters to Wolfe from relatives.
  (4) Letters to Wolfe from other correspondents.
  (6) Canceled checks and bank statements.
  (10) Manuscript fragments found with the correspondence.

HCL*46AM-13. Letters from Thomas Wolfe to Aline Bernstein.

HCL*46AM-14. Letters from Thomas Wolfe to Elizabeth Nowell.

HCL*46AM-15. Letters from Thomas Wolfe to other correspondents. Included are manuscript drafts, typescript carbons, and unfinished letters.

Letters from Thomas Wolfe to Maxwell Perkins and John Hall Wheelock. In the files of Charles Scribner's Sons.

Letters from Thomas Wolfe to Frederick Wolfe, Benjamin Wolfe, and Mrs. Mabel Wolfe Wheaton; to Horace Williams, James Holly Hanford, and Frederick Koch. The University of North Carolina Library.

Letters from Maxwell Perkins to John Terry. The University of North Carolina Library.

The Thomas Wolfe Collection of the Pack Memorial Library, Asheville, North Carolina. Letters, legal documents, photographs, and newspaper clippings.

HCL*46A 102-836, 862-873. Thomas Wolfe's personal library of books in English, French, and German. Included are textbooks from the Orange St. School, the North State Fitting School, the University of North Carolina, Harvard University, and New York University.

HCL*48A-1. An interview with Mrs. Mabel Wolfe Wheaton by Paul Beath and Duncan Emerick. Seven discs, 33⅓ R.P.M., recorded at the Library of Congress, February 23, 1947.

HCL*AC9 W8 327 9291(b). Thomas Wolfe. *Look Homeward, Angel.* Inscribed by the author for Aline Bernstein.

HCL*AC9 W8 327 9350. Thomas Wolfe. *Of Time and the River.* Inscribed by the author for Aline Bernstein.

Harvard University Archives, UA III 5.78.10 1st Series. Harvard Appointment Office folder for Thomas Wolfe.

Harvard University Archives, UAV 101.201.10. Harvard Registrar's Office folder for Thomas Wolfe.

II. PUBLISHED WORKS

A. *Works of Thomas Wolfe*

The Crisis In Industry. Chapel Hill: The University of North Carolina, 1919.

"The Return of Buck Gavin," in *Carolina Folk Plays, Second Series,* ed. Frederick Koch. New York: Henry Holt and Company, 1924.

Look Homeward, Angel. New York: Charles Scribner's Sons, 1929.

Of Time and the River. New York: Charles Scribner's Sons, 1935.

From Death to Morning. New York: Charles Scribner's Sons, 1935.

The Story of a Novel. New York: Charles Scribner's Sons, 1936. [Citations in notes taken from *The Viking Portable Thomas Wolfe,* ed. Maxwell Geismar. New York: The Viking Press, 1947]

"Fame and the Poet," *American Mercury,* XXXIX (October, 1936), 149-54.

"Prologue to America," *Vogue,* XCI (February, 1938), 63-66, 150-53, 161.

A Note on Experts: Dexter Vespasian Joyner. New York: House of Books, 1939.

The Web and the Rock. New York: Harper and Brothers, 1939.

You Can't Go Home Again. New York: Harper and Brothers, 1940.

The Hills Beyond. New York: Harper and Brothers, 1941.

"The Third Night," in *Carolina Folk Plays, First, Second, and Third Series*, ed. Frederick Koch. New York: Henry Holt and Company, 1941.

Thomas Wolfe's Letters to his Mother, ed. John Skally Terry. New York: Charles Scribner's Sons, 1943.

"Writing Is My Life" [Letters of Thomas Wolfe to Mrs. J. M. Roberts], *Atlantic Monthly*, CLXXVIII (December, 1946), 60-66; CLXXIX (January, 1947), 39-45; CLXXIX (February, 1947), 55-61.

Mannerhouse. New York: Harper and Brothers, 1948.

Western Journal. Pittsburgh: The University of Pittsburgh Press, 1951.

"Justice is Blind," in *The Enigma of Thomas Wolfe*, ed. Richard Walser. Cambridge, Mass.: Harvard University Press, 1953.

The Correspondence of Thomas Wolfe and Homer Andrew Watt, ed. Oscar Cargill and Thomas Clark Pollock. New York: New York University Press, 1954.

The Letters of Thomas Wolfe, ed. Elizabeth Nowell. New York: Charles Scribner's Sons, 1956.

Welcome to Our City, Esquire, XLVIII (October, 1957), 57-83.

The Short Novels of Thomas Wolfe, ed. C. Hugh Holman. New York: Charles Scribner's Sons, 1961.

B. *Other Works*

Adams, Agatha Boyd. *Thomas Wolfe: Carolina Student*. Chapel Hill: The University of North Carolina Library, 1950.

Adams, J. Donald. Review of *You Can't Go Home Again, New York Times Book Review*, September 22, 1940, p. 1.

Addresses by Eric Axel Karlfeldt and Sinclair Lewis on the Occasion of the Award of the Nobel Prize. New York: Privately printed, n. d.

Asheville Citizen, November 16, 1906; June 1 and 2, 1916; September 10, 1937.

Aswell, Edward C. "A Note on Thomas Wolfe," in *The Hills Beyond*. New York: Harper and Brothers, 1941.

———. Introduction to *Look Homeward, Angel: II. The Adventures of Young Gant*. New York: New American Library, 1948.

———. "Thomas Wolfe Did Not Kill Maxwell Perkins," *Saturday Review of Literature*, XXXIV (October 6, 1951), 16-17, 44-46.

Barber, Philip. "Tom Wolfe Writes a Play," *Harper's Magazine*, CCXVI (May, 1958), 71-76.

Barr, Stringfellow. "The Dandridges and the Gants," *Virginia Quarterly Review*, VI (April, 1930), 310-13.

Basso, Hamilton. Review of *From Death to Morning, New Republic,* LXXVI (January 1, 1936), 232.

———. "Thomas Wolfe: A Summing Up," *New Republic,* CIII (September 23, 1940), 422.

Beach, Joseph Warren. *American Fiction 1920-1940.* New York: The Macmillan Company, 1941.

Benét, Stephen Vincent. "Thomas Wolfe's Torrent of Recollection," *Saturday Review of Literature,* XXII (September 21, 1940), 5. Reprinted in Walser, *The Enigma of Thomas Wolfe.*

Bentley, Phyllis. *Some Observations on the Art of Narrative.* New York: The Macmillan Company, 1941.

Bernstein, Aline. *An Actor's Daughter.* New York: Alfred A. Knopf, 1941.

———. *The Journey Down.* New York: Alfred A. Knopf, 1938.

———. *Three Blue Suits.* New York: Equinox House, 1933.

Bishop, John Peale. *The Collected Essays of John Peale Bishop,* ed. Edmund Wilson. New York: Charles Scribner's Sons, 1948.

Braswell, William. "Thomas Wolfe Lectures and Takes a Holiday," *College English,* I (October, 1939), 11-22. Reprinted in Walser, *The Enigma of Thomas Wolfe.*

Bridgers, Ann Preston. "Thomas Wolfe, A Legend of Man's Hunger in His Youth," *Saturday Review of Literature,* XVII (April 6, 1935), 599-600, 609.

Burgum, Edwin Berry. "Thomas Wolfe's Discovery of America," *Virginia Quarterly Review,* XX (Summer, 1946), 421-37. Reprinted in Walser, *The Enigma of Thomas Wolfe.*

Canby, Henry Seidel. "River of Youth," *Saturday Review of Literature,* XI (March 9, 1935), 529-30. Reprinted in Walser, *The Enigma of Thomas Wolfe.*

Cargill, Oscar, and Pollock, Thomas Clark. *Thomas Wolfe at Washington Square.* New York: New York University Press, 1954.

Carpenter, Frederic. Letter to the Editor, *Saturday Review of Literature,* XIII (January 25, 1936), 9.

Chamberlain, John. Review of *Of Time and the River, Current History,* XLII (April, 1935), iii.

Church, Margaret. "Thomas Wolfe: Dark Time," *Publications of the Modern Language Association,* LXIV (September, 1949), 629-38.

Cowley, Malcolm. "Thomas Wolfe," *Atlantic Monthly,* CC (November, 1957), 202-12.

———. "Thomas Wolfe's Legacy," *New Republic,* XXXIX (July 19, 1939), 311-12.

Cowley, Malcolm. "Unshaken Friend," *New Yorker,* XX (April 1, 1944), 28-36; (April 8, 1944) 30-43.

Daniels, Jonathan. Review of *Look Homeward, Angel, Raleigh News and Observer,* October 10, 1929.

————. *Tar Heels.* New York: Dodd, Mead, and Company, 1941.

Davenport, Basil. Review of *Look Homeward, Angel, Saturday Review of Literature,* VI (December 21, 1929), 584.

De Voto, Bernard. "Genius is Not Enough," *Saturday Review of Literature,* XIII (April 25, 1936), 3-4, 14-15. Reprinted in Walser, *The Enigma of Thomas Wolfe.*

Delakas, Daniel L. "Thomas Wolfe and Anatole France: A Study of Some Unfinished Experiments," *Comparative Literature,* XV (Winter, 1957), 33-50.

Dickson, Frank A. "Look Homeward, Angel." *The Anderson [South Carolina] Independent,* July 9, 17, 24, 31, August 7, 14, 21, 28, September 4, 1948.

Dodd, Martha. *Through Embassy Eyes.* New York: Harcourt, Brace and Company, 1939.

Dykeman, Wilma. *The French Broad.* ("Rivers of America Series.") New York: Rinehart and Company, 1955.

Fadiman, Clifton. Review of *Of Time and the River, New Yorker,* X (March 9, 1935), 79-82. Reprinted in Walser, *The Enigma of Thomas Wolfe.*

————. Review of *The Web and the Rock, New Yorker,* XV, (June 24, 1939), 69-70.

Fagin, N. Bryllion. "In Search of an American *Cherry Orchard,*" *Texas Quarterly,* I (Summer-Autumn, 1958), 132-41.

Fifield, William. "Tom Wolfe Slept Here," *Story,* XXII (March-April, 1943), 9-16.

Frenz, Horst. "A German Home for *Mannerhouse,*" *Theater Arts,* XL (August, 1956), 63, 95-96.

Friede, Donald. *The Mechanical Angel.* New York: Alfred A. Knopf, 1948.

Frye, Northrop. *Anatomy of Criticism.* Princeton: Princeton University Press, 1957.

Geismar, Maxwell. *Writers in Crisis.* Boston: Houghton Mifflin Company, 1942.

Greenlaw, Edwin. *The Province of Literary History.* Baltimore: The Johns Hopkins Press, 1931.

Gould, Gerald. Review of *Look Homeward, Angel, London Observer,* August 17, 1930.

Gurko, Leo. *The Angry Decade*. New York: Dodd, Mead, and Company, 1947.

Hanford, James Holly. "Edwin Greenlaw and the Study of Literature," *Studies in Philology*, XXIX (April, 1932), 141-48.

Hanford, Pamela Johnson. *Hungry Gulliver*. New York: Charles Scribner's Sons, 1948.

Hart, Henry. Review of *You Can't Go Home Again*, *New Masses*, XXXVII (October 22, 1940), 25-26.

Hellman, Geoffrey E. "Everything Is Mobile," *New Yorker*, XVII (October 4, 1941), 25-33.

Hoffman, Frederick J. *Freudianism and the Literary Mind*. Baton Rouge: Louisiana State University Press, 1945.

Holman, C. Hugh. *Thomas Wolfe*. ("University of Minnesota Pamphlets on American Writers.") Minneapolis: The University of Minnesota Press, 1960.

———. "Thomas Wolfe, a Bibliographical Study," *Texas Studies in Language and Literature*, I (Autumn, 1959), 427-45.

Hutsell, James K. "As They Recall Thomas Wolfe," *Southern Packet*, IV (April, 1948), 4, 9-10.

———. "Thomas Wolfe and Altamont," *Southern Packet*, IV (April, 1948), 1-4, 7-8.

Jack, Peter Munro. Review of *From Death to Morning*, *New York Times Book Review*, November 24, 1935, p. 6.

Jones, Howard Mumford. Review of *The Web and the Rock*, *Boston Transcript*, July 1, 1939.

———. "Social Notes on the South," *Virginia Quarterly Review*, XI (July, 1935), 452-57.

Jung, C. G. *Psychology of the Unconscious*. Translated and with an introduction by Beatrice M. Hinkle. New York: Moffat, Yard and Company, 1916.

Kahl, Joseph. *American Class Structure*. New York: Rinehart and Company, 1957.

Kazin, Alfred. *On Native Grounds*. New York: Reynal and Hitchcock, 1942.

Kennedy, William F. "Economic Ideas in Contemporary Literature— The Novels of Thomas Wolfe," *Southern Economic Journal*, XX (July, 1953), 35-50.

Kussy, Bella. "The Vitalist Trend and Thomas Wolfe," *Sewanee Review*, L (July-September, 1942), 306-24.

Latimer, Margery. Review of *Look Homeward, Angel*, *New York Herald-Tribune Books*, November 3, 1929, p. 20.

Ledig-Rowolt, H. M. "Thomas Wolfe in Berlin," *American Scholar,* XXII (Spring, 1953), 185-201.

Lowes, John Livingston. *The Road to Xanadu.* Boston: Houghton Mifflin Company, 1927.

Macauley, Thurston. "Thomas Wolfe: A Writer's Problems," *Publishers' Weekly,* CXXXIV (December 24, 1938), 2150-52.

McCoy, George. "Asheville and Thomas Wolfe," *North Carolina Historical Review,* XXX (April, 1953), 200-17.

McElderry, Bruce R., Jr. "The Durable Humor of *Look Homeward, Angel,*" *Arizona Quarterly,* XI (Summer, 1955), 123-28.

Martin, F. David. "The Artist, Autobiography, and Thomas Wolfe," *Bucknell Review,* V (March, 1955), 15-28.

Meade, Martha N. *Asheville in the Land of the Sky.* Richmond: The Dietz Press, 1942.

Middlebrook, L. Ruth. "Reminiscences of Tom Wolfe," *American Mercury,* LXIII (November, 1946), 544-49.

Miller, Edward. "Gulping the Great West," [*Portland*] *Oregonian,* July 31 and August 7, 1938.

Muller, Herbert. *Thomas Wolfe.* Norfolk, Conn.: New Directions Books, 1947.

North Carolina, A Guide to the Old North State. ("American Guide Series.") Federal Writers' Project of the Federal Works Agency, Works Progress Administration. Chapel Hill: The University of North Carolina Press, 1939.

Norwood, Hayden. *The Marble Man's Wife.* New York: Charles Scribner's Sons, 1947.

Nowell, Elizabeth. *Thomas Wolfe: A Biography.* New York: Doubleday and Company, 1960.

Paterson, Isobel. "Turns with a Bookworm," *New York Herald-Tribune Books,* February 24, 1935.

Perkins, Maxwell. "Thomas Wolfe," *Harvard Library Bulletin,* I (Autumn, 1947), 269-77.

[Perkins, Maxwell]. *Editor to Author, The Letters of Maxwell Perkins,* ed. John Hall Wheelock. New York: Charles Scribner's Sons, 1950.

Pfister, Karin. *Zeit und Wirklichkeit bei Thomas Wolfe.* Heidelberg: Carl Winter, Universitätsverlag, 1954.

Rascoe, Burton. Review of *You Can't Go Home Again, American Mercury,* LI (December, 1940), 493-94.

Raynolds, Robert. Review of *Look Homeward, Angel, Scribner's Magazine,* LXXXVI (December, 1929), 2.

Reeves, Paschal. "The Humor of Thomas Wolfe," *Southern Folklore Quarterly,* XXIV (June, 1960), 109-20.

Roberts, J. M., Jr. Letter to the Editor, *Life*, LXI (October 8, 1956), 22.

Russell, Bertrand. "Non-Materialistic Naturalism," *Kenyon Review*, IV (Autumn, 1942), 361-65.

Rubin, Louis. *Thomas Wolfe, The Weather of His Youth*. Baton Rouge: Louisiana State University Press, 1955.

Sayler, Oliver M. *Our American Theater*. New York: Brentano's, 1923.

Scott, Evelyn. "Colossal Fragment," *Scribner's Magazine*, XCVII (June, 1935), 2.

Sloane, William. "Literary Prospecting," *Saturday Review of Literature*, XIII (December 3, 1938), 3-4, 15-22.

Solon, S. L. "The Ordeal of Thomas Wolfe," *Modern Quarterly*, XI (Winter, 1939), 45-53.

Sondley, F. A. *Asheville and Buncombe County*. Asheville: Privately printed, 1922.

Stearns, Monroe M. "The Metaphysics of Thomas Wolfe," *College English*, VI (February, 1945), 193-99.

Stevens, George. "Always Looking Homeward," *Saturday Review of Literature*, XX (June 24, 1939), 5-6.

Stoney, George. "Eugene Returns to Pulpit Hill," *Carolina Magazine*, VI (October, 1938), 11-14.

Taylor, Walter F. "Thomas Wolfe and the Middle-Class Tradition," *South Atlantic Quarterly*, LII (October, 1953), 543-54.

Trilling, Lionel. *The Liberal Imagination*. New York: The Viking Press, 1950.

"Two Die as Blast Rocks the Marguery and Routs Guests," *New York Times*, January 4, 1960, pp. 1-2.

Swinnerton, Frank. Review of *Look Homeward, Angel*, London *Evening News*, August 8, 1930.

"U. S. Voice," *Time*, XXV (March 11, 1935), 77.

Volkening, Henry T. "Tom Wolfe: Penance No More," *Virginia Quarterly Review*, XV (Spring, 1939), 196-215. Reprinted in Walser, *The Enigma of Thomas Wolfe*.

Wallace, Margaret. Review of *Look Homeward, Angel*, New York *Times Book Review*, October 27, 1929, p. 7.

Walser, Richard (ed.). *The Enigma of Thomas Wolfe: Biographical and Critical Selections*. Cambridge, Mass.: Harvard University Press, 1953.

Warren, Robert P. "A Note on the Hamlet of Thomas Wolfe," *American Review*, V (September, 1935), 191-208. Reprinted in Walser, *The Enigma of Thomas Wolfe*.

Watkins, Floyd. "De Dry Bones in the Valley," *Southern Folklore Quarterly*, XX (June, 1956), 136-49.

———. "Thomas Wolfe and the Nashville Agrarians," *Georgia Review*, VII (Winter, 1953), 410-23.

———. *Thomas Wolfe's Characters*. Norman, Okla.: The University of Oklahoma Press, 1957.

Weigle, Edith. Review of *From Death to Morning*, *Chicago Daily Tribune*, December 14, 1935.

Wheaton, Mabel Wolfe, and Blythe, Legette. *Thomas Wolfe and His Family*. New York: Doubleday and Company, 1961.

Williams, Horace. *The Education of Horace Williams*. Chapel Hill: Privately printed, 1936.

———. *The Evolution of Logic*. Chapel Hill: Privately printed, 1925.

———. *Logic for Living*. New York: Philosophical Library, 1951.

———. *Modern Logic*. Chapel Hill: Privately printed, 1927.

Winston, Robert. *Horace Williams, Gadfly of Chapel Hill*: The University of North Carolina Press, 1942.

Wolfe, Fred. Letter to the Editor, *New York Times Book Review*, July 31, 1960, p. 18.

INDEX

Abernethy, Milton, 46
Adams, Agatha Boyd, 39
Addison, Joseph, 42
Aeschylus, 41, 68
Agricola, 40
Aldington, Richard, 215
Ambleside, 102
American Mercury, publishes "The Bell Remembered," 305; publishes "April, Late April," 339; mentioned, 181, 302
"An Angel on the Porch," 178
Anima Poetae, 63
Anna Karenina, 89
Antaeus, 207-9, 221
Apology, 40
"April, Late April," echoes *The Waste Land,* 237; mentioned, 339
Aristotle, 68
Arlen, Michael, 215
Arles, 218
Armstrong, Anne, 363
Arnold, Matthew, 68, 118
Around the World with Captain Parker, 32
Asheville, described, 21-3; real estate boom, 77-8; bank fails, 220-1; Wolfe's return, 343-5, 354-6, 383; mentioned, 21-30 *passim,* 213, 319, 377
Asheville Citizen, prints parts of "Passage to England," 98; prints "London Tower," 103; mentioned, 32, 36
Aswell, Edward, edits "The Party at Jack's," 347-8; meets Wolfe, 362-3; edits W&R and YCGHA, 388-413, 403-6; rearranges Wolfe's outline of his last novel, 415-36; mentioned, 3, 360, 378, 383, 386, 396

Babbitt, Irving, 59
Bacon, Francis, 43
Baker, George Pierce, Wolfe enrolls in English 47 given by, 59; criticizes Wolfe's dramas, 71-3; emphasizes compression and control, 78-82; suggests that Wolfe has not the proper talents for a dramatist, 86; mentioned, 97, 114, 124, 160. *See also* 47 Workshop

Balzac, Honoré de, 89
Barr, Stringfellow, 180-1
Barry, Philip, 113
Basso, Hamilton, criticizes Wolfe's conception of short story in FDTM, 285; Wolfe meets friends of in New Orleans, 334; attacks Harper, 410; mentioned, 338, 345, 355
Baxter, Warner, 290
Beach, Joseph Warren, 4
Beaumont, Francis, 68
Beer, Thomas, gives Wolfe idea for "Death the Proud Brother," 251; mentioned, 162
The Beginning of the Middle Ages, 68
"The Bell Remembered," 305
Benét, William Rose, 155, 181
Bennett, Arnold, 6
Bentley, Phyllis, 412
Bergson, Henri, influence on Wolfe's philosophy, 53; analogy of time and life, 128; influence on LHA, 144n, 145n; mentioned, 9
Berkeley, George, 50
Berlin, 326
Bernard, W. S., 40
Bernstein, Aline, helps Wolfe find a producer for *Welcome to Our City,* 106; introduces Wolfe to psychology, 111-5; with Wolfe in Europe, 120; returns to New York, 148; strained relationship with Wolfe, 152-8 *passim;* tries to place LHA with various publishers, 162; quarrel with Wolfe, 166-9; LHA dedication, 179; Wolfe uses their affair as material for his novel, 204; break with Wolfe, 217; attempted suicide, 222; becomes "Esther Jack," 223; mentioned, 12, 85, 171, 174-9 *passim,* 184, 188, 215, 264
Bernstein, Theodore, 224
Bible, 32, 34, 104, 249
Bishop, Donald, 39
Bishop, John Peale, 271
Blake, William, 249
Bonn, 169
Book of Common Prayer, 32

DA